The Purchase of the Danish West Indies

The Purchase of the Danish West Indies

CHARLES CALLAN TANSILL

GREENWOOD PRESS, PUBLISHERS
NEW YORK   1968

CONTENTS

Contents

Chapter VII

PREFACE

This study is largely the result of many conversations that I had with Professor John H. Latané, formerly Head of the Department of History in The Johns Hopkins University, who confirmed my belief that there is evident need of intensive research into the problems of American policy in the Caribbean. I deeply regret that the recent death of Dr. Latané will deprive me of his valuable counsel during the period when this volume will be going through press.

I owe a special debt of gratitude to Chancellor and Mrs. Lucius C. Clark, of the American University, for their kindly interest which has made it possible for me to continue my research activities. To Dean Walter M. Splawn, and to Dr. Ellery C. Stowell, of the American University, I am also indebted for that assistance which only colleagues can give.

Every scholar who does research work in Washington realizes the great rôle that has been played by Dr. Herbert Putnam, the Librarian of Congress, in making available the vast resources of the library that is under his competent charge. Especially helpful to historians is Mr. Martin Roberts, Superintendent of the Main Reading Room, and Dr. J. Franklin Jameson, Chief of the Division of Manuscripts. I am also under obligation to Dr. T. P. Martin and to Dr. Curtis Garrison of this same division.

PREFACE

I have had two personal friends in particular who have lent me encouragement when I most needed it— Mr. J. L. Sherwood and Mr. Samuel E. Collegeman. And in this connection I cannot forget the much-needed assistance of Mrs. Charles S. McCarthy, of Mr. and Mrs. B. R. Parker, of Mr. Lester H. Woolsey, of Mr. Waldo W. Young, and of Mr. Grant Olson.

In the Department of State the Historical Adviser, Mr. Hunter Miller, has shown me unusual courtesy, while in this same division the effective aid granted to all investigators by Mrs. Natalia Summers has become a tradition. I am also indebted to Miss Amy Holland, Miss Julia Bland, Miss Alice Brown, Miss Eileen Berrall and to Mr. R. L. Luthin for assistance.

Mrs. Edith Kermit Roosevelt was so gracious as to permit me to roam untrammeled through the Roosevelt Papers in the Library of Congress, while Mr. John Campbell White granted me the privilege of examining the manuscripts of his father, Henry White. Similar privileges were also granted me by Mrs. William Jennings Bryan and Mrs. Robert Lansing.

There are certain friends I should like to mention who have been of distinct service in many ways. Among them are Dr. and Mrs. Daniel Davis, Mr. Charles Warren, Dr. C. O. Paullin, Dr. James A. Robertson, Mrs. Alice Ruddy, Dr. and Mrs. Frederick L. Benton, Miss Frances Hitchcock, Mr. Allen R. Boyd, Professor Allan Nevins, and Professor A. T. Volwiler.

At this point I wish also to record the assistance given me by the Social Science Research Council through a timely grant-in-aid.

PREFACE

There are certain distinguished scholars in Europe who have greatly contributed to the value of this volume. My esteemed friends in Germany, Dr. Alfred von Wegerer and Dr. Alfred Vagts, made it possible for me to secure access to the materials in the German Foreign Office. In Denmark the archives in the Foreign Office were opened through the good offices of that eminent Danish scholar, Dr. Aage Friis. I wish also to acknowledge my indebtedness to Dr. Hejls, Keeper of the Royal Archives, to Mrs. Elisabeth Hude, and to Mr. J. O. Bro-Jorgensen.

I have been fortunate indeed in having the constant encouragement of my father and my mother, and as the years have dragged their weary length along, my wife has aided me not only in extensive researches, typing and proof-reading, but with cheering counsel that made the task seem worth while.

CHARLES C. TANSILL.

Washington, D. C.,
January, 1932.

INTRODUCTION

SEWARD'S CARIBBEAN POLICY

Seward's policy in the Caribbean was essentially defensive, and was largely an expression of his ardent desire to safeguard the future of America against the attacks of envious foreign foes. His experience as Secretary of State in the Lincoln Cabinet had shown him all too clearly the hazards of foreign intervention during a period of national crisis. In case of future strife it was only from maritime nations like England and France that America need apprehend any serious challenge, and it so happened that both these nations had numerous colonial possessions in the Caribbean which could serve as bases of operations against the American coasts. To Seward it seemed obvious that the United States should endeavor either to purchase from these powers some of their possessions, or should secure from other nations certain islands in the Caribbean which could serve as outposts of American defense. But neither Congress nor the American public was disposed to follow Seward in these schemes of territorial expansion, so in the Caribbean he achieved nothing.[1]

[1] For an interesting survey of the forces that militated against post-war imperialism, see Professor T. C. Smith, "Expansion after the Civil War, 1865-1871," *Political Science Quarterly*, vol. 16, pp. 412 ff.

This lack of achievement, however, did not mean that Seward was lacking in those diplomatic arts that ordinarily bring success. His best biographer assures us that Seward "holds the first place among all our Secretaries of State,"[2] and there are many students who would agree with this estimate. It was his misfortune that his program of expansion was conceived during a period of political and economic readjustment that necessitated greater emphasis upon domestic rather than foreign policies: reconstruction came before expansion. Seward, however, never allowed adversity to dampen his ardor, so despite repeated rebuffs, he actively strove to secure for the United States some naval base in the Caribbean which would answer all the demands that interested naval officers were constantly making upon him. And in this regard it should be noted that Seward had long been an imperialist who considered American expansion as the chief canon in the creed of American patriotism. In the decades prior to the Civil War he had boldly prophesied the resistless roll of successive waves of American pioneers into the friendly Arctic or into lands below the equator. Manifest destiny was his by-word, and when he became Secretary of State he sought to give substance to his beliefs.

America's needs were of paramount importance, and were worthy of unceasing efforts that led him into negotiations with four foreign countries whose pos-

[2] Frederic Bancroft, *The Life of William H. Seward* (N. Y. 1900), vol. 2, p. 528.

sessions he greatly desired. In this study only the Danish-American phase of Seward's Caribbean policy will be treated. In a second volume to be published later, there will be an extended account of Seward's attempt to secure the islands of Culebra and Culebrita from Spain, the island of St. Bartholomew from Sweden, and from the Dominican Republic the use of Samana Bay as a naval base.

CHAPTER I

ANOTHER CASE OF "SEWARD'S FOLLY"—THE TREATY
OF OCTOBER 24, 1867

Seward's desire for expansion in the Caribbean had
ample support from American naval officers. During
the Civil War the difficulties encountered in securing
supplies of coal in foreign ports had indicated to the
officials of the Navy Department the advantage of
having a naval base in the Caribbean. Such an outlying
possession would serve not only as a coaling station for
American warships, but would also be a convenient
place to which naval officers could bring their prizes for
adjudication by an admiralty court.

In the annual report of the Navy Department for the
year 1865, there was inserted a paragraph that must
have warmed the hearts of American imperialists. After
indicating the evident need for more adequate protection for our fast developing commerce, the report
pointed out the necessity for naval stations abroad:

"There are circumstances which render it necessary
that a commercial and naval people should have coaling
stations and ports for supplies at one or more important
points on those seas and oceans where there are important interests to be protected, or naval power is to be
maintained. Steamers cannot carry the same amount of
supplies as the sailing vessels of former days, and the
coal which is indispensable to their efficiency must, particularly in time of war, be furnished or obtainable at

brief intervals, and in the immediate vicinity of their cruising grounds. A prudent regard for our future interests and welfare would seem to dictate the expediency of securing some eligible locations for the purpose indicated."[1]

According to the *Diary* of Gideon Welles, the Secretary of the Navy under Presidents Lincoln and Johnson, this report of the Navy Department for 1865,

"roused the Secretary of State, and he began when the War was over to press the purchase. . . . The Danes wish to sell and first edged in the matter gently. The Secretary of State did not give the matter earnest attention, but the Navy Department in our war, feeling the want of a station in the West Indies, has favored the subject."[2]

Gideon Welles is correct in asserting that the officers in the American navy were eager for the acquisition of a naval station in the West Indies, but it would appear that Seward was interested in a program of expansion many months previous to the publication of the *Report* of the Navy Department for the year 1865. According to Olive Risley Seward, an adopted daughter of Secretary Seward, both President Lincoln and the Secretary of State were early convinced of the value of a depot in the Caribbean, and upon one occasion they

"summoned Vice Admiral Porter for consultation in regard to the matter. Admiral Porter procured the necessary charts and descriptions of the region from the Hydrographic Bureau, and laid them before the President and Secretary. . . . Admiral Porter strongly

[1] *Ex. Doc.* 1, 39 Cong., 1 sess., p. xv.
[2] Vol. 2, p. 466 (N. Y. 1911).

advised their acquisition, and prepared a memoir on the subject of the Danish islands."[3]

It is certain that during the continuance of the Civil War, Seward was often fearful of the designs of European powers with reference to certain islands in the Caribbean. Spanish intrigues in Santo Domingo served to heighten this suspicion and, in 1864, the establishment of Maximilian's empire in Mexico seemed as a new menace to American supremacy in the Western Hemisphere. By some Americans it was feared that Prussian aggrandisement resulting from the war against Denmark in 1864, might lead Austria to demand the Danish West Indies by way of compensation. This contingency appeared very threatening to Bradford R. Wood, the American Minister to Denmark, who wrote to Seward a letter of warning. To his mind the partial dismemberment of Denmark might be considered as an accomplished fact, but

"as France will object to the absorption of Denmark by Germany without a *quid pro quo* (the Rhenish provinces for instance), and Russia, to her alliance with Sweden, she is somewhat in the position of Mahomet's coffin. What share of the plunder will go to Austria remains to be seen. The Danish West Indies are very convenient to the new Empire of Mexico, and our Monroe Doctrine for the present, in abeyance, I hope Grant will soon make it a living principle."[4]

[3] "A Diplomatic Episode," *Scribner's Magazine*, new series, vol. 2, p. 586.

[4] Bradford R. Wood to W. H. Seward, July 15, 1864, MS. Dept. of State, *Denmark, Desp.*, vol. 8.

But whatever suspicions Seward may have harbored relative to the aggressive designs of certain European powers in the Caribbean, it was apparent to him that as long as the Civil War continued the United States would have to be content to play a passive rôle. By December, 1864, however, the success of Northern arms seemed assured, so Seward made ready for an adventure in imperialism. He had already discussed with President Lincoln the general features of his program, and had gained his assent. Indeed, the President was ready to lend active assistance. On January 2, 1865, the annual New Year's reception was held at the White House, and as the members of the Diplomatic Corps filed past the President, Lincoln beamed with special favor upon the Danish Minister, General Raasloff. In Europe such marked attention would have been highly significant, but Raasloff, who had resided in the United States for more than a decade, and whose contact with Lincoln had been intimate and friendly, did not seem to realize that the President was practising one of the gestures of diplomacy.[5] Seward was now ready to enter upon the scene.

[5] In General Raasloff's report to Mr. Bluhme, Danish Privy Councillor, January 9, 1865, of his conversation with Seward on January 7, 1865, mention is made of Lincoln's friendly attitude. Thus: "I ought to mention that when the diplomatic corps on the second instant extended the usual New Year's wishes to the President, President Lincoln treated me with unusual friendliness and honored me with a long conversation, which, although it was merely of a general nature, yet was of an extremely cordial character." MS. *Udenrigsministeriet*, Copenhagen, hereafter cited as D.F.O. (Danish Foreign Office).

On January 7, 1865, M. de Geoffroy, the chargé d'affaires of France, gave a dinner to some of his friends. In American diplomacy, dinners were an important factor in shaping American policy from the days when Jefferson had inflicted his rule of pell-mell upon the unappreciative British Minister, Anthony Merry, to the period just before the Civil War when the astute Lord Elgin is supposed to have "floated" the Treaty of Washington through an adverse but thirsty American Senate by means of certain liquid delights.[6] This dinner of M. de Geoffroy was again to make manifest a happy union of culinary and diplomatic arts.

It is possible that Seward had conveyed to General Raasloff an intimation that upon this occasion business should precede pleasure, for on the evening of the dinner party both General Raasloff and Secretary Seward presented themselves at the residence of M. de Geoffroy a half hour before dinner was announced. Finding the drawing-room deserted, they repaired to a convenient sofa and Seward promptly unburdened himself. The United States, it appeared, had been compelled by the Civil War to develop into a great maritime power,

"and consequently the possession of a harbor and depot in the West Indies had become a necessity; he [Seward] had for some time desired to make this overture but he could not do so as long as Denmark was at war; now that Country being at peace the right moment was, in his opinion, at hand; that he had (for motives of dis-

[6] Charles C. Tansill. *The Canadian Reciprocity Treaty of 1854* (Baltimore, 1922), pp. 76 ff.

cretion) not tried to obtain any preliminary information about the condition and value of the islands, but that eventual negotiations would be carried on by the United States in the most generous, chivalrous, and delicate manner; that the United States would not desire to see the islands in the hands of any other power; that the material advantages to be derived from annexation to the United States would render the population of the islands well disposed to the transfer; that absolute secrecy was of the highest importance; if any divulgation took place he would make the Danish Minister responsible for it; that the proposition was made with the approval of the President (Lincoln)."[7]

General Raasloff was quite taken aback by Seward's proposition, but he finally found voice enough to murmur that the inhabitants of the Danish West Indies appeared "happy and contented under Danish rule." Seward did not contest the verity of this statement: he did believe, however, that the inhabitants might be even happier under American rule.

On January 9, 1865, General Raasloff wrote to Mr. Bluhme, of the Danish Privy Council and made a detailed report of his conversation with Seward on January 7. This report closely coincides with the account given in the *Memorandum* in the Department of State. At the conclusion of his communication, General Raasloff made the following general observations:

[7] In the Department of State there is a lengthy *memorandum* which reproduces all the conversations between Seward and Raasloff concerning the acquisition of the Danish West Indies. See *Reports of Bureau Officers,* vol. 4, 1860-1873.

"On the whole, Mr. Seward expressed himself with affection and warmth, and endeavored carefully to avoid any expression which might have given umbrage to me as the representative of the King of Denmark. Our conversation has given me the impression that it is the vital wish of the United States to see this proposal accepted, and that in any event this matter will be dealt with by the United States with the greatest possible liberality and delicacy. I am convinced that the proposal is made in all sincerity and with the approval of the President, and I believe that the American Government will be capable of eventually bringing this problem to a solution. . . . In case that Mr. Seward's proposal is deemed advisable to take into consideration, I beg to express my conviction that a negotiation concerning the disposal of the islands to the United States may be completed quickly and with a financially satisfactory result."[8]

On February 4, after Seward had returned from the well-known Peace Conference at Fortress Monroe, Raasloff called at the Department of State and was informed by the Secretary that

"he adhered to the proposition he had made on the 7th of January, unalterably, and that he had not since then spoken or written to anybody about this matter."[9]

The Danish Government was greatly surprised that the United States should be so deeply interested in the acquisition of the Danish West Indies, and although it was important to preserve the most friendly relations with the American Government, yet the sacrifice of these possessions was at that time out of the question.

[8] Raasloff to Bluhme, January 9, 1865, MS. D. F. O.
[9] Raasloff to Bluhme, February 6, 1865, MS. D. F. O.

On February 24, 1865, the Danish Foreign Office instructed Raasloff to the effect that

"it would now be contrary to the feelings of the King voluntarily to dispose of a portion of his subjects. However, on an occasion such as this, personal feelings should not be the sole factor. From a political point of view it is always justifiable seriously to consider the advantages which a proposed transaction seems to promise. . . . Therefore, although the Royal Government cannot *at present* accept the proposal made in behalf of the United States, yet it would clearly be a complete miscalculation of Denmark's financial and political position at this moment to decide, without the most careful consideration, upon a refusal of such a well meant offer. Therefore, I request that when you answer Mr. Seward in accordance with this instruction, you will add that the Royal Government would regard with favor, at some future date, the renewal of this proposal."[10]

On the afternoon of April 5, 1865, Seward went for a drive with his family. They had gone but a short distance when the horses became frightened, and Seward, in attempting to leave the carriage, was thrown violently to the ground and severely injured.[11] On April 12, General Raasloff called at the Department of State in order to communicate the substance of the instruction he had recently received from his government. Seward, however, was still confined to his bed, so the Danish Minister informed Frederick W. Seward, the Assistant Secretary of State, of the disinclination

[10] Quaade to Raasloff, February 24, 1865, MS. D. F. O.
[11] Frederick W. Seward, *Seward at Washington, 1861-1872* (N. Y. 1891), pp. 270 ff.

of the Royal Government to part with its colonial possessions.[12]

On the night of April 14, President Lincoln was assassinated, and both Secretary Seward and his son, Frederick, received dangerous wounds at the hands of one of the accomplices of John Wilkes Booth. Under these circumstances there was little opportunity for many weeks of any renewal of the negotiations for the purchase of the Danish West Indies. In the meantime, however, General Raasloff received from the Danish Foreign Office additional instructions dated May 25, 1865. These were drafted by Mr. Vedel, Director of the Ministry of Foreign Affairs, and they emphasized the necessity of sounding out the Governments of France and England before any definitive steps could be taken with reference to the cession of the Danish West Indies. It was the opinion of Mr. Vedel that it would be

"highly inadvisable to carry on the negotiation with North America without having in advance made sure as to the reaction of the western maritime powers towards such a step of the Royal Government, and therefore I have already written to the Royal Envoys in London and Paris requesting them secretly to sound out the sentiment with regard to this matter. However, I do not think that I could advise His Majesty, particularly under present conditions, to open negotiations with all three powers simultaneously, if, after all, the Royal Government *should* decide to dispose of the islands. For, on one side, it seems to me that there is at this moment such an uncertainty as to the North American policy that I consider it dangerous, not only for

[12] *Memorandum,* MS. Dept. of State, April 12, 1865, *Reports of Bureau Officers,* vol. 4, 1860-1873.

Denmark but for the political situation in general, to
compel the new President to decide as to the application
of the Monroe Doctrine with regard to the transfer of
a West Indian island to a European power. . . . Under
these conditions I do not see that there is anything to
do at present but to wait for the reports that I expect
to receive from London and Paris in answer to my
above-mentioned suggestion, and the information you
might be able to give me concerning the character of
the policy that North America will adopt towards
Europe. When these data are at hand, the Royal Government will make its decision, and I suppose that
negotiations with the representatives may then follow
without any great difficulty or much loss of time."[13]

From the tenor of these instructions, General Raasloff realized that it would be best to let the negotiation
slumber for a while. On August 27, he had a conference
with Seward, but on this occasion there was no allusion
to the question of the purchase of the Danish West
Indies, nor "was the matter brought up by either of
them at any of their subsequent and rather frequent
social interviews."[14]

On November 6, 1865, a new Ministry was installed
in Copenhagen, and opposition to the sale of the Danish
West Indies began appreciably to diminish. Also,
because of international complications, a new feeling
of friendliness towards the United States began to
develop. On December 16, 1865, George H. Yeaman,
the American Minister to Denmark, wrote an interesting despatch to Seward in which he described the
state of public opinion in Copenhagen. There was, of

[13] Vedel to Raasloff, May 25, 1865, MS. D. F. O.
[14] *Memorandum*, MS. Dept. of State, *op. cit.*

course, much bitterness expressed towards both Austria and Prussia because of their seizure of the provinces of Schleswig and Holstein. But in addition, there was sharp animosity felt towards Great Britain

"because that power is deemed to have stood by and permitted the alleged outrage after having pledged herself to prevent it. The popular feeling against Great Britain is marked, and as that power is deemed to be our rival, with a possibility of soon becoming our enemy, there is a corresponding expression of friendship for the United States, and a frequently expressed wish that we may get into war with that power, thinking as they do that we would surely beat her in the contest."[15]

It may well have been that this unfriendly feeling towards Great Britain was one of the reasons why the Danish Government was now willing to open negotiations with the United States concerning the cession of the Danish islands. It was readily appreciated, however, that such negotiations might involve Denmark in difficulties with both France and Great Britain, and the gravity of the situation was pointed out to General Raasloff by Mr. Vedel in his instructions of December 2, 1865.[16] His greatest apprehension with reference to

[15] Yeaman to Seward, December 16, 1865, MS. Dept. of State, *Denmark, Desp.*, vol. 8.

[16] From a careful study of the manuscripts in the British Foreign Office it is apparent that on April 12, 1865, Sir Augustus Paget, the British Minister at Copenhagen, decided to write to Lord John Russell, the British Foreign Secretary, and acquaint him with certain rumors he had heard relative to proposals by the United States to Denmark for the purchase of the Danish West Indies. Sir Augustus had inquired of Mr.

the sale of the Danish islands to the United States was
active hostility that was certain to be manifested by

"the western powers relative to the transfer to the
United States of the best harbor and the most important center of the Antilles, . . . as such a center may
create incalculable dangers for the European maritime
powers, not only in case of a possible war between
America and Europe, but even in time of peace, due to
the conditions among the negroes in the West Indies.
Our relations to England have been made doubly difficult, because some time ago Lord Russell received,
apparently from Washington, some information concerning America's wish to purchase the islands, and he
has therefore immediately made to General Buelow a

Quaade, at the Danish Foreign Office, as to the verity of these
rumors, and had been informed that "some time since, a sort
of vague intimation had been given, through an indirect
channel that if the Danish Government should be willing to
sell their West Indian Islands, the United States might possibly
be disposed to purchase." The Danish Government had returned a negative reply to this indirect proposal, and also
assured Sir Augustus that they would not entertain such a
proposition "without giving due notice to Her Majesty's Government." Indeed, Mr. Quaade expressed the belief that he
"should consider it an act of treachery towards the Powers of
Europe if Denmark were to enter into negotiations for the
transfer of her West Indian Colonies without previously informing them of her intention to do so." See Augustus Paget
to Earl Russell, April 12, 1865, *Secret and Confidential,* MS. F. O.
22/327. On April 19, 1865, Earl Russell instructed Sir Augustus
Paget to "convey to M. Quaade the thanks of Her Majesty's
Government for the assurances" given with reference to the
transfer of the Danish West Indies. MS. F. O. 22/326, no. 27.
Needless to say, these statements of Mr. Quaade to Sir
Augustus Paget were about as worthless as his assurances, but
they served a useful purpose.

kind of protest against a sale, which does not take English interests into consideration. The Government has, of course, defended itself against this unreasonable requirement. However, you will easily understand that during the present political situation it is very serious for us to take a step which would deprive us of the sympathy of the western powers, although we would not by such action expose ourselves to any positive danger. . . . I have presented briefly these different aspects so that you may see what difficulties we shall eventually have to conquer. They are, however, not unconquerable, particularly if it be true that America is really inclined to make a sincere offer of such an amount as you have earlier suggested. The higher the sum, the stronger the inclination will be for the government to decide upon the sale, and the less will be the difficulties, particularly if the western powers should find that there is in this economic consideration an essential motive for us to sell the islands.

"The first consideration, then will be the financial benefit we might derive from the sale. You are therefore instructed to renew your earlier conversations with Mr. Seward concerning this matter, and to inform him that your Government has asked you confidentially to urge him to make a definite offer for the islands."[17]

On December 29, General Raasloff had an interview with Secretary Seward, during the course of which he informed him that the Danish Government was not

"absolutely unwilling to entertain the proposition made by the Secretary of State on the 7th of January last for the transfer of the Danish West Indies to the United States, but that very grave considerations militated against such a transaction, and that under these circumstances his Government desired to know how large a sum the United States was prepared to offer for those

[17] Vedel to Raasloff, December 2, 1865, MS. D. F. O.

islands: that it would in a great measure depend upon the liberality of the offer to be made by the United States whether Denmark could or could not engage in negotiations with the United States for that transaction."[18]

Seward appeared pleasantly surprised when he learned that the Danish Government was inclined to open negotiations for the cession of the islands, but he soon "composed himself" and then expressed a doubt as to whether "the present moment was opportune for such a transaction." When he requested time for further consideration, Raasloff assured him that there was no necessity for an immediate answer.[19]

Seward then explained to the Danish Minister how new circumstances had arisen since the conversation on the sofa at the residence of M. de Geoffroy. At that time President Lincoln was in favor of the proposed purchase of the Danish islands, but the accession of Andrew Johnson to the presidential office had altered the situation. It was believed that the new President was favorable to the purchase, but inasmuch as Mr. Seward was leaving Washington on December 30, for a trip to the West Indies, the Secretary of State would have no opportunity of "conversing upon the matter with Mr. Johnson before his departure." Seward further explained that he intended to visit Havana and "perhaps also St. Thomas," but he informed General Raasloff that his visit to the Danish West Indies would

[18] *Memorandum,* MS. Dept. of State, *op. cit.*
[19] Raasloff to Count Frijs, December 25, 1865, MS. D. F. O.

have "no connection whatever with the proposed purchase."[20] It was to be merely a quest for health.

Raasloff accepted this assurance at face value because he knew that an

"intimate friend of Mr. Seward, the well known politician in New York state, Mr. Thurlow Weed . . . some years ago spent a winter on the island of Santa Cruz . . . and has often advised Mr. Seward to visit our islands."[21]

Some of the members of President Johnson's Cabinet, however, had quite a different idea as to the real reason for Seward's trip to the Caribbean. In the *Diary* of Gideon Welles there is the following acrid comment:

"Seward is preparing to take a cruise and will leave tomorrow for the West Indies in the steamer De Soto. There has been much mystery in this premeditated excursion. I am amused and yet half-disgusted with Seward's nonsense. He applied to me some weeks since for a public naval vessel to proceed to Havana, and perhaps beyond. Without inquiries, I take it for granted he goes on public business, or he would not ask for a public vessel. . . . When it was settled he should have a vessel, he talked of a family excursion. Wanted relaxation, wanted Fred should go, said he wanted to get away from the receptions, etc., of the New Year. . . . To-day he took me aside and made some inquiries about St. Thomas, which during the war I had said might be a desirable acquisition as a coaling station and central point in the West Indies. His action and talk indicate anticipated trouble and perhaps complications, the

[20] *Memorandum,* MS. Dept. of State, *op. cit.*

[21] Raasloff to Count Frijs, December 25, 1865, MS. D. F. O. For an account of Seward's cruise, see Frederick W. Seward, *Seward at Washington,* 1861-1872, pp. 302-310.

development or *denouement* of which he cares not to be here to witness." [22]

Seward returned from this Caribbean cruise on January 28, 1866, and on the following day he arranged an interview with General Raasloff. The Danish Minister found him "very well, happy, and thoroughly satisfied with his visit to our islands." [23] Seward opened the interview by requesting General Raasloff to repeat the communication he had made to him during their conference on December 29. After the General had complied with this request, Seward then informed him that he was now prepared to lay the matter before the President and those members of the Cabinet who were especially interested in the proposed purchase. He further stated that he would make a careful study of the precedents in the case, such as the Louisiana Purchase and the Florida Treaty, with a "view of finding the proper basis for the contemplated negotiation about the price which the United States might offer for the D. W. Islands."

Before closing the interview, Seward inquired whether General Raasloff was acquainted with "the expectations of his Government" with reference to the purchase price of the Danish islands. The General confessed his ignorance of the exact amount which his Government might ask for the islands in question, but it seemed to him that a mere twenty-five millions of dollars was "a reasonable price, and at all events his

[22] Vol. 2, 1864-1866, p. 406.
[23] Raasloff to Count Frijs, February 8, 1866, MS. D. F. O.

Government would certainly not be willing to negotiate about the transfer unless a somewhat liberal and acceptable offer was made by the United States." In the event that his own government should ask him to name a price for the islands, Raasloff informed Seward that he would probably "propose 20 millions as the absolute minimum price."

At the termination of the interview, both Seward and Raasloff agreed "that the conditions at present seem very favorable," and they promised "that as soon as one of them should learn anything new, he would communicate it to the other."[24]

On February 8, 1866, Raasloff paid a visit to the Department of State and was informed by Seward that President Johnson had been consulted about the purchase of the Danish islands. As a result ·of this consultation it had been decided by the President and Secretary of State to let the negotiation "rest a short while with a view of avoiding that it should be connected in the public mind with the journey of the Secretary of State to the West Indies." Seward then disclosed the fact that he had been importuned by certain persons to

"acquire a harbor on the island of Santo Domingo by intervening, either in the Dominican revolt against Spain, or in the civil war in Haiti, but that he had not desired to follow such unprincipled advice."[25]

[24] *Memorandum,* MS. Dept. of State, *op. cit.* Also, Raasloff's despatch to Count Frijs, February 8, 1866, MS. D. F. O.

[25] Raasloff to Count Frijs, February 8, 1866, MS. D. F. O. Also, *Memorandum,* MS. Dept. of State, *op. cit.*

One of the main reasons why Seward was not disposed to intervene in Santo Domingo was because of
the bright outlook for acquiring the Danish islands, and
his cruise in the Caribbean had confirmed his early
opinion as to their value as a naval base. This cruise,
however, had again aroused the suspicions of France
and Great Britain with reference to American policy.
On February 3, 1866, Lord Clarendon, the British
Foreign Secretary, instructed Mr. George Petre, the
British representative at Copenhagen, to inquire whether
Seward's visit to St. Thomas had any political significance.[26]

As soon as Mr. Petre received this instruction he at
once placed the matter before Count Frijs, the Danish
Foreign Minister, who assured him, "without the
slightest hesitation," that neither had there been

"nor were there at present any negotiations whatever
between Denmark and the United States for cession
of the Island of St. Thomas; that Denmark had not
the slightest intention at the present moment of disposing of any of her Colonies, or of any portion of
them, and that to the best of his belief the visit of Mr.
Seward was dictated by no other motives than those of
pleasure or convenience."

Mr. Petre regarded this explicit declaration as "very
satisfactory" with reference to the present state of
affairs, but he thought that it would be better still if
Count Frijs would give him the same assurance for the

[26] Lord Clarendon to Mr. George Petre, February 3, 1866,
MS. F. O. 22/334.

future. To this, however, the Count demurred, for he
regarded it within

"the sphere of possibility, though not of probability,
that the United States may on some future occasion
make such brilliant offers to Denmark for the purchase
of her Colonies as to dispose her to entertain them; but
under any circumstances the known objections entertained by Her Majesty's Government and that of
France would not fail to have great weight with the
Danish Government."[27]

These assurances on the part of Count Frijs had
little weight with the British Prime Minister, Lord
John Russell, who made the following marginal comment on Lord Clarendon's instruction to Mr. Petre,
February 3, 1866:

"The Danish Minister told me that if Denmark chose
to sell the Island the fact wd. be communicated but
that the right of Denmark to do so was he thought clear
and indisputable. I have little doubt the sale is intended
in the treasury of the Danish Exchequer, if Seward
offers a good price."[28]

The future was to prove the truth of this forecast
on the part of Lord John Russell, and if Seward had
known how seriously the British Government was
taking these rumors as to the probable purchase of the
Danish islands by the United States, he would have
pushed the matter more vigorously. As it was, the
rumors proved disturbing both to Seward and Raasloff,

[27] Petre to the Earl of Clarendon, February 15, 1866, MS.
F. O. 22/335, no. 16.

[28] Clarendon to Petre, February 3, 1866, MS. F. O. 22/334,
no. 9.

especially one that appeared in the New York *Herald* and was then reprinted in the *Daily National Intelligencer* on March 2, 1866. According to this newspaper notice it was apparent that Seward's recent trip to the Caribbean had a definite political motive back of it. This motive was nothing less than to secure a naval station on the island of St. Thomas, and the New York *Herald* expressed the belief that Seward was so pleased with this Danish island that he immediately entered into negotiations with the Danish Government "by which the object has been accomplished."

On March 2, 1866, Seward and Raasloff had a conference for the purpose of discussing the effect of these rumors upon the proposed negotiations between Denmark and the United States. Seward expressed his readiness publicly to deny the truth of the rumor as reported in the New York *Herald,* but it was finally decided "to let this rumor die in the same way as all the other rumors had died that were connected with Mr. Seward's trip to the West Indies." Seward then observed that it was his opinion that secrecy and speed were essential to the success of the negotiations:

"It is evident," remarked the Secretary, "that the moment I begin to talk about this matter which, at this moment is yet entirely confidential between you and me, it becomes extremely difficult to preserve the secret, and it is neither in your interest nor in mine that the affair should be known before it becomes absolutely necessary ; and as soon as you shall have received positive instructions, I shall be prepared to take up the affair."[29]

[29] *Memorandum,* MS. Dept. of State, *op. cit.*

The whole attitude of Seward in this affair convinced Raasloff that the "United States eagerly and sincerely wishes to buy our islands, that she will pay a good price for them, and that the completion of the transaction will not meet insurmountable difficulties in Congress."[30] This favorable attitude on the part of the American Government proved so alluring to Raasloff that he did not wait for positive instructions from his Government before taking up the matter again with Seward. On March 16, 1866, another interview was arranged with the Secretary of State in which Raasloff readily admitted

"that he had nothing new of special interest to communicate; that the position of his Government to this affair had not undergone any change since their last interview (March 2d), and that he should not have sought a conversation with the Secretary of State if he had not received the impression in the last named interview, that the Secretary of State expected the Danish Government to give to this matter a more definite shape before he, the Secretary of State could submit it to the President and bring about an action of the United States Government."

For this reason, Raasloff considered it in accordance

"with the spirit of their previous understanding to say, that since the visit of the Secretary of State to the Danish West India Islands, which had given rise to so many rumors, the Danish Government was not more than formerly disposed to proceed differently in this matter, and that the Danish Government still expected a positive offer from that of the United States."

[30] Raasloff to Count Frijs, March 3, 1866, MS. D. F. O.

At the conclusion of the interview, Seward assured the Danish Minister that he himself

"desired the acquisition of the Islands for political and commercial reasons as much as ever before; that, as yet, he had only spoken to the President about it, and that he hoped, within a few weeks to be able to make some such definite offer which the Danish Government expected from him."[31]

On March 18, 1866, Raasloff sent a long report to Mr. Vedel, Director of the Ministry of Foreign Affairs, about the general situation in Washington. It was his opinion that the "most opportune time" to have pushed through the treaty of cession had already passed. The foreign relations of the United States were not enjoying a smooth course, and friction had already developed between it and both France and England. In view of the threatening possibilities with reference to those powers, it was difficult to predict the future. One thing was certain, however, and that was that both France and England would protest against the sale of the islands to the United States. Therefore, if the Danish Government decided to negotiate a treaty of cession, it would have to be done "quickly and definitively."[32]

Some ten days later, March 29, 1866, Seward and Raasloff again discussed the question of the cession of the Danish islands to the United States. After the usual preliminaries, Seward informed the Danish Minister that he had been so busy with domestic problems that

---

[31] *Memorandum*, MS. Dept. of State, *op. cit.*
[32] Raasloff to Vedel, March 18, 1866, MS. D. F. O.

there had been no opportunity to discuss the matter
with the President and Cabinet. Moreover, he was distinctly puzzled as to how to present the problem to them,
for their first question would be:

" 'What sum does Denmark demand?' It would be
very difficult to make them understand and accept the
viewpoint that in this case the buyer would have to
make the offer—just opposite to the usual procedure."

Raasloff then directed Seward's attention to the fact
that the "matter in question was very different from an
ordinary commercial transaction." In this case, Denmark had not offered the islands for sale, but had
merely declared a willingness seriously to consider a
"definite offer." If Seward was really anxious about
securing the islands why could he not make an offer
that Raasloff would treat as entirely confidential? To
this proposal, however, Seward strongly demurred:

"No," said the Secretary of State, "if I mention to
you a sum which we would be ready to pay, then I
must have a clear and definite agreement with the President and my colleagues. . . . In that event the matter
would no longer be secret. . . . In that regard your
Government apparently is better off than ours."

This little speech made but slight impression upon
Raasloff, who reported to Count Frijs as follows:

"I am pretty sure that it is not necessary for Mr.
Seward to present the matter to the entire Cabinet
before he can make us a definite offer, but I believe that
an understanding with the President . . . would be
sufficient. As the President has the sole responsibility,
and as in matters of far greater importance he acts

according to his desires without consulting the members of his Cabinet, I am inclined to believe that Mr. Seward . . . will delay the matter . . . not so much because he expects in this way to obtain more favorable terms, but because he wishes to boast of a little diplomatic victory. As a matter of fact I have . . . been con-firmed in my conviction that the size of the amount (within certain limits, of course) will not be a stumbling-block, and that the President himself is inter-ested in the project."[33]

In accordance with his conversation with General Raasloff, Seward on the following day, March 30, brought the question of the purchase of the Danish West Indies before the Cabinet for discussion. In the *Diary* of Gideon Welles there is the following illus-trative entry:

"Mr. Seward brought up in the Cabinet to-day, the subject of the purchase of the Danish islands in the West Indies, particularly St. Thomas. . . . I do not think there has been overmuch shrewdness in the trans-action on our part as yet. It would have been better for Seward to have remained away from the islands, but should we acquire it his visit will undoubtedly become historical, and it will not afflict him, perhaps, if the country pays largely for the record of his name and visit. He proposes to offer ten millions for all the Danish islands. I think it a large sum. At least double what I would have offered when the islands were wanted, and three times as much as I am willing the Government should give now. In fact I doubt if Congress would purchase for three millions, and I must see Seward and tell him my opinion."[34]

[33] Raasloff to Frijs, March 30, 1866, MS. D. F. O.
[34] Vol. 2, pp. 466-467.

From the entries in Welles's *Diary* it would seem that at this time the Cabinet refrained from taking any definite action as to the exact price to be offered for the Danish West Indies. This fact proved somewhat embarrassing to Seward when he met the Danish Minister on April 6. He could still state, however, that the United States was anxious to make the purchase, but he added that his Government

"declined to offer a certain sum for those possessions, but expected a proposition to that effect from the Danish Government, which proposition would then be earnestly and kindly considered."

When General Raasloff inquired whether this communication was to be considered as confidential, Seward replied:

"Yes, it is confidential, but it is at the same time authentic; this matter has been regularly considered by the Executive."[35]

The Danish Minister then expressed a desire to know whether the refusal of the Secretary of State to name a definite sum for the purchase of the Danish West Indies was meant to be definite and final. Mr. Seward's reply was emphatic. His refusal was

[35] *Memorandum*, MS. Dept. of State, *op. cit.* On April 2, 1866, Welles called to see Seward and informed him "that he had named too high a price for the Danish islands; that five millions was, I apprehended, more than our people would feel like giving; that I would not offer more than three. He thanked me; said he would inquire their lowest terms, that Raasloff was anxious to sell, etc., but thought not less than five millions would be required." See Gideon Welles, *Diary,* vol. 2, p. 473.

"entirely definite, and he added, that if the Danish Government should not be willing to adopt the proposed course with a view of arriving at an understanding, it would probably be better to let the whole matter drop."[36]

In the meantime, on March 9, and April 9, 1866, Yeaman had written to Seward relative to the continued rumors in American and European newspapers to the effect that the United States was anxious to secure St. Thomas as a naval station, and that Seward's cruise to the West Indies had distinct political significance.[37] On April 20, Seward wrote to Yeaman to inform him that

"only speculative diplomatists could suppose that the Secretary of State, however desirous he might be to purchase an island in American seas dependent upon a European Government, would personally go for that purpose to the island which was to be bought, instead of addressing himself, . . . through the Minister of the United States to the Government which should own the island."[38]

Seward, however, failed to mention, in this instruction to Yeaman, that for more than a year he had been discussing the question of the purchase with the Danish Minister, and that President Johnson and his Cabinet were even then considering the matter.[39]

---

[36] *Memorandum,* MS. Dept. of State, *op. cit.*

[37] MS. Dept. of State, *Denmark, Desp.,* vol. 8.

[38] MS. Dept. of State, *Denmark, Inst.,* vol. 14.

[39] One of the reasons that Seward did not inform Yeaman of the progress of the negotiations for the purchase of the Danish West Indies was the fact that on April 6, 1866, he had in-

On April 22, 1866, General Raasloff once more declined to name a definite sum for the cession of the
Danish West Indies. Seward was equally coy, although
he admitted

"that he had now in his mind a sum which the United
States Government might pay for those islands and
that that sum was larger than the one he had in his mind
when he made the first overture to the Danish Minister
on the 7th of January, 1865, and he explained this by
the present improved condition of the finances of the
country."[40]

After this cryptic utterance, Seward endeavored to
quicken the interest of the Danish Minister in the
negotiation. The matter had made important progress
since January 7, 1865, since it had "been made the
subject of regular consideration in the Cabinet." It
was not a mere question of "dollars and cents," the
main difficulties in the way of such a purchase were the
complications arising out of "domestic politics." President Johnson and his Cabinet had several times discussed the purchase of the Danish West Indies, the
final decision being that it was proper for the Danish
Government to name the price. Seward further inti-

---

formed General Raasloff of the inquiries of Mr. Yeaman, and
he had assured the Danish Minister on that occasion that Mr.
Yeaman would receive no direct answer to his query, "the
Danish Minister present being the only person outside of the
Government of the United States to whom any communi-
cation whatever about this affair had been, or would be made."
See *Memorandum*, MS. Dept. of State, *op. cit.*

[40] *Memorandum*, MS. Dept. of State, *op. cit.*

mated that as Secretary of State he had not yet "made a single step in this matter which implied a real responsibility."[41]

If Seward wished to excite alarm in the mind of the Danish Minister relative to the fate of the negotiation, he certainly succeeded in his purpose. General Raasloff felt that he could interpret Seward's declaration in no other sense than that the Secretary of State was "no longer willing to incur any serious responsibility for the sake of this project." Such an attitude offended the sensibilities of the Danish Minister, who promptly informed the Secretary of State that "in his opinion, the Secretary of State had not acted rightly in bringing forward this matter without being at the same time determined to carry it out consistently."

To General Raasloff it seemed that Seward was trying to reverse the usual practice of diplomacy. The Secretary of State had made the first overture to the Danish Minister on January 7, 1865, and it appeared to the representative of the Danish Government that some definite offer from Seward was no more than a "plain logical consequence" of the steps already taken by the American Secretary of State. The Secretary's change of attitude had "shaken the Danish Minister's belief" in Seward's sincerity, and Raasloff thought it would not be surprising if the Danish Government would share this same view.

But these plain words had little effect upon Seward, who closed the interview

[41] *Memorandum,* MS. Dept. of State, *op. cit.*

"with the remark that, in his opinion the project was not in any bad position, but that he thought it advisable to await the answer of the Danish Government to the communication made by the Secretary of State to the Danish Minister in the interview which took place on the 6th of April."[42]

The answer of the Danish Government was distinctly discouraging to the continuance of the negotiations. After a careful survey of all the factors in the case, Mr. Vedel, the Director of the Danish Ministry of Foreign Affairs, thought that "more than ever," he should adhere to his opinion that it was not expedient at that time to cede the Danish islands to the United States. It was evident that both France and England would be strongly opposed to the acquisition by the United States of colonial possessions in the Caribbean. England herself might well insist that the Danish Ambassador at London, General Buelow, had definitely promised that his Government would not part with its islands. Of course, this promise had never been actually given, and Buelow had written a note to the British Government in which he had endeavoured to dissipate the false impression under which they apparently labored. But nevertheless, British objections had to be given some consideration, and it was decidedly worth while to cultivate the good will of France and England, especially since the Schleswig-Holstein question was still unsettled.

[42] *Memorandum,* MS. Dept. of State, *op. cit.* See also the report of Raasloff to Count Frijs, April 24, 1866, MS. D. F. O.

The best policy for Denmark to follow, thought Mr. Vedel, would be to postpone the negotiations for the sale of the islands until a more propitious moment. The desire of America to acquire the islands would "hardly be lessened by waiting," and the value of St. Thomas as a naval station would probably increase each year. It would be important, however, to be careful lest the United States become distrustful of the Danish Government, and thus render it difficult at a later date to negotiate for the cession of the islands.[43]

After Raasloff had received these instructions and had learned of the disinclination of the Danish Government to conclude negotiations for the sale of their islands to the United States, he was fearful that any abrupt termination of his conversations with Seward might give umbrage to the Secretary of State. Therefore, on June 14, 1866, he called at the Department of State and informed Seward that there were certain "grave difficulties" that the Danish Government would have to face in carrying on negotiations for the sale of the islands. In view of this situation it seemed best for him to return to Copenhagen for consultation with the Minister of Foreign Affairs.

Seward was not surprised that strong opposition to the sale of the islands had developed in Denmark, but he sought to convince Raasloff that not only on the side of the Danish Government did serious objections lie against the negotiation, but that in America the way was equally difficult. Indeed, he was certain that if he

[43] Mr. Vedel to Raasloff, May 18, 1866, MS. D. F. O.

should commit a "single mistake" in the conduct of the negotiations, then all would be lost. He could hardly hope to convince the "President and the other members of the Cabinet that this affair was connected with greater difficulties for the Danish Government than for that of the United States." He would, however, "make a new effort in that direction and try to get the President and his colleagues to allow him to make an offer to the Danish Government."[44]

Two weeks later, June 28, 1866, the Danish Minister called at the Department of State in order to acquaint Seward of his early departure for Copenhagen. Seward then informed him of the failure of his efforts to induce the President or the members of the Cabinet to "consent to any new step being taken by him in this affair." He was certain, however, that "the Executive could always count upon the assistance of Congress in matters of this kind, provided the proceedings had been correct." The Government of the United States still retained a strong desire to secure possession of the Danish West Indies, and when the Danish Minister returned to the United States with "positive instructions" the Secretary of State would be prepared "to engage in a definite negotiation."[45]

On this same day, Rear-Admiral W. B. Shubrick in answer to a formal request, submitted to Gideon Welles, the Secretary of the Navy, a report on "The Necessity for Coaling Stations for supplying our Steam Vessels

[44] *Memorandum,* MS. Dept. of State, *op. cit.*
[45] *Memorandum,* MS. Dept. of State, *op. cit.*

of War, bound from the United States around Cape St. Roque to the south coast of Brazil, and around Cape Horn."

Steam having taken the place of wind as a propulsive power in all cases where time is valuable and speed of importance, it was the opinion of the Rear-Admiral that provision should at once be made

"for an ample supply of the superior anthracite coal of our country at suitable distances on the long routes which our vessels of war will be called upon to take in the service of the country. . . . The public service has already suffered injury as well as inconvenience from want of attention to this subject. . . .

"The remedy for these evils is to have on this important route our own *coaling stations,* at which should be kept at all times a full supply of the best quality of anthracite coal. These coaling stations should be at distances which can be reached in succession in from seven to ten days steaming. The harbors at these stations should be easy of ingress and egress. We should not be dependent for their use on the courtesy of any other power; in other words they should be our colonies under our own flag.

"The first of these stations after leaving the United States should be somewhere in the West Indies, and so far as my own experience goes in those seas, and from the examination of charts and other authorities, I am of opinion that the best position will be found in the group of the Virgin Islands, and those of them belonging to the Kingdom of Denmark. These are three principal islands, Saint Thomas, Santa Croix and St. John's, and a number of islets. The best island, that of St. Thomas, is well known to many officers of our Navy as having a fine harbor, capacious, secure, and easy of ingress and egress.

"It is believed that the whole group might be purchased from Denmark for a sum inconsiderable in comparison with the advantages which would accrue to the United States from their possession."[46]

Apparently, Seward wished to confirm this report of Rear-Admiral Shubrick, by a similar report from some high military officer, for on July 6, 1866, he wrote to Edwin M. Stanton, Secretary of War, as follows:

"It is deemed desirable to ascertain officially and authentically the value to the United States, especially for military and naval purposes, of the Danish West India Islands, supposing that we should acquire a title to them. I will consequently thank you to detail an officer to proceed thither for the purpose of examining and reporting upon the subject, or to adopt such other measures as to you may seem best to that end. It is presumed to be unnecessary to add that it is essential for the success of the object that the steps with reference to it should not be prematurely disclosed."[47]

But Seward soon realized that it would take some weeks for a military officer to visit the Virgin Islands and then submit a definitive report on their value. Inasmuch as the Danish Minister was about to depart for Copenhagen, it would be wise, thought Seward, to let him carry back to Denmark with him a tentative offer from the United States relative to the purchase of the Danish West Indies. For more than a year Seward had evaded giving the Danish Minister any clear intimation as to the probable sum the United States would offer for the islands, and now before coming to any conclu-

[46] Shubrick to Welles, June 28, 1866, *Gideon Welles Papers*, Library of Congress, vol. 61.

[47] *Edwin M. Stanton Papers*, Library of Congress, vol. 30.

sion he thought it advisable to seek the advice of military and naval experts. The report which Rear-Admiral Shubrick sent to Secretary Welles, June 28, 1866, had stressed the advantages of the Virgin Islands from the viewpoint of naval needs, and no attempt had been made to translate the value of the islands in dollars and cents. Perhaps it would be best to request the joint opinion of a high military and a high naval officer, such opinion to be given at once and not on the basis of extended study. Therefore, on July 7, 1866, the day after his letter to Stanton, Seward prepared the following memorandum:

"Confidential.
"The Secretary of State presents his compliments to Major-General Delafield and to Rear-Admiral Shubrick, and will thank them to state, for the information of the President, the greatest and the least amount of money which, in their opinion, it would be advisable to offer for the Danish West India Islands."[48]

Two days later, July 9, 1866, Richard Delafield, Brevet Major-General and Chief Engineer of the United States Army, made a brief report to Seward. In this report he indicated that the Danish West Indies were only "a source of debt" to Denmark, and that if the King of Denmark were given "$3,000,000 in bonds bearing 5 per cent. interest he will be well paid for his sovereignty," and if paid $5,000,000 therefore, he would realize "more than his Government can in any way derive by holding a prize that can be taken from him

[48] MS. Miscellaneous Letters, Dept. of State, July, 1866, pt. 1.

at any moment he becomes at war with a strong maritime nation."[49]

Rear-Admiral Shubrick submitted a separate report to Seward on July 10. It was his opinion that the

"least sum to be offered should be Four Millions of Dollars, and the greatest sum to be offered should be Seven Millions of Dollars."[50]

On the basis of these reports Seward had a latitude of from three millions to seven millions, and born imperialist that he was, it is easy to understand how he placed the greater faith in the report of Shubrick. On July 12, 1866, Raasloff wrote to Seward and requested an audience for the purpose of taking leave of absence from the United States. On July 17, the audience was held, and as soon as Raasloff was seated, Seward sent for the Assistant Secretary of State, Mr. Frederick W. Seward, who lost no time in appearing with a short note addressed to the Danish Minister. The letter contained the long sought-for offer on the part of the United States for the Danish West Indies. It was phrased as follows:

DEPARTMENT OF STATE, Washington, July 17, 1866.
"Confidential.
"SIR:—I have the honor to propose to you that the United States will negotiate with the King of Denmark for the purchase of the Danish Islands in the West Indies, namely, St. Thomas and the adjacent islets, Santa Cruz and St. John.

[49] *Sen. Doc.* 231, 56 Cong., 2 sess., pt. 8, pp. 177-178.
[50] *MS. Miscellaneous Letters,* Dept. of State, July, 1866, pt. 1.

"The United States would be willing to pay for the same five millions of dollars in gold, payable in this country—negotiation to be by Treaty, which you will of course understand will require the constitutional ratification of the Senate.

"Insomuch as you propose to visit Copenhagen, the United States Minister at that place will be instructed to converse with you, or with your Government on the subject, but should your Government conclude to negotiate, the proceeding will be expected to be concluded here, and not elsewhere.

"Accept, sir, the renewed assurance of my high consideration.

WILLIAM H. SEWARD.

"His Excellency General Raasloff.[51]

Seward then informed Raasloff that the American Minister at Copenhagen, Mr. George H. Yeaman, would be instructed to observe "the utmost discretion about this matter and to take no step whatever in regard to it before the Danish Minister should have arrived in Copenhagen." When Raasloff remarked that for reasons of health he intended to make a visit to Switzerland, and therefore some time would elapse before he should reach Copenhagen, Seward replied that "he was not pressed for an answer, and that he should now leave it entirely with the Danish Government to negotiate how and when they thought proper."[52]

On the same day of his interview with Raasloff, Seward sent to Yeaman a copy of his confidential letter

[51] MS. Dept. of State, *Danish Legation, Notes to,* vol. 6. See also, Raasloff to Frijs, July 20, 1866, MS. D. F. O.

[52] *Memorandum*, MS. Dept. of State, *op. cit.*

to the Danish Minister, and instructed him not to allude to the matter unless first brought up by the Danish Government.[53]

General Raasloff's stay in Switzerland was only a brief one, and when he arrived in Copenhagen on September 28, 1866, he was invited to take a seat in the Danish Cabinet as Minister of War. In writing to Seward on September 29, he speaks of his reluctance to accept a Cabinet post because this might render it necessary for someone else

"to complete the interesting negotiation we have been carrying on for nearly two years. . . . I trust however that the negotiations I attended to will be brought to a happy end. I have taken upon myself to assure Count

[53] Seward to Yeaman, July 17, 1866, MS. Dept. of State, *Denmark, Inst.,* vol. 14. In the *Diary* of Colonel William G. Moore, private secretary to President Johnson, there is the following interesting entry with reference to the attitude of Secretary Stanton towards the purchase of the Danish West Indies: "July 14, 1866. The Secretary of War is a most valuable man and if he were not controlled by impulses, would exert great power and balance. He has a most eminently legal mind and can study a legal proposition with greater balance than another would, all the way through. But this balance which he sometimes exhibits is external and unaccountable. Take for instance the proposition to purchase the Island of Saint Thomas from Denmark. It has been brought before the Cabinet several times and has on each occasion been postponed on account of his violent opposition to the project, he declaring that it was only a pile of rocks in the sea which he would not have as a gift. At a Cabinet meeting yesterday, however, he was most earnest in advocating the purchase of the islands, and thought that $10,000,000 would not be an exorbitant price for it." The *Diary* of Colonel Moore is in the Manuscript Division of the Library of Congress.

Frijs that you would deal liberally and generously with us and I think I shall succeed in bringing about a decision and the necessary action. I shall see the King to-day and will then solicit that my post in the U. S. will be kept open for me while I am in the Cabinet, and it will thus only be a question of time when I shall return to Washington."[54]

On September 30, Yeaman wrote to Seward that Raasloff was "sincerely in favor" of the cession to the United States of the Danish West Indies, and it was his opinion that Raasloff's elevation to the office of Secretary of War in the Danish Cabinet would "facilitate the progress of affairs." Raasloff had intimated that the Danish Government was favorable to the negotiation, but had added that they "must have some assurance of the confirmation of the Rigsraad," which would probably meet in November.[55]

On October 21, Raasloff wrote again to Seward in order to express his regret that he was unable at that moment "to communicate any progress in regard to the matter which you allude to, but it is under discussion, and I hope soon to have something definite to report."[56]

As the weeks hurried by and neither Yeaman nor Raasloff reported any further progress in the negotiations, Seward became more and more impatient. His son Frederick, the Assistant Secretary of State, was preparing to go to Santo Domingo to secure the lease

[54] MS. Dept. of State, *Denmark, Notes*, vol. 4.
[55] MS. Dept. of State, *Denmark, Desp.*, vol. 8.
[56] MS. Dept. of State, *Denmark, Notes*, vol. 4.

or sale of the Gulf and Peninsula of Samana to the United States to serve as a naval station.[57] Before closing definitely with Santo Domingo, Seward wished to have an exact report on how affairs stood with Denmark relative to the Danish West Indies. Therefore, on January 12, 1867, Seward sent the following message by cable, and in cipher, to Yeaman at Copenhagen:

"Tell Raasloff haste important."[58]

This brief instruction reached Yeaman on the following day, but unfortunately, after a frenzied search through the Legation archives, Yeaman was unable to discover any key to cipher messages. He at once telegraphed to Berlin, but the American Minister there was in the same fix, so it was necessary to get in touch with London.[59] Finally, on January 19, by way of London, Yeaman received a translation of Seward's cable instruction of January 12.[60]

On the following day, Yeaman had an interview with Raasloff and communicated to him Seward's delayed cable instruction. The Minister of War assured the American Minister that "the matter was making progress, but that Count Frijs, being cautious and a little slow in such things, felt some hesitation about taking the final step."

[57] MS. Dept. of State, *Special Agents,* vol. 1.
[58] MS. Dept. of State, *Denmark, Inst.,* vol. 14.
[59] MS. Dept. of State, *Denmark, Desp.,* vol. 9.
[60] MS. Dept. of State, Yeaman to Seward, Jan. 21, 1867. *Denmark, Desp.,* vol. 9.

When Yeaman inquired if there "were any impediments other than the objection or hesitation felt in the Danish Cabinet," Raasloff informed him that he knew of "none." He did raise the question, however, of the ratification of any treaty after March 4, Congress being adjourned after that date. Yeaman then explained how the President could request the Senate to remain in session for the transaction of executive business. But the Minister of War, who had long been the representative of Denmark in the United States, was familiar with American constitutional procedure, and he expressed some fears that even though the Senate consented to the ratification of the treaty, the House of Representatives might not appropriate the money necessary to fulfil the treaty obligations. Yeaman sought to quiet such fears. He was certain that "there could not possibly be any difficulty about that, as Congress would assuredly not refuse the necessary appropriation."[61]

On January 14, 1867, two days after his cable to Yeaman, Seward wrote to Raasloff to urge haste in the pending negotiations.[62] On February 5, Raasloff replied by a letter which he entrusted to a friend to deliver to the Secretary of State. He wished Mr. Seward to know that he had

"not lost sight of the matter you mention, but am pushing it gently. There is however one difficulty in the way which might perhaps be removed by a single

[61] Yeaman to Seward, January 21, 1867, MS. Dept. of State, *Denmark, Desp.,* vol. 9.

[62] Seward to Raasloff, January 14, 1867, MS. Dept. of State, *Danish Legation, Notes to,* vol. 6.

word said by you to the trusty and confidential friend who will hand you this letter;—a word indicating the terms on which the affair can be arranged—from your point of view. My friend, of course, knows nothing of the contents of this letter, and I must leave with you how far you will or can say that word to him." [63]

Some ten days later, February 16, 1867, General Raasloff called to see Mr. Yeaman and questioned the American Minister very closely concerning the probable effects of the conflict between the President and Congress. He was especially anxious to know whether the removal of President Johnson through impeachment proceedings would mean the resignation of Seward as Secretary of State. Yeaman agreed that such a course would be very likely, but as to the success of the impeachment trial it was largely a matter for speculation, and the Danish Minister of War could guess about the outcome just as accurately as could the American Minister.

When Raasloff further questioned Yeaman about the likelihood of another civil war in America, and whether the contest between the Executive and Congress would depress the gold market, the American Minister replied:

"The only clear and definite opinion I have about the whole thing is that there will be no more fighting, that there will be a President and a Secretary, that the government will go on, and will have gold enough in the treasury for all its purposes." [64]

[63] Raasloff to Seward, February 5, 1867, MS. Dept. of State, *Denmark, Notes,* vol. 4.

[64] Yeaman to Seward, February 16, 1867, MS. Dept. of State, *Denmark, Desp.,* vol. 9.

Raasloff finally wished to know if there were any political significance in the visit of Frederick W. Seward to Santo Domingo. When Yeaman disclaimed any official knowledge of the purpose of the Assistant Secretary of State in making his brief sojourn in the Caribbean, Raasloff sagely remarked: "There is something in that trip."

Yeaman had hoped that Frederick Seward's visit to Santo Domingo would hasten the course of the negotiations for the Danish West Indies, but it had no apparent result. The failure of the Dominican mission lessened the need for a quick response from the Danish Government, but Seward again became restive after weeks of delay, so on March 8, 1867, he sent the following cable to Yeaman, *via* London:

"Want yea or nay now. We can read Danish politicians here as well as Danish politicians can read American in Copenhagen." [65]

This cable was received by Mr. Yeaman on March 12, who immediately secured an interview with General

[65] Seward to Charles Francis Adams, March 8, 1867, MS. Dept. of State, *Denmark, Inst.,* vol. 14. Seward's anxiety to push the negotiations led him to consider in February, 1867, the appointment of a special agent to Denmark to hasten the action of the Danish Government. According to the *Diary* of Gideon Welles, Seward and Stanton "had made arrangements to send General Meigs to Denmark to purchase or negotiate for St. Thomas. I doubted the necessity; but the President ended the matter by saying he was opposed to the practice, which was being introduced, of sending officers on traveling excursions for their personal benefit at the Government's expense." See entry in *Diary* under date of February 8, 1867, vol. 3, p. 40.

Raasloff. When the Minister of War was asked if any progress had recently been made relative to the cession of the Danish West Indies to the United States, he replied in a disappointingly laconic fashion: "None material." He did admit, however, that Count Frijs favored the negotiation, but did "not feel quite ready yet." Indeed, nothing much could be accomplished until the American Government should make a more liberal offer. The sum mentioned in Seward's letter to General Raasloff was considered as "pro forma'" only, and was entirely too inadequate to be seriously considered.[66]

On March 28, 1867, after Seward had received Mr. Yeaman's despatch of March 13, setting forth the fact that the Danish Government wished the United States to make a more liberal offer, the Secretary of State wrote a confidential instruction to the American Minister at Copenhagen requesting him to ascertain from

"General Raasloff whether the United States may expect to be favored with a communication, formal or informal, from the Government of Denmark concerning the matter within a short time. If he shall answer in the negative, you will then say that you are authorized to submit to the Minister for Foreign Affairs an offer for the purchase of the Danish West India islands in the terms of the note before referred to. You will make such a communication to the Minister for Foreign Affairs in a confidential manner and will communicate his reply."[67]

[66] Yeaman to Seward, March 13, 1867, MS. Dept. of State, *Denmark, Desp.*, vol. 9.

[67] Seward to Yeaman, March 28, 1867, MS. Dept. of State, *Denmark, Inst.*, vol. 14.

On April 23, Mr. Yeaman called upon General Raasloff in accordance with Seward's instructions, and the
Minister of War expressed the opinion that a reply to
Mr. Seward's inquiry of March 28 might soon be expected. Raasloff then alluded to the price offered by
Mr. Seward in his letter of July 17, 1866. Such an offer
he believed was not more than half what it should be,
and he slyly intimated that

"Mr. Seward understood his people too well to risk
his reputation by offering as much in the beginning as
he really intended to give." [68]

Four days later, April 27, 1867, Yeaman again wrote
to Seward and emphasized the opinion that the negotiation "should be concluded with the present Government, and as soon as possible." There was evident
danger that news of the negotiations might reach the
ears of foreign diplomats, and there was no doubt but
that "England, France, and Spain would use all possible
efforts to thwart the design." Besides, there was the
additional menace of an unfriendly Cabinet succeeding
the present Danish Cabinet which was favorable to the
cession. In case the new military bills before the Rigsdag would be defeated, the Cabinet would resign, and
there was also the possibility that in the event of a war
between France and Prussia it would be impossible to
restrain the strong feeling in favor of France, and thus
the present Danish Cabinet which inclined towards

[68] Yeaman to Seward, April 24, 1867, MS. Dept. of State,
Denmark, Desp., vol. 9.

neutrality would be compelled to resign in favor of a more militant one.[69]

On April 29, Yeaman had an extended conversation with Raasloff and many aspects of the negotiation were discussed. One thing was certain—the Danish Cabinet was ready to take up the matter seriously, and General Raasloff was convinced that the Rigsdag would confirm whatever treaty the Government concluded. There was no discounting the fact that the proposed treaty would give umbrage to both England and France, but it was hoped that this could be compensated for in a closer "alliance with Russia and the United States." As to the price offered by the United States for the islands, it was apparent that such an offer was made by Seward only as a starting point. In Raasloff's opinion it would be necessary for the American Government to be liberal, and Yeaman believed that "$10,000,000 is about the amount this Government would expect to be offered and feel justified in accepting."[70]

There was one point to which special heed would have to be given. With reference to Santa Cruz, there was, on the part of the Danish Government, a "well-defined obligation to offer it to France first, if ever the Government was willing to sell." Therefore, it would be necessary to confine the negotiations to the cession of the islands of St. Thomas and St. John.

[69] Yeaman to Seward, April 27, 1867, MS. Dept. of State, *Denmark, Desp.,* vol. 9.

[70] Yeaman to Seward, April 29, 1867, MS. Dept. of State, *Denmark, Desp.,* vol. 9.

In the event that the negotiations reached a success-
ful conclusion, it would be required by the Danish
Government that a plebiscite be held in the Danish West
Indies to determine whether the people in the islands
desired the transfer of sovereignty to the United
States.[71]

It was at this point in the progress of the negotiations that Seward became convinced that the services
of a special agent would be of value in bringing the
matter to a speedy conclusion. Already, in the early
part of February, 1867, he had thought it wise to send
General M. C. Meigs to Copenhagen to assist the
American Minister, Mr. Yeaman, in the treaty negotiations, but at that time President Johnson had vetoed
the suggestion because he was "opposed to the practice
of sending officers on traveling excursions for their
personal benefit at the Government's expense." But, by
April 30, of this same year, events so shaped themselves that the President was ready to assent to
Seward's second suggestion of a special agent commissioned to expedite the negotiations with Denmark.

At the close of the Civil War it was deemed highly
advisable to have better cable communications with
Europe, so a Russian-American company called the
"Western Union Russian Extension Company," was
formed for the purpose of laying a cable that would
connect Siberia and Russian America with the United
States. Great things were expected of this projected
cable and telegraph line, and in the spring of 1867,

[71] Yeaman to Seward, April 30, 1867, *ibid.*

Senator James R. Doolittle, of Wisconsin, was sent to St. Petersburg as the American representative of this joint Russian-American company.[72]

Seward was of the opinion that Doolittle might be able to render distinct service to the United States if he would arrange to stop at Copenhagen and talk with Count Frijs, the Danish Minister for Foreign Affairs. In a communication addressed to Doolittle, April 30, 1867, Seward requested him to call on Mr. Yeaman and General Raasloff, and endeavour to ascertain what obstacles were retarding the conclusion of a treaty for the cession of the Danish West Indies.[73] One week later, May 8, 1867, Seward sent the following confidential memorandum to Senator Doolittle:

"See the President. Tell him that I propose that you informally stop at Copenhagen and see if you can hurry up the purchase of the Danish West India Islands (including St. Thomas and Santa Cruz). The price offered is five millions which we always stood ready to advance to ten millions. With a view to be able to do this we have, as the President knows, stopped upon Samana in St. Domingo. If you find that you can succeed for ten millions and no less, say so to Danish Government. If you find you cannot, then say nothing about it."[74]

It is interesting to note that Seward had finally made up his mind to offer as high as ten millions for the

[72] Seward, Olive Risley. "A Diplomatic Episode," *Scribner's Magazine*, new series, vol. 2, pp. 591-592. See also J. D. Reid, *The Telegraph in America* (N. Y. 1886), chap. 39.

[73] MS. Dept. of State, *Special Missions*, vol. 3.

[74] Seward to Doolittle, May 8, 1867, MS. Dept. of State, *Special Missions*, vol. 3.

Danish West Indies. It is even more interesting to note that he had "always stood ready to advance to ten millions." For many months the Danish Government had played a game of procrastination in order to induce Seward to make an offer of that amount, and here he calmly announces to Doolittle that he had long had this particular sum in mind. It is no wonder that the negotiations had languished!

On May 16, 1867, Seward, without waiting to hear the outcome of the Doolittle mission, sent the following peremptory telegram to Yeaman:

"If Denmark do not desire to sell, she will not, and so an end. If she desires to sell to the United States let her name price and conditions. Plebiscite not important. Would prove inconvenient and unnecessary. Still may be yielded. We presume Denmark will not now refuse us and then sell to European monarchical power. If so we should protest. No transfer of colonies in West Indies between European Powers can be indifferent to United States. Time essential because we may any day conclude arrangements in another quarter. In that case we desist from our offer but do not agree to alienation of Danish Islands to another power. Doolittle will see you. Show him this. All ready here."[75]

As soon as Yeaman received this cablegram from Seward he arranged an interview with both General Raasloff and Count Frijs in order to discuss the situation. Count Frijs opened the interview by declaring that the offer contained in Seward's confidential note to General Raasloff of July 17, 1866, had been carefully

[75] Seward to Yeaman, May 16, 1867, MS. Dept. of State, *Denmark, Inst.,* vol. 14.

considered by the Danish Cabinet and had been unanimously rejected. However, in compliance with Secretary Seward's desires, the Danish Government

"would make another proposition, *viz.*, that Denmark would cede the group of islands in question to the United States for 15 million dollars in gold—the two islands of St. Thomas and St. John for 10 million, and Santa Cruz for 5 million, the United States having the privilege of accepting the first offer and refusing the second."

In explanation of this proposition, Count Frijs then spoke to Yeaman as follows:

"The reason for this was that it was thought necessary to have France's consent to the sale of Santa Cruz. According to our constitution, it was absolutely necessary to have the Rigsdag approve the transaction; furthermore we should insist on the consent of the population. I [Frijs] gave it as my opinion that if the authorities came to an agreement about the transaction, it would be desirable to wind up the negotiations as soon as possible, to avoid the protests and remonstrances from other Powers. With all due consideration for the American Government, I [Frijs] favored the suggestion that the negotiations be held in Copenhagen, since in this case one would be able to lay the final agreement before the Rigsdag without any loss of time, and the separate special points could be settled better here." [76]

At the close of this interview with General Raasloff and Count Frijs, Yeaman cabled as follows to Seward:

[76] *Memorandum* in Danish Foreign Office giving records of conversations between Yeaman, General Raasloff, and Count Frijs. This *memorandum* covers the dates from May 2, 1867, until October 4 of that year.

"Danish Government says fifteen millions for all, or ten millions for St. Thomas and St. John. Consent of people there to be had. Negotiations to be here. Rigsdag adjourns next month. I write this date."[77]

In a lengthy despatch to Seward, Yeaman tells in detail how the Danish Government finally came to the point of indicating what sum they would accept for the cession of the Danish West Indies. Count Frijs, the Danish Minister of Foreign Affairs, was willing to sell the three islands to the United States, but the consent of France would have to be secured with reference to Santa Cruz. If this consent was withheld, Denmark would keep the island rather than sell it to France.[78]

On May 21, 1867, Seward brought up before the Cabinet the question of the purchase of the Danish West Indies, and formally presented the offer of the Danish Government. The comment in the *Diary* of Welles is significant:

"Seward presents a telegraphic correspondence with Raasloff, now at Copenhagen, and a memorandum given to Senator Doolittle relative to the purchase of the Danish West India Islands. Denmark wants $15,000,000 for the whole or $10,000,000 for St. Thomas, with consent of the inhabitants to the transfer. Seward sent a dispatch to Yeaman, our Minister to offer $5,000,000, ultimatum $10,000,000. Any expression of inhabitants must be before treaty. McCulloch and myself expressed surprise that more than $5,000,000 had been or should be offered. McCulloch said he believed something had been said about going up to

[77] Yeaman to Seward, May 17, 1867, MS. Dept. of State, *Denmark, Desp.*, vol. 9.

[78] Yeaman to Seward, May 17, 1867, *ibid.*

$7,500,000 for the whole. I stated that I preferred not
to purchase even at $5,000,000. At all events, would not
go beyond that. During the War I had felt that a station
in the West Indies was desirable, but we should experience no such want again. . . . Attorney-General
Stanbery preferred to take Snake Island than to buy an
inhabited island. Seward is anxious to make a purchase
somewhere. Has loose, indefinite, and selfish notions.
It is more the glory of Seward than the true interests of
the country, I apprehend."[79]

On May 23, the question of the purchase was again
presented to the Cabinet for discussion. Upon this
occasion Seward

"submitted a modified proposition to Denmark for the
purchase of her West India Islands, making $7,500,000
an ultimatum. McCulloch, Stanbery, and myself
[Welles] thought it best to guard the Treasury at this
time; that we wanted money more than West Indian
people. Seward was very earnest. It was necessary to
get these islands, or a foothold in the West Indies as a
preservative measure, as a means of security. It would
insure peace. He had talked with the Senators. Grimes
and Wade were earnestly for it, and of course others
were. Stanton, Randall, and Browning went with him.
I stated we had no need of a station in time of peace.
We could take any of the islands from any power with
which we might be at war."[80]

Having secured the consent of the majority of the
Cabinet to his modified proposition to Denmark,
Seward on May 23, 1867, sent the following cipher
cable to Yeaman:

[79] Vol. 3, pp. 95-96.
[80] Gideon Welles, *Diary*, vol. 3, pp. 97-98.

"Denmark's delay has induced parallel negotiations elsewhere. Less anxious now. Nevertheless negotiate. Ultimata, all islands seven and half millions gold. No more. Tell Doolittle. Treaty to be signed, ratified by Denmark absolutely before 4th August or negotiation ended. Consent of islands not necessary."[81]

On May 27, Seward enclosed in his instruction of that date to Yeaman, a copy of a draft treaty for the purchase of the islands. The three islands of St. Thomas, St. John and Santa Cruz were to be ceded to the United States for the sum of $7,500,000. The inhabitants might return to Denmark within two years, but if they chose to remain in the islands they would have the privilege of becoming citizens of the United States, or if they should prefer not to forswear their natural allegiance, they might stay and enjoy all the rights and immunities of citizens of the United States. The cession of the territory was to be free and unincumbered by any reservations, privileges, franchises, grants, or possessions by any associated companies, whether corporate or incorporate, Danish or any other, or by any parties except merely private individual property holders. There was no provision for a plebiscite by which the inhabitants could voice their wishes with reference to the purchase.[82]

On May 28, Yeaman received Seward's cablegram, and immediately despatched a note to Count Frijs which embodied Seward's instructions. On the follow-

[81] MS. Dept. of State, *Denmark, Inst.,* vol. 14.
[82] Seward to Yeaman, May 27, 1867, MS. Dept. of State, *Denmark, Inst.,* vol. 14.

ing day Count Frijs intimated to him that he feared there would be some difficulty about the cession of Santa Cruz. General Raasloff was more explicit, and he assured Yeaman that the answer of the Danish Government "would be negative."[83]

On June 6, Senator Doolittle arrived in Copenhagen, and at once called to see Mr. Yeaman. Then flanked by the American Minister, Senator Doolittle next secured an interview with General Raasloff, but in this case two heads were no better than one. The General was polite but firm. After giving courteous attention to the remarks of the Senator, he informed him that "the offer of seven millions and a half" would "not be acceptable." He did signify, however, that "another sum—eleven millions and a quarter—would certainly be acceptable, and enable them immediately to close and ratify the treaty." It was even possible, he added that so low a sum as "ten or ten and a half millions' might be considered by the Danish Government.[84]

On June 13, Yeaman had an interview with Count Frijs, the Minister of Foreign Affairs, with reference to Seward's offer of seven and a half million dollars for all the islands. Count Frijs was in doubt as to the exact tenor of the reply that was to be made to Seward's

---

[83] Yeaman to Seward, June 7, 1867, MS. Dept. of State, *Denmark, Desp.*, vol. 9. A copy of this draft treaty is contained in *Sen. Doc.* No. 231, 56th Congr., 2d sess., pt. 8, pp. 170-171.

[84] Yeaman to Seward, June 7, 1867, MS. Dept. of State, *Denmark, Desp.*, vol. 9.

offer, but he promised action within a few days.[85] On
June 16, Count Frijs and General Raasloff discussed
the entire question with Mr. Yeaman in great detail.
First of all, Mr. Seward's offer of May 23 was definitely declined. On the other hand, the Danish Government would "accept seven and a half millions for the
two islands of St. Thomas and St. John, and half that
sum for Santa Cruz, the two offers being distinct and
independent, and might be accepted or rejected sev-
erally, each as an entire proposition."[86]

Seward had next required that the convention "must
be signed and ratified on behalf of Denmark on or
before the 4th of August next." This condition was
likewise declined by Count Frijs, but he was willing
that Denmark "be bound equally with the United States
to exchange ratifications within a given time."

A third stipulation of the Secretary of State met a
like fate. Seward wished Count Frijs to agree that
the United States could reserve the right to "withdraw
its proposition and end the negotiation at any time
before notice is received of its ratification by Denmark."
The Danish Minister of Foreign Affairs regarded such
a reservation as unequal unless "Denmark had the same
right." To his mind, every step in the negotiation
"ought to be equally binding upon both parties, and
further observed that in any view it was an unusual and
might be a very inconvenient position."

85 Yeaman to Seward, June 13, 1867, *ibid.*
86 Yeaman to Seward, June 17, 1867, *ibid.*

In spite of Seward's opposition, Count Frijs made it very clear to Yeaman that the Danish Government would insist upon a plebiscite in the Danish West Indies. The modern custom in Europe "upon that subject was so uniform as to amount almost to a rule of public law." In addition "to this the people and the Government of Denmark were just at this moment intensely interested in the subject of a vote of the people of North Schleswig, under a provision of the Treaty of Prague, to determine for themselves their final and permanent relations with Denmark."[87]

In a private letter to Seward, June 17, 1867, Yeaman confided to the Secretary of State his personal estimate of the situation. He had long been of the opinion that the Danish Government would not consider any offer for the purchase of the Danish West Indies unless the amount was at least ten millions of dollars. Mr. Yeaman also indicated that Senator Doolittle greatly regretted that Mr. Seward had changed his views since the Senator had left Washington, and had reduced the amount offered to Denmark from ten millions to seven and a half millions. Otherwise, the Senator believed "that a treaty might have been negotiated."[88]

On July 2, 1867, Seward brought before the Cabinet a proposition to purchase only the islands of St. Thomas and St. John from Denmark for the sum of seven and

[87] Yeaman to Seward, MS. Dept. of State, June 17, 1867, *Denmark, Desp.,* vol. 9. See also the aforementioned *Memorandum* in the Danish Foreign Office which recounts the conversations of Count Frijs with Mr. Yeaman.

[88] MS. Dept. of State, *Denmark, Desp.,* vol. 9.

a half millions of dollars. It was apparent that he saw the necessity of receding from the position taken in his cablegram of May 23. It is also clear that his vacillating course had been the chief obstacle in the way of concluding the negotiations for a treaty.

In the Cabinet meeting on July 2,

"Stanton and Randall strongly supported him [Seward]. McCulloch doubted; was willing the subject should be presented and submitted to the Senate, though, if himself a Senator, would vote against it. Stanbery claimed not to be sufficiently posted to act, but his impressions were against it. I was perhaps strongest in opposition of any; stated we wanted these islands for no present purpose. . . . Seward, a little nettled by my views, said we wanted a station in the West Indies for naval coaling purposes, and we could not have Samana—that was ended. I said I was glad of it . . . and I wished this Danish matter was ended also. Still, as the others assented, and the Secretary of State urged its importance for ulterior purposes which he claims the Senate will sanction with unanimity, I would not oppose its going to that body."[89]

Having secured the sanction of the Cabinet, Seward, on this same day, July 2, sent the following cable to Charles Francis Adams:

"Tell Yeaman close with Denmark's offer, St. Thomas, St. John, seven and half million. Report brief, quick, by cable. Send treaty ratified immediately."[90]

Two days later, July 4, he sent another cablegram to Adams:

[89] Gideon Welles. *Diary,* vol. 3, pp. 124-25.
[90] MS. Dept. of State, *Denmark, Inst.,* vol. 14.

"Tell Yeaman waive August ratification. Report."[91]

On July 6, Yeaman received Seward's cablegram instructing him to close with Denmark's offer and immediately advised General Raasloff of Seward's acceptance. A few days later he talked over the matter at length with Count Frijs, and strongly urged a speedy conclusion of the negotiations. But he soon discovered that "one can not easily hasten affairs of any sort in Denmark. In everything, from cobbler to King, they are the most deliberate and leisurely people in the world." He also found out that the Danish Government was very tenacious in the matter of the holding of a plebiscite in the islands, and Yeaman decided that rather than jeopardize the negotiations he would yield on that point.[92]

[91] *Ibid.*

[92] Yeaman to Seward, July 12, 1867, MS. Dept. of State, *Denmark, Desp.,* vol. 9. In the MS. *Memorandum* in the Danish Foreign Office which gives the gist of the conversations leading up to the treaty with the United States, Count Frijs remarks as follows concerning the question of the holding of a plebiscite in the Danish islands: "Between July 6 and July 12, we [Frijs and Yeaman] had several conversations in which it turned out that the consent of the population was the main difficulty. Mr. Yeaman insisted that his government would much prefer an absolute transfer; that nothing should be done that might open the door to hostile influences, and that it would serve the interests of neither government to have the project fail after the agreement was signed. His instructions did not authorize him to agree to a plebiscite, and the latter would endanger the agreement in Washington as well as in the islands. In principle, neither he nor his government were against a plebiscite, but they wished to avoid jealous intrigues. To this I [Frijs] answered that there would be very little time

On July 11, 1867, Raasloff wrote to Seward to inform him as to the progress of the negotiations. It was his belief that inasmuch as the Danish counter-proposition had been accepted by the American Government, the matter of the purchase was really "settled in principle." However, to

"retain the Legislature here and to draw the documents in great haste, cannot be done, and would in my opinion, do no good; some weeks will be required, we being as you are doubtless aware by this time,—slow people but sure, and then we can ratify, you first or we first, as it may happen."[93]

It was the matter of a plebiscite that was now to delay the negotiations still further. Throughout the whole course of conversations and exchanges of notes, the Danish Government had clung to the idea that a vote would have to be taken in the islands in order that the inhabitants could signify their approval or disapproval of the cession. Yeaman understood the insistence of Count Frijs upon this point, and was willing to yield

---

or opportunity for such intrigues; that it would be easier and more certain to obtain the ratification of the Rigsdag if the population had given its consent by vote. (July 17, 1867) Conference at my home. Present Mr. Yeaman, General Raasloff, and myself [Frijs]. Mr. Yeaman announced that he withdrew his request of ratification in August, and we agreed that the plebiscite was now our only point of difference. We discussed this point thoroughly, and I did not waver from my opinion. . . . I emphasized that I must insist on the vote on account of other matters, especially the Schleswig question."

[93] MS. Dept. of State, *Denmark, Notes*, vol. 4.

to Danish wishes in this regard. Thinking it wiser, however, to ascertain the wishes of Seward at this particular moment, he sent the following cablegram to the Secretary of State:

"Looks very favorable. Count engaged in Rigsdag; treats next week after adjournment. Shall I agree to a vote of the Islands? How long will Congress sit?"[94]

On the following day, July 16, 1867, Seward replied by way of London:

"Do not agree to submit question. Congress soon adjourns."[95]

When Yeaman received this cablegram of July 16, it appeared to him that his only course was "to propose at the next interview to negotiate the treaty unconditionally. This will leave it for them to consider whether the Danish Government shall take the vote of its own motion and for its own information. I very earnestly hope . . . that this will not break the negotiation."[96]

As soon as Seward received this word from the American Minister, he wrote to inform him that he had correctly understood the telegraphic instructions of July 16. He was then authorized

[94] Yeaman to Seward, July 15, 1867, MS. Dept. of State, *Denmark, Desp.,* vol. 9.

[95] MS. Dept. of State, *Denmark, Inst.,* vol. 14.

[96] Yeaman to Seward, July 22, 1867, MS. Dept. of State, *Denmark, Desp.,* vol. 9.

"to say that, in the opinion of this Department, promptness in the pending negotiation is essential to its success and the acceptance of its results."[97]

On August 1, Yeaman had an interview with Frijs, and suggested to him "that there was not more than enough time left between this and the October sessions of Congress and the Rigsdag to complete the matter and get it to Washington." Frijs remarked that the matter of the plebiscite was now "the difficulty in the case."[98]

A week later, August 7, General Raasloff called to see Mr. Yeaman, and he seemed certain "that the vote could not be avoided." He then asked whether the Government of the United States was considering negotiating not only for the islands of St. Thomas and St. John, but also for the island of Santa Cruz. On the following day he repeated the same question in the following note:

"I beg to reiterate what I said to you yesterday, *viz.*, that we consider our counter proposition as having been accepted by the United States Government as a whole, although the telegraphic answer mentions only that part of it which can and will be immediately acted upon. It would be well, however, to have that point also settled between us. We shall on the first point act speedily as soon as we shall be properly prepared. I shall soon call upon you again."[99]

[97] Seward to Yeaman, August 7, 1867, MS. Dept. of State. *Denmark, Inst.,* vol. 14.

[98] Yeaman to Seward, August 8, 1867, MS. Dept. of State, *Denmark, Desp.,* vol. 9.

[99] *Ibid.* It is apparent from the private letters of Mr. Yeaman that the American Minister regarded Senator Doolittle as a nuisance rather than a help. The newspapers in America and

Yeaman could only refer these inquiries to the Department of State for instructions. But with reference to the question of the vote in the islands he continued his conferences with Count Frijs. On August 10, the Danish Minister of Foreign Affairs "expressed his preference that, without agreeing in the treaty to submit the question of cession to a vote of the people of the islands in such form as to make the vote decisive as a condition, yet to allude to it in such manner as to show the fact of the intention of the Government to take the vote." Mr. Yeaman declined to agree to this upon the ground "that any such reference of statement in the treaty might be construed as an agreement to submit." Count Frijs then expressed the opinion "that it could be so worded as to avoid that construction," and he requested Mr. Yeaman to accept such a suggestion *ad referendum.* The American Minister readily accepted this suggestion, but expressed the hope that the treaty would be ready for submission at Washington and Copenhagen in December.[100]

But there was another element that now intervened to delay the negotiations. In Europe a war loomed between France and Prussia, and the Danish Cabinet

---

in Europe gave a good deal of notice to Doolittle's movements, and in Yeaman's eyes, this fact derogated from any usefulness the Senator might have had as special agent. See Yeaman to Doolittle, August 8, 1867, MS. Dept. of State, *Denmark, Desp.,* vol. 9. Also, Yeaman to Seward, June 20, 1867, and July 4, 1867, MS. Dept. of State, *Denmark, Desp.,* vol. 9.

[100] Yeaman to Seward, August 17, 1867, MS. Dept. of State, *Denmark, Desp.,* vol. 9.

was in favor of maintaining a neutral stand in case such a contingency actually came to pass. So strong however, was public sentiment in favor of participation with France, that a Ministerial crisis was at hand, and all consideration of the cession of the Danish West Indies had to be postponed.[101]

On August 28, 1867, Seward sent to Yeaman the following cablegram by way of London:

"Adhere to instructions. No engagement about third part."[102]

This cablegram apparently referred to the decision of Seward to confine the negotiations to securing only the cession of the two islands of St. Thomas and St. John, and not to carry on a parallel negotiation for the island of Santa Cruz. Strange to say, there is no mention in the despatches of Yeaman of the receipt of this instruction of August 28. A few days later, September 3, 1867, Seward sent another cablegram in cipher to Yeaman which directly referred to the plebiscite in the islands:

"In no case must vote be mentioned in treaty. If outside of treaty Denmark orders popular vote then your 81 is right."[103]

[101] Yeaman to Seward, August 22, 1867, *ibid.* In a despatch to Seward, September 2, 1867, Yeaman states that the late Ministerial crisis has "been disposed of," and that the present Cabinet "will remain in office."

[102] MS. Dept. of State, *Denmark, Inst.,* vol. 14.

[103] MS. Dept. of State, *ibid.*

It happened, however, that Yeaman did not have any key to aid him in deciphering this cablegram, so he was forced to send it to London for translation. But Mr. Adams, at London, advised Yeaman that there was no key at London,[104] so as late as September 27, we find Yeaman still complaining to Seward that he has been "unable to decipher satisfactorily" the cablegram of September 3.[105]

In the meantime, on September 13, Admiral Farragut arrived at Copenhagen with an American fleet, and a round of festivities ensued. As early as April 30, 1867, General Raasloff had intimated to Mr. Yeaman that a visit from an American fleet would greatly expedite matters by helping to mould a public sentiment friendly to the United States.[106] Mr. Seward was too astute a diplomat to overlook any favorable factors, so the outstanding naval hero of the American Civil War, Admiral Farragut, was instructed to call at Copenhagen and pay his respects to the Danish Government. He received a warm welcome from the Danes, and Mr. Yeaman was enthusiastic in his appreciation of

"the extremely happy and favorable impression which the accomplished officers of the Admiral's fleet have made on this Court and on public opinion here. They are an honor to the American name and the American naval service, and wherever they have gone, the effect of their visit and their intercourse with Society has

104 Yeaman to Seward, Sept. 16, 1867, MS. Dept. of State, *Denmark, Desp.,* vol. 9.

105 Yeaman to Seward, Sept. 27, 1867, MS. Dept. of State, *Denmark, Desp.,* vol. 9.

106 Yeaman to Seward, April 30, 1867, *ibid.*

been an unmixed advantage to our reputation and to our political interests."[107]

On September 23, Seward sent a long instruction which dealt largely with the question as to whether the United States would negotiate not only for the islands of St. Thomas and St. John, but also for Saint Croix. In his despatches of August 8, and September 5, Yeaman had stressed the desire of the Danish Government to include the island of Saint Croix in the negotiations, and now Seward wished to settle this point once and for all. President Johnson had always been of the opinion that "the division of our original proposition, so as to exclude Santa Cruz from the negotiation, would prove a hindrance to Denmark." Moreover, he still believed that "our proposition was well conceived, having reference to our situation at the time it was made." But now circumstances had changed. Imperialism was on the wane in the United States, and the delays which had attended the negotiations for the Danish West Indies had "contributed to still further alleviate the national desire for enlargement of territory." The best that could now be done would be "to accept the two upon the terms which seem to have been agreed upon." Indeed, if the negotiations dragged on much longer it might well "wear out the popular desire for even that measure of partial acquisition." General Raasloff had adverted to the fact that the Danes were

[107] Yeaman to Seward, Sept. 21, 1867, *ibid.* See also James E. Montgomery, *The Cruise of Admiral D. G. Farragut in the Flagship Franklin* (N. Y. 1869), pp. 118ff.

a cautious people who moved very slowly: it would be well for him to remember that in the United States all political movements "require vigor and promptitude."[108]

Nearly a week later, September 28, Seward wrote Yeaman a confidential letter in much the same tenor as his instruction of the 23d. Procrastination in the negotiations had "abated an interest which was at its height when we came successfuly out of a severe civil war." No longer was there any "absolute need for a naval station in the West Indies." Besides, "other and cheaper projects are widely regarded as feasible and equally or more advantageous." If the Danish Government were really anxious to negotiate for the sale of Santa Cruz, let it "send us a protocol through your Legation, to be dealt with as on consultation we shall find practicable and expedient."[109]

On the previous day, September 27, Yeaman had written to Seward that the Danish Government insisted upon inserting in the projected treaty a clause as follows:

"It is, however, understood and agreed that His Majesty the King of Denmark, before proceeding to the ratification of this convention, reserves to himself to give the native population of the above-named islands an opportunity of expressing their adhesion to this cession."[110]

[108] Seward to Yeaman, September 23, 1867, MS. Dept. of State, *Denmark, Inst.,* vol. 14.

[109] *Ibid.*

[110] Yeaman to Seward, September 27, 1867, MS. Dept. of State, *Denmark, Desp.,* vol. 9.

It was apparent to Yeaman that the question of a plebiscite in the islands would have to be decided in favor of the contention of the Danish Government. He had "urged against it every possible argument and consideration," but without success. On October 2, after an interview with Count Frijs in which the Minister of Foreign Affairs stoutly upheld the necessity of conceding the inhabitants of the Danish West Indies an opportunity of expressing their wishes,[111] Mr. Yeaman resolved to send Mr. Seward the following cablegram:

"Denmark quite ready to conclude, if vote mentioned in Treaty. Considers favorable vote sure. Desires explicit acceptance of Santa Cruz."[112]

On the following day, October 3, 1867, Yeaman wrote to tell Seward that the French Minister had called upon Count Frijs to ascertain whether "the constant reports about the sale of the West Indies were true." The Count had answered "that propositions had been made but that the parties were not in accord."[113] But the French Minister, well versed in the language of diplomacy, was not satisfied with such an evasive answer, so on October 4, Yeaman believed that a crisis was at hand. It was evident that the Danish Government would not sign any treaty which did not include some reservation as to a plebiscite in the islands, and Yeaman was certain that the vote in the islands would

[111] Yeaman to Seward, October 3, 1867, MS. Dept. of State, *Denmark, Desp.*, vol. 9.

[112] Yeaman to Seward, October 2, 1867, *ibid.*

[113] Yeaman to Seward, October 3, 1867, *ibid.*

be in favor of annexation to the United States. In desperation, Yeaman finally decided to send the following cablegram to Seward:

"France knows our offer and remonstrates. Denmark expects other remonstrances. Prompt action desirable. Vote in treaty indispensable."[114]

Seward, in the meantime, on this same day, October 4, 1867, sent a cablegram to Yeaman in answer to the cablegram which the American Minister had sent on October 2. Seward's cablegram read as follows:

"No condition of vote in treaty. If Denmark wants to negotiate for Santa Cruz by separate treaty send draft here for consideration."[115]

Yeaman's cablegram reached the Department of State on October 5, and Seward, realizing the gravity of the situation, sent a second cablegram, reversing the one of the previous day. This last cablegram read:

"Concede popular vote."[116]

Seward now believed that he had removed the last obstacle to a speedy conclusion of a treaty ceding the Danish West Indies to the United States, but misfortune still attended his efforts. On October 5, Yeaman had received Seward's first cablegram which refused to accept the idea of a plebiscite in the islands. On the following evening he received Seward's second

[114] Yeaman to Seward, October 4, 1867, *ibid.*
[115] Seward to Yeaman, October 4, 1867, MS. Dept. of State, *Denmark, Inst.,* vol. 14.
[116] Seward to Yeaman, October 5, 1867, *ibid.*

cablegram, but was unable to decipher it "with any
certainty." Since September 4, he had received three
cablegrams in cipher, two of which he had not been able
to read. In the cipher that the State Department had sent
him there were numerous inconsistencies. For instance,
the cipher for *certain* also meant *doubt,* while the cipher
for *Santa Cruz* also meant *South Carolina.* Of Seward's
last cablegram, Yeaman had received four copies, but
they were "all different, no two being alike."[117] However, the American Minister, after much labor and deep
thought, decided that the intent of the cablegram must
have been "affirmative," and that the Secretary of State
had finally conceded the popular vote.[118]

But now that the American Government had conceded everything, some of the Danish officials thought
it might be possible to exact even further conditions.
To Yeaman such an attitude seemed inexcusable, so he
informed General Raasloff that "some of his colleagues
were under the impression that the United States
wanted the islands so much that they would accept
them on any terms whatever." Such an impression

[117] On October 28, 1867, Seward wrote to Yeaman and explained to him some of the difficulties of cipher making.
Seward was "indebted" to Yeaman for his criticisms "on the
new cipher," and they would be "borne in mind." The new
cipher, it seemed, had been entrusted to a man "somewhat
advanced in life," who was obliged "to do the work by lamp-
light at his own home." It was not unreasonable, therefore,
"to expect a few errors." MS. Dept. of State, *Denmark, Inst.,*
vol. 14.

[118] Yeaman to Seward, October 7, 1867, MS. Dept. of State,
Denmark, Desp., vol. 9.

was entirely false, and if the General wished the negotiations to be successful it was high time that such a
delusion be promptly corrected.

On this same day that Yeaman warned General Raasloff that there were limits to the concessions that
America would grant in order to secure the Danish
islands, Count Frijs, the Danish Minister for Foreign
Affairs, submitted a detailed report to King Christian
concerning the question of the cession. Three days
later, October 18, 1867, His Majesty formally approved
the report of Count Frijs, and thereby gave his consent
to the transfer of the Danish West Indies to the United
States. In the first part of his report, Count Frijs discussed the objections that could be raised against the
cession. It was believed that certain dangers might
result from the opposition of France and England to
the acquisition by the United States of a naval station
in the Caribbean, so it had been considered expedient to
delay the conclusion of any treaty of cession until either
the French or British Governments indicated their
approval of the sale of the islands, or until their friendship was less important to Denmark. The unsettled
question of North Schleswig had also led the Danish
Foreign Office to refrain from pushing the negotiations
to a conclusion. Thus the matter had stood

"until in July of the last year Your Majesty's former
envoy in Washington left America. On the 17th of the
same month, shortly before his departure, General
Raasloff received from Mr. Seward a confidential note
in which the latter made, at last, a definite offer,
namely, five million dollars in gold for all of the islands.

. . . With respect to this proposal, and after consultation with General Raasloff . . . I [Frijs] have had during the last five months a series of interviews with Mr. Yeaman which have served to let the matter assume . . . a more definite and favorable character. . . . The price is now fixed at seven and one-half million dollars in gold for the two islands, St. Thomas and St. John. Santa Cruz is excluded from the sale, at least at present, because with respect to this island Denmark has special obligations to the French Government. We also insist upon the consent of the population as a necessary requirement for the execution of the sale, partly because the Danish Government will not separate from the Danish state a population which desires to remain a part of it, and partly because by doing otherwise we would place ourselves in definite opposition to those principles which we so strongly insist upon in regard to Prussia in the matter of North Schleswig.

"I have succeeded . . . in securing acceptance of these points, and . . . in agreement with my colleagues, with the exception of the Secretary of the Navy . . . I have come to the conclusion most respectfully to advise Your Majesty not to . . . delay the conclusion of a treaty which offers . . . such considerable advantages to the State Treasury at a time when we are— and probably in still higher degree will be—in need of cash. The Royal Government is particularly afraid that the outbreak of a war in American waters would seriously endanger the neutrality of our West Indian islands, so that if we do not seize the opportunity now offered to us we incur the risk of losing the islands without any reward whatsoever."[119]

[119] *Recommendation most respectfully submitted to His Majesty, King Christian, concerning a Treaty with the United States of North America about the Disposal of the Islands of St. Thomas and St. John, October 15, 1867, approved and signed by His Majesty,* October 18, 1867, MS. D. F. O.

Yeaman did not know that the Danish King had approved, on October 18, the report of Count Frijs which favored the sale of the islands to the United States, so it appeared to the American Minister that the negotiation was "progressing slowly." To his mind there were numerous reasons for this delay. Some of the Danish officials who were not actively opposed to the cession were inclined to be excessively cautious, while the Assistant Secretary of Foreign Affairs had striven in every way to defeat the treaty. And there had been some weight to his objections. For instance, soon after Seward had made his trip to the West Indies in 1866,

"Lord Russell, then at the head of the cabinet of London, approached the Danish minister in London on the subject, and the result of the interview was a promise by the Danish Minister that nothing would be done without first letting the British Government know it. This was naturally felt here to be an embarrassment, but can be avoided, if necessary, upon the ground that such a promise was unauthorized and can not be held to bind the Danish Government."[120]

Another cause of delay in arriving at a definite convention was the difficulty in settling the status of the inhabitants of the islands after annexation to the United States, so after many discussions of this problem it was decided to adopt the 8th article of the treaty of Guadalupe Hidalgo as a model. But the most serious difficulty of all was with reference to Article 5 in Seward's draft

[120] Yeaman to Seward, October 25, 1867, MS. Dept. of State, *Denmark, Desp.*, vol. 9.

treaty. The Danish Government deemed the language of the draft treaty "much too sweeping," and more especially as liable to the construction that it absolutely abrogated and dissolved

"all previous grants, franchises, possessions, companies, and corporations in any way desiring title or existence from the Government, which would be as unnecessary as unjust."

Mr. Yeaman urged that the expressions and limitations objected to could only be taken

"with reference to the legal administration and political sovereignty over the 'territory and islands' so declared to be free and unencumbered especially when taken with the provision already agreed to that private rights should be protected. And I referred them to such monopolies and semi-sovereign corporations as had controlled large regions in America and Asia, and to grants or permits for the coolie trade, with none of which the United States would be encumbered."

The Danish Government then assured the American Minister that "nothing of the kind existed in the Danish West Indies, and with this assurance they seemed to think the provision was useless, besides being liable to the misconstruction above named." Then, Mr. Yeaman, in order to defer to these objections, drafted an alternative article which Count Frijs accepted and the negotiations were at length brought to a close by the signature of a treaty bearing the date of October 24, 1867.[121]

121 Yeaman to Seward, October 25, 1867, *ibid.*

In his despatch to Seward of October 26, 1867, Yeaman expressed his ardent appreciation of the rôle played by General Raasloff in effecting this end. It was his belief

"that most of the labor, and the most difficult conduct of the negotiation from the Danish side have been by . . . the General. Always earnest and zealous for his own government, General Raasloff's moderation, activity and quickness of perception have undoubtedly very greatly aided the progress of the business, so much so that I may say that it appears to me doubtful whether it could have been brought to a successful conclusion without his connection with it."[122]

[122] MS. Dept. of State, *Denmark, Desp.*, vol. 9. A copy of the treaty is given in Sidney Andrews, the *St. Thomas Treaty* (N. Y. 1869), pp. 22-24.

CHAPTER II

THE STRUGGLE FOR RATIFICATION

The treaty of October 24, 1867, was a monument to Seward's patience and spirit of conciliation. The slow processes of Danish diplomacy would have exhausted many statesmen in the early stages of the negotiation, while the persistent refusal of the Danish Government to compromise on certain American demands would have caused some Secretaries of State to abandon the project. But Seward viewed American expansion in the Caribbean as necessary to national defense, and though he had often shown himself to be a mere partisan politician, yet in his rôle as Secretary of State he regarded things from a national angle and all his efforts were directed towards paving the way for American leadership. Developing America would soon have her commerce scattered over all the seven seas and Seward was determined that such hostages to fortune should be protected by an adequate navy with convenient naval stations. To fail to provide these necessary naval bases would be unintelligent and unpatriotic, and few people have ever accused Seward of lacking in mental alertness or in love of country.[1]

[1] It will be remembered (see *ante,* pp. 15-16) that in April, 1865, M. Quaade, of the Danish Foreign Office, had assured the British Minister at Copenhagen that the Danish Government would not entertain any proposition to sell the Danish islands to

It was because of this infusion of patriotism in his
diplomacy that made Seward so tenacious in the matter
of securing the Danish West Indies, and he was prepared to adopt any expedient that would serve his purpose. On October 1, 1867, General Raasloff had assured
Yeaman that the treaty would soon be signed and that
it would be well for the American Government to be
ready promptly to send an agent to the Danish West
Indies to explain to the inhabitants the advantages of
annexation to the United States. Seward understood
the value of this suggestion, and when Yeaman sent a
cablegram to the State Department advising the Secre-

---

the United States "without giving due notice to Her Majesty's
Government." It would appear that this assurance was an
empty formality, for there is no record in the British Foreign
Office of any notice given to the British Government concerning the beginning of the negotiations for the cession of
the islands. On November 4, 1867, Mr. Charles A. Murray,
the British Minister at Copenhagen, wrote to Lord Stanley,
the British Foreign Secretary, that he had just been informed by Count Frijs of the conclusion of a treaty between
the United States and Denmark, October 24, 1867, providing
for the sale of the Danish West Indies. F. O. 22/342, no. 48.
On November 7, 1867, Mr. Murray again wrote to Lord
Stanley with reference to the Danish-American treaty. He
had ascertained the exact amount which the United States was
to pay for the islands, and he expressed the opinion that the
Danish Rigsdag would ratify the treaty without any difficulties
being raised against it. Finally, on November 20, 1867, in a
confidential despatch to Lord Stanley, Mr. Murray entered
into a detailed discussion of the probable cession of the island
of St. Croix to the United States, and of the objections that
might be raised by the French Government. F. O. 22/342, nos.
49, 51.

tary of State to send an agent to St. Thomas and St. John "immediately,"[2] Seward at once wrote to his friend, the Rev. Charles Hawley, at Auburn, New York, and commissioned him to proceed to the Danish West Indies to meet a commissioner from the Danish Government.

In his letter of instructions to Mr. Hawley, Seward had indicated the line of argument for the American Commissioner to take with the inhabitants. Thus

"It is presumed that you will be at no loss for arguments to show those who may have votes upon the subject the advantages which they would derive from transferring their allegiance to the United States should they think proper to remain in the islands. The market of this country, even now, is an eligible one for their products. It must become much more so in the event of their annexation. As one of the purposes of this Government in the acquisition is to secure a naval station, the inhabitants of the islands will derive benefits from that, which it is needless to expatiate upon. If, too, they should become a part of the domain of the United States, they and their posterity will have the same right to protection by a powerful government in war and to those advantages in time of peace which are enjoyed by other citizens."[3]

On November 12, Mr. Hawley reached St. Thomas, and found that the principal topic of conversation was whether the United States, in case of annexation, would continue "St. Thomas a free port." If the merchants

[2] Yeaman to Seward, October 25, 1867, MS. Dept. of State, *Denmark, Desp.,* vol. 9.

[3] Seward to Charles Hawley, October 26, 1867, MS. Dept. of State, *Special Missions,* vol. 3.

and others connected with the business relations of the islands could be assured "that there would be no change in this regard, and that their trade with the other islands would be maintained with its present advantages, the formidable objection to the transfer would be obviated. The whole issue, as they contemplate it, resolves itself into a question of trade."[4]

On November 15, 1867, Seward wrote to Mr. Hawley to enclose a copy of the treaty of October 24. This procedure, he realized, involved a "peculiar risk." Treaties, before ratification, "are properly regarded as confidential in their nature." Mr. Hawley, therefore,

[4] Hawley to Seward, November 13, 1867, MS. Dept. of State, *Special Agents Series* (unbound). While Mr. Hawley was on his way to the Danish West Indies, Seward received a long letter from Vice-Admiral David D. Porter, November 6, 1867, with reference to the islands of St. Thomas and St. John. It was Porter's belief that the island of St. Thomas held "the most prominent position in the West Indies as a naval and commercial station. It is situated . . . right in the track of all vessels from Europe, Brazil, East Indies, and the Pacific Ocean, bound to the West India islands or to the United States. It is a point where all vessels touch for supplies, when needed, coming from any of the above stations. It is a central point from which any or all of the West India islands can be assailed, while it is impervious to attack from landing parties, and can be fortified to any extent. . . . There is no harbor in the West Indies better fitted than St. Thomas for a naval station. Its harbor and that of St. John, and the harbors formed by Water Island, would contain all the vessels of the largest navy in the world, where they would be protected at all times from bad weather and be secure against an enemy. . . . In fine, I think St. Thomas is the keystone to the arch of the West Indies: it commands them all." *Miscellaneous Letters,* MS. Dept. of State, November, 1867, pt. 1.

must be extremely circumspect in his handling of such a document, but he must be prepared to "enlighten the consuls and naval officers of the United States" with whom he might come in contact.[5]

By the time the treaty reached Mr. Hawley, that gentleman had already undergone some harrowing experiences that proved that the ways of the diplomat may be as hard as those of the transgressor. On November 17, Mr. Chamberlain Carstensen, the Danish Commissioner, reached St. Thomas, and on the following day at three P. M., the Danish Commissioner, the Danish Governor of the islands, and the American Commissioner met in Christiansted to discuss the provisions of the treaty of cession. Hardly had the Commissioners and the Governor assembled in Government House, when they felt "the violent shock of an earthquake," and they rushed into the street in time to see a great tidal wave sweeping upon the town. The United States Ship "Monongahela," which had carried Mr. Hawley to Christiansted, was carried from her anchorage in the harbor up into the town and left "high and dry on the water side of Bay street."[6] In the town itself indescribable terror seized the populace. Many fled to the hills behind the town, while others searched the

[5] MS. Dept. of State, *Special Missions,* vol. 3.

[6] Hawley to Seward, November 22, 1867, MS. Dept. of State, *Special Agents Series* (unbound). In the New York *Tribune* for January 20, 1868, there is a graphic description of the earthquake and tidal wave written by the *Tribune's* correspondent in the islands.

wreckage for survivors. It was apparent to the Commissioners that it was no day for a conference, so Mr. Hawley left immediately for Fredericksted where the situation was even worse.

It had been hoped by both Commissioners that the quake of November 18 would not be followed by other shocks, but the earth tremors continued day after day, so Mr. Hawley felt that in the tense atmosphere of the islands it was difficult to settle the details necessary to carry the treaty into execution. He soon discovered that the mercantile interest would "be a unit against the transfer, without some assurance from the United States that, for a specified period at least, the present privileges and immunities enjoyed by the port will remain undisturbed." If the trade of St. Thomas were brought under the operation of American revenue laws it would undoubtedly "destroy at a blow its commercial importance."

Feeling that it was necessary to quiet the fears of the inhabitants, Hawley informed both Commissioner Carstensen and Governor Birch that "the principal design of the United States in acquiring these islands being the establishment of a naval depot," he had "no doubt" but that the American Government would be disposed to adopt a liberal commercial policy towards its new possessions, and permit them to retain "all the rights and immunities not in conflict with the common interest."[7]

[7] Hawley to Seward, November 22, 1867, MS. Dept. of State, *Special Agents Series* (unbound).

On November 25, Hawley, Commissioner Carstensen, and Governor Birch, repaired to St. Thomas, where, on the following day, they held an "informal conference" with the leading merchants. The merchants frankly admitted that "certain advantages" would be gained by annexation to the United States, but they pressed for assurances that St. Thomas would remain a free port. Mr. Hawley, of course, was in no position to give such assurances. He did attempt to explain to them, however, the limitations of the treaty-making power: all regulations "pertaining to the imposition of duties belonged to Congress," and therefore it would be regarded as "an encroachment upon the province of the legislative department" if any promises were given by Mr. Seward relative to the retention of commercial privileges. He felt quite certain, nonetheless, that the American Congress would "deal generously with the existing privileges by appropriate legislation."[8]

But the merchants of St. Thomas were not content with mere promises of generous treatment, so after the Danish Commissioner had read to them the text of the royal proclamation notifying them of the treaty of cession, October 24, 1867, and expressing deep sorrow because of the "severment" of long-existing ties, there was a decided expression of opinion that the vote in the islands would be opposed to the cession unless the American Government would give a pledge to re-

[8] Hawley to Seward, November 29, 1867, MS. Dept. of State, *Special Agents Series* (unbound).

tain the commercial privileges of St. Thomas "for a
period of at least fifteen or twenty years."[9]   Under
these circumstances it seemed wise to postpone the
plebiscite until after Commissioner Carstensen had
talked over the situation with Secretary Seward at
Washington.

On the eve of the departure of Commissioner Carstensen for the United States, he received two communications of importance. One was from the merchants
of St. Thomas, in which they enjoined upon him the
necessity of keeping St. Thomas a free port. If such
a privilege were not retained, then the "whole scene,
as it now exhibits itself, will be changed."   Fortunes
would fall, properties would be depreciated, and ruin
would descend upon the island.[10]

The other communication was a long letter from
Governor Birch to the Commissioner, in which all the
points at issue were carefully considered.[11]   Birch then
enclosed a draft of additional articles to the treaty of
October 24, 1867. The first article specifically reserved
to St. Thomas the status of a free port for a period
of twenty years. The second article provided that the
Danish common and statute law in force in the islands,
would remain in force until alterations be made by
new legislative enactments "after previous delibera-

[9] E. H. Perkins, U. S. Consul, St. Croix, W. I., to Seward,
December 4, 1867, *Sen. Doc.* 231, 56 Cong., 2 sess., pt. 8, pp.
208-209. There is a copy of the royal proclamation in this
Senate document 231, pp. 209-210.

[10] *Sen. Doc.* 231, 56 Cong., 2 sess., pt. 8, p. 215.

[11] *Ibid.*, pp. 211-214.

tion in the council existing at the time in the islands for the treatment of legislative and other like matters." The third article was meant merely to clarify the language of article 5, of the treaty of October 24. It specifically provided that "concessions or grants given from time to time by the Danish Government for conducting or carrying on certain establishments or industrial occupations, shall remain in force until they expire or be withdrawn or recalled from the same circumstances that would have justified such withdrawal or recall had the islands continued to be subject to Denmark." Such was also to be the case with those "rights or privileges which have been granted or bestowed by the Danish Government to certain communities or establishments in the islands." [12]

Armed with these elaborate instructions and with the draft of the additional articles to the treaty of October 24, Carstensen sailed from St. Thomas with Mr. Hawley. They arrived in Washington on December 13, and the Danish Commissioner immediately consulted with Mr. Seward with reference to the additional articles suggested by Governor Birch. Seward returned a formal answer by means of a note addressed to Mr. Hawley, December 16, 1867. First, Mr. Hawley was instructed to inform the royal commissioner that

"In so great a transaction as the cession of territory and dominion by one sovereign to another it is difficult,

[12] Governor Birch to Chamberlain Carstensen, St. Thomas, December 4, 1867, MS. Dept. of State, *Special Agents Series* (unbound).

if not impossible, to adjust minute arrangements in detail concerning the future government of the ceded territory. All reservations and conditions made by the ceding sovereign necessarily impair the sovereignty of the receiving power, and equally tend to embarrass its legislation and to lay the foundation of ultimate difference and controversy between the contracting powers."[13]

Seward next proceeded to instruct the Danish Commissioner in the essentials of American constitutional practice. The Constitution of the United States reserves to the

"Senate the power to ratify, and to refuse to ratify, the treaty made by the President, and the constitution of Denmark equally reserves to the legislature of Denmark the same absolute control over the subject. While the respective chief magistrates concluding the treaty might well suppose that they possess sufficient ability to adjust such details by contract, the assumption that they could so adjust them as to obtain the consent of the two ratifying bodies, and foreclose future legislative action by the Congress of the United States indefinitely, or for a term of years, would be exceedingly presumptuous."

After thus rejecting the first additional article proposed by Governor Birch relative to making St. Thomas a free port for twenty years, Seward then declined to give the two other additional articles any serious consideration. His disposal of them took the form of a righteous sermon upon the benefits of American rule. The American constitutional system was established

[13] MS. Dept of State, *Special Missions,* vol. 3.

"upon the principle that every people incorporated into the American Union by annexation, or even by conquest, acquire, in the act of annexation, their due and equal share in the protection of the United States and of the liberties and rights of American citizens. Another principle is found at the base of the American Constitution, which is that every community which is received into the national family secures rights and privileges of local self-government with due representation in the councils of the Federal Union."

He was of the opinion that no portion of the American people can need, or reasonably desire

"any higher or broader guaranties for the protection of life, liberty, and property than those which the Constitution of the United States affords equally and indiscriminately to all the States and the whole American people. The United States are an aggregation of forty-seven distinct political communities, thirty-seven of which are States and ten preparing to be States. . . . All these political communities have at some time belonged to foreign states and empires. Such has been the benignant operation of self-government in the United States that no one of these distinct communities could now be induced to assume independence, much less to return to its ancient allegiance, or to accept of any other sovereign."[14]

In view of the late Civil War in the United States, during which the entire southern portion of the Federal Union strove desperately to break away from the

[14] Seward to Hawley, December 16, 1867, MS. Dept. of State, *Special Missions* vol. 3. On this same day, December 16, 1867, Seward sent a cipher telegram to Yeaman as follows: "We have declined either to negotiate here or to again open negotiations at Copenhagen about supplementary articles to treaty." See MS. Dept. of State, *Denmark, Inst.,* vol. 14.

northern portion, it may well have been that Commissioner Carstensen had some doubts as to the verity of Seward's homily on "the benignant operation of self-government in the United States." There could be no question, however, that it was hopeless to expect any favorable action on the additional articles drafted by Governor Birch. In view of this obvious fact, Carstensen confined his efforts to conversations with Seward, Sumner and other members of the Senate Foreign Relations Committee, with members of the House of Representatives, and with many persons of influence in Washington. And there was much need of these conversations, for the situation would have puzzled the most seasoned diplomat.

As far back as September 23, 1867, Seward had warned Yeaman that the negotiation was in danger because of the declining interest in the United States in imperialism, and as evidence of this fact, Mr. C. C. Washburn, of Wisconsin, introduced in the House of Representatives the following resolution:

"*Resolved,* That in the present financial condition of the country, any further purchases of territory are inexpedient, and this House will hold itself under no obligation to vote money to pay for any such purchase unless there is greater present necessity for the same than now exists."[15]

In a short speech introducing his resolution, November 25, 1867, Mr. Washburn adverted to recent rumors

[15] *Congressional Globe,* 40 Cong., 1 sess., November 25, 1867, p. 792.

"that the Secretary of State has been making another purchase without consulting any one, in the absence of any public sentiment requiring it, or of any demand from any quarter. I intend that that action shall be covered by the resolution. I intend to serve notice upon the Kingdom of Denmark that this House will not pay for that purchase; and I mean to serve notice upon the world that we will pay for no purchase that the Secretary of State, on his own motion, may see proper to make—that no purpose will be sanctioned that is not demanded by the public sentiment and the best interests of the country."[16]

After a short debate the resolution was passed by the House of Representatives by the overwhelming vote of 93 ayes to 43 nays. But despite such a clear expression of opinion by the lower house of Congress, President Johnson remained heartily in favor of the Danish treaty, and in his third annual message to Congress, December 3, 1867, he strongly argued in favor of such an acquisition.[17]

It was difficult, therefore, for Carstensen to make a decision. He had completely failed to secure any acceptance of the desires of the inhabitants of St. Thomas with reference to retaining for that island its privileges as a free port. Moreover, the instructions given in Governor Birch's letter of December 4, could not possibly be carried out. Apparently, there was a serious difference in opinion between the President and the House of Representatives about the value of colonial

[16] *Ibid.*, p. 792.
[17] Jas. D. Richardson. *Messages and Papers of the Presidents,* vol. 6, p. 580.

possessions. But no word of warning was conveyed to him by any member of the Senate Committee on Foreign Relations, so Carstensen decided to return to St. Thomas and St. John and order the plebiscite to be taken.

But Carstensen was not the only one to be puzzled by the conflicting currents in American political circles. The resolution in the House of Representatives, November 25, against any further purchases of territory, caused considerable anxiety in Copenhagen as to the fate of the treaty. Count Frijs had previously intimated to Mr. Yeaman that

"after hearing from a favorable vote of the islands, Denmark would be fully committed, and that he thought it would then be proper he should hear from the Senate before going to the Rigsdag with the treaty."

The Count further expressed himself as believing that it would now be "necessary" to hear from "the House upon the subject." Yeaman, however, assured the Danish Minister of Foreign Affairs that he did not remember "a case in which the House had refused money to carry a ratified treaty into effect."[18]

The warm approval expressed by President Johnson of the treaty of October 24, 1867, seemed to confirm Yeaman's optimistic predictions. In his message of December 3, Johnson had discussed at length the advisability of securing naval stations in the Caribbean. After indicating the disadvantages suffered by the

[18] Yeaman to Seward, December 13, 1867, *Confidential*, MS. Dept. of State, *Denmark, Desp.*, vol. 9.

United States during the Civil War because of the lack
of naval bases in the West Indies, the President then
observed:

"The duty of obtaining such an outpost peacefully
and lawfully, while neither doing or menacing injury
to other states, earnestly engaged the attention of the
executive department before the close of the war, and
it has not been lost sight of since that time. . . . With
the possession of such a station by the United States,
neither we nor any other American nation need longer
apprehend injury or offense from any trans-atlantic
enemy. I agree with our early statesmen that the West
Indies naturally gravitate to, and may be expected
ultimately to be absorbed by, the continental States,
including our own. . . . The islands of St. Thomas and
St. John, which constitute a part of the group called
the Virgin Islands, seemed to offer us advantages immediately desirable, while their acquisition could be secured in harmony with the principles to which I have
alluded. A treaty has therefore been concluded with
the King of Denmark for the cession of those islands,
and will be submitted to the Senate for consideration."[19]

While at Washington it was becoming more and
more uncertain as to whether the treaty of October
24, would be ratified, General Raasloff wrote to Seward
on November 27, 1867, and inquired about negotiations
for a new treaty which would provide for the cession
to the United States of the island of Santa Cruz.
Seward replied to this new overture in an instruction
to Yeaman, December 30, 1867. After adverting to
the "strong current of economical sentiment" that was

[19] Jas. D. Richardson. *Messages and Papers of the Presidents,* vol. 6 (Washington, 1897), pp. 579-580.

daily gathering strength in America, he expressed the
fear that the "treaty for St. Thomas and St. John is not
unlikely to labor in the Senate just as the transaction
itself has labored in the country."[20]   Although public
opinion in the United States was strongly in favor of

[20] In many quarters in the United States, strong opposition
was developing against the treaty of October 24, 1867. The following excerpts from an editorial in the New York *Tribune,*
December 19, 1867, indicate the attitude of a very large number of Americans at that time: "Congress has been repeatedly
in session while this dicker was in progress, and might have
been called at any other time. Yet its advice or concurrence
was never asked. There has been no pretence of deferring to
its authority. . . . If Congress should succumb to this glaring
usurpation and weakly vote the money, it were absurd to elect
another Congress. We may better hand over the Government
and the Treasury to the President, and bid him do with each
as he shall see fit."

On December 31, 1867, the *Tribune* published another item
of interest with reference to the Danish-American treaty. This
item is copied from the New York *Evening Post,* and is as
follows: "It appears that the new Danish Minister, who
arrived a few days ago, was unaware that there was any difference between the Executive and Congress regarding the purchase of the Island of St. Thomas. His friends say that Secretary Seward had so represented the matters to the Danish
Government as to leave the impression that the treaty would
be quickly ratified by this Government. Immediately after his
arrival here, the Minister called upon Mr. Seward to consult
with him in regard to the matter, but the latter pleaded an
extraordinary pressure of public business, and bowed the
Danish Minister out very politely, and up to the present time
he has been unable to gain another audience, or to learn officially the condition of the treaty. This is a true statement of
the case, as learned from persons connected with a foreign
legation here [Washington], and among the foreign ministers
the matter has excited considerable comment."

adopting any means necessary for the confirmation of the Monroe Doctrine, yet the "recent terrible displays of hurricanes and earthquakes in the lands and waters" of the Virgin Islands had led many persons to question the advantages of the treaty of October 24. Under these circumstances it would be necessary for Denmark to take the initiative in the matter of treating for the cession of Santa Cruz. Any negotiation, "to have a prospect of success, must be opened by Denmark, not at Copenhagen," but at Washington. Moreover, the whole question "including price must be considered entirely open, free from all former discussion. No reservation of plantation or of law could be allowed."[21]

After Seward had settled this question of a separate negotiation for the island of Santa Cruz, he next took up the question of how much influence the House of Representatives had in moulding American foreign policy. In an instruction to Yeaman, January 2, 1868, he reviewed the topic in much the same manner that he had adopted in the spring of 1864 when the House of Representatives had passed a resolution declaring that "Congress has a constitutional right to an authoritative voice in declaring and prescribing the foreign policy of the United States.[22] Seward now remarked that it is

"neither convenient nor customary with the Executive Department to discuss or give explanations concerning

[21] MS. Dept. of State, *Denmark, Inst.,* vol. 14.

[22] *Congressional Globe,* vol. 34, pt. 2, 38 Cong., 1 sess., pp. 1408, pt. 3, p. 2475. Also, C. C. Tansill, "War Powers of the President of the United States, etc." *Political Science Quarterly,* March, 1930, pp. 21-23.

the expressions of opinions which are made in incidental debates and resolutions, from time to time, in either
or both of the Legislative bodies, at least until they
assume the practical form of a law. When they assume
that form, they are constitutionally submitted to the
President for his consideration, and he is not only
entitled, but he is obliged to announce his concurrence
or nonconcurrence with the will of the Legislature. It
would not be becoming for me to entertain correspondence with a foreign State concerning incidental debates
and resolutions in regard to the Treaty for the two
Danish Islands, while it is undergoing constitutional
consideration in the Senate and in Congress."

In conclusion Seward delivered the following rebuke
to the Danish Government:

"I may add that I think that it belongs to the Executive of Denmark, so that it always proceeds in good
faith towards the United States, to determine when and
how it will submit the Treaty for the consideration and
ratification of the Rigsdag; and when he shall so have
submitted it, that the current debates it shall call forth
in the Danish Legislature will not probably be made
the subject of attention by the President of the United
States."[23]

[23] Seward to Yeaman, January 2, 1868, MS. Dept. of State.
Denmark, Inst., vol. 14. On this same day that Seward was
preparing his lecture to Count Frijs, the Baltimore *Sun,* January 2, 1868, published a significant excerpt from the London
Morning Star, which showed how the cession of the Danish
islands was viewed in certain British circles. Pertinent portions of this excerpt are as follows: "The acquisition by the
United States of the West India Islands of St. Thomas and
St. John is an event of sufficient gravity to warrant an examination into the motives of the nation which has acquired a
foothold in that region, and of the probable future results on
the scattered communities of those seas belonging to different

There was really, however, very little need for Seward to prepare such a lecture for Count Frijs and General Raasloff. They had been most conciliatory, and had already expressed to Yeaman their "most lively and entire satisfaction" with regard to Seward's letter to Mr. Hawley, December 16, 1867. Indeed, they openly expressed their regret that Commissioner Carstensen had thought a trip to Washington necessary, and that Governor Birch should have deemed it incumbent upon him to "cause additional propositions to be made."[24] It had only been quite natural for them to express some misgivings as to the fate of the treaty in view of the lively domestic dissensions existing in America.

Everything now waited upon the outcome of the plebiscite in the islands of St. Thomas and St. John. On January 4, 1868, Commissioner Carstensen called the leading business men of St. Thomas into a conference, and at the close of the meeting he read to them the passages in Mr. Seward's letter to Mr. Hawley,

---

European powers. . . . Certainly in a war with the United States, . . . the possession of these two Islands would entirely alter the balance of power which has hitherto subsisted between this country and America. We do not point out these results in any spirit of hostility to the United States, but rather to show the blindness and stupidity of the traditional policy of the Foreign Office."

For excerpts taken from the London *Times* with reference to the cession of the Danish islands to the United States, see the Philadelphia *Press,* January 2, 1868.

[24] Yeaman to Seward, January 8, 1868, MS. Dept. of State, *Denmark, Desp.,* vol. 9.

December 16, 1867, in which the Secretary of State had stressed the generous policy the United States would adopt toward the islanders. These fair words had great influence, so on January 9, when the plebiscite was held in the island of St. Thomas, the vote was 1,039 votes in favor of annexation, and only 22 votes against such a measure. On the following day the vote was held in St. John, where the vote was even more conclusive: 205 votes in favor of annexation, and none against it.[25]

On January 18, Seward cabled to Yeaman that the news of the favorable vote in St. Thomas and St. John had been received with satisfaction by the President, and had been communicated at once to the Senate.[26] Ten days later, Yeaman wrote to inform Seward that the treaty had been "voted for by the Folksthing,"[27]

[25] E. H. Perkins, U. S. Consul at St. Thomas, to Seward, January 13, 1868, *Sen. Doc.* 231, 56 Cong., 2 sess., pt. 8, pp. 219-220. Also extracts from the St. Thomas *Tidende,* January 4, and January 11, 1868, in *Sen. Doc.* 231, pp. 220-221.

[26] MS. Dept. of State, *Denmark, Inst.,* vol. 14.

[27] Yeaman to Seward, January 28, 1868, MS. Dept. of State, *Denmark, Desp.,* vol. 9. The treaty was ratified by the Folkething on January 25, 1868, without a dissenting vote, and on January 29, it passed the Landsthing by a unanimous vote. On January 8, 1868, Seward appeared before the Senate Committee on Foreign Relations and read a long memorandum relative to the negotiations he had conducted in regard to Alaska, Samana Bay, and the islands of St. Thomas and St. John. According to the Washington correspondent of the New York *Tribune,* "almost the entire session was taken up in the reading of the document, so that the Committee did not have an opportunity of conferring together respecting their views thereon. The idea is pretty general in the Senate that it

the lower house of the Rigsdag, and on January 31, he wrote that the treaty had been ratified on the previous day by the Landsthing, and had received the signature of the King (January 31).[28] On this same day Yeaman sent the following cablegram to Seward:

"Treaty sent to Washington; ratified by Rigsdag and signed by King. Several European powers hope it will fail in Congress."[29]

Under the terms of Article VI. of the treaty of October 24, 1867, the ratifications were to be exchanged within four months after the date of the signature of the treaty. This meant, of course, February 24, 1868, so on February 19, de Bille, the Danish chargé d'affaires at Washington, announced to Seward that he was ready

---

[the Danish treaty] will not get a dozen votes in that body. After leaving the Senate Committee, the Secretary of State appeared before the House Committee, and read the document to them. The Committee are understood to be opposed to the Danish treaty." See New York *Tribune*, January 8, 1868. The Philadelphia *Press*, January 9, 1868, in commenting upon Seward's appearance before the Senate Foreign Relations Committee on January 8, remarked that the Secretary of State "urged the adoption of the [Danish] treaty in very moderate terms, and two members of the Senate committee are strongly impressed with the idea that he is quite willing it should be defeated. It seems certain anyhow that the committee will not report favorably upon it." See also, Baltimore *American and Commercial Advertiser*, January 11, 1868, for similar comments relative to Seward's indifference to the fate of the Danish treaty.

[28] Yeaman to Seward, January 31, 1868, MS. Dept of State. *Denmark, Desp.*, vol. 9.

[29] Yeaman to Seward, January 31, 1868, *ibid.*

for the exchange.[30]   On the following day, February 20, Seward replied to de Bille to the effect that the treaty of October 24, 1867, was still "under consideration in the Senate of the United States," and here the matter rested.[31]

In Denmark the action of the Rigsdag had been very prompt and favorable, but in the Senate of the United States a policy of deliberate inactivity seemed to prevail.   On December 3, 1867, President Johnson sent the treaty to the Senate for its advice and consent,[32] but when February 24 came, that body had failed to take any action.   Such an attitude greatly worried Yeaman who expressed his fears as to the fate of the treaty.   Seward, however, attempted to make light of this inactivity, and in an instruction to the American Minister at Copenhagen he assured him that even though the Senate had thus far refrained from any real consideration of the treaty, such delay should not lead to inferences "unfavorable" to the success of the convention.   On January 8, 1868, a special envoy from the Dominican Republic had arrived in the United States with the information that his Government had "reconsidered its rejection of our propositions for the purchase of Samana, and desired now to agree upon terms of cession."   It was, of course, due to the Senate and to the country,

[30] MS. Dept. of State, *Denmark, Notes from,* vol. 4.
[31] MS. Dept. of State, *Denmark, Notes to,* vol. 6.
[32] Jas. D. Richardson, *Messages and Papers of the Presidents,* vol. 6, p. 581.

"to give a fair consideration to the Dominican proposition. That subject is therefore, now under discussion in this Department. It is not unlikely that the Senate will prefer to wait for the result of my conferences with the Dominican Minister before proceeding to a final consideration of the Danish Treaty. Certainly the treaty for St. Thomas and St. John, loses nothing in popular favor by a free examination upon its merits."[33]

As the months passed by and the Senate still took no action relative to the treaty with Denmark, Seward's facile explanations of the Senate's inactivity carried less and less weight. On March 6, 1868, Yeaman wrote to the Secretary of State to inform him how the delay in the ratification of the treaty had seriously weakened the Danish Ministry. Many members of the Rigsdag were growing increasingly curious as to the probable fate of the treaty in the Senate, but Count Frijs and General Raasloff were still optimistic about the result.[34]

This optimism of Count Frijs is revealed in an instruction that he sent to Captain Bille on March 27, 1868. The main obstruction to any speedy ratification of the Treaty of October 24, seemed to be the impeach-

[33] Seward to Yeaman, January 29, 1868, MS. Dept. of State, *Denmark, Inst.,* vol. 14. Seward's assurances were to be received in Denmark with a firm belief in their verity. On January 21, 1868, Mr. Charles A. Murray, the British Minister at Copenhagen, wrote to Lord Stanley that on the previous day he had had an interview with Count Frijs, who had informed him that "he could not foresee any difficulty with regard to the ratification of the agreement concluded here for the sale of the Islands of St. Thomas and St. John." F. O. 22/349, no. 6.

[34] MS. Dept. of State, *Denmark, Desp.,* vol. 9.

ment proceedings against President Johnson. However, if the President were acquitted, it then appeared to Count Frijs that Johnson and Seward would

"find themselves so strengthened by this victory that it will be easy for them to carry the treaty through, and even if he should be found guilty and the Republicans come into power, it seems unlikely . . . that they should wish to drop a matter which certainly offers great advantages for America's future. . . . It would be of the greatest interest to me [Frijs] to be informed of Mr. Wade's opinion about foreign affairs in general as well as the West Indian treaty in particular. Of course I do not mean his pronouncements at the present time, since he is not likely to feel greatly inclined to approve a transaction that has been concluded by President Johnson, but his probable attitude towards the matter when he will be able to consider it impartially. If there is any chance of Charles Sumner being Minister of Foreign Affairs, I am confident that he has enough political ability to feel favorably towards our treaty. Seeing from your cablegram that he is among the many political personages with whom you have been able to establish a connection, I presume I shall learn from you whether or not my opinion in this matter is well-founded."[35]

This Danish optimism was very gratifying to Seward who tried to reassure Count Frijs and General Raasloff by expressing the opinion that the delay in ratification of the treaty was to be attributed, he believed to the

"intervention of our exciting domestic question of a political nature, which has from the beginning of the

[35] Count Frijs to Captain Bille, March 27, 1868, no. 3, MS. *D. F. O.*

session absorbed, and still continues to absorb, the attention of both Houses of Congress."[36]

With special reference to General Raasloff, who felt personally responsible for the signature of the treaty, Seward expressed his deep interest in the "welfare and reputation" of the Minister of War, and he intended to hand Mr. Yeaman's letter to Mr. Sumner for his confidential perusal.[37]

In the following month, renewed pressure upon Mr. Sumner in behalf of General Raasloff was exerted by George William Curtis, who wrote to the Chairman of the Senate Foreign Relations Committee a note of inquiry:

"I have reason to know that General de Raasloff, the Danish Minister of War and so long Danish Minister here, is extremely anxious about the fate of the St. Thomas treaty. I think that he would even make a special mission to this country if it should be thought useful to secure the ratification of the Treaty. Will you have the great kindness to tell me—so far as you can—your opinion of the probable ratification of the treaty, and whether you think the presence in this country of a special Danish envoy, essential or necessary."[38]

Sumner's answer to Curtis is not available, but it is apparent that the friends of the treaty recognized that the success of that project depended largely upon personal considerations.

[36] Seward to Yeaman, April 10, 1868, *Private,* MS. Dept. of State, *Denmark, Inst.,* vol. 14.

[37] *Ibid.*

[38] Curtis to Sumner, May 20, 1868, *Sumner Papers,* Harvard College Library.

On May 18, 1868, the question of the cession of Santa Cruz to the United States again arose. Mr. Yeaman wrote to Seward that Count Frijs had confidentially communicated to him the information that France would "interpose no obstacle" to such a negotiation.[39] On June 5, Yeaman wrote that the people of Santa Cruz had petitioned the Danish Government to "give effect to the desire of the inhabitants of that island for its annexation to the United States,"[40] and the following week, June 11, 1868, he wrote that the petition had been received, and he believed that if the

"Government of the United States now deems it desirable, a negotiation could be opened for that island, with much better prospect of success than formerly, and possibly on better terms."[41]   .

On June 29, 1868, Seward replied to this new overture on the part of the Danish Government relative to the cession of the island of Santa Cruz to the United States. In the early part of his instruction he discussed the reasons for the delay in the ratification of the treaty of October 24. It was largely due to the fact that "important domestic questions" had arisen which "engrossed the attention of Congress and the country during the present year to the exclusion of external policies." The House of Representatives had thus far failed to vote the appropriation necessary to carry out the treaty with Russia for the purchase of

[39] Yeaman to Seward, May 18, 1868, MS. Dept. of State, *Denmark, Desp.*, vol. 10.
[40] Yeaman to Seward, June 5, 1868, *ibid.*
[41] Yeaman to Seward, June 11, 1868, *ibid.*

Alaska, and several other important treaties had been postponed. Judging from these indications, he was of the opinion that the Danish treaty would "be left for consideration until the next session of Congress." It would be better, therefore, to hold in reserve the suggestion of Mr. Yeaman "in regard to the Island of Santa Cruz." In the meantime, the American Minister might

"unofficially and informally, and without committing this Department, ascertain and communicate any change of sentiment that may exist on the part of the Danish Government in regard to the transfer of the last mentioned island. This communication is made for your own information. It is not expected that its contents will be formally communicated to the Danish Government."[42]

As the session of the American Congress was drawing near to a close, the Danish Minister of Foreign Affairs felt a growing interest in the question of the ratification of the treaty of October 24, 1867. The domestic situation in the United States greatly perturbed the Danish Cabinet, and Count Frijs, in particular, was trying in every way to read the riddle of American politics. The open quarrel between President Johnson and Congress had resulted in the impeachment trial that had recently come to an unsuccessful conclusion. Continuance of this friction would make it very difficult to secure the consent of the Senate to any treaties that had been negotiated by the Johnson ad-

[42] Seward to Yeaman, June 29, 1868, MS. Dept. of State, *Denmark, Inst.*, vol. 14.

ministration, and this very uncertain prospect was often commented upon by Count Frijs in his instructions to Captain F. Bille, the Danish chargé d'affaires in Washington. In this regard the following communication from Frijs to Bille is typical:

"Considering only our interests, I cannot but think that the affair against the President has been settled in exactly the way which is the least favorable to us. Far from feeling beaten, the anti-governmental opposition in the Senate is now exerting itself to the utmost to revenge its defeat and strengthen its prospects for the future by working against the President's policies. Unfortunately for us, this opposition is powerful and ruthless enough to reject a project which reveals the government's more far-sighted judgment of the requirements of America's future interests. Thus I realize that the wisest course for us to follow under the present circumstances is to wait for better times, and not make the situation still more difficult by urging an immediate settlement. Yet Your Honor will understand how very disagreeable this delay is for the Royal Government in consideration of the meeting of the Rigsdag in the fall, and especially in view of the West Indian islands.

"Since, for this reason, I feel it my duty to leave no stone unturned which might clear the situation. I must urge Your Honor to seek a confidential conversation with Mr. Seward who, I am convinced, wishes as ardently as I to have the treaty ratified as soon as possible. You will tell him that the Royal Government has all reason for surprise, having observed the stipulations of the treaty concerning ratification, while the American Government has as yet taken no step to redeem its given word. He will easily realize the precarious position in which the Royal Government finds itself, especially after the population has voiced its opinion in the matter."[43]

[43] Count Frijs to Captain F. Bille, July 9, 1868, MS. *D. F. O.*

The next move of Count Frijs was to inquire of Mr. Yeaman, at the weekly diplomatic interview on July 23, 1868, whether he had any further news upon the subject. The American Minister replied that he "had no facts to communicate" that the Minister of Foreign Affairs was not already in possession of. He did, however, repeat his previous statement as to the "supposed causes of delay." Count Frijs then assured Mr. Yeaman that he had "entire confidence" in the "loyalty of the intentions and the views of the Government of the United States," but he felt constrained to remark that the matter was "none the less embarrassing to the Danish Government."[44]

On August 6, 1868, the Danish Minister of Foreign Affairs referred to the proposed cession of the island of Santa Cruz, and remarked that the "Danish Government, before offering to open any negotiation would prefer to know whether the Government of the United States still desired the acquisition of that island." Mr. Yeaman was diplomatically indefinite in his reply. He could only say that any suggestion from Count Frijs would be "duly and attentively considered" by Mr. Seward. Personally, it seemed to the American Minister that the openly expressed desire on the part of the inhabitants of Santa Cruz for annexation to the United States would justify Denmark in "either making or receiving any modified propositions" on the subject of the cession. In concluding the discussion, Count Frijs

[44] Yeaman to Seward, July 23, 1868, MS. Dept. of State, *Denmark, Desp.*, vol. 10.

observed that "he would further consider what might be done in the matter of Santa Cruz," but at present he did not see how the negotiations for St. Thomas and St. John could be "conveniently or usefully connected" with a negotiation for Santa Cruz.[45]

Some ten days later, August 17, 1868, Seward wrote a private and confidential letter to Yeaman on the subject of the cession of Santa Cruz. He believed that there was "manifest in the public mind something of a reaction in favor of the recent treaty acquisitions of Alaska and St. Thomas." He did not think that this reaction was as yet "sufficiently strong" to justify an expectation that the addition of Santa Cruz with an increase of the purchase money stipulated in the treaty of October 24, would render it "more acceptable to the Senate and Congress."[46]

It took Seward's naturally cheerful eye to detect any growing sentiment in favor of the St. Thomas treaty, and the Senate, not possessing such clairvoyance, refused to take any action with reference to the convention. As a consequence, when Congress adjourned in July, 1868, the time within which the ratifications were to have been exchanged had long expired, so that in order to revive the treaty it would be necessary to sign an additional article extending the time limit prescribed by Article VI. This failure of the Senate to act had placed the Danish Government in a

[45] Yeaman to Seward, August 8, 1868, *ibid*.
[46] Seward to Yeaman, August 17, 1868, MS. Dept. of State, *Denmark, Inst.,* vol. 14.

most embarrassing position. The plebiscite in the islands had been taken, the Rigsdag had ratified the treaty, and it had been signed by the King. Every obligation had been faithfully and punctually carried out. America's policy of inaction was of such doubtful propriety that on August 6, Count Frijs remarked to Mr. Yeaman that the "strict rights" of the Danish Government in regard to the treaty were "apparent," and for that reason it could "take a very strong position" with reference to it. But he had hastened to add that his Government was not "disposed to raise that question, or to interrupt the consideration of the matter at Washington."[47] It was to be expected, therefore, that when Congress adjourned without taking any action relative to the treaty, the Danish Government thought the time had come for further explanations.

Seward, therefore, began to discuss with de Bille, the Danish chargé, the feasibility of an additional article extending the time for the exchange of ratifications. On August 25, 1868, he placed in the hands of de Bille a draft of the proposed additional article postponing for a year the date of ratification. He assigned as the reason for proposing such a long period, that it was "necessary to do so in order to enable us to submit the Treaty to the Senate which will begin on the 4th of March next, if the Senate which is to reassemble in December, should for any reason omit or

[47] Yeaman to Seward, August 8, 1868, MS. Dept. of State. *Denmark, Desp.,* vol. 10.

delay a consideration of that subject until its prescribed adjournment on the 3d of March."[48]

There was some opposition in the Danish Cabinet to this additional article, so in order to answer inquiries in the Rigsdag, Count Frijs requested Mr. Yeaman to submit to him a confidential note explaining the reasons for the delay in the United States. On September 17, Yeaman sent to the Danish Minister of Foreign Relations the confidential note as requested, and in it he reviewed at length the domestic dissensions in the United States. He did express the belief, however, that "some delay would work beneficially," and that now many questions had been settled, the "presence of which was unfavorable to the consideration of the treaty."[49]

On October 11, 1868, de Bille informed Seward that he was ready to sign the additional article. He wished, however, to inform the Secretary of State, that the Danish Government hoped to see the ratifications completed before "the complete expiration of the year during which the Government of the King consents to hold itself bound by the Treaty of the 24th of October."[50]

On October 15, when Seward signed the additional article to the treaty, he gave formal assurances to the Danish chargé that

[48] Seward to Yeaman, August 27, 1868, MS. Dept. of State, *Denmark, Inst.,* vol. 14.

[49] Yeaman to Seward, September 18, 1868, MS. Dept. of State, *Denmark, Desp.,* vol. 10.

[50] De Bille to Seward, October 11, 1868, *Denmark, Notes from,* vol. 4.

"such further proceedings as are necessary to give full effect to the Treaty referred to, will be taken with good faith and diligence on the part of the United States."[51]

Now that the treaty was saved by the signature of the additional article extending the date of ratifications, both Mr. Yeaman and General Raasloff set about devising methods for securing favorable consideration by the American Senate. Mr. Yeaman professed great belief in the personal equation. He thought that it is very seldom that any important question is decided strictly upon its merits. Many times indirect pressure is necessary to secure the passage of even the most salutary laws. It seemed to him, therefore, that the presence of General Raasloff in Washington might greatly facilitate the ratification of the treaty. The General was known to possess a most agreeable personality; he had a ready command of the English language, and his wide circle of friends included members of both Houses of Congress. Mr. Yeaman had sounded out General Raasloff who was quite willing to undertake the trip to Washington if "it was believed it would do any good," and Count Frijs, who at first was opposed to such a step, was now ready to give his consent provided that Mr. Seward was not opposed to it.[52]

When Seward received this despatch from Yeaman concerning General Raasloff's visit to the United States, he immediately sent the following cablegram in cipher:

[51] Seward to de Bille, October 15, 1868, MS. Dept. of State, *Denmark, Notes to,* vol. 6. See also J. D. Richardson, *Messages and Papers of the Presidents,* vol. 6, p. 693.

[52] Yeaman to Seward, November 1, 1868, MS. Dept. of State, *Denmark, Desp.,* vol. 10.

"No material objection."[53]

On November 28, 1868, he also sent a private letter to Yeaman in which he indicated the main difficulty in the way of accomplishing any project during the last days of a presidential administration. The periodical reconstruction "of the Executive Administration always brings on, when the Presidential election is passed, and before a newly chosen administration comes in, a condition of uncertainty and suspense." The outgoing administration

"cannot venture upon matters of which no result can be expected during its continuance, while the shadow of the incoming administration is too obscure to indicate any important policy. . . . We are now entering this condition of *quasi interregnum*. Prudence and patience are needful but there is no ground to apprehend any serious difficulty or danger of any kind from any question."[54]

It was evident from the neutral tone of Seward's cablegram to Yeaman of November 17, that the Secretary of State did not have any high hopes as to the success of Raasloff's visit to the United States,[55] but

[53] Seward to Yeaman, November 17, 1868, MS. Dept. of State, *Denmark, Inst.*, vol. 14.

[54] Seward to Yeaman, November 28, 1868, MS. Dept. of State, *Denmark, Inst.*, vol. 14.

[55] Although Seward was losing hope as to the ratification of the treaty, Yeaman, at Copenhagen, remained optimistic. On November 11, 1868, Mr. G. S. Strachey, the British representative at Copenhagen, wrote to Lord Stanley with reference to a recent conversation with Mr. Yeaman: "The American Minister continues to believe that the United States will

the Danish Minister of War felt himself so deeply involved in the fate of the treaty that he dared not wait any longer. The Danish Cabinet reluctantly granted him a three months leave of absence in order that he might visit the United States for the special purpose of using his "personal influence" in an endeavor to convince dubious Senators that the treaty of October 24 would redound greatly to America's benefit. At the same time, the Danish Cabinet agreed upon instructions to Captain Bille, at Washington, which empowered him now to offer to the United States the cession of the island of Saint Croix in addition to the islands of St. Thomas and St. John. The policy which dictated this new offer from Denmark to the United States was made clear in the following instructions that Count Frijs sent to Captain Bille:

"We have had intimations from men who are closely connected with the present [American] Government, and from others who are expected to obtain influence with the new Government, about the possibility that

ultimately purchase the Islands of St. Thomas and St. John. But he has no other ground for his opinion than the general fact that from the acquisition of Louisiana downwards, every proposal to add new territory to the Union has been violently arraigned and invariably accepted. He insists on the great value of St. Thomas as a naval station for the United States navy in case of war with England, which consideration decided Mr. Seward to the Treaty. Mr. Yeaman finished his recent remarks to me on this subject, by advising the suggestion of Your Lordship, that if the Islands did not become American they might easily and advantageously become English." MS. F. O. 22/349, no. 4.

the matter might be given new impetus if Santa Cruz were included in the agreement. It is very important to obtain a reliable opinion about this. Those who think that the financial side of the affair has exercised the strongest influence on the attitude and feelings of Congress, will consider it necessary, in order to push the matter, to lower the price for Santa Cruz. . . . If the final issue should depend altogether on the eventual reduction of the agreed-upon price for Santa Cruz, you are authorized by me and the Government, to assent, as a last resort, to a cut of even half of the price for Santa Cruz, but only if the new Government headed by Grant will adopt the matter as its own, and with all their might urge a speedy settlement.

"The opinion has been expressed that the opposition against the Treaty of October 24, has been based much more on personal than on genuine motives, and that, in reality, the opposition has been used only as a convenient weapon against the President and his Government. Now that this fight has terminated in the victory of the Republican Party, it is assumed that neither the new Government nor the Senate will fail to appreciate the great importance of the treaty for the future of the United States, and that they will, therefore, be pleased to find a pretence to switch the matter into a new course opposite to that one in which it has until now been blocked. The extension of the treaty to include Santa Cruz will probably serve as a means to this end, because it might then be claimed that the whole question is assuming a new character."[56]

General Raasloff now made hurried preparations to leave Copenhagen in the last week of November, 1868, so that he would arrive in the United States shortly after Congress convened. He delayed his trip slightly

[56] Count Frijs to Captain Bille, November 26, 1868, MS. D. F. O.

by paying a visit to London in order to discuss the situation with his old American friend, Anson Burlingame, who had just arrived in Europe as the representative of China to the Western Powers. Raasloff was well aware of the fact that Burlingame was intimately acquainted with Charles Sumner, the chairman of the Senate Committee on Foreign Relations, so he cherished the hope that a note from Burlingame might be of some assistance. It was for this reason that, on December 4, 1868, Burlingame addressed a private letter to Sumner, a portion of which is as follows:

"Our mutual friend Genl. Raasloff has confided to me the object of his visit to the United States. Can you aid him? He has committed himself to us in such a way by vouching for our good faith, that if his treaty is not ratified he will feel it to be his duty to resign his high post of Minister of War, not because it will be required, but from delicacy. His personal *status* is not of course to be weighed against justice or the interests of the United States."[57]

Raasloff arrived in Washington on December 19, 1868, and in his own words, found the situation "highly unfavourable" with regard to the Danish treaty. Party passions that had been aroused by the impeachment of President Johnson had not subsided, and the relations between Secretary Seward and Senator Sumner were so strained that "they evaded as much as possible coming into personal contact with each other." This fact deprived Raasloff of the assistance he had counted

[57] Burlingame to Sumner, December 4, 1868, MS. *Sumner Papers*, Harvard College Library.

on from Seward, and forced him to rely largely on his own efforts to secure the ratification of the treaty. Disappointed, but not dispirited, Raasloff began to concentrate all his attention upon Sumner, who was known to be hostile to any further American expansion. On January 1, 1869, he wrote to the Massachusetts Senator a carefully worded New Year's greeting:

"Allow me first and foremost to tender you my sincerest wishes for a happy new year. It will doubtless bring to you much labor and heavy responsibilities, but I trust that it will also bring you much satisfaction and success, especially the kind of success which I know you value most of all and which marks the progress of civilization not only in this country but all over the world."[58]

After this friendly greeting, Raasloff asked Sumner to have New Year's dinner with him, and during the following weeks these dinner invitations came thick and fast. On January 7, 1869, Raasloff wrote to ask Sumner to go with him to see Senator Harlan, of Iowa, who was a member of the Senate Committee on Foreign Relations,[59] and on January 19, he expressed the hope that

"in fairness to Denmark, the fate of our treaty will not be decided (at least not unfavorably), before your Committee have taken testimony about the value of the islands, and before I shall have had an opportunity of fairly meeting the objections—if any."[60]

[58] Raasloff to Sumner, January 1, 1869, MS. *Sumner Papers.*
[59] Raasloff to Sumner, January 7, 1869, *ibid.*
[60] Raasloff to Sumner, January 19, 1869, *ibid.*

On January 26, and January 28, 1869, Sumner procured for Raasloff the privilege of appearing before the
Senate Committee on Foreign Relations in order that
the arguments in favor of the treaty should have their
strongest expression.   Raasloff greatly appreciated
Sumner's kindness in this regard, so on February 1, he
wrote to Sumner to express his gratitude for the
"patient hearing" given him by the Senate Committee.
In this same letter he voices the hope that the Committee would,—

"in view of the doubt expressed in some quarters in
regard to the value of St. Thomas and St. John as a
naval station and depot, and as a commercial center,—
let competent men appear before them and hear their
testimony upon that point." [61]

Although Raasloff had presented his strongest arguments to the Senate Committee on Foreign Relations
relative to the obligations of the American Government
to ratify the treaty of October 24, yet it was apparent
to the Danish chargé, Captain Bille, that the Senate
Committee remained unconvinced.   In a despatch to
Count Frijs, January 28, 1869, after discussing the
appearance of Raasloff before the Committee on
Foreign Relations, Bille expresses the opinion that

"it will hardly be possible to do more than has already
been done to further the affair at its present stage.
Things seem to have reached such a point that it is considered nearly as difficult to reject the treaty as to ratify
it.   Whether the result of this will be that either of
these alternatives will finally be chosen—or whether it

[91] Raasloff to Sumner, February 1, 1869, MS. *Sumner
Papers.*

will be preferred to let the matter rest until after the 4th of March—about this I shall shortly be able to report. It is very difficult to perceive which of these alternatives is most desirable for us. On one hand there is always, during negotiations like these, a point where the pressure may be supposed to have attained its maximum and where any further postponement means losing ground. On the other hand, it is no less precarious to precipitate the settlement of the affair, when it has been intimated that it might gain in certainty by being delayed a short time."[62]

A week later, February 5, 1869, Captain Bille wrote to Count Frijs to inform him that

"the uncertainty regarding the immediate result of the efforts to dispose the Senate Committee to favor the ratification of the St. Thomas treaty cannot be said to exist any longer. Unfortunately, it has been replaced by the fact that there is a prevailing, if not yet a positively pronounced determination, to reject the treaty. That this determination was not carried out in the Committee meeting of Tuesday, when it seems to have been ripe, is due principally to a request made by General Raasloff, who requested the production of certain missing parts of the correspondence from the Department of State, and asked the Committee to wait for the communication of these as well as for a new, official memorial, illustrating the affair from the viewpoint of the Danish Government. In this way, time will be gained until the case shall have its last chance after the appointment of the new Secretary of State and the advent of the new administration.

". . . I fear to speak with too great a confidence with reference to the expectations that may be attached to this change. One may, however, find a negative consolation in the fact that nobody is able to form an accurate guess as to the situation after the change in the

[62] Bille to Count Frijs, January 28, 1869, MS. D. F. O.

Presidency. There is, at present, no small amount of ill-humor in the Republican Party because of the total independence maintained by General Grant, who does not communicate his views and plans to any important person. Only after the formation of his Cabinet will it appear whether the result of this momentary dissatisfaction will be a coolness towards the Radicals, who have never regarded General Grant with absolute confidence.

"This circumstance contains a contingency that may have much influence on the approaching situation. It may be that the executive power will make a successful attempt to liberate itself from the absolute dependence upon Congress to which the present administration has been tied. But it is also possible that such an attempt will fail and that the actual control of the Government will continue to be located in the Senate.

"As we are so near the moment where we will necessarily be enlightened as to these circumstances, I shall confine myself to the following indications: on the 10th instant the votes for the President will be counted in the Senate, and it is to be assumed that General Grant will then, after his definite nomination, take his stand more firmly.

". . . It is a fact that the idea that the question of expansion into the West Indies cannot be evaded much longer, gains more ground each day, and although at the present moment the actual position of the St. Thomas treaty in the Senate seems weak, yet the treaty itself cannot be said to lose ground in public estimation. The press expresses itself rather feebly against it, and leading organs admit articles which recommend the ratification of the treaty far more forcefully than is strictly permitted by the political views of the papers. On the whole, there are symptoms which make me inclined to believe that the tide of public feeling will soon change perceptibly, and that the political situation will be essentially altered. Still, I cannot hide that also in the circumstances intimated above, there may be grave dangers as to the safe carrying through of our treaty."[63]

General Raasloff shared Captain Bille's belief that everything would depend on the attitude taken by the administration of President Grant with reference to the Danish treaty. Through "numerous interviews with Mr. Sumner and other leading Senators," and through conferences "with the Committee for Foreign Affairs of the Senate," Raasloff had become "convinced that there was at that moment no possibility of obtaining the desired ratification."[64] But this fact did not prevent him from making further efforts to enlighten the Senate Committee. Being of the opinion that the testimony of naval officers would have unusual weight with the members of the Committee, he applied to Captain Gustavus V. Fox, former Assistant Secretary of the Navy Department, for a letter to Sumner in which the advantages to the United States from the cession of the Danish islands would be clearly indicated. But Fox was uncertain as to the proper procedure in this regard, so on January 31, 1869, he wrote to Sumner to inquire if the Committee would make a formal request for a report from him in regard to the cession. Such action by the Committee would provide him with an opportunity to send in a studied reply which would cover every aspect of the situation.[65]

[63] Bille to Count Frijs, February 5, 1869, MS. D. F. O.
[64] Raasloff to Baron Rosenorn-Lehn, Secretary for Foreign Affairs, September 29, 1880, MS. D. F. O.
[65] Fox to Sumner, January 31, 1869, MS. *Sumner Papers*.

In accordance with this suggestion, on February 19, Sumner wrote to Fox to request his expert opinion with reference to the value of St. Thomas and St. John as naval stations. In his reply of February 27, 1869, Fox sent a long document which reviewed at length every advantage America could derive from the treaty. The harbor of St. Thomas was one of the "best in the West Indies, admirable for naval purposes, and fully equal to all the requirements of the commerce of those seas." And not only could St. Thomas serve every commercial purpose, but the harbor was eminently suitable for defence. Moreover, the naval experience of the Civil War taught unmistakably that "in future wars steam power only can be used successfully against an enemy's commerce." Therefore, it was patent that the nations having "naval depots and surplus coal will occupy a commanding position in a maritime struggle." The reasons which made it "wise and patriotic" for Mr. Lincoln to open negotiations in January 1865, were still in operation. New grounds for

"favoring the object come constantly into notice, and our country can hardly fulfil the great destinies expected of her, unless she secures, when the opportunity is presented, a position which by strategic art will serve as an outwork to the coast of our Union, and give additional efficiency to the means of defending our commerce and our Atlantic and Pacific communications."[66]

Meanwhile, General Raasloff spared no effort to gather all possible information relative to the probable

[66] James Parton, *The Danish Islands,* pp. 72-76.

fate of the treaty. On February 5, 1869, he wrote at
length to Senator Doolittle who had assisted in the
negotiations leading up to the treaty of October 24.
Someone who "insisted upon being well-informed," had
just assured General Raasloff

"that the Com. for f. Relations had—before the Christmas holidays and recess, agreed to reject the St.
Thomas treaty immediately after the recess. He says
that the members of the Com. had talked the matter
over with Mr. Sumner, and that they were all agreed.
My arrival—he further stated—had prevented this execution of the preliminary decision the Com. had come
to, and that now the Com, would prefer to let the matter
lay over to the next administration after 4th of March.
This latter assertion, being essentially in accordance
with what you wrote to me last week in answer to my
inquiry, I believe to be well founded, but it is never-
the less important for me to know *for certain* whether
his first assertion is also correct, and I would feel
greatly obliged to you if you would ascertain the fact
for me. If the Com. have abandoned their first plan
they cannot be entirely unwilling, I imagine, to speak
out about it. I prefer now myself to let the matter pass
over until after the 4th of March, and I should be
happy to know that the Com. will not again change
and suddenly act adversely, without waiting for the
Memorandum which I have promised them and which
. am now preparing." [67]

The following week Raasloff became convinced that
"one of the difficulties in the way of the St. Thomas
Treaty is the prevailing ignorance of the facts con-
ected with its negotiation." Therefore, on February

[67] Raasloff to Doolittle, February 5, 1869, MS. *Doolittle
apers,* Library of Congress.

11, he wrote to Sumner to request that the Senator let him have as many copies as possible of the printed documents relating to the treaty.[68] If these could be distributed wisely they might lead to a change in public sentiment.

This letter is typical of the Raasloff-Sumner correspondence, and reveals the extent to which Raasloff often went in his requests for assistance. He had early realized that Sumner was strongly opposed to the Danish treaty, and he expressed to Commissioner Carstensen his regret that he "could not win the sympathy of that statesman for the transaction."[69] But despite Sumner's opposition, Raasloff recognized that the chairman of the Senate Committee on Foreign Relations was a gentleman of the highest integrity, and that personal objections, no matter how weighty, would not prevent Sumner from using his influence to give the treaty a searching and candid examination. Not only did Raasloff ask for documents for distribution, but he repeatedly sent pamphlets and memoranda to Sumner to pass around to the other members of the Foreign Relations Committee. The above correspondence between Sumner and Captain Gustavus Fox indicate how far Sumner was willing to go in order that argu ments favorable to the treaty would have a chance for consideration before the Committee.

Indeed, the Senator from Massachusetts showed definite forbearance with reference to General Raa

[68] Raasloff to Sumner, February 11, 1869, *Sumner Papers.*
[69] Edward L. Pierce, *Memoir and Letters of Charles Sumn* (Boston, 1894), vol. 4, p. 620.

loff's tactics. As soon as the General reached America in December, 1868, he engaged the services of Sidney Andrews, an able newspaper correspondent, for the purpose of bringing before the American public the alleged advantages of the Danish treaty.[70] On January 11, 1869, Andrews published his first article in the *Boston Daily Advertiser,* and other articles appeared in the same paper until February 22. In the article that was published on February 8, Andrews does not hesitate to criticize Sumner. In December, 1867, the Danish Commissioner, C. R. Carstensen, had arrived in the United States to consult with Seward and other officials with reference to additional articles to the treaty of October 24, and with regard to taking a plebiscite in the Danish islands. If he had been warned by any responsible officials that the treaty would probably suffer defeat in the Senate it is very likely that he would not have returned to the islands to order the vote, and it is not likely that the Danish Government would have ratified the convention. It was for this reason that Andrews scores Sumner on February 8, and a part of his indictment is as follows:

"Can the Senate show guiltless hands? A word from that body while Mr. Carstensen was here in December,

[70] It is interesting to note that these articles were afterwards printed in pamphlet form by the Danish Commissioner C. T. Carstensen, and were given wide distribution. See Sidney Andrews, *The St. Thomas Treaty* (N. Y. 1869). With reference to Andrews see the article by S. Harrell, in the *Dictionary of American Biography* (edited by Allen Johnson), N. Y. 1928), vol. I, pp. 297-98.

1867, a simple resolution of warning from the Committee on Foreign Relations, would have stopped the proceedings in the islands. That word was not uttered, that resolution was not offered: can the Senate throw stones at Mr. Seward's glass house?"

In his article of February 22, he is even more critical. After discussing the steps leading up to the signature of the treaty he comes to the conclusion that Seward's diplomacy followed a very "crooked course." His opinion of the way in which the Senate had acted was little better. Thus:

"The way of the Senate was not an honorable way— indeed, it was a way the United States cannot afford to have any future Senate take. It received the Danish treaty from the President early in the session of 1867-68. The Government of Denmark knew, all the while, that action upon that document was required at the hands of this body. It had a right to ask that this action be taken within the time named in the treaty itself. Yet, in all the twelve weeks, from December 3, 1867, to February 24, 1868, nothing was done. The Danish Commissioner and Rev. Dr. Hawley came here the first week in December and remained two or three weeks. The Committee on Foreign Relations, which had the matter in charge, might properly enough have acted during their visit; if the islands were not wanted, we could have said so at once, and thus have made an end of the whole business. The committee said nothing; did not even hint its purpose of inaction. . . . February went by, and then followed the months to July, in the end of which Congress adjourned. The Senate had not passed upon the question of ratification—even Mr. Sumner's committee had not passed upon the question. . . . Mr. Sumner's committee held the convention for nine months, neither saying anything or doing anything; and no member of the body called for a report on the question it had been charged to consider. The way of this committee and this Senate is a way we have a right to demand shall never again be followed."

But Sidney Andrews was not the only publicist that General Raasloff engaged to defend the treaty before the American public. He promptly hired James Parton, an author of note, to write a pamphlet entiled *The Danish Islands*. This pamphlet was published in 1869, and its tenor is similar to that of the articles of Mr. Andrews. He carefully rehearses the negotiations leading up to the treaty, and then arrives at the conclusion that the United States is "bound in honor" to carry out the terms of the convention. Raasloff gave him many confidential documents, and told him of conversations he had had with important officials. The following excerpt is typical of these reported conversations:

"A distinguished Senator put a searching question some time since to General Raasloff:—

"'In your opinion,' asked the Senator, 'would the United States have a right to complain if your Rigsdag had refused their consent to the ratification of the St. Thomas treaty?'

"An excellent question. The reply of the General was interesting and deserves consideration.

"'If,' said he, 'the Rigsdag had refused their consent to the ratification of the treaty with the United States, the Danish Government would have dissolved that body, and appealed to the people by means of a general election; and if the new Rigsdag, elected on that question, should likewise have refused their consent, the Cabinet ministers would have resigned their offices. But even though we should in that manner have given you all the satisfaction our government had it in their power to give, you would, in my opinion, still have a right to complain of us for having trifled with you in having neglected to secure beforehand the ratification of a solemn treaty entered into with you; and that your right to complain would have been greater still, if, implicitly confiding in the good faith of Denmark, the United States had *irrevocably committed themselves* by the adoption and execution of important measures which could not be deferred without rendering impossible the punctual exchange of ratifications within the term stipulated by the treaty itself!' "[71]

The defence of the Danish treaty by Andrews and Parton took place in 1869. In the previous year the Danish Government had already secured the services of Robert J. Walker, an American statesman of unusual ability, for the purpose of influencing American public opinion in regard to the cession of the Danish islands. The sole evidence of Walker's activity is an article published in the Washington *Daily Morning Chronicle*,

[71] Parton, J., *The Danish Islands*, p. 53. This was really an exchange of question and answer before the Senate Foreign Relations Committee upon the appearance of General Raasloff on January 26 and 28, 1869. In Raasloff's letter to Baron Rosenorn-Lehn, September 29, 1880, there is the following account of how James Parton came to write his pamphlet on the Danish islands: "Incidentally, I ought to mention the treatise by Parton, *The Danish Islands*, which was written during my stay in Washington. It was composed under my supervision, use being made of the material collected by me, and it is a masterpiece of its kind. Unfortunately, however, it does no go beyond the end of the year 1868." MS. D. F. O.

January 28, 1868, in which he strongly argues for the purchase of St. Thomas.[72]

In addition to this formidable trio of defenders, Raasloff also had some sort of an arrangement with the Marquis Charles A. de Chambrun, a lawyer of ability and a social lion in the city of Washington. But despite such an array of talent, it was not possible to secure even a favorable report from the Senate Committee on Foreign Relations. The general outlook should have been very discouraging to Raasloff and Captain Bille, but they continued to entertain hopes that the Grant administration might do them justice. It was with this idea in mind that Bille, on March 18, finally called to see the new Secretary of State, Mr. Hamilton Fish. After a brief survey of the negotiations leading up to the treaty and the prompt action of the Danish Government in ratifying it, Captain Bille

[72] In discussing Walker's last years, Professor William E. Dodd, in his brochure entitled *Robert J. Walker, Imperialist* (Chicago, 1914), p. 39, observes as follows: "Our hero closed his career as he had begun it — true to his extreme nationalist ideals and unscrupulous imperialism." At the same time that Walker was publishing his article in favor of the purchase of the Danish islands by the United States, the Danish Government, January, 1868, addressed a note to the French Minister of Foreign Relations, requesting him to use his good offices to secure the ratification of the Danish treaty by the American Senate. The Marquis de Moustier promptly replied that he would be glad to come to the aid of Denmark, "qui avait le bon droit pour lui, mais qu'il croyait impossible, dans le moment, de rien effectuer à Washington, où le congrés était très hostile au président." See Jules Hansen. *Les Coulisses de la Diplomatie* (Paris, 1880), p. 163.

then inquired as to the attitude of the new administration in this matter. Mr. Fish explained to Captain Bille that he "had had no opportunity of following this affair attentively," and for that reason his decision would have to be given later.

As a result of this interview, Bille felt somewhat heartened, and in a despatch to Count Frijs, March 23, 1869, he sets forth the reasons for the encouragement that he now felt:

"It has only now become possible to find a reliable means of making the energetic effort to carry the treaty through to which Your Excellency has exhorted the Legation for more than a year. It seems now that for the first time our assertions and our views produce the idea of a responsibility incurred by disregarding them. I do not doubt that Mr. Seward embraced the idea of the dominion of the United States in West Indian waters with a constant partiality. On the other hand, however, I believe that the liability towards the Danish Government had small weight in his deliberations compared to the obstacles he encountered when proceeding to carry it out, and he did not hesitate—at the expense of our affair—to try another chance that would lead him to the same goal, if that should contain one more favorable element than the St. Thomas treaty. The Senate, on their side, liberated themselves so much the easier from every responsibility in the matter, as it created a new inconvenience, and found a new charge against the Government of President Johnson by doing so.

"There was, therefore, no particular point in the executive power where it proved possible to place an effective lever to conquer the passive opposition that during a whole year prevented the St. Thomas treaty from being taken into serious consideration, and a significant proof of the fruitlessness of all endeavors in

that respect may probably be found in the fact that
the treaty was never so near its definite defeat as when
. . . General Raasloff's personal and energetic advocacy
of the treaty during the last days of the Johnson administration, pushed the matter towards a final decision.
Individually, every one was probably ready to acknowledge the abstract right of Denmark to complain of the
rejection of the treaty, yet collectively, they were ready
to vote against the ratification, disclaiming all the while
every responsibility in that respect. As this became
clear, it was then deemed better to postpone the decision
and await the attitude of the new administration.

". . . President Grant's administration possesses the
feeling of the obligation of leading the politics of a
large country and the faculty for doing so. Even within
its limited sphere of power it is capable of using great
force to enable it to carry through what it considers as
important, and one may now hope for a *bona fide* deliberation, without secondary considerations or precon-
ceived party views. In consequence of this situation,
then, the foremost aim has been to win over the members of the administration to a favorable view of the
treaty, and there is every reason to believe that an
opinion definitely pronounced by the Cabinet will favorably influence the possibility of the Senate's consent
to the ratification.

"At the present time the general spirit of the Cabinet
seems to be favorable if not positively decided. One
seems to feel that the President ought to give the
matter his support if our arguments cannot be refuted
by sound reasons. A prominent member of the Government, General Rawlins, seems to be decidedly in
favor of the acquisition of the Islands. With reference
to the Secretary of State, the impression of my first
interview does not permit me to expect to find a quickly
convinced and eager partisan of the treaty. However,
he has the advantage of being absolutely free in arriving at his decision, and *may,* without being at variance
with already expressed views, defend the ratification

from a diplomatic as well as from a more general political point of view."[73]

These high hopes of Bille were, however, soon dispelled. Shortly after Bille had had his interview with Secretary Fish, General Raasloff sought an audience with President Grant, and when the subject of the acquisition of the Danish West Indies was broached, Grant at once indicated his distaste for the Treaty of October 24. "That," he remarked, "is entirely Seward's plan, with which I desire absolutely nothing to do."[74] So unmistakable was the opposition of the President, that General Raasloff decided it would be better to have the Senate continue its policy of inaction. Therefore, on March 28, 1869, Secretary Fish sent the following note to Charles Sumner:

"Dear Sumner,—

Raasloff does not wish any action on his treaty. He will probably see you.   H. F."[75]

As indicated by Secretary Fish, General Raasloff did hasten to see Sumner in order to inform him in person of the decision that had been reached to postpone action on the Danish treaty. Sumner thoroughly appreciated the embarrassing position in which Raasloff was placed with reference to the failure of his efforts in regard to the treaty. Therefore, in an attempt to assuage the

[73] Bille to Count Frijs, March 23, 1869, MS. D. F. O.

[74] Jules Hansen, op. cit., p, 167. See also Senator Patterson's letter to E. L. Pierce, November 23, 1887, Pierce Papers, Harvard College Library.

[75] E. L. Pierce, Memoir and Letters of Charles Sumner, vol. 4, p. 620.

wounded feelings of his Danish friend, Sumner decided to present him with a much prized portrait of the Danish sculptor, Thorwaldsen. On March 28, Raasloff, in acknowledging this gift, assured Sumner that it would always be "very dear" to him as a *"souvenir d'amite."* [76]

Shortly after this exchange of courtesies, Raasloff left for Copenhagen. When he arrived in Denmark he discovered that several telegraph companies that had laid cables to England, to Norway, and to Russia, were being consolidated into one company, and the "seat of administration" was to be Copenhagen. It was deemed a fitting occasion for a grand celebration, and Raasloff was asked to make a speech at a large public banquet held on May 13, 1869. [77] During the course of his

[76] Raasloff to Sumner, March 28, 1869, *Sumner Papers.*

[77] In commenting upon this speech of General Raasloff, Sir Charles L. Wyke, the British Minister at Copenhagen, wrote to Lord Clarendon, the British Foreign Secretary on May 19, 1869, as follows: "The Danish Minister of War, formerly Envoy at Washington, has returned from a visit to the United States, where he has been trying to promote the Ratification of the Danish West Indies sale Treaty. Some days ago, at a public dinner, General Raasloff declared his firm belief that the American Senate will eventually sanction the payment in question. He added that he would stand or fall with a Treaty, for whose approval by the Cabinet and Rigsdag he felt himself *partly* responsible. The General also said that the rejection of the Treaty would be a heavy blow to the political and financial credit of the United States. If the General actually expects the Treaty to be ratified, he is almost the only person in Denmark who indulges in such a belief. I presume, however, that his speech was meant less for Copenhagen than for Washington, where his words might be expected to produce a certain effect." MS. F. O. 22/357, no. 37.

speech he reviewed his impressions of the United States, and discussed in detail the reasons why the treaty of October 24, had not been promptly ratified by the Senate of the United States. When he reached Washington in December, 1868, he

"did not find the state of public affairs in the United States in a normal condition. . . . Mr. Johnson had not the same hold upon the affection, nor the same claim upon the gratitude of the people, as his predecessor. The relations between him and the legislative bodies ere long assumed a character of unfriendliness which continued until the recent change of administration. . . . On my arrival in Washington I found party spirit running high and the administration enjoying but little confidence and credit. The general unpopularity of which it was the object made itself felt with regard to all its transactions, and consequently also influenced the view taken by the public of the treaty with Denmark. Although the circumstances in no wise justify the delay that has attended the ratification of the treaty of October 24, 1867, yet they appear to me in some measure to explain it and incline me to apply to this case the words of Chateaubriand: 'Si l'on pouvait tout comprendre, il faudrait tout pardonner.'

"Nowhere in the United States did I find a lack of friendship for Denmark, and many were the expressions of sincere regret at the delay in the ratification of the treaty. . . . It must however not be forgotten that the treaty has not been rejected—its ratification has only been postponed, and that it is so is owing to the stand taken by some few wise statesmen foremost among whom is my friend the Honorable Charles Sumner, one of the most prominent and experienced statesmen of the age. . . . Besides, a decided change for the better has of late taken place in the condition of public affairs in the United States. The passions so long prevailing are now gradually subsiding, and the public having become acquainted with all the facts connected with the negotiations preceding our treaty, the chief hindrance for the ratification—which all along has consisted in the total ignorance of the public as to those facts—may now be looked upon as being satisfactorily removed.

"I am confident therefore, from my knowledge of the sense of right so deeply rooted in the American character, that justice will be done to us, and that my American friends will bear me out in the implicit confidence in their loyalty which I have never, even under the most trying circumstances, allowed to be shaken. But while in view of the circumstances before mentioned, I can explain the delay in the ratification of our treaty, I should be utterly unable to comprehend—as matters now stand—any further postponement beyond the next meeting of Congress."[78]

With the Danish Government still hoping for the ratification of the treaty of October 24, 1867, it was but natural that the Danish chargé, Bille, should address a note to Fish on September 25, 1869, and inquire if the Secretary of State was ready to sign an additional article extending the time for the exchange of ratifications. Fish, on the same day, replied that he was ready to sign the additional article at any time that Bille should be "in possession of full powers."[79] On October 12, Bille wrote that he had received "full powers" from his Government,[80] so on October 14, the addi-

[78] A copy of General Raasloff's speech was enclosed in Yeaman's dispatch to Seward, May 19, 1869, MS. Dept. of State, *Denmark, Desp.,* vol. 10.

[79] Fish to Bille, September 25, 1869, MS. Dept. of State, *Denmark, Notes to,* vol. 6.

[80] Bille to Fish, October 12, 1869, MS. Dept. of State, *Denmark, Notes from,* vol. 4.

tional article extending for six months the period for the exchange of ratifications, was signed.

It should have been apparent to the Danish Government that the treaty was doomed to defeat, and Raasloff must have been an invincible optimist to continue to hope for its ratification. But not for one moment did he abandon his efforts in its behalf, and once again he appealed to Anson Burlingame to use his good offices with Sumner. As a result of this intercession, Burlingame, on November 1, 1869, wrote to Sumner as follows:

"In Denmark I met our old friend Genl. Raasloff, who made known to me the situation of the Treaty matter now pending.

"The General, naturally, feels deeply upon the subject, as do all the officials in Denmark. If the Treaty shall not be approved by the Senate, the General with a portion of his colleagues will resign and state their question to the civilized world. Their case as stated by themselves, is strong.

"That the islands are valuable, that they (the Danes) have made commitments with their inhabitants of a humiliating character if the Treaty shall be rejected— that our action under the circumstances would be for ratification or violence—that we would not reject if Denmark were strong.

"I do not presume to advise, but write to you, as I said to the Danes, that if there is doubt, Mr. Sumner will give the benefit of it to the weaker party."[81]

But all these efforts, direct and indirect, were fruitless, for on March 22, 1870, the Senate Committee on Foreign Relations reported the treaty of October 24,

[81] Burlingame to Sumner, November 1, 1869, *Sumner Papers.*

with the recommendation "that the Senate do not advise and consent to the ratification of the same."[82]

It was evident to the Danish Government that the
report of the Senate Foreign Relations Committee was
equivalent to a rejection of the treaty, so on April 17,
1870, General Raasloff tendered his resignation as Secretary of War.[83] On May 5, the General, in a speech
in the Folkething, the lower house of the Danish Rigs-

---

[82] *Sen. Doc.* 231, 56 Cong., 2 sess., pp. 224-25. With reference to the effect of the adverse report of the Senate Foreign
Relations Committee upon the Danish Government, the following despatch of March 24, 1870, from Sir Charles Wyke to Lord
Clarendon, is illustrative: "A telegram was received yesterday evening from the Danish Minister Resident at Washington reporting that the Committee in the Senate for examining
into all questions connected with Foreign Affairs had reported
against the Ratification of the Treaty with Denmark for the
purchase of the Island of St. Thomas in the West Indies.
This is a terrible blow to the Danish Government, which in
their estimates for the Naval and Military defence of the
Country had counted upon the receipt of five millions and a
half of dollars payable in gold that they were to have received
for the Island. Added to this, they consider themselves hardly
used in having been urged at the time by Mr. Seward to part
with this possession of the Danish Crown, which is now again
thrown upon their hands after taking measures to induce the
population there to pronounce in favor of their transfer to
the United States." MS. F. O. 22/365, no. 18.

The minutes of the Senate Committee on Foreign Relations
as given to E. L. Pierce by Senator John Sherman, read as
follows: "1869. Laid on Table, March 30, the understanding
being that this was equivalent to rejection and was a gentler
method of effecting it. January 25—February 1, 1870—considered. March 22, 1870, reported adversely."

[83] Yeaman to Fish, April 19, 1870, MS. Dept of State, *Denmark, Desp.,* vol. 10.

dag, explained the reasons for his resignation. He was aware of the fact that he had done his utmost to persuade the Danish Government

"into the making of this convention, and . . . of having invariably offered to guarantee, that the United States would, as conscientiously as we ourselves, fulfill every obligation. . . . I will not undertake to justify my course of action, or that of the Government, in regard to the negotiation for the cession of the Danish West India Islands, . . . but what I feel at this moment is, that the issue of this unfortunate affair has—at least for the present—deprived me of the courage and confidence in myself without which I could not, and ought not, to continue to fill the responsible offices hitherto entrusted to me."[84]

On May 19, 1870, the Danish Cabinet, as a whole, tendered their resignations to the King, and although the immediate occasion for this collective resignation was the defeat in the Folkething of a bill to reorganize the army, it was generally understood that the failure of the St. Thomas negotiations was the real cause of this action.[85]

In Europe the failure of the Senate to consent to the ratification of the treaty of October 24, caused widespread comment. In some quarters it was interpreted as an indication of American ill-faith in the conduct of foreign relations. In this regard the following comments of Jules Hansen, the well known Danish publicist, are pertinent:

[84] Yeaman to Fish, May 14, 1870, *ibid.*, enclosing copy of General Raasloff's speech of May 5,

[85] Yeaman to Fish, May 20, 1870, MS. Dept of State, *Denmark, Desp.*, vol. 10.

"Le Sénat américain, par son étrange attitude en cette circonstance, a fait litière des égards qui sont dus même de la part de la plus grande puissance au plus petit État; d'autant plus que c'était l'Amérique qui avait pris la première initiative et engagé le Danemark a entamer les négociations. On ne sait ce que l'on doit le plus blâmer: ou de l'absence de tout sentiment du devoir au sein du comité du Sénat; ou de la légéreté et du sans-gêne du ministre Seward, qui devait être bien au courant de la situation et savoir au moment où il concluait la convention, que selon toute probabilité il ne pourrait pas en obtenir la ratification; ou enfin du cynisme du président Grant et de l'indifference de son secretaire, M. Fish, a l'egard d'un engagement international pris par le gouvernement des États-Unis. Car, si le président Johnson, dans le dernière année de son administration, se trouvait impuissant vis-à-vis du Congres, le gouvernement du général Grant était au contraire très-fort, et rien ne lui eût été plus facile que d'amener le Sénat à remplir son devoir constitutionnel, en donnant ou en refusant sa sanction au traité. Il importe d'instruire le public des véritables particularités de cette affaire, et de bien faire ressortir ce qu'il y a eu d'injuste et d'inexcusable dans la conduite des États-Unis a l'égard du Danemark."[86]

But it was not only in Europe that the Senate's dubious action aroused criticism. In the United States there were others beside Parton, Andrews, and Walker who expressed the opinion that Denmark had not been justly treated. In the *North American Review* for July, 1870, Henry Adams assailed with trenchant pen

[86] *Les Coulisses de la Diplomatie,* p. 168. These comments of Hansen are of particular interest because of his intimate familiarity with the condition of affairs in Denmark. They appeared in 1880, just one decade after the rejection of the treaty.

the foreign policy of the Grant administration, which abandoned the St. Thomas treaty only to negotiate with the Dominican Republic for the annexation of that Republic to the United States. Such conduct was indefensible:

"From the first moment of the new administration the policy of active interference in the Antilles was forced upon its attention in a manner which left no chance of escape. The St. Thomas treaty, under which a popular vote had already been taken and the island formally transferred to an authorized agent of the United States government, had been for some six months reposing on the table of the Senate Committee of Foreign Relations. If the government meant to pursue a policy of annexation in the Antilles, it was peculiarly bound, by every obligation of international decency and of common self-respect, to begin with the ratification of this treaty. Indeed, there may be a grave doubt whether the obligation to ratify was not absolute and irrespective of conditions, but in any case the refusal to ratify this treaty was only to be excused on the understánding that it implied a reversal of the policy of annexation. . . . The refusal to ratify the St. Thomas treaty was a strong measure which gravely compromised the dignity of the government and found its only excuse in the firm conviction that any annexation to the southward of the continent was a danger and a mistake."[87]

The article, however, that evoked the largest response in the United States was one by Olive Risley Seward, an adopted daughter of the famous Secretary of State.

[87] Pp. 55-56. Woodrow Wilson, in his *Congressional Government* (N. Y. 1885), pp. 50-51, has a sharp criticism of the action of the Senate for refusing to ratify the St. Thomas treaty.

This article appeared in *Scribner's Magazine* for November, 1887, and was entitled "A Diplomatic Episode."

In the course of her article Miss Seward criticizes Sumner very severely for his attitude with reference to the Danish treaty. She seems to regard Sumner's gift to Raasloff of the portrait of Thorwaldsen as one calculated completely to deceive the ingenuous Danish Minister of War. Her account of this episode is eminently readable:

"Mr. Sumner still preserved his silence, but General de Raasloff, feeling unusually sure that he could not on any known grounds refuse to report favorably on the treaty, was confirmed in this opinion by an incident which seemed to him significant, and which occurred the day before he left Washington. In Mr. Sumner's art collection there was one picture which he valued very highly, a striking and beautiful portrait of the Danish sculptor, Thorwaldsen, painted from life by the American artist, Rembrandt Peale. It hung in Mr. Sumner's dining-room, and was often the subject of conversation at those dinners so famous in Washington political social history. General de Raasloff rather envied his friend the possession of this rare picture, which he thought should belong to the Thorwaldsen collection in Copenhagen. Mr. Sumner had playfully said to him in the summer of 1866, 'When the St. Thomas treaty is concluded and we have annexed the Danish Antilles, you shall have the Peale portrait.' General de Raasloff being often at Mr. Sumner's table during his sojourn in Washington in 1868 and 1869, reminded his host of this joking promise, and Mr. Sumner always replied that he adhered to it. Early one morning, General de Raasloff saw Mr. Sumner trudging up the street with a large package under his arm, and hastened to open his door. 'There is your picture, Raasloff, and God bless you,' said Mr.

Sumner; then wrung the general's hand and turned away. It was the Thorwaldsen portrait. Interpreting this and other incidents in their favorable sense, General de Raasloff went away, satisfied on the whole with the results of his mission."[88]

Despite its readable qualities, Miss Seward's article is obviously faulty in its interpretations. Raasloff had early informed the Danish Commissioner, Carstensen, of his inability to make Sumner an advocate of the treaty of October 24, and on the evening of January 11, 1869, Sumner told Raasloff frankly that there was little probability that a meeting with the members of the Senate Foreign Relations Committee would accomplish anything. At that time he had also expressed himself to Raasloff as follows: "I am sorry for you; you are in a tight place."[89]

In a note from General Raasloff to Sumner on January 12, and in another communication of a few days later, the Danish Minister of War confessed that he "was fully prepared for the worst."[90] If he interpreted Sumner's gift in March as a token that the Chairman of the Senate Foreign Relations Committee had finally swung round in favor of the treaty, it must then be patent that the former Danish Minister to the United States lacked downright common sense.

On May 13, 1869, Raasloff made the speech in Copenhagen in which he gave high praise to Sumner,

[88] Pp. 599-600.

[89] E. L. Pierce, *Memoir and Letters of Charles Sumner*, vol. 4, p. 620.

[90] *ibid.*, p. 620.

and in a private letter to Sumner of May 16, he re-hearses the nice things he had said about his American friend. In conclusion he remarks as follows:

"I did not say as the telegraph (I am told) has it that you were in favor of ratifying the St. Thomas treaty, but I said that you had done more than anybody else to save the treaty from an untimely death."[91]

If we take these expressions of ardent friendship at *par value* it seems apparent that Raasloff had a genuine regard for Sumner, and did not blame him for the failure of the treaty. But if we place any credence in the remarks of the Marquis de Chambrun in a letter to the biographer of Sumner, E. L. Pierce, January 20, 1888, it would be necessary to revise our opinions as to the quality of the friendship that Raasloff felt for Sumner. Chambrun had helped Miss Seward pre-pare her article in *Scribner's Magazine,* and he in-formed Pierce that Raasloff had written many letters highly critical of Sumner. These letters Chambrun had not shown to Miss Seward lest the young lady be more critical of Sumner than she had been.

It was quite a surprise to Pierce to know that Raas-loff had written to Chambrun a series of letters in-veighing against Sumner, so he expressed his surprise that Raasloff could do so after having paid Sumner such extravagant compliments in his speech in Copen-hagen on May 13, 1869. This apparent inconsistency is explained by Chambrun as follows:

[91] *Sumner Papers.*

"As for the speech of Raasloff you refer to, I know why he made it; it was for the only purpose of placing Mr. Sumner in the position where he should be obliged to act. Therefore you cannot rely on that speech, which was preceded by bitter expressions of disappointment, and followed by renewed expressions of the same sort."

Chambrun then proceeds to justify Miss Seward's criticisms of Sumner in the article that appeared in *Scribner's Magazine,* in November, 1887. It was not Chambrun's intention

"to deny Mr. Sumner's right to oppose the Danish islands purchase; even to change his mind about it; nobody undertakes to question why he changed it, but I have told Mr. Sumner repeatedly that he was mistaken in the practical course he adopted. I wanted to be perfectly clear on this point, because in a controversy of this kind, . . . Miss Seward is fully prepared, and I am still in a position to produce Raasloff's letters—inasmuch as I was his counsel in that sad affair, I happen to know more than almost everybody else about that side of the case. I will state to you also that Count Frijs who was then Prime Minister of Denmark and one of the warmest friends of Raasloff, has written lately to Miss Seward a letter where he wholly sustains her positions."[92]

In his reply to Chambrun, January 23, 1888, Pierce does not mince words. He greatly regrets to learn what Chambrun says of Raasloff, for Pierce had supposed that he was an honest man, but

"if he spoke at Copenhagen and wrote to Sumner in one way and wrote to you in another, he was not an

[92] Chambrun to Pierce, January 20, 1888, MS. *Pierce Papers,* Harvard College Library.

honest man. A diplomatist may be astute and skillful, but he is bound like all of us to the common rules of truth, with no right to say one thing to one and the opposite to another."

His opinion of Miss Seward is equally critical. Her practice of

"making a quotation from his speech and stopping where the next sentence was a complimentary tribute to Sumner . . . is sheer trickery. It may be womanly in here eye, but certainly it is not manly in mine. A right minded person would have made her issue when Sumner was alive and could speak for himself, and not waited till he had been more than thirteen years in his grave. If I had not the courage to meet a man in his life time, I would spare his memory when dead."[93]

But notwithstanding the fact that Miss Seward's article was written with an evident animus against Sumner and therefore not to be wholly relied upon, yet it did in an indirect way render a distinct service to students of American diplomacy. Mr. E. L. Pierce, the biographer of Sumner, was so incensed at Miss Seward's interpretation of the events connected with the St. Thomas treaty that he wrote to the members of the Senate Foreign Relations Committee who served with Sumner, and inquired as to the real reasons for the rejection of that convention. Their replies to him

[93] *Pierce Papers*. A careful reading of Raasloff's letter to Baron Rosenorn-Lehn, September 29, 1880, MS. D. F. O., might well incline one to believe that Raasloff did feel aggrieved towards Sumner for his opposition to the St. Thomas treaty, and that he *did* write to Chambrun certain letters which were sharply critical of the Massachusetts Senator.

constitute a very full explanation of the adverse report of the Senate committee. In a letter to Pierce, November 19, 1887, Carl Schurz wrote as follows:

"I became a member of the Senate on the day of Grant's first inauguration, but I was not a member of the Foreign Relations Committee during the first session of Congress following. Neither was at that time my intercourse with Sumner as confidential as it subsequently became. There was, as far as I can remember, but little talk about the St. Thomas affair. There may have been some prejudice against the treaty as a work of the Johnson administration. But the main difficulty it had to meet was undoubtedly an instinctive reluctance among Northern Senators to acquire territory in the tropics, the possession of which would be a constant incitement for further acquisition in that region, and finally develop a policy highly dangerous to free institutions of government—in short the same instinct which at a later period defeated the annexation of Santo Domingo."[94]

On November 23, 1887, Senator J. W. Patterson wrote at length to Pierce. He had read Miss Seward's article with a

"good deal of interest and more surprise. Her information relative to diplomatic matters during Mr. Seward's administration of the State Department, seems to be quite complete from the Sec's. standpoint, but very defective from the standpoint of the Senate and the public. . . . The Senate generally, I believe, regarded the treaty for the purchase of St. John and St. Thomas about as Gen. Grant did—one of Seward's schemes, and determined to have nothing to do with it. Some denied the constitutionality and most rejected the policy of entering upon a system of annexing non-

[94] *Pierce Papers.*

contiguous territory and outlying islands to the United States. The vote of the islands on the question of annexation could have been carried either way, and though perhaps a politic provision looking to the interests of the home government, was regarded by Senators as a mere farce, that should have little or no weight in determining their action. . . . There might have been some advantages in having a coaling station in the West Indies in time of peace, but to put it in a condition of defense and to maintain that condition in time of war, to say nothing of the seven and a half millions of purchase money, would have been an addition to the national debt which no possible advantages from its acquisition could have justified. In time of war it would have been a constant temptation to an enemy.

"To defend such an outlying dependency would have demanded a great increase of the military and naval force of the country, or would have left our entire Atlantic coast in a defenseless condition by drawing away the naval force for the protection of the islands. Besides, lying as they do in the track of European commerce, we should have been pretty likely, at no distant day, to have become involved in the complications and dangers of European politics.

". . . But as if to make the rejection of the treaty certain, a hurricane swept over the islands and an earthquake nearly shook them to pieces. A refluent wave, caused by this convulsion, lifted up the vessels lying in the harbor and among the rest, one or two U. S. ships, and carried them inland. . . . Immediately every one began to make fun of the treaty, as one for the annexation of hurricanes and earthquakes, and the subject was fairly 'laughed out of the Court.'

"The reason why the Senate did not act promptly on the treaty, but allowed it to die on its hands, was a desire, if possible, to save the liberal ministry of Denmark which had been drawn into this measure, against the natural effects of its rejection."[95]

[95] *Pierce Papers.*

Simon Cameron had also read Miss Seward's article, but he was not in agreement with her interpretation. The rejection of the treaty of October 24, was after all

"quite a simple matter—there was no mystery about it. No person on the Foreign Affairs Committee was in favor of the treaty. The case of Alaska was very different. One of the chief motives was to show our regard for Russia for the part she had taken during the war, and to strengthen the North Western possessions. The St. Thomas purchase made no impression upon the Committee or upon the public either."[96]

Justin Morrill was even more laconic. He believed that in 1869-70, there was a

"general reluctance about establishing colonies, and the inopportune earthquake was disastrous to the treaty. I think now the Senate made a mistake but that was not my opinion 20 years ago."[97]

The last reply to Pierce's inquiries was that of James Harlan, of Iowa. Pierce had asked specific questions, and Harlan answers them *ad seriatim:*

"First. Why the Committee were against the ratification?
Because they did not think the property offered for sale worth the price asked for it. The land was chiefly owned and occupied by private holders, whose rights would of course have to be protected. There were no public buildings, fortifications or other public property worth cataloguing. Hence as a mere commercial transaction the proposed purchase at the price named would have been great folly. Its future government and protection would also have involved large annual expenditures without the prospect of any pecuniary returns.

[96] Cameron to Pierce, December 9, 1887, *Pierce Papers.*
[97] Morrill to Pierce, December 23, 1887, *Pierce Papers.*

And after careful examination the committee arrived at the conclusion that as a naval depot and coaling station its possession would be of doubtful value to the United States. Hence the transfer of this island by Denmark to the United States would have carried to us little except the naked sovereignty. In the opinion of the Committee this had no pecuniary value. And as it did not appear to them to be especially desirable as a military station, they decided, unanimously, I think, not to recommend the ratification of the treaty.

"You inquire,

"Second, why there was delay in acting on it?

According to my recollection there was no unusual delay; and there did not appear to be any public necessity for unusual haste. The extension of time first fixed by the two contracting parties to a treaty for the exchange of ratifications, has been frequently (as in this case), extended. In such matters the consumption of ample time in deliberation is not regarded as a discourtesy. In this case, the committee were not, I think, dilatory. Ample but only necessary time was taken to make the necessary investigations and inquiries, and for the interchange of views. And when they decided not to recommend the ratification it was thought that it would seem less harsh towards the other power to permit the time for exchanging ratifications to expire than to formally reject the proposed cession.

"You ask,

"Thirdly, Whether Mr. Sumner (the Chairman of the Committee) did not act fairly?

No one who ever knew Mr. Sumner could have any doubt on that point. He was the soul of candor and frankness. But if he had been disposed to act otherwise, in the case referred to, he could not have trifled with the Senate Committee on Foreign Affairs as then constituted."[98]

[98] James Harlan to Pierce, January 14, 1888, *Pierce Papers.* In 1889, Mr. E. L. Pierce published a small pamphlet entitled "A Diplomatic Fiasco" in which he reviews the whole story of the Danish treaty.

These frank letters from the members of the Foreign Relations Committee make it abundantly clear that
the treaty of October 24 was regarded by them as a
scheme of Secretary Seward's which merited scant
consideration. The many arguments that had been
raised in official circles against the purchase of the
islands are clearly indicated in the above correspondence, and they are faithfully reproduced in a long letter from General Raasloff to Baron Rosenorn-Lehn,
September 29, 1880. The gist of Raasloff's letter is
given in the following chapter of this book,[99] but it is
worth while here to point out that the Danish envoy
realized that hostility to the Danish treaty was not confined to the American Senate. Neither President Grant
nor Secretary Fish was favorably inclined towards
the acquisition of the Danish islands. They preferred
to negotiate for the annexation of the Dominican Republic to the United States, and the resulting breach
of faith with Denmark aroused the indignation of
Henry Adams who voiced his sentiments in an article
in the *North American Review* from which we have
already quoted. Strange to say, Woodrow Wilson mis-
read this article and assumed that Adams threw the
whole responsibility for the failure of the Danish treaty
upon the Senate. Wilson then subscribed to this false
interpretation of the Adams article and in his epoch-
making *Congressional Government* he discourses
learnedly upon the *treaty-marring* powers of the Senate.[100]   In later years, another prominent publicist,

[99] See *post.*, pp. 355-57.
[100] Pp. 50-51.

Professor Willis Fletcher Johnson, adopted the same viewpoint, and absolves the Grant administration from any responsibility in this matter of the rejection of the Danish treaty. It is his belief that the chief reason for the defeat of the treaty

"was factional and personal spite. Sumner was then chairman of the Foreign Relations Committee of the Senate, which had the treaty in hand, and he and the other Republican leaders who controlled the Senate were bitterly hostile to President Johnson, whom, at that time, they were aiming to impeach and remove from office. They were almost equally bitter against Seward, because he had remained at the head of Johnson's cabinet. . . . It did not matter that the proposal had originated with Lincoln. It did not matter that it promised to be of incalculable advantage to the United States. To Senators blind with passionate hate it was enough that it was Johnson's and Seward's treaty; away with it!"[101]

In the last pages of this chapter I have indicated how both Grant and Fish were opposed to the Danish treaty, and in that regard were in harmony with the Senate. I have also rehearsed the many arguments that had been raised against it. Sumner was too large a personality and too great a statesman to be controlled in this matter by mere partisan spite, and yet the tradition still persists that the Danish treaty was rejected because of some personal quarrel between the Massachusetts Senator and the President of the United States. This tradition, however, has variant forms, and in January,

[101] *North American Review,* July-December, 1916, pp. 381-90.

1902, the New York *Times* published a version which ascribed the defeat of the treaty to a quarrel between Sumner and President Grant. This new interpretation aroused the ire of a distinguished Massachusetts lawyer who, during the troublous years from 1867-1870, had served as Sumner's private secretary. In the following letter to the *Times,* Mr. Moorfield Storey pays his respects to this latest version of the Sumner legend:

"To the Editor of the New York *Times:*
"My attention has been called to a passage in the article entitled 'The Danish Islands,' published in your issue of January 25, in which you say, speaking of the treaty negotiated by Mr. Seward for the purchase of the Danish Islands: 'It fell through simply because Charles Sumner, then Chairman of the Foreign Committee of the Senate, happened to be engaged in a personal quarrel with the President, whom the treaty offered him an opportunity of annoying. Accordingly he pigeon-holed the treaty for months, the Government had to ask Denmark to prolong the time set for ratification, and, when, the treaty was finally brought up in the Senate, it was rejected.'

"I was Mr. Sumner's secretary at the time and familiar with the facts, and the statement in your article is entirely inaccurate. This treaty was submitted to the Senate in December, 1867, and was never popular. The House of Representatives on the 25th of November, 1867, passed a resolution by more than two-thirds vote protesting against any further purchase of territory, and the Committee on Foreign Relations of the Senate was opposed to it from the beginning. President Grant, when he came into office, expressed his disapproval of it, and the Senate Committee, after giving the Danish Ambassador every opportunity of presenting its merits, laid the treaty on the table, March 30, 1869, only a few weeks after General Grant came into office, before any difference had occurred between General Grant and Mr. Sumner.

"The records of the Committee made when the treaty was laid on the table contain this minute: 'The understanding being that this was equivalent to a rejection and was a gentler method of effecting it.' A simple comparison of dates will show that the dispute between General Grant and Mr. Sumner had nothing whatever to do with the action of the Senate Committee on the Danish treaty.

Moorfield Storey."[102]

The real reason for the rejection of the Danish treaty was the evident disinclination of the American public to follow Seward in his schemes for colonial dominion.[103] There was still a vast American hinterland that called for development, and American capital and American energy could best be employed in domestic undertakings. Moreover, the American navy was soon allowed to dwindle to insignificant proportions and its demands for naval stations were given little heed. The imperialism which became the accepted state policy of Great Britain and France during the seventies and eighties seemed sharply opposed to American traditions, and it was not until the turn of the century that the call of the Caribbean grew so insistent that it could not be denied.

[102] New York Times, February 5, 1902.

[103] American opposition to the purchase of the Danish islands inspired Bret Harte to write one of his worst poems, *St. Thomas,* which was written in 1868. See *Poetical Works of Bret Harte* (N. Y. 1902), pp. 43-44. The following lines indicate its character:

"Very fair and full of promise
Lay the island of St. Thomas:
Ocean o'er its reefs and bars
Hid its elemental scars;

*   *   *   *   *   *

Then said William Henry Seward
As he cast his eye to leeward,
'Quite important to our commerce
Is this island of St. Thomas.'

Said the Mountain ranges, 'Thank'ee
But we cannot stand the Yankee

*   *   *   *   *   *

Said the Sea, its white teeth gnashing
Through its coral-reef lips flashing

*   *   *   *   *   *

Said the black-browed Hurricane
Brooding down the Spanish Main,
'Shall I see my forces, zounds!
Measured by square inch and pounds.'

*   *   *   *   *   *

So the Mountains shook and thundered,
And the Hurricane came sweeping,

*   *   *   *   *   *

Till one morn, when Mr. Seward
Cast his weather eye to leeward,
There was not an inch of dry land
Left to make his recent island."

[104] As a typical expression of the feeling in Denmark relative to the action of the Grant administration and of the American Senate with reference to the treaty of October 24, 1867, the following excerpt from the Copenhagen *Dagbladet*, April 24, 1869 is of interest. "Notwithstanding all that has

happened and all that has been neglected, we maintain the firm belief that the treaty will be ultimately acknowledged by the Americans. Denmark has not hitherto been treated by the United States with that consideration which it is proper for friendly powers to show toward one another in their international intercourse, and which, least of all, should be disregarded by a great country in its relations with a smaller one. But, if the agreement should now be pushed aside, it would be an insult to us so great, that we refuse to believe in its possibility as long as there is a shadow of hope left. . . . It is not our province to discuss international law with the American people, or to instruct the United States Senate about its constitutional duties. But we have a right to tell them how the Danish people regard this manner of proceeding, in a case which is of vital importance to our native land. And the impression we have received is this—that the Americans are about to forget two important principles: First, that in foreign relations there can be no such thing as parties or internal controversies, but that every government whatever its domestic relations may be, in its actions represents and binds the country. Secondly, that this obligation to preserve the continuity during all changes of government, and to acknowledge the unity of its different branches in relations with foreign powers, becomes greater in proportion as the degree of freedom upon which the country is established, increases. . . If there have ever been international relations in which a party could be said to be 'bound by honor,' that is really the case with the United States in its relations to Denmark, regarding the West India islands."

CHAPTER III

WATCHFUL WAITING IN THE CARIBBEAN

Although President Grant had bluntly informed General Raasloff that he regarded the treaty with Denmark as "entirely Seward's plan," with which he wished "absolutely nothing to do," yet during the course of his two administrations he and Secretary Fish were ever fearful that some other power might try to secure the Danish West Indies for a naval base. Of course, such an attitude was a perfect example of a "dog-in-the-manger" policy, but the American Government could always save its face by invoking the Monroe Doctrine with its prohibitions of any increase of European influence in the American hemisphere.

The first scare with reference to European expansion came in the summer of 1871. On August 22, 1871 Fisher Ames, the American consul at Santo Domingo City, wrote an alarming despatch to the American Secretary of State. He had learned from

"a reliable source that the Prussian Government have made propositions to this Government for acquiring the Bay and Peninsula of Samana, and for eventual annexation of the whole Republic."[1]

No sooner had Hamilton Fish received this despatch than he at once cabled to George Bancroft, the American Minister at Berlin, to "ascertain if there be an

[1] Fisher Ames to Fish, August 22, 1871, MS. Dept. of State, *Santo Domingo, Consular Letters,* vol. 7.

foundation for these rumors."[2] When Bancroft received this peremptory instruction he immediately repaired to the German Foreign Office, and on that same day he cabled back to Fish as follows:

"Rumor untrue, utterly denied."[3]

In his official despatch of September 25, Bancroft went into further details relative to the attitude of the German Government with reference to the islands in the Caribbean. Not only was there no intention on the part of that government to make "acquisitions in America," but furthermore, German statesmen were "from principle opposed to any such idea."[4]

In this regard Bancroft was undoubtedly making a correct report of Bismarck's policy at that time. There were numerous internal questions that demanded solution before Germany could embark upon a program of overseas expansion, so it was many years later that the great chancellor adopted imperialism as a part of his political creed.[5]

[2] Fish to Bancroft, September 22, 1871, MS. Dept. of State, *Prussia, Inst.,* vol. 15.

[3] Bancroft to Fish, September 23, 1871, MS. Dept. of State, *Germany, Desp.,* vol. 1.

[4] Bancroft to Fish, September 25, 1871, MS. Dept. of State, *Germany, Desp.,* vol. 1.

[5] In this connection the following statement in Dr. Mary E. Townsend's monograph, *Origins of Modern German Colonialism,* 1871-1885, p. 55, is quite pertinent: "During the years 1870 to 1875, the Government extended and increased the consular service and practiced 'diplomatic guardianship' everywhere; but it emphatically refused and discouraged each explicit demand for the establishment of a protectorate or naval base or for the acquisition of territory." (N. Y. 1921.)

Secretary Fish, however, was not easily convinced by Bancroft's disquisition on German policy, for on November 25, 1871, he wrote to advise the American Minister of certain rumors to the effect that Germany was endeavouring to purchase the island of Curaçoa. Bancroft was instructed to make "cautious" inquiries, and report at once to the Department of State.[6]

The American Minister lost no time in seeking an interview with the German "Minister who has most to do with foreign commercial affairs," and on January 5, 1872, he reported to Secretary Fish the following assurances of that German official:

"I am wholly opposed to the entanglement of Germany in schemes of colonization. As long as you see me holding a place in the ministry, engaged in public affairs, you may be certain that no such scheme is on foot. If I could realize my utmost wishes I should wish only coaling stations, and perhaps here and there a factory for the residence of an agent."[7]

We fully realize nowadays that these assurances were entirely sincere, and that Secretary Fish would have saved himself many worries had he accepted them at face value, but the fate of the Danish West Indies seemed tied up with one of the thorniest problems that had ever vexed European chancelleries—the so-called Schleswig-Holstein Question. Palmerston, in his usual

[6] Fish to Bancroft, November 25, 1871, MS. Dept. of State, *Prussia, Inst.,* vol. 15.

[7] Bancroft to Fish, January 5, 1872, MS. Dept. of State, *Germany, Desp.,* vol. 1.

jaunty style, once observed that there were only three persons in all Europe who had been completely familiar with the details of this question—the British Prince Consort who was dead, a German professor who was in a lunatic asylum, and himself, who had forgotten all about it.[8] But if Palmerston's only contribution to the settlement of this age-old problem was a mere witticism, there was another statesman in Europe who had worked out a solution which he believed would prove quite lasting. Bismarck was ready in the autumn of 1863 to apply the test of force, and by a treaty of January 16, 1864, he bound the Austrian Government to active co-operation in a program of joint control over the two Duchies of Schleswig and Holstein. As anticipated, such a program was not acceptable to the Danish Government, and in the war that followed both the Duchies were wrested from Denmark. In the division of the spoils, Austria was to extend her administration over Holstein, while Prussia was to administer Schleswig. It was apparent to Bismarck that such an arrangement could only be temporary. In 1866, difficulties with Austria led to the Six Weeks' War from which Prussia emerged as the leading German state. Under the terms of the Treaty of Prague, August 23, 1866, the Emperor of Austria renounced all his rights in the Duchies, but this did not leave to Prussia an undisputable title to every portion of them because of the following reservation in Article V:

[8] C. Grant Robinson, *Bismarck* (London, 1918), p. 156.

"The inhabitants of North Sleswick shall be again reunited with Denmark if they should express such a desire in a vote freely given."[9]

It was soon apparent, however, that this stipulated plebiscite would never be held, so the Danish Government then began to cherish a faint hope that an exchange might be arranged whereby the Danish West Indies could be traded to the new German Empire for North Schleswig. And despite the fact that Bismarck did not favor such an exchange, yet the rumors of such an arrangement were very numerous throughout the next few decades.[10]

As early as the spring of 1873, rumors began to circulate that the Danish Government was willing to cede the island of St. Thomas to Germany in exchange for North Schleswig. On April 22, 1873, the American

[9] *British and Foreign State Papers,* vol. 56, p. 1050.

[10] With reference to the Schleswig-Holstein question see F. de Jessen, ed., *Manuel Historique de la Question du Slesvig* (Copenhagen, 1906) ; Aage Friis, *Det Nordslesvigske Sporgsmaal,* 1864-1879 (Copenhagen, 1921, 1925) ; Aage Friis, *Den Danske Regering og Nordslesvigs Genforening med Danmark* (Copenhagen, 1921) ; Jules Hansen, *Les Coulisses de la Diplomatie* (Paris, 1880) ; M. Mackeprang, *Nordslesvig* (Copenhagen, 1910). For the German viewpoint, see E. Daenell, *Historische Zeitschrift,* vol. 115, pp. 162 ff ; and Karl Jansen and Karl Samwer, *Schleswig-Holstein Befreiung* (Wiesbaden, 1897). For Bismarck's policy with reference to Schleswig-Holstein, see *Bismarck und die Nordschleswigsche Frage,* 1864-1879 (Berlin, 1925), ed. by W. Platzhoff, K. Rheindorf, and J. Tiedje. With reference to Prussian administration in North Schleswig, see the interesting article by Professor L. M. Larson, "Prussianism in North Sleswick," *American Historical Review,* January, 1919, pp. 227-252.

consul at St. Thomas wrote to Secretary Fish to inform him of conditions in the island, and during the course of his despatch he observed that there was a rumor in the island that "Denmark is seeking to barter St. Thomas for that portion of Schleswig taken by Prussia in 1864, and which is said to come from high Danish authority in St. Croix."[11]

This rumor evidently worried Secretary Fish, for, on June 25, 1873, he had a conversation with Mr. Cramer, who was returning to Copenhagen, in which he requested him to ascertain whether there was any truth in this report. This instruction was duly carried out by Mr. Cramer as soon as he reached Denmark. After making "careful inquiries" he discovered that none of his "trustworthy Danish informants seem to place any credence in it." Indeed, they firmly believed that the Danish Government

"would entertain no proposition looking toward such a settlement of the 'North Slesvig Question,' for they look upon the ultimate possession of North Slesvig as their absolute right."

Cramer had also discussed the matter with the German Minister at Copenhagen, who had informed him

"that there was no truth in the said rumor; at least he knew absolutely nothing as to whether such a proposition had ever been made by the one or the other of the two Governments."[12]

[11] Thomas J. Brady to Fish, April 22, 1873, MS. Dept. of State, *West Indies, Consular Letters*, vol. 10.

[12] Cramer to Fish, July 28, 1873, MS. Dept. of State, *Denmark, Desp.*, vol. 12.

On August 7, 1873, Cramer had an interview with the Danish Minister for Foreign Affairs during which he frankly asked the Minister whether there was any truth in the rumors relative to St. Thomas and North Schleswig. The Minister

"faintly smiled and said that that was an old rumor, and then expressed his regrets that Prussia had not ere this settled that question in accordance with the provisions of Article V. of the Treaty of Prague. . . . I simply observed that it was desirable that the North Slesvig Question should be settled in a manner perfectly satisfactory to both parties, and then put the question again to him: 'There is then no truth in the aforementioned rumor?' He faintly shook his head, and in about a minute answered by simply re-expressing the wish on the part of Denmark for a settlement of the vexed question in accordance with the provisions of the Treaty referred to."[13]

Some weeks after Cramer sent this despatch to Secretary Fish, George Bancroft, the American Minister at Berlin, wrote to the Secretary of State to assure him that the rumors in connection with St. Thomas were "totally devoid of foundation." The German Government had "not the least wish to own colonies," but "on the contrary," her policy was decidedly against such acquisitions.[14]

These assurances, however, did not dissipate the fears of Secretary Fish, who appeared to believe that

[13] Cramer to Fish, August 8, 1873, MS. Dept. of State, *Denmark, Desp.*, vol. 12.
[14] Bancroft to Fish, September 15, 1873, MS. Dept. of State, *Germany, Desp.*, vol. 4.

Bancroft's warm German sympathies and personal friendship with Bismarck might affect his judgment. These fears were further aroused when the foreign press began to allude quite frequently to the possibility of an arrangement between Denmark and Germany. In this regard the following excerpt from the Paris *Journal des Debats,* November 28, 1873, is typical:

"The Schleswig question has assumed a new and wholly unexpected phase. It is written from Copenhagen to the *Dannewirke,* that, according to reports circulated in official circles, Prussia has proposed to Denmark a new method of arrangement. She will be disposed to give up the northern districts of this Duchy, that is to say, all the Danish part, in exchange for the colonies that Denmark possesses in the Antilles. . . . The German papers allege that these colonies are of little interest to Denmark, and they add by way of gratuitous advice, that in the hands of Prussia they would be at any given moment a disagreeable neighbor for the French colonies of Guadeloupe and Martinique. . . . Will Denmark allow herself to be caught by this bait?"

In Europe these rumors were given definite credence, and the French Government began to bestir itself to prevent any such exchange. On January 3, 1874, General Le Flo, the French Ambassador at St. Petersburg, called on Marshall Jewell, the American Minister, and informed him that

"he had an official despatch from his government that negotiations were said to be now going on at Copenhagen looking to the retrocession to Denmark of North Sleswig, including the island of Alsen, and even the fortified line of Duppeln, in accordance with the treaty

of Prague. As a compensation therefore, Germany is
to acquire the Danish islands of St. Thomas and St.
John in the West Indies. He understood the offer to
come from Germany and that the Danish Government
was listening to it not unfavorably."[15]

The French Ambassador further informed the American Minister that the French Government was strongly
opposed to such a transfer, and suggested a joint protest on the part of the two governments.

Mr. Jewell was greatly disturbed at the thought of
such an arrangement. To his mind it was clearly an
infringement on the Monroe Doctrine and should be
strongly opposed. With this idea in mind, on January
3, 1874, he sent the following cablegram to Secretary
Fish:

"French ambassador gives me official report from
Copenhagen that Germany proposes to Denmark to
fulfill the Treaty of Prague and cede North Slesvig in
exchange for West Indian Islands—St. Thomas and
St. John. Danish Government listens to project. French
Government strongly disapproves German establishment in American waters."[16]

Fish promptly took alarm at this news from St.
Petersburg. On January 5, 1874, he hurriedly despatched a cablegram to Mr. Schenck, the American
Minister at the Court of St. James, in which he instructed him to

[15] Marshall Jewell to Secretary Fish, January 3, 1874, MS.
Dept. of State, *Russia, Despatches,* vol. 25.
[16] Jewell to Fish, January 3, 1874, MS. Dept. of State,
Russia, Desp., vol. 25.

"telegraph and send also by mail to our Minister at Berlin and at Copenhagen the following: A report reaches here that Germany is in treaty with Denmark for the acquisition of her West India Islands, proposing to fulfill her existing Treaty, and to cede North Schleswig. Inquire discreetly and ascertain the truth of the report. A transfer of the possession of those islands to another European Power could not be regarded with favor by this Government. You will also communicate the above by mail to Washburne, and you and he will cautiously enquire and will discreetly use the information as to the policy of this Government."[17]

Schenck received Fish's cablegram on January 6, and immediately transmitted copies of this instruction to the American Ministers at Copenhagen, Berlin and at Paris. From Bancroft came the usual assurances:

"As to St. Thomas, Germany does not want it; would not accept it as a gift; has no hankering after that or any other West India colony; from principle avoids them; wishes at most a coaling station in Asiatic seas, and that only in case it can be enjoyed in security without being made a military post. This statement I have had often from every member of the government that could by any possibility have charge of any negotiation made for the acquisition of territory."[18]

[17] Fish to Schenck, January 5, 1874, MS. Dept. of State, *Great Britain, Inst.,* vol. 23.

[18] Bancroft to Fish, January 9, 1874, MS. Dept. of State, *Germany, Desp.,* vol. 4. In a second despatch of January 12, 1874, Bancroft further states that he is "very certain that the idea has never been entertained on either the side of Denmark or of Germany to transfer St. Thomas to the latter power. As to the present, I cannot find the slightest reason to believe that any such negotiation is on foot or even in contemplation."

From Denmark the news was not so reassuring. After receiving Secretary Fish's instruction on January 7, Mr. Cramer had a lengthy conversation with the editor of one of the leading newspapers in Copenhagen. The editor did not place much faith in the rumor regarding the transfer of St. Thomas to Germany, but he did admit

"that nearly a year ago a Prussian official had been here and semi-officially talked about this subject, that is, he was trying to sound the opinion of the Danish Government and people concerning it. I [Cramer] asked him further: 'Since Denmark looks upon the restoration of North-Schleswig to her as her right, would the Danish people consent to such an exchange as is indicated in the report?' He replied in the affirmative."

The tenor of this conversation gave cold comfort to the American Minister who straightway called on the Danish Minister for Foreign Affairs in order to elicit further information concerning the alleged negotiations. The Minister seemed surprised that Mr. Cramer should be so deeply interested in the truth of such a rumor, whereupon the American Minister observed that every intelligent American was interested in such a transfer of sovereignty because it was contrary

"to the so-called Monroe Doctrine, a Doctrine strongly believed in by them. He asked me what my Government thought about it? Not wishing to make an official declaration without further instructions from the Department, I observed that I supposed the Government of the United States, like the people thereof, would not look with favor upon the transfer of the Danish West India Islands to another European Power. He then said: 'I can quiet you on this subject. For the present there is nothing of it. But let our conversation on this subject be confidential.' "

As a result of this conversation with the Minister for Foreign Affairs, Mr. Cramer arrived at the following conclusions:

"That a proposition for the exchange of the Danish West India Islands for North Schleswig had been made in some form or other by the one or the other of the two parties directly concerned in it. That some negotiations had been carried on by the two parties on that subject, but led to no result for the present. That Denmark seems so anxious for the repossession of North Schleswig that she would doubtless be willing to cede her West India Islands for it."[19]

A few days later, January 14, 1874, Cramer sent a despatch that should have relieved some of the anxieties of Secretary Fish. The American Minister had taken a little stroll with the German chargé d'affaires at Copenhagen who had categorically denied that there was any basis for the recent rumors.[20]

From Washburne, at Paris, the news was equally quieting. The American Minister had endeavored

"to ascertain from well informed sources . . . if there was any truth in this report. From the best information I can get, the project, if ever entertained, has been abandoned."[21]

[19] Cramer to Fish, January 9, 1874, MS. Dept. of State, *Denmark, Desp.*, vol. 12.

[20] Cramer to Fish, January 14, 1874, MS. Dept. of State, *Denmark, Desp.*, vol. 12.

[21] Washburne to Fish, January 28, 1874, MS. Dept. of State, *France, Desp., Confidential*, vol. 74.

But there were still some discordant notes, and Secretary Fish was not to be without some apprehensions. On January 2, 1874, the American consul at St. Thomas wrote a despatch that was distinctly of the same tenor as the cablegram and despatch from Marshall Jewell at St. Petersburg on January 3. It appeared that in the island of St. Thomas there was

"a ferment of excitement over the rumor of the negotiations pending for a transfer of the Danish West Indies to Germany in exchange for some portions of Schleswig. . . . The great majority of the people of this Island, and I believe of the islands of St. Croix and St. John, are bitterly opposed to this contemplated transfer, and I have been approached by many since my return to know if my Government would not interfere to prevent it, or herself open negotiations for the purchase of the Islands. I could give them no encouragement, and great disappointment is the result."[22]

It was a difficult situation for Secretary Fish, and so uncertain was he with reference to the actual state of affairs concerning the alleged transfer of St. Thomas for North Schleswig, that he decided on February 11, 1874, again to warn Bancroft to be watchful for any resumption of negotiations between Germany and Denmark.[23]

For some months the bogey of German expansion in the Caribbean was banished from American minds, but in the summer of 1874, new rumors were circulated to

[22] Brady to J. C. Bancroft Davis, Assistant Secretary of State, *West Indies, Consular Letters,* vol. 10.

[23] Fish to Bancroft, February 11, 1874, MS. Dept. of State, *Germany, Inst.,* vol. 15.

the effect that the German Government was trying to secure from Spain the cession of Porto Rico. So persistent were these rumors that Caleb Cushing, the American Minister at Madrid, secured from the Spanish Minister of State, M. Ulloa, a positive denial of such a cession.[24] In Germany the rumor continued to be given space in the press, and finally, J. C. Bancroft Davis, the new American Minister at Berlin, took the matter up with von Buelow, the Principal Secretary for Foreign Affairs. Buelow was quite conciliatory and assured Davis that the rumors respecting Porto Rico were "entirely unfounded." He then spoke

"warmly and strongly of the wish of this government to maintain the most cordial relations with us, and of his own purpose to continue to do everything in his power to accomplish it."[25]

From Demark there came another rumor of German intrigue. According to the American Minister at Copenhagen there were stories afloat that Bismarck had proposed to the King of Denmark to cede to him North Schleswig, provided Denmark would enter the German Federation, place its navy at the disposal of the Emperor, and open its ports, home and colonial, to the German navy on terms of equality. The German Minister at Copenhagen promptly branded this story as a fabrication, but Count Barratow, the Secretary of the

[24] Cushing to Fish, September 16, 1874, MS. Dept. of State, *Spain, Desp.*, vol. 71.

[25] J. C. B. Davis to Fish, October 14, 1874, MS. Dept. of State, *Germany, Desp.*, vol. 5.

Russian Legation in Copenhagen, expressed the opinion that the German Government "had for some time been feeling its way in this matter, but that it had as yet made no *official* proposition to Denmark in relation to it."[26]

The American Minister himself inclined to the view that such an arrangement would never be accepted by Denmark. Besides, the United States and Russia would

"scarcely give their consent . . . for it would, no doubt, be regarded by the former as a virtual violation of the 'Monroe Doctrine,' and by the latter as a surrender to Germany of the key to the Baltic sea."

In the spring of the following year when new rumors made their appearance with reference to the exchange of St. Thomas for North Schleswig, the American Minister at Copenhagen wrote to Secretary Fish and repeated his disbelief in the possibility of such a transfer. To his mind there were two "insuperable difficulties" that would effectually block any scheme of that sort. First of all, there would be a "protest of the United States Government against such an arrangement, and 2d, the unwillingness on the part of the German Government to accept such a proposition, for its diplomatic representative here has repeatedly declared to me that they do not want the Danish possessions in the West Indies."[27]

[26] Cramer to Fish, October 30, 1874, MS. Dept. of State, *Denmark, Desp.,* vol. 12.

[27] Cramer to Fish, March 12, 1875, MS. Dept. of State, *Denmark, Desp.,* vol. 13.

But Secretary Fish refused to have his suspicions dispelled by this line of reasoning.   Perhaps where there was "so much smoke there must be some fire," and it needed only another warning despatch to awaken renewed vigilance. On December 16, 1875, Caleb Cushing advised Secretary Fish that much curiosity was aroused in Madrid by "reports, coming from Paris, of alleged negotiations at Copenhagen by Germany for the purchase of the island of St. Thomas and of opposition thereto by the United States."[28]

Secretary Fish took no chances that these rumors reported by Caleb Cushing might be mere diplomatic gossip.   On January 12, 1876, he wrote to Cramer at Copenhagen, to inform him of the contents of Cushing's despatch, and then instructed him "make inquiry as to the truth of the above report."[29]

Upon the receipt of this instruction there was nothing for Cramer to do but arrange for an interview with the Danish Minister for Foreign Affairs in order to make the required inquiry. The question of the proposed exchange of St. Thomas for North Schleswig had now become a delicate matter for the American Minister to handle. Repeated denials of such an arrangement had failed to satisfy the American Government, and yet any further inquiries might well seem to impeach the veracity of the Danish Foreign Min-

[28] Caleb Cushing to Fish, December, 16, 1875, *Spain, Desp.*, vol. 82. MS. Dept. of State.

[29] Fish to Cramer, January 12, 1876, MS. Dept. of State, *Denmark, Inst.*, vol. 15.

ister. Mr. Cramer, however, was received with the
"usual kindness and courtesy," and after exchanging
a few commonplaces, he directly put the question about
the alleged negotiations for trading St. Thomas for
North Schleswig. The Minister slightly nodded his
head in a negative gesture, and remarked

"that this was an old report, and for aught he knew,
it was probable that the Prussian Government started
it. . . . (He said 'the Prussian Government,' instead of
the German Government) but that there was nothing
in it. These last words he spoke in an undertone. He
evidently did not like to speak on the subject. Nor
did I press the subject any further."[30]

This assurance of the Danish Foreign Minister received confirmation some two weeks later when the
British Minister at Copenhagen informed Cramer that
the British Ambassador at Berlin had been instructed
to inquire into the truth of the St. Thomas-Schleswig-
Holstein rumor, and that the German Foreign Office
had

"positively denied that any negotiations are being carried on between the German and Danish Governments
looking towards the acquisition, in any manner, by Germany of St. Thomas. He further remarked that also
at this capital the truth of the said report is officially
denied."[31]

A few days later, February 19, Cramer wrote a long
despatch to Fish in which he recounted a very inter

[30] Cramer to Fish, January 31, 1876, MS. Dept. of State
Denmark, Desp., vol. 13.
[31] Cramer to Fish, February 14, 1876, MS. Dept. of State
Denmark, Desp, vol. 13.

esting conversation he had had on the previous night with the Crown Prince of Denmark. On the evening of February 18, the Prime Minister gave a diplomatic dinner, at which were present not only the representatives of the foreign governments accredited to the Danish Court, but also the members of the Danish Cabinet and the Danish Crown Prince. After the dinner the guests reassembled in the parlors. The Crown Prince then approached the different diplomats and after conversing with each of them he happened to notice where the American Minister was located. Immediately he crossed the room, and after a few civilities, he

"commenced to speak of his own accord, of the 'North Schleswig-St. Thomas' reports that have gone the rounds of the European press. He said in substance the following: He felt very sorry that the report about the purchase, or exchange, by Germany, of St. Thomas for North Schleswig had again been started. He would tell me how it originated, provided I would promise not to mention his name as the source of my information. I gave him the desired promise with the proviso that I should be permitted to communicate the information confidentially to my Government, knowing, as His Royal Highness may, perhaps, be aware, that it took a great interest in this matter. He then said that the present King of Sweden and Norway, while on a visit to the Emperor of Germany in Berlin, in June last, voluntarily and of his own accord broached to the Emperor the plan of exchanging North Schleswig for the Island of St. Thomas. He (the Swedish King) thought that opportunity a good one for using his good offices in proposing a settlement of the North Schleswig Question in the manner indicated. He thought he was doing both parties a favor. But, continued the Crown Prince, nothing came of that proposition; and there is now no foundation in fact for the report recently started anew in regard to this matter."[32]

It is interesting to note that the truth of this revelation of the Danish Crown Prince to the American Minister is strikingly confirmed in one of the documents contained in the recently published volume entitled, *Bismarck und die Nordschleswigsche Frage*, 1864-1879. In a "promemoria" of the German Foreign Minister, von Buelow, a record is kept of a conversation he had had with Oscar II, the King of Norway and Sweden, on June 1, 1875. After some remarks on the general European situation, the King adverted to the Schleswig-Holstein Question. For Norway and Sweden

"it was not a vital question, and good relations with Germany did not depend upon it. 'Do as you can and wish, I shall always remain your friend. I am merely complying with an obligation of my conscience, when, in referring to this question I mention the possibility of a settlement.' The King then observed that in a sense he was a messenger—that he had openly promised in Copenhagen to straighten out the difficulties. He would repeat to me what he had said to Prince Bismarck in this connection. Should Germany desire a colony or a naval station in America, no other location would be as suitable as the Danish islands of St. Thomas, St. Croix, and St. John. St. Thomas in particular had an excellent harbor which in all the West Indies was the nearest to Europe. He, the King, knew that in Denmark there was a desire to exchange these islands for North-Schleswig. . . . When I [Buelow] remained silent, the King remarked that naturally he

[32] Cramer to Fish, February 19, 1876, MS. Dept. of State, *Denmark, Desp.*, vol. 13.

did not now expect an answer, and that he had received none from the Chancellor."[33]

While the Department of State at Washington was awaiting these assurances from Mr. Cramer, at Copenhagen, it had also instituted inquiries at Berlin in this same connection. On December 15, 1875, Secretary Fish had instructed Nicholas Fish, at Berlin, to make a "careful inquiry" into the truth of a rumor that Germany was negotiating for the purchase of the island of St. Thomas.[34]

In response to this inquiry, von Buelow gave Nicholas Fish

"a most explicit denial of the rumor, and said that these rumors were being constantly put in circulation by speculators in different quarters of the globe, but that the policy of Prince Bismarck was opposed to any such acquisition and that where proposals had been made to this government to purchase such colonial possessions, whether in the Atlantic or Pacific, in America or in Africa, they had been invariably declined. He added that they knew too well the responsibilities such outlying stations would entail, and that they did not deem them consistent with the policy of Germany."[35]

But no sooner had the German Government denied any aggressive intent with reference to the island of

[33] *Bismarck und die Nordschleswigsche Frage,* 1864-1879, ed. by W. Platzhoff, K. Rheindorf, and J. Tiedje (Berlin, 1925), pp. 401-402.

[34] Fish to Nicholas Fish, December 15, 1875, MS. Dept. of State, *Germany, Inst.,* vol. 16.

[35] Nicholas Fish to Hamilton Fish, January 13, 1876, *Germany, Desp.,* vol. 11.

St. Thomas, when Secretary Fish instructed the American Minister at Berlin to make even further inquiries. This time it referred to the island of Santo Domingo. On December 21, 1875, Charles R. Douglass, the American consul at Puerto Plata, Santo Domingo, wrote to Secretary Fish to report that he had seen letters from Paris and Hamburg, addressed to General Luperon, wherein it was stated

"that Minister Garrido, recently appointed by the Dominican Government to negotiate a loan abroad, having failed in his efforts, had accepted an offer from the German Government of the lease of Samana Bay for ninety-nine years, for the sum of one million dollars, and that the Dominican Government has accordingly acquiesced in the arrangement."[36]

This warning of Mr. Douglass was identical with that of Mr. Fisher Ames, who, as American consul at Santo Domingo in August, 1871, had sent to Secretary Fish an alarming despatch concerning alleged German schemes to secure Samana Bay. In September, 1871, George Bancroft, the American Minister at Berlin, had reported the most explicit assurances from the German Government that there was no truth in such a rumor, but Fish had remained apprehensive. Now, some four years later, the Secretary of State still thought it worth while to make another formal inquiry. On February 9, 1876, he instructed J. C. Bancroft Davis, the nephew of George Bancroft, to inquire "as to the correctness

[36] Chas. R. Douglass to Fish, December 21, 1875, *Puerto Plata, Santo Domingo, Consular Letters,* vol. i.

of the statement" of consul Douglass, and "report the result to the Department."[37]

In accordance with instructions, Bancroft Davis went to the German Foreign Office, and when he read to von Buelow the instruction that he had just received from Washington, "a look of blank amazement" came over the face of the Foreign Secretary, and

"he exclaimed in English: 'It is a lie—all a lie from beginning to end—not one word of truth in it. It is a lie of a tropical growth!' He then went on to say that he had had similar enquiries made to him before respecting reports of German attempts at acquisition. Not long since he believed that Mr. Fish had asked him such a question in regard to another of the West Indian Islands—he thought it was St. Thomas, and he had assured him that there was no truth in it. Some ten years since, he said, when the North German Bund was formed, the subject of colonizing and of foreign acquisitions of territory had been carefully considered . . . and a conclusion had been arrived at, that it was not for the interest of Germany to make such acquisitions. This conclusion had received the sanction of Prince Bismarck and of Mr. Delbruck, and of the Emperor; and the policy then inaugurated would not be reversed while they had anything to do with administering the government. It was true that since that time Germany had received several offers of territory—in Asia, in South Africa, and in San Domingo: but these offers had been declined."[38]

This very positive denial on the part of the German Foreign Secretary of any desire on the part of the

[37] Fish to Bancroft Davis, February 9, 1876, MS. Dept. of State, *Germany, Inst.,* vol. 16.

[38] Bancroft Davis, to Fish, February 25, 1876, MS. Dept. of State, *Germany, Desp.,* vol. 12.

German Government to secure colonies in the Caribbean seemed to satisfy Secretary Fish, and during the rest of his term of office recurrent rumors were given scant consideration. But American vigilance was not relaxed under the succeeding administration of President Hayes, with Mr. William M. Evarts as Secretary of State. In the summer of 1879, the usual storm warnings came from the Caribbean. On July 1, 1879, Mr. V. V. Smith, the American consul at St. Thomas, wrote to the Acting Secretary of State, F. W. Seward, with reference to rumors that

"negotiations are pending between Denmark and some government not named, for the sale of St. Thomas. I know that Denmark is anxious to dispose of her West India possessions. In the event that the Isthmus Canal should be completed, this Island would become a very important place, and its possession by either England or France is almost certain, unless the United States should interfere."[39]

As soon as Mr. Evarts received this despatch from St. Thomas he at once instructed Mr. Cramer, at Copenhagen, to make a "judicious inquiry on the subject," and then to inform the Department "at the earliest convenient date."[44]

When Mr. Cramer received this instruction late Saturday afternoon, August 9, 1879, he did not wait until the following Thursday (the day reserved for diplomatic conferences), but on Monday he presented him-

[39] V. V. Smith to F. W. Seward, July 1, 1879, MS. Dept. of State, *St. Thomas, Consular Letters*, vol. 11.

[40] Evarts to Cramer, July 18, 1879, MS. Dept. of State, *Denmark, Inst.*, vol. 15.

self at the Foreign Office and inquired as to the truth
of the rumor that France, Great Britain, or some other
nation was negotiating for the Danish West Indies.
The Foreign Minister replied "with perfect candor
that there is no truth in the report, and that no negotiations are pending with any Government on the subject
in question." The Foreign Minister then took advantage of this opening to ask whether "the Government
of the United States had any thought of opening such
negotiations."

Mr. Cramer, somewhat taken aback, confessed that
"he knew nothing" of the intentions of his Government
in that regard. Such a question, however, did awaken
his interest in the possibility of the acquisition of these
islands by the United States, and he informed Mr.
Evarts that he believed that Denmark would be willing to re-open negotiations for their purchase.[41]

In a later despatch, September 23, 1879, Cramer expressed the opinion that Denmark was really anxious
to sell the islands. In October, 1878, there had been
a serious negro uprising on the island of Santa Cruz
which made it necessary for the Danish Government
to increase the garrison on the island, and thus considerably increased the expenses of administration.
From the other two islands, St. Thomas and St. John,
the Danish Government derived no profit, and therefore, there was little reason in keeping them. In view
of this situation, Mr. Cramer was of the opinion that,

[41] Cramer to Evarts, August 11, 1879, MS. Dept. of State,
Denmark, Desp., vol. 14.

"if any one of the European Powers were to make a fair offer, however small it might comparatively be, the Danish Government would be willing to accept it, and thus get rid of islands that are only a source of annoyance and expense to Denmark." With specific reference to the attitude of Great Britain, Mr. Cramer believed that there was distinct danger that the British Government might come to an agreement with Denmark "irrespective of the protests of the Government of the United States." Hence,

"it would be no wonder, if under the circumstances of the case such a transaction should in all secrecy be effected between the two Governments, unless the Government of the United States should offer to Denmark more favorable terms. It is a notable sign that the British Minister at this capital has been spending the summer in England . . . while the Danish Minister in London, who spends his summers usually in Denmark, remained all summer at his post."[42]

But notwithstanding these fears on the part of Mr. Cramer, or his warmly expressed belief that the United States should acquire the islands, the Department of State was not ready to open negotiations for their purchase. Mr. Hunter, the Acting Secretary of State, expressed satisfaction at the news that the Danish Government was not carrying on any negotiations for the sale of the islands to any other power, for such action could not be regarded "with indifference" by the United States. Nevertheless, Mr. Hunter thought that

[42] Cramer to Evarts, September 23, 1879, MS. Dept. of State, *Denmark, Desp.,* vol. 14.

"at this time it would be premature to express any opinion as to the probability of reopening the negotiations for their transfer to the United States, but the subject is one of interest and importance, and as such, will receive careful consideration."[43]

In the year 1880 American suspicions of European expansion in the Caribbean became centered on France, and for a short time there is a cessation of the rumors relative to German intrigue. This shift in American attitude was probably produced by the widespread talk in Europe of a proposed canal across the isthmus of Panama. On May 15, 1879, there assembled at Paris an International Scientific Congress, consisting of 136 delegates from various countries. The purpose of this congress was to determine the most feasible route for an isthmian canal, and also whether it was to be a lock-canal or a sea-level one. The predominant nationality represented at the congress was French, and the meetings were presided over by the eminent French engineer, Ferdinand de Lesseps. After a short session a decision was reached in favor of a sea-level canal to be constructed across the isthmus of Panama. On October 20, 1879, the Universal Interoceanic Canal Company was organized, millions of shares were sold to eager investors, and in February, 1881, the work of actual construction was formally inaugurated.[44]

[43] Hunter to Cramer, September 1, 1879, MS. Dept. of State, *Denmark, Inst.,* vol. 15. See also the instruction of Hunter to Cramer, October 31, 1879.

[44] W. F. Johnson, *Four Centuries of the Panama Canal* (N. Y. 1906), pp. 78-98.

It was but natural that such an important undertaking, sponsored and controlled by French citizens,
should be viewed with evident concern by the American
Government. For years there had been an anxious
desire to secure control over all possible canal routes
in North and Central America. It was regarded as a
corollary of the Monroe Doctrine that American control should be exercised over any inter-oceanic canal in
the Western Hemisphere, and this note was distinctly
sounded by President Hayes in a special message to
Congress, March 8, 1880:

"I deem it proper to state briefly my opinion as to the
policy of the United States with respect to the construction of an interoceanic canal by any route across
the American Isthmus. The policy of this country is a
canal under American control. The United States can
not consent to the surrender of this control to any
European power or to any combination of European
powers."[45]

In order that France should be in a position ad-
equately to protect this vast enterprise it seemed more
than likely that she would endeavor to secure additional
islands in the Caribbean as naval bases. In 1877, in
direct defiance of the Monroe Doctrine, the French
Government had acquired the island of St. Bartholomew from Sweden. Could it be possible that negotiations were now under way with Denmark to purchase
the Danish West Indies?

[45] Jas. D. Richardson, *Messages and Papers of the Presidents,* vol. 7, pp. 585-586.

In the late summer of 1880, rumors to this effect began to be circulated, and Mr. Evarts, not wishing to be presented with a *fait accompli,* as had been the case with the island of St. Bartholomew, sent, on August 24, 1880, th ᶠollowing cablegram to Mr. E. F. Noyes, the American Minister at Paris:

"It is rumored in the West Indies that France is negotiating for purchase of Danish Islands. Ascertain facts." [46]

Four days later, Mr. Noyes replied:

"Minister for Foreign Affairs is absent. Am assured by his confidential Secretary there is no foundation for rumor about the Danish Islands. No negotiation is pending, not contemplated." [47]

On the very day that Secretary Evarts sent his instruction to Mr. Noyes, August 24, 1880, there appeared in the New York *Herald* [48] a report that the

[46] Evarts to Noyes, August 24, 1880, MS. Dept. of State, *France, Inst.,* vol. 20.

[47] Noyes to Evarts, August 28, 1880, MS. Dept. of State, *France, Desp.,* vol. 86. See also Noyes to Evarts, August 30, 1880, *Desp.,* vol. 86.

[48] The report in the New York *Herald* is from the Washington correspondent under date of August 23, 1880, and is partly as follows: "The report from Havana that the French are in treaty with the Danes for the islands of St. Thomas, St. Croix and St. John is not credited in administration quarters. During the Presidency of General Grant it became necessary to inform the Danish government that any attempt to transfer her colonial possessions on this continent to another European nation would be regarded as an unfriendly act and treated as such. It has been necessary since the present administration

French Government was actually negotiating with the Danish Government relative to the cession of the Danish West Indies. A copy of the *Herald* containing this item was sent by an unknown person to Mr. Cramer, the American Minister at Copenhagen, who without waiting for instructions, immediately set about making inquiries concerning this rumor. At the Danish Foreign Office he met the Minister of Foreign Affairs just as the latter was leaving for the day. During the course of a short walk with the Minister, Mr. Cramer alluded to the rumor in the *Herald,* and indicated his interest in such a report. The Minister then replied

"that his attention had been drawn to it a few days ago, but he could frankly say that there is no truth in it whatever, that no negotiations are pending between the Government of Denmark and France, or between his Government and that of any other country on the subject of the transfer of these islands, though he confessed that they are not only no source of income to the State Treasury, but the cause of actual expense." [49]

came into power to reiterate the so-called Grant doctrine, and if necessary it will again be done." In an editorial of the same date, August 24, 1880, the following statement is of interest. "It is too late now to inquire if our breach of faith in 1868 was well or ill considered for the national interests. By declining to complete the bargain we renounced the benefit of the Monroe Doctrine as regards those islands, and have no right to complain if France . . . shall now choose to augment her colonies in the Antilles. We can have no jealousy of our sister Republic, to which we are bound by so many ties."

[49] Cramer to Evarts, September 11, 1880, MS. Dept. of State, *Denmark, Desp.,* vol. 14. See also W. Hunter, Acting Secretary of State, to Cramer, October 9, 1880, approving Cramer's actions. *Denmark, Inst.,* vol. 15.

The Danish Minister of Foreign Affairs was perfectly correct in his statement to the American Minister with reference to any pending negotiations with France. Not only was Denmark unprepared for the cession of the Danish West Indies to any European power, but instead, she was seriously considering the possibility of selling the islands to the American Government. In August, of 1880, the Danish Secretary for Foreign Affairs, Lehnsbaron Rosenorn-Lehn, wrote to General Raasloff, the former Danish Minister to the United States, an inquiry as to the whole history of the failure of the treaty with the United States for the cession of the Danish West Indies. On September 10, 1880, Raasloff wrote the Secretary an abbreviated account of the situation in 1867-1870. Before the Foreign Secretary had received this letter from Raasloff, Mr. Cramer, the American Minister, had dropped by the Danish Foreign Office and inquired about the rumors of the cession of the Danish West Indies to France. That inquiry seemed to enlist even more deeply the interest of the Danish Foreign Secretary in the project of selling the islands to the United States, so without any further ado, he wrote a second letter to Raasloff, September 16, 1880, and frankly asked for his advice in detail.

Raasloff, then at Baden Baden, replied at great length on September 29, 1880. First of all, he discussed the reasons why the American Government had not ratified the treaty of October 24, 1867. When he reached the United States in December, 1868, on a special mission to endeavor to persuade the American Senate

to consent to the ratification of the treaty, he realized
that there was at that moment

"no possibility to obtain the desired ratification. In
fact, the case was that the Senate *would not* sanction
the Convention, nor was it, in one sense, *able* to do so.
The reasons for this were principally the following
ones: The Senate was altogether definitely indisposed
to sanction anything that had been done by Mr. Seward.
The purchase of St. Thomas had become very unpopular after the earthquake and the hurricane, and after
these natural catastrophes the purchase sum seemed unreasonably high to everybody. Alaska had meanwhile
been acquired and at a price which in the opinion of
most people was far too high. Under these circumstances it would be considered impossible to induce the
House of Representatives to grant the purchase money.
The ratification of the treaty by the Senate would probably thus produce a conflict of competence between the
two assemblies, a conflict that would be so much more
dangerous, as the question whether the House is *in duty
bound* to grant money which is to be raised according
to a treaty adopted by the Government and the Senate,
is one of the most difficult ones, and is generally regarded as insoluble. And finally, several of the
Senators, among these Mr. Sumner, regarded any
acquisition of land in the south as dangerous to the
interior peace of the country."

These reasons, although actually decisive, were not,
however, of such a nature that they could be urged

"officially towards Denmark, and men such as Mr.
Sumner perceived this perfectly well; as, however, no
arguments except these have ever been seriously advanced to me, and as, moreover, I do not know where
one would be able to find them, I must arrive at the
conviction (expressed in my report of the 10th instant),
'that the Government of the United States would not

be able to provide good reasons, viz., reasons that it ventures to state officially and that would be acknowledged by the law of nations, to refuse to ratify the Convention in question.' Through the conferences mentioned above, however, we recognized, on *both* sides, that it would be impossible for the Senate to declare itself *against* the ratification of the Convention; for, that this should happen, a Committee report would have to be written, in which such a decision had to be accounted for by good reasons, and to write such a report was a moral impossibility for Mr. Sumner (and would be so for the present President of the Committee in question), *partly* because he, as already stated, had no really good reasons at his disposal, but *partly* also because a short time before he had written a report on the subject of the Alaska Treaty in which he had put forward so many general reasons that might be applied direct to the St. Thomas Treaty, *in favor of its ratification,* so that he could not possibly argue in the exactly opposite direction regarding the St. Thomas Treaty immediately afterwards, without utterly contradicting himself and exposing himself and his Committee to a crushing criticism."

Because of this difficult position in which the American Government was placed, General Raasloff had hoped that the Grant administration would recognize the obligations of the United States towards Denmark and ratify the treaty of October 24, 1867. He discovered, however, that both President Grant and Secretary Fish were

'totally unacquainted with foreign relations generally, and with the St. Thomas affair in particular, and were strongly influenced by their animosity against Mr. Seward. . . . From the reports of the Danish Legation Your Excellency will be acquainted with the fact that the administration of General Grant, represented by

Mr. Fish, quite definitely refused to use its influence to persuade the Senate to make a resolution regarding the St. Thomas Treaty, and that it—having at one time (this, however, in direct opposition to what Mr. Fish had pronounced to Chamberlain Bille a few days before as his decided and unchangeable determination) agreed that there should be fixed a new term for the exchange of the ratifications, viz., from October 14, 1869, to April 14, 1870—let this matter drop without giving any reason except that he, Mr. Fish, 'was not authorized to proceed further with reference thereto."

But this ungenerous treatment of Denmark at the hands of the Grant administration was now a thing of the past, and General Raasloff ventured the opinion that a new "proposal from the Danish Government, requesting a final settlement of this affair, would be answered by the Government of the United States in an obliging sense." He was inclined to this opinion because of the change in public opinion in the United States during the past decade, and also because of the change in presidential administration. Raasloff had no definite knowledge as to the attitude of President Hayes with reference to Seward's plans for American expansion in the Caribbean, but he did know that the present Secretary of State, Mr. Evarts,

"was always one of his [Seward's] friends and ad herents, and I [Raasloff] remember quite distinctly that in 1869 I had a satisfactory conversation with him about the St. Thomas treaty. At that time thi had no practical importance; still it might possibly hav some now. In my opinion, then, there is good reaso to believe that, if moved to do so by a definite reque from the Danish Government, the present adminis tration or its successor will submit the affair to a dis passionate investigation and deal with it accordingly; by doing so, it cannot fail to be convinced (if, as I presume, it has not already long ago arrived at this conclusion) that Denmark suffered a great wrong in this affair, and that an absolute undeserved humiliation was inflicted upon it, that the behavior of the administration of General Grant was anything but correct, and that the good reputation of the United States and the prestige of the American Government can only suffer if this affair should be made the subject of a controversy between the two Governments. . . . In case the administration and the Senate, as assumed above, agree, it will not be difficult to obtain the sanction of the House too, because for one thing it will be disposed to listen to the same considerations and regards as the other two parties involved, and for another, it will be easy to bring about again a public opinion in favor of the acquisition of the Danish Islands if the purchase money is fixed at an essentially lower amount than stipulated previously."[50]

This long letter from Raasloff to the Danish Minister for Foreign Relations is of great value in throwing light upon the efforts that were made by the Danish Government to secure, in 1868-69, the ratification of the treaty for the cession of the Danish West Indies to the United States. It is of interest to note that even after the lapse of ten years, General Raasloff still felt very deeply upon the whole subject, and now, in 1880, thought that the American Government would finally recognize the obligation that it owed to Denmark and would proceed to the ratification of the treaty. His suggestion to the Foreign Office to re-open the nego-

[50] Raasloff to Rosenorn-Lehn, September 29, 1880, MS. D. F. O.

tiations with the United States seems to have been read with interest but not to have been acted upon. There is no record of any Danish overture to the American Government at this time.

In 1884, the old rumor of an exchange of North Schleswig for the Danish West Indies was revived in a St. Thomas newspaper, and on August 21, 1884, Mr. J. J. Buck, of Emporia, Kansas, wrote to the Department of State to sound a warning against German intrigue. According to Mr. Buck there was no doubt but that negotiations were actually pending between Denmark and Germany looking towards this exchange. In order to guard against any such contingency. the Department of State instructed Mr. Wickham Hoffman, the American Minister at Copenhagen, to make discreet inquiries and to report to the Department.[51] Mr. Hoffman did not think it worth while to dignify a newspaper "canard" by inquiring directly of the Minister for Foreign Affairs if this report was correct, but he did elicit from an official in the Foreign Office an assurance that "there is not one word of truth in the report."[52]

A few days later, Hoffman wrote another despatch to Secretary Frelinghuysen in which he reported a conversation that he had had with the British Minister at Copenhagen. The rumor of the exchange of North

[51] John Davis, Acting Secretary of State, to Wickham Hoffman, September 10, 1884, MS, Dept. of State, *Confidential, Denmark, Inst.,* vol. 15.
[52] Hoffman to Frelinghuysen, October 2, 1884, MS. Dept. of State, *Denmark, Desp.,* vol. 14.

Schleswig for the Danish West Indies had been brought to the attention of the British Minister who had made inquiries at the Danish Foreign Office, and who had been informed that the rumor was "wholly unfounded."[53]

These assurances temporarily set at rest this most persistent rumor about German desires for a naval base in the Caribbean, but in 1890, Mr. Clark E. Carr, the American Minister at Copenhagen, gave it a new lease of life. In a despatch to Secretary Blaine, June 24, 1890, he mentions a rumor "that negotiations are pending between the Sovereigns of Germany and Denmark for an exchange of Territory by which Germany will surrender to Denmark a portion of Schleswig and Denmark, in turn, cede to Germany her West India Islands."

It seemed very apparent to Mr. Carr that the Danes

"would make almost any sacrifice to repossess themselves of that portion of Schleswig which, in language and religion and customs and sympathy, remains Danish. I have become satisfied that no amount of money and no other territory would be accepted by the Danes in exchange for their West India possessions with so much satisfaction as they would receive the portion of Schleswig to which I have referred."[54]

This despatch of Mr. Carr did not seem greatly to disturb the Department of State, and the rumor of

[53] Hoffman to Frelinghuysen, October 7, 1884, MS. Dept. of State, *Denmark, Desp.*, vol. 14.

[54] Carr to Blaine, June 24, 1890, MS. Dept. of State, *Confidential, Denmark, Desp.*, vol. 14.

such an exchange was allowed to die a natural death. In the following summer, however, Mr. Carr once more adverted to the Danish West Indies, and this time he opened up the question of the sale of these islands to the United States. On July 17, 1891, he wrote a long despatch to Secretary Blaine in which he recounted some interesting conversations he had recently had with Colonel C. H. Arendrup, the Governor of the Danish West Indies. Arendrup was at that time on a visit to Copenhagen, and he and Mr. Carr chanced to discuss the recurrent rumors of the transfer of the Danish West Indies to some European power. Arendrup finally inquired whether there was "any desire or disposition on the part of our Government at this time to obtain a foothold in the West Indies." Carr replied that inasmuch as it seemed "probable that there would soon be a ship canal across the isthmus to connect the two oceans, there had in some quarters been expressions favorable to such acquisition," but that so far as he knew, "it had taken no definite shape."

On July 8, 1891, Governor Arendrup called to see Mr. Carr and informed him that Mr. Estrup, the Danish Prime Minister, had expressed

"a willingness on his part now to carry out the provisions of the treaty of 1867 which was ratified by Denmark and failed to be ratified by the Senate of the United States. Governor Arendrup stated that Mr. Estrup further said that it was his opinion that in case the United States should so desire, the Danish Government would now be willing to sell to the United States the Islands of St. Thomas and St. John upon the terms of the treaty of 1867, and also said that in case the United States should now desire to have those islands, the treaty of 1867 could be revived."

In reply, Mr. Carr pleaded a lack of instructions with reference to a revival of the treaty of 1867, but he promised that he would notify his government of these conversations.[55] When his despatch reached Washington it was carefully read by Secretary Blaine who then wrote to President Harrison in regard to it. With reference to the purchase of the Danish West Indies, Blaine states that his

"prepossessions are all against it until we are by fate in possession of the larger West Indies. They are very small, of no great commercial value, and in case of war we would be required to defend them and to defend them at great cost. At the same time they lack strategic value. They are destined to become ours, but among the last of the West Indies that would be taken."[56]

Carr, however, was not to be discouraged by Blaine's lack of enthusiasm. Ever since the Civil War prominent naval officers had expressed a desire to see the American Government secure naval bases in the Caribbean. Perhaps it might be well to work through the Secretary of the Navy! With this idea in mind, Carr wrote to Benjamin F. Tracy on July 13, 1892, and canvassed the situation from beginning to end.

[55] Carr to Blaine, July 17, 1891, MS. Dept. of State, *Denmark, Desp.*, vol. 14.
[56] Blaine to Harrison, August 10, 1891, *Harrison MSS.,* Library of Congress.

After telling of his conversations with Governor Arendrup, and of the willingness of the Danish Prime Minister, Mr. Estrup, to receive overtures from the United States, Mr. Carr then endeavors to show Mr. Tracy how important the islands would be for naval purposes:

"I have thought that perhaps, in the policy of building up a Navy, so successfully inaugurated and carried into effect by you, the desirability of the acquisition of so important a Harbor as that of St. Thomas, with the advantages it presents for a coaling station, and for a place of refuge for our naval and merchant ships, would be apparent to all Americans. Certainly, if there was any reason whatever for acquiring these Islands twenty-five years ago, with the prospect of a Canal across the Isthmus, and with the new condition of Commerce and of naval affairs, it is far more important at this time. . . . Perhaps it would be important that the matter be so accomplished as to preclude the influence of any European Government. I suppose that it would be possible, should any action be regarded as desirable, to ascertain through individual Members of the Senate, what would be the probable action of that Body."[57]

Later on, in November, 1892, Carr wrote to John W. Foster, who had succeeded Blaine as Secretary of State, and put the matter of the sale of the islands to the United States directly before him. Mr. Carr was now unofficially authorized to inform the American Secretary of State that

[57] Carr to Benjamin F. Tracy, Secretary of the Navy, July 13, 1892, *Tracy Papers,* Library of Congress.

"a proposal from the Government of the United States to revive the convention of 1867 . . . would receive favorable consideration from the Danish Government, the meaning of which is, that the Danish Government will now if desired cede those Islands to the United States upon the terms of the convention of 1867."

Mr. Carr then went on to explain how this matter of the revival of the convention of 1867 had arisen. It appeared that he had called upon Mr. Estrup, the Danish Prime Minister, in order to request a loan of the Icelandic sagas which give an account of the discovery of America by the Norsemen. These manuscripts were to be placed on exhibition at the great Columbian Exposition to be held in the United States. In the course of the conversation the matter of the cession of the Danish West Indies came up, and Mr. Estrup remarked that he would "now be willing to cede those islands to the United States and indicated that he would be willing to do so upon the terms then agreed upon, i. e., 1867." Mr. Carr mentioned his lack of instructions and also adverted to the fact that in March, 1893, there would be a change in presidential administrations. Mr. Estrup, however, appeared so deeply interested in the sale of the islands to the United States that he refused to be discouraged, and on November 22, 1892, he called by the American Legation to advise Mr. Carr that the Danish Minister for Foreign Affairs would take up the matter at once.

On that same afternoon, when Mr. Carr visited the Foreign Office, the Minister, Mr. Reedtz-Thott, assured him of his readiness to receive a proposal from the

United States. Later, it was decided to consult the King concerning the opening of negotiations, and on Friday, November 25, the Minister waited upon Mr. Carr to inform him of the royal consent to await overtures from the United States.[58]

On the following day, November 29, Mr. Carr wrote a personal letter to Secretary Foster in which he stressed the importance of the islands for naval bases in the Caribbean. It was his belief that the United States

"must have a station in that region and that it will be found that this is the best one available, and that it will be sought for on our part soon, and that this administration should take the initiative. This can now be done if desired, but should the President not be inclined to do so, we are not, as you will see, committed in the least. It seems to me that it would be wise for the President to take up the matter of receiving such a station in his message to Congress, but of course I would not presume to advise him. . . . Whatever may be thought of the matter I hope that you will so instruct me that I may be able to show Mr. Estrup and Baron Reedtz-Thott that you are not indifferent to their feelings in the matter and that you appreciate the suggestions they have confidentially made in our private unofficial interviews."[59]

Secretary Foster was far more favorable towards the acquisition of the Danish West Indies than Mr. Blaine had been, but the administration was fast drawing to a close and it seemed impossible to complete any nego-

[58] Carr to Foster, November 28, 1892, MS. Dept. of State *Denmark, Desp.,* vol. 14.

[59] Carr to Foster, November 29, 1892, MS. Dept. of State, *Denmark, Desp.,* vol. 14.

tiation before March 4, 1893. He took pains to congratulate Mr. Carr upon

"the skill and tact with which you have received the
approach of the Danish Government on the subject,
and, while ascertaining the disposition of the Danish
Government, have in no way committed the Government of the United States. The question of the acquisition of the Islands is one of far-reaching and national
importance, the extent of which is appreciated by no
one more than the President. As his administration is,
however, drawing to its close, he considers it inadvisable to express any views or indicate any policy, the
consummation of which he could not effect. . . . You
are therefore instructed to convey verbally to these
gentlemen [Mr. Estrup and Baron Reedtz-Thott] the
sentiments of the President."[60]

It seems very likely that shortly after Secretary
Foster sent this instruction to Mr. Carr he must have
received additional evidence indicating the importance
of initiating negotiations with Denmark, for on December 31, 1892, he cabled to Carr to "take no action on
instruction number one twenty-eight, the number of
the instruction of December 20, for present."[61] But
on February 4, 1893, he sent a second instruction to
Carr which read:

"You can execute instruction one twenty-eight at
convenient opportunity."[62]

[60] Foster to Carr, December 20, 1892, MS. Dept. of State,
Denmark, Inst., vol. 15.

[61] Foster to Carr, December 31, 1892, MS. Dept. of State
Denmark, Inst., vol. 15.

[62] Foster to Carr, February 4, 1893, MS. Dept. of State,
Denmark, Inst., vol. 15.

After receiving this latter instruction, Mr. Carr at once informed both Mr. Estrup and Baron Reedtz-Thott of the views of the President. Neither of them seemed surprised at this decision not to open negotiations at such a late date, but they did suggest that perhaps the pending negotiations between the United States and Hawaii had something to do with this reluctance on the part of the American Government. In this regard Mr. Carr remained discreetly silent, although it did appear to him that "with a canal across the Isthmus, the acquisition of Hawaii makes it even more important that we should have a station in the West Indies."[63]

After Mr. Carr had finished reading to Baron Reedtz-Thott the instruction from Secretary Foster of February 4, the Danish Foreign Minister made a careful memorandum of the whole incident, part of which reads as follows:

"In the beginnng of the month of December, 1892, the American Minister, Mr. Carr, addressed himself to me, calling my attention to the fact that the acquisition of St. Thomas must be highly important to the North American Free States. For this reason he was anxious to know the attitude of the Danish Government towards a renewal of the negotiations that had at an earlier date been interrupted, concerning the cession of St. Thomas. I directed Mr. Carr to discuss this matter with the President of the Council. . . . Mr. Carr then had an interview with the President of the Council who, as agreed upon between us, answered Mr.

[63] Carr to Foster, February 22, 1893, MS. Dept. of State, *Denmark, Desp.*, vol. 14.

Carr that as the American Government had taken no steps in this direction, the Danish Government would confine itself *to take the matter into its gracious consideration in case negotiations . . . were initiated by the American Government*. Mr. Carr declared himself to be fully satisfied with this answer, and from that time until today nothing has been heard of the matter. Today Mr. Carr read to me a communication in which the American Foreign Minister, after the orders of the President, says that the American Government is fully aware of the importance of the Island of St. Thomas and of the interest that it would present to the United States to acquire this island—that further, the President highly appreciates the position that the President of the Council and the Foreign Minister have held in this matter, but that time is so advanced that the President does not perceive the possibility of carrying this affair through before his going out of office in the month of March of this year, and therefore does not think it right to take it up."[64]

On March 7, 1893, shortly after the accession of Mr. Cleveland to the presidential office, Baron Reedtz-Thott sent a confidential instruction to Count Sponneck, the Danish Minister in Washington, in which he discussed the possibility of a cession of the Danish West Indies to the United States. After reviewing the conversations that had been held with Mr. Carr, the American Minister at Copenhagen, he alluded to the refusal of President Harrison to initiate negotiations. Thus, it appeared, the matter was settled for the present, but in Mr. Carr's opinion, the acquisition of the Danish West Indies was of such significance to the

[64] Memorandum of Baron Reedtz-Thott, February 9, 1893, MS. D. F. O.

United States that the question would be taken up
again at the earliest possible moment by the new
Secretary of State. It also seemed quite possible to
Baron Reedtz-Thott that Secretary Gresham would
"touch upon this matter," and in that event Count
Sponneck was instructed to "foster" the idea of a sale
to the United States. In case Secretary Gresham should
respond favorably, it would be important to have the
negotiations

"carried on before Mr. Carr has been replaced by another Minister who will be as unfamiliar with the affair
itself as with the personalities and the conditions in
this country."[65]

Secretary Gresham, however, appeared indifferent
in regard to the Danish West Indies, but public
opinion in the United States was becoming more and
more interested in the region of the Caribbean. The
question of an isthmian canal under American control
continued to attract public notice, and in 1890, the
Maritime Canal Company had actually commenced
operations at Greytown. Although the financial panic
of 1893 made it impossible to secure the additional
capital necessary to carry on the construction of a
canal through Nicaragua, yet it seemed only a matter
of a few years when the American Government itself
would assume the responsibility of such an undertaking. And in case the United States should decide to
build a canal across the isthmus of Nicaragua, it was

[65] Baron Reedtz-Thott to Count Sponneck, March 7, 1893,
MS. D. F. O.

vital that adequate provision be made for its future defence.

Prominent publicists began to discuss various methods of defence for this projected canal, some of whom were of the opinion that it would require American control over some of the islands in the Caribbean. The most distinguished of these publicists was Captain Alfred T. Mahan, a famous authority on naval history. In an article entitled "The Isthmus and Sea Power," published in the *Atlantic Monthly,* September, 1893, Captain Mahan discusses the many dangers that would threaten an American-built isthmian canal:

"Under this increased importance of the Isthmus, we cannot safely anticipate for the future the cheap acquiescence which, under very different circumstances, has been yielded in the past to our demands. Already it is notorious that European powers are betraying symptoms of increased sensitiveness as to the value of the Caribbean positions, and are strengthening their grip upon those they now hold. Moral considerations undoubtedly count for more than they did, and nations are more reluctant to enter into war; but still, the policy of states is determined by the balance of advantages, and it behooves us to know what our policy is to be, and what advantages are needed to turn in our favor the scale of negotiations and the general current of events. . . . If . . . we determine that our interest and dignity require that our rights should depend upon the will of no other state, but upon our own power to enforce them, we must gird ourselves to admit that freedom of interoceanic transit depends upon the predominance in a maritime region — the Caribbean Sea — through which pass all the approaches to the Isthmus. . . . At present the positions of the Caribbean are occupied by foreign powers, nor may we, however disposed to acquisition, obtain them by means other than righteous; but a distinct advance will have been made when public opinion is convinced that we need them, and should not exert our utmost ingenuity to dodge them when flung at our head."[66]

Two years later the United States became involved with Great Britain in a very serious dispute relative to the delimitation of the boundary line between British Guiana and Venezuela. Inasmuch as this dispute involved the Monroe Doctrine there was strong support throughout the United States of the bold stand taken by President Cleveland and Secretary Olney, and we have such an ardent Republican as Theodore Roosevelt writing to Olney as follows:

"I must write you just a line to say how heartily I rejoiced at the Venezuela message. I earnestly hope our people won't back down in any way."[67]

There were many resolutions introduced into Congress calling for a strict enforcement of the Monroe Doctrine, and these finally resulted in the concurrent resolution reported from the Senate Foreign Relations Committee on January 20, 1896. After calling attention to Monroe's message to Congress, December 2, 1823, the concurrent resolution declared that

[66] A. T. Mahan, *The Interest of America in Sea Power, Present and Future* (Boston, 1898), pp. 101-103.

[67] Roosevelt to Olney, December 20, 1895, *Olney Papers,* Library of Congress. See also Henry James, *Richard Olney* (N. Y. 1923), pp. 96-142; R. M. McElroy, *Grover Cleveland* (N. Y. 1923), pp. 173-202, vol. 2; A. L. P. Dennis, *Adventures in American Diplomacy* (N. Y. 1928), chap. i.

"the United States of America reaffirms and confirms the doctrine and principles promulgated by President Monroe in his message . . . and declares that it will assert and maintain that doctrine and principles, and will regard any infringement thereof, and particularly any attempt by any European power to take or acquire any new or additional territory on the American continents, or any island adjacent thereto, or any right of sovereignty or dominion in the same in any case or instance as to which the United States shall deem such an attempt to be dangerous to its peace or safety by or through force, purchase, cession, occupation, pledge, colonization, protectorate, or by control of the easement in any canal or any other means of transit across the American Isthmus . . . as the manifestation of an unfriendly disposition toward the United States and as an interposition which it would be impossible in any form for the United States to regard with indifference."[68]

But even before this resolution was reported out from the Senate Foreign Relations Committee, Senator Henry Cabot Lodge had already on January 3, 1896, submitted the following resolution:

"Resolved, That the Committee on Foreign Relations be directed to inquire and report to the Senate whether the islands of St. Croix, St. John, and St. Thomas, in the West Indies, can be now purchased from the Danish Government, as provided by the treaty signed at Copenhagen in October, 1867, and whether if these islands are not purchased by the United States it is probable that they will be sold by the Danish Government to some other power."[69]

[68] *Congressional Record,* vol. 28, pt. 1, p. 783.

[69] *Ibid.,* vol. 28, pt. 1, p. 782. According to an article in the New York *Herald,* it was on account of a rumor that the Danish West Indies were about to be sold to a European power—presumably Great Britain—that Senator Lodge was led to introduce his resolution. See issue of January 17, 1896.

In discussing the reasons for the introduction of his resolution, Senator Lodge remarked that

"the reason for acquiring the West India Islands, apart from the question of general policy which I have stated, is obvious in the fact that they furnish an admirable naval station for us in the West Indies and have small populations."[70]

It is very likely that Mr. Lodge's anxiety concerning the sale of the Danish West Indies to a European power was largely produced by a cablegram from Havana, of December 23, 1895, which was published in the American newspapers on the following day. This cablegram reported an interview with a distinguished Danish journalist, Henrik Cavling, the editor of the Copenhagen *Politiken*. With reference to the Danish West Indies, Mr. Cavling is quoted as saying that Germany wants either

"Cuba or St. Thomas, and has been negotiating with Denmark for the latter island. The Danish government is anxious to sell, but the Danish people are opposed to the sale to Germany or any other European Power. Mr. Cavling thinks that the United States should own both St. Thomas and Santa Cruz, and use them as a naval station when the Panama or Nicaragua Canal is completed. The question of disposing of the islands will be discussed this winter in the Danish Storthing. If the islands are not sold he says their independence will be granted. In this case, the inhabitants, a majority of whom are English speaking, will probably ask for a British protectorate."[71]

[70] New York *Herald*, January 17, 1896
[71] New York *Herald*, December 24, 1895.

As soon as the report of this interview with Mr. Cavling reached Denmark, newspaper editors in Copenhagen immediately began to inquire of Mr. John E. Risley, the American Minister, and of the Danish Foreign Office as to the truth of rumors concerning the sale of the Danish West Indies to the United States. But both Mr. Risley and the Foreign Office remained discreetly silent, although Mr. Vedel, the Director General of the Ministry of Foreign Affairs, informed Mr. Risley that Mr. Cavling was only

"a self-appointed agent, and had not authority nor instigation from the Foreign Office, nor was there any negotiation whatever pending between Denmark and Germany for the sale or transfer of the islands."

Mr. Risley then inquired whether the Danish Government was inclined to re-open negotiations for the sale of the islands to the United States. Mr. Vedel replied that the Danish Government could not propose to re-open negotiations "but if the United States should choose to do so, he was of the opinion that his Government would be inclined to sell them, though he was personally opposed to it."[72]

While these views were being exchanged at Copenhagen, similar conversations were being carried on at Washington between Secretary Olney and Mr. Brun, the Danish Minister. On January 13, 1896, Olney wrote to Brun to inquire whether there was any truth in the rumors relative to the sale of the Danish West

[72] Risley to Olney, January 14, 1896, MS. Dept. of State, *Denmark, Desp.,* vol. 21.

Indies.[73]   On January 16, Brun replied that he was "absolument sans instructions quant a la materiere en question. J'ai cependent porté les bruits, qui ont couru, à la connaissance de mon Gouvernement et dans le cas ou une reponse me parviendrait, je ne manquerai pas d'en informer Votre Excellence."[74]

Brun also lost no time in sending two cablegrams to the Danish Government.   In the first cablegram he stated that the Secretary of State had asked him "unofficially by letter whether the accounts that the Danish Antilles are for sale are well founded?"   The second cablegram was equally brief: "Sénat saisi enquête possibilité achat Antilles danoises ou vente à autre puissance."

The Danish Foreign Secretary at once replied as follows: "Dispositions du gouvernement n'ont pas varié."   As soon as Brun received this cablegram he wrote as follows to Olney:

"Mon Gouvernement me fait savoir aujourd'hui que ses dispositions au sujet de l'objet de Votre lettre du 13 courant n'ont pas varié.   Pensent être agreeable à Votre Excellence en Lui faisant part de cette communication, je Vous prie, Monsieur, le Secretaire d'Etat, d'agreir l'expression de mes sentiments respecteux."[75]

[73] The personal notes that Secretary Olney wrote to Brun with reference to the sale of the Danish West Indies are not preserved either in the Department of State or in the *Olney Papers* in the Library of Congress.

[74] Brun to Olney, January 16, 1896, MS. *Olney Papers*, Library of Congress.

[75] Brun to Olney, January 18, 1896, MS. *Olney Papers*, Library of Congress.

Olney then wrote to Brun to ask whether the Danish Minister had sent to the Department of State the exact text of the note from the Danish Foreign Office. Brun immediately replied that he had "transmis la dépêche de mon Gouvernement textuellement telle que je l'ai reçue moi-même." [76]

Two days earlier, January 18, 1896, Mr. Risley had a long conversation with the Danish Minister for Foreign Affairs in which the rumors that had been spread by Mr. Cavling were thoroughly canvassed. The Minister then took great pains to assure Mr. Risley that

"no one had been authorized to offer the Islands for sale to any power whatever; nor would they be offered for sale. The Minister continued, however, to say that if the United States should make an offer for them he could assure me that it would be fairly considered; that the great publicity given to the subject would no doubt increase the difficulties here, and make it more difficult to carry the matter through to success; and there might possibly be an objection from France as to the island of St. Croix, from whom it was acquired some 200 years ago: he thought not, but deemed it right to mention the possibility, as it was better to have everything as clearly understood as possible before proceeding further." [77]

On January 20, 1896, the Danish Foreign Secretary sent an instruction of similar import to the Danish Minister at Washington. First of all, he explained the meaning of his short telegram to Mr. Brun which

[76] Brun to Olney, January 20, 1896, MS. *Olney Papers,* Library of Congress.

[77] Risley to Olney, January 18, 1896, MS. Department of State, *Denmark, Desp.,* vol. 21.

had read: "Dispositions du gouvernement n'ont pas
varié." What he had desired to express

"by these words is the fact that the attitude of the
Royal Government towards the question of an alienation of the Danish West Indies is still that of which
Your Excellency is already aware, nothing having occurred which has enabled the Government to change
the attitude that it has maintained since the treaty was
concluded with the Government of the United States
in 1869 was not ratified by the North American Senate.
For one thing, the Royal Government does not offer
the Danish West Indies 'for sale.' It has not taken,
nor does it intend to take, any initiative towards the
alienation of these colonies, either to North America
or to any European power, and I need scarcely tell
you that when the question now seems to be put forward through the endeavors of an unresponsible political franc-tireur [Mr. Cavling, editor of the Copenhagen *Politiken*], the Royal Government is an absolute
stranger to the proceedings of this individual, and only
knows of it through what it has learned from the newspapers. Let me add to this that no more has any foreign power intimated, much less made any offer to the
Royal Government, of purchasing the Islands. On the
other hand, the same general reasons which in 1868
decided the Government to accept the offer of the
Government of the United States still exist. In case,
then, that any proposal should be made, from any side,
to the Royal Government concerning this, such a proposal would be taken into serious consideration here.
I must, however, at this very early stage remark that
in case such a communication should come forward
from the Government of the United States, one would
have to require the very strictest possible guarantee
that we shall not run the risk of repeating the experience of 1869, and further that the Royal Government
will not be able to consent to a transaction that might
be regarded as a demonstration against some other

friendly power, or as taking sides, even indirectly, in some other present political question that does not touch the Danish State, and where it might, under certain circumstances, have to guard an absolutely neutral attitude." [78]

When Secretary Olney learned definitively from the Danish Minister that there were no negotiations being carried on for the sale of the Danish West Indies to a European power, he dismissed the subject from his mind for the time being and turned to other more important questions that clamored for settlement. But there were many public men who had come to the conclusion that these islands should be purchased as soon as possible, and who constantly worked towards that end. One of the most prominent and indefatigable of these was Senator Henry Cabot Lodge, who lost no opportunity to keep this question before the public eye. Although Secretary Olney was a member of an opposing political party, Lodge wrote to him repeatedly with reference to the situation in the Caribbean, and also sent to him such correspondence as the Senator thought might prove influential in moulding the Secretary's thought. Thus, on March 23, 1896, we find him writing to Olney, and enclosing a letter from Mr. J. J. Storrow, which

"I think will interest you and which I will ask you to have the kindness to return to me after you have read it. Mr. Storrow is a wise and conservative man and I think his opinion in regard to the importance of

[78] Danish Minister for Foreign Affairs to Royal Minister at Washington, January 20, 1896, MS. D. F. O.

the Danish Islands carries a good deal of weight. I
hope you will not forget that matter among the greater
things."

Mr. Storrow's letter was very brief. He sincerely
hoped that the United States would soon acquire the
island of St. Thomas. To say

"nothing of its international value, it will be a notable
help towards extending our commerce with the West
Indies. It needs but a glance at the shops, in the
English Islands especially, and but a little talk with
the people to learn not only that they get a large proportion of things from the United States, but that
they look to us for those things they care most for."[79]

As the summer of 1896 approached, Senator Lodge
redoubled his efforts, and it is certainly true that he
was at least partly responsible for the planks in the
Republican platform relative to American foreign
policy. According to this platform the Republican
Party reasserted the Monroe Doctrine "in its full extent." Indeed, the platform went even further and
looked "forward to the eventual withdrawal of the
European powers from this hemisphere," in this way
repeating Sumner's desire for a "hemispheric flag
withdrawal."

But not content with this vigorous warning to
Europe to stay out of the Caribbean and adjacent regions, the platform contained a plank that specifically
called for the purchase of the Danish West Indies in

[79] Lodge to Olney, March 23, 1896, and J. J. Storrow to
Lodge, March 9, 1896, *Olney Papers*, Library of Congress.

order to secure for the United States a "proper and much-needed naval station in the West Indies."[80]

After the Republican victory in the elections of 1896, Senator Lodge felt more certain of his ground, and shortly after the inauguration of President McKinley he adopted every expedient to awaken national interest in the need of a naval station in the West Indies. With this end in view, on March 18, 1897, he re-introduced his resolution of January 3, 1896, which directed the Senate Committee on Foreign Relations to inquire whether the islands of St. Croix, St. John and St. Thomas could be purchased from the Danish Government as provided for by the treaty of October 24, 1867.[81]

This resolution evoked but little favorable response in the Senate, but there was prompt response and assistance in other quarters. In *Harper's Magazine* for September, 1897, Captain Mahan brought out a timely article entitled "A Twentieth-Century Outlook," in which he strongly argued for American expansion in the Caribbean in order to protect the projected isthmian canal. According to Mahan, it was evident that

[80] Edward Stanwood. *A History of the Presidency* (N. Y. 1912), vol. 1, pp. 535-36. In the platform of the Democratic Party for 1896 there was no mention of the purchase of the Danish West Indies, but there was a plank that stated that "the Monroe Doctrine, as originally declared and as interpreted by succeeding Presidents, is a permanent part of the foreign policy of the United States, and must at all times be maintained."

[81] *Congressional Record*, vol. 30, pt. 1, p. 52.

"wherever situated, whether at Panama or at Nicaragua, the fundamental meaning of the canal will be
that it advances by thousands of miles the frontiers
of European civilization in general, and of the United
States in particular; that it knits together the whole
system of American states enjoying that civilization as
in no other way they can be bound. In the Caribbean
Archipelago—the very domain of sea power, if ever
region could be called so—are the natural home and
center of those influences by which such a maritime
highway as a canal must be controlled, even as the control of the Suez Canal rests in the Mediterranean."[82]

Again, in the *Harper's Magazine* for the month of
October, Captain Mahan continued his arguments for
the need of an American naval station in the Caribbean. In this second article, "Strategic Features of
the Caribbean Sea and the Gulf of Mexico," he clearly
indicates the importance of the island of St. Thomas
in building up a defensive barrier in the Caribbean.[83]

This consistent propaganda in favor of the purchase
of the Danish West Indies attracted attention not only
in the United States but also in Denmark itself. In
December, 1896, a naturalized American named Niels
Grön, visited Copenhagen, and in the early part of
January, 1897, he had some conversations with Mr.
Vedel, the Director General of the Ministry of Foreign Affairs, with reference to the sale of the islands
to the United States. Mr. Vedel became so interested
in the subject that he brought the matter to the at-

[82] A. T. Mahan, *The Interest of America in Sea Power*,
pp. 260-61.

[83] A. T. Mahan, *The Interest of America in Sea Power*, pp.
276-299.

tention of Capt. E. Bluhme, chairman of the committee in the Folkething on West Indian affairs. Bluhme shared this interest and immediately called upon Mr. Grön and suggested that he return to the United States in order to ascertain whether the American Government would be inclined to purchase the Danish islands. Capt. Bluhme also assured Mr. Grön that he believed the Danish Government would "back him up" if he succeeded "in raising the issue."

With this encouragement, Grön returned to the United States where he made a careful study of the situation. In October, 1897, he returned to Copenhagen and reported his conviction that the American Government would be willing to open negotiations. He soon found, however, that the Danish Government was still very sensitive about the failure of the treaty of 1867, and would take no official initiative in the matter. It was finally decided to organize a representative committee of nine prominent Danish citizens to take charge of this delicate negotiation.[84] This committee, in the opinion of Mr. Grön, was the most powerful and most representative committee ever formed in Denmark, and having agreed upon a plan of procedure, had "no difficulty in securing from the prime minister and the Government the desired authority," which, in turn, they delegated to Mr. Grön.

[84] The committee was composed of the following members: Captain E. Bluhme, General J. J. Bahnson, Count M. Krag-Juel-Vind-Frijs, Octavius Hansen, Gustave Hansen, C. Hage, G. A. Hageman, C. Carstensen, and V. Horup.

It was soon realized that these informal negotiations might consume a long period of time and would necessitate a large expenditure of money. In order to meet this difficulty, Count Frijs suggested that in the event that a sale to the United States was actually effected, then a definite percentage of the purchase price should be paid to Mr. Grön and to those whom he should select as his associates in America. The committee thereupon agreed to fix this honorarium that was to go to Grön and his associates at ten per cent. of the purchase price of the islands, and the only financial responsibility of the Danish committee was to raise 5,000 kroner, or £275.

It was left entirely to the judgment of Mr. Grön to select any one he desired to form his American committee, although Mr. Hagemann did suggest the name of his friend, Mr. Henry H. Rogers, of the Standard Oil Company. This suggestion was gladly accepted by Mr. Grön, and as soon as he reached New York he appointed Mr. Rogers and Mr. Charles R. Flint as his American associates. These appointments were made in the early part of January, 1898, and the committee at once began to sound the officials in the Department of State. On March 23, Grön tried to convince Mr. Kasson, of the Department of State, that $7,500,000 was merely a nominal sum for such valuable islands as St. Thomas, St. John, and Santa Cruz, but Mr. Kasson held out for a smaller figure.   At length, Mr. Grön gave in and assured Mr. Kasson that notwithstanding the fact that he had no "official authority," yet he was certain that the Danish Government would accept an offer of $5,000,000.[85]

Shortly after this conversation between Mr. Kasson and Mr. Grön, Senator Lodge introduced on March 31, 1898, a bill providing for the purchase of the Danish West Indies on such terms as the President might in his discretion deem advisable. Five million dollars, or so much thereof as may be necessary was to be appropriated for the purchase.[86]

Along with this bill for the purchase of the Danish West Indies there was submitted by Senator Lodge a long report giving the history of the relations between Denmark and the United States relative to these islands. In conclusion the report observes as follows:

"The Danish Islands could easily be governed as a Territory—could be readily defended from attack, occupy a commanding strategic position, and are of incalculable value to the United States, not only as a part of the National defense, but as removing by their possession a very probable cause of foreign complications."[87]

On April 1, there was a long and acrimonious debate in the Senate concerning the acquisition of the Danish

[85] This account of the Grön mission to the United States is based upon the long statement of Grön on pages 46-47, of *House Report* No. 2749, 57 Cong., 1 sess., and on the book written by Miss Mathilde Lutken, entitled *Potentia* (Copenhagen, 1912). Miss Lutken claims that the book is written with the aid of the private papers of Niels Grön, but there is little information which is not contained in the statement published by Grön in the above-mentioned *House Report*.

[86] Senate Bill 4303, *Cong. Record.* vol. 31, pt. 4, p. 3409.

[87] *Sen. Ex. Rep.* No. 1, 57 Cong., 1 sess., p. 19.

islands. Senators Perkins and Elkins attacked the idea of purchase because they believed that it would involve the United States in heavy expenditures and unnecessary entanglements. Senator Teller thought that with the imminence of a war with Spain threatening America, the moment was not propitious for purchasing islands in the Caribbean. Senators Bacon, Gorman, and Pettigrew, also opposed any action on the bill introduced by Senator Lodge, Mr. Pettigrew remarking that

"he was willing to support the Administration in all reasonable and just measures in preparation for what appeared an inevitable war, but that he did not intend because of his loyalty in this respect to be induced to give his adherence to a measure that did not appeal to his judgment. The islands were fully 1500 miles from our coast, and to attempt to acquire them now would be in violation of our policy of not annexing territory which is not contiguous. . . . He said Senator Lodge had had a report in favor of the policy now undertaken in his desk for a year, and that the friends of the measure sought to get it through now under the stress of war pressure."

Senator Lodge replied briefly to this attack by admitting his "long advocacy of the acquisition of the Danish possessions." He then stated that he had "called upon the President with reference to the purchase of the islands, and not only he, but the naval officials, had concurred in the opinion that their possession would be of inestimable value in case of hostilities in the West Indies."[88]

[88] New York Times, April 1, 1898.

In the meantime, on March 25, 1898, Cornelius N. Bliss, the Secretary of the Interior, telegraphed to Mr. Rogers that the question of purchasing the Danish West Indies would be discussed in the Cabinet meeting on that day.   Mr. Grön at once called a meeting of his associates, and at 2:30 that afternoon, Mr. John D. Long, the Secretary of the Navy, told Mr. Grön over the telephone that "the matter had been favorably considered in the Cabinet and that the President had referred it to Mr. Kasson."   At four o'clock Mr. Kasson telephoned to Mr. Grön to suggest that he leave at once for Denmark, and on the following morning Mr. Grön sailed.[89]   When he reached Copenhagen, however, war was about to break out between the United States and Spain, and the Danish Government refused to conclude the negotiation because it would be a "diplomatic discourtesy to Spain."

Although it was apparent in the later summer of 1898 that the United States would secure an excellent

[89] *House Report* No. 2749, 57 Cong., 1 sess., p. 47.   On March 31, 1898, the New York *Times* published an editorial which strongly favored the purchase of the Danish islands. It was evident that "a very strong case might be made out . . . for our acquisition of St. Thomas 'on general principles.' But, of course the case is immensely strengthened by the particular exigency which now presents itself.   The island lies just to the eastward and within sight of Porto Rico and in the track of the traffic between Spain and what remains of her American possessions. . . . Apparently nothing should or could prevent that consummation purchase by the United States unless Denmark puts an exorbitant price upon a piece of property which is of less than no use to her.   But this is not to be assumed."

naval station either in Porto Rico or in Cuba, still the
interest in the purchase of the Danish West Indies
did not disappear, and Senator Cushman K. Davis,
while serving at Paris on the American Peace Commission, confided to Mr. Grön, October 19, 1898, that
"the United States must and will have the harbor of
St. Thomas."[90]   After learning of this statement, the
Danish Committee that had been directing the unofficial negotiations of Mr. Grön, advised him in November, 1898, to "have the matter brought up in America
whenever the opportune moment should appear."   It
was while Mr. Grön was in America attempting to
carry out these instructions that a certain Captain
Christmas Dirckinck Holmfeld appeared upon the
scene and thus ushered in the strange interlude that
is the subject of the next chapter.

[90] *H. Rep.*, 2749, op. cit., p. 47. In an interesting autobiography entitled, *Memories of an Active Life* (N. Y. 1923), pp.
184-185, Mr. Charles R. Flint tells of his relations with Mr.
Niels Grön and Mr. H. H. Rogers with reference to the proposed annexation of the Danish West Indies. Thus: "When
it seemed impossible to avoid war with Spain, President
McKinley sent for me. . . . President McKinley, not wanting
it to appear that the United States was actively preparing for
war, decided to take advantage of my being in a position to
negotiate for war vessels without it being manifest that such
negotiations were in the interest of the United States. I had
been able to deliver to Japan the Armstrong cruiser *Esmeralda,*
. . .so that when I followed President McKinley's instructions the natural inference was that I was acting for Japan.
. . . Utilizing the cable I immediately located every available
warship in the world. . . . I then brought up the question of
the purchase of the Danish West Indies. The King of Denmark . . . appointed a committee of prominent Danes with

power to sell the Islands, and that Committee sent an agent to H. H. Rogers and myself to request us to offer them to the United States Government. I remarked to the President that Bradford, who was then in charge of coal supplies, had said that the Danish West Indies would be of great value in the event of war with Spain, and I said that Mr. Rogers and I had been requested to offer to sell those islands to the United States Government. The President then asked me to name the price. I replied: 'Five million dollars.' He answered: 'I will have a bill introduced in the Senate tomorrow authorizing the purchase.' The bill was prepared, but Senator Elkins made it manifest that he would oppose it, and, as the President wanted all legislation regarding the war to be unanimous, the bill was withdrawn."

CHAPTER IV

A Strange Interlude—The Christmas Mission

In the early months of 1899 when Niels Grön had
resumed his task of trying in an unofficial way to arrange for a cession of the Danish West Indies to the
United States, there was a movement in Copenhagen
to effect this same end. On February 11, 1899, Mr.
Swenson, the American Minister at Copenhagen, wrote
to Secretary Hay to inform him that a Danish citizen
"of high commercial and political standing," had recently called at the Legation to acquaint him of the
fact that the Danish Government was ready to sell
those islands to the United States for a "bagatelle—
possibly one million dollars." The reason for this inclination to sell was because of the growing cost of
the administration of the islands which was creating
an annual deficit of some 500,000 kroner. Also, the
islands had little strategic value to Denmark but were
of evident importance to the United States especially
in view of the proposed construction of an isthmian
canal.

Swenson believed it wise to follow up this bit of
diplomatic kite-flying, so he repaired at once to the
Foreign Office to discuss the situation. When he inquired whether he should write to the Secretary of
State and advise him of the favorable disposition on
the part of the Danish Government, both the Danish

Foreign Minister and the Director General of the Foreign Office expressed the opinion that their Government would receive "in a most friendly spirit such offer as the United States might wish to make for the islands." In this regard Mr. Swenson thought that the islands could be bought for about $1,500,000.[1]

While Secretary Hay was considering just how to follow up these advances there appeared in Washington to a colorful adventurer named Captain Walter von Christmas Dirckinck-Holmfeld. Captain Christmas had been dismissed from the Danish Navy for certain indiscretions, and in looking around for some means to recoup his fortunes he decided to develop the commercial possibilities of the fine harbor of Coral Bay on the east side of the island of St. John. It was impossible to secure adequate capital in Denmark, so Christmas went to Germany where he succeeded in establishing a syndicate known as "Die Kolonial und Handelsgesellschaft St. Jun." While it would be difficult for the German Government to secure the island of St. John by direct purchase from Denmark, yet American opposition could be obviated by indirect methods. Through purchases by the Hamburg-American Line of the water-front in the harbor of Coral Bay, complete control could be secured over the naval facilities in one of the best ports in the West Indies. All that was lacking were certain concessions from the Danish Government. When these could not be secured,

[1] Swenson to Hay, February 11, 1899, MS. Dept of State, Denmark, Desp., vol. 22.

Captain Christmas abandoned his undertaking, and learning of the efforts of the Danish Committee to arrange for the sale of the islands through the agency of Niels Grön, he decided to engage in this new venture.[2]

It will be remembered that the Danish Committee had agreed that Niels Grön and his American Committee should have as a reward for their labors a commission of ten per cent. of the purchase price of the islands. This feature is what attracted the notice of Captain Christmas, and he believed that Grön and his American associates had tired of their task and would place little opposition in the way of a new attempt to dispose of the islands. Confident of his abil-

[2] See the report of Captain Christmas to the Danish Government, October 1, 1900, in *H. Rep.*, no. 2749, 57 Cong., 1 sess., pp. 2 ff., and New York *Times*, May 1, 1900. I was suspicious of the printed text of this report of Captain Christmas, so I secured the services of an able Danish scholar, Mrs. Elizabeth Hude, of Copenhagen, to compare the original copy of the Christmas *Report* in the Danish Foreign Office with the printed copy in *House Report*, no. 2749, and at once discovered that in some cases there are wide divergencies. Where these divergencies have been of considerable moment, I have used the original version. In the *Dansk Biografisk Haandleksikon* (Copenhagen, 1920), p. 323, there is a short biography of Captain Christmas. I have been assured by Mr. J. O. Bro-Jorgensen, a well-informed Danish scholar, that Captain Christmas was not a "mere adventurer." His dismissal from the Danish Navy in 1894 was generally regarded in Denmark as an "unreasonably hard punishment for quite an ordinary military oversight." This dismissal was later "recalled," and he "was discharged with assurances of royal favour." Captain Christmas died in 1924.

ity to arrange for the cession of the islands to the United States, Christmas interviewed one of the Danish officials named Herr Schlichtkrull, who definitely encouraged him to carry on the project. Christmas next had a conversation with the Danish Prime Minister who was very skeptical concerning the possibility of accomplishing "anything in America." But when Christmas inquired as to whether he could count on the same commission that had been promised to Niels Grön and his associates, the Prime Minister assumed a "very obliging attitude" and assured him that the commission would be "precisely the same." He also expressed to Christmas his abhorrence

"for the political situation in America, which made it necessary to offer money in order to bring a political action, like that of transferring the islands, to a successful termination, but that he had long ago discovered the necessity for making such a money sacrifice, and he was ready to grant it."

With reference to the purchase price of the islands, the Prime Minister would not commit himself. He did, however, unburden himself to Christmas as follows:

"It is not at all the idea to sell the islands. To that thought is His Majesty opposed. What could be done is to arrange a transfer on such conditions that we sustain no loss, but it must not appear that we *sell* . . . It must constantly be remembered that what must be done is to get the American Government to take the first step towards acquiring the islands. The Danish Government is absolutely ignorant of your journey and undertaking."[3]

[3] *Christmas Report,* MS. D. F. O.

In October, 1899, Christmas left for the United States, and as soon as he arrived in New York he immediately got in touch with a lawyer named Carl Fischer-Hansen. In his correspondence with Mr. Fischer-Hansen, Christmas had already referred to his project for the sale of the Danish West Indies to the United States, and now he disclosed to him the fact that he had had "an interview with Prime Minister Hörring," who had assured him that if he could "bring about some overt act on the part of America," he would then be appointed as a "special agent for the sale."

Captain Christmas then inquired whether Mr. Fischer-Hansen would be willing to co-operate in this undertaking. When Mr. Fischer-Hansen expressed a desire to know just what would be expected of him, Christmas replied:

"If you and I divide the work between us, I would take care of the Danish end. I would be Denmark's representative to receive anything that America might send there, and you, on the other hand, are to open the work here and see that America does make some offer and take the initiative."

At this point Mr. Fischer-Hansen became interested in the matter of compensation, whereupon Captain Christmas remarked that everything depended on "the price America would pay." Captain Christmas then hastened to assure Fischer-Hansen that Denmark would "pay liberally."[4]

[4] *H. Rep.*, 2749, pp. 65-66.

Fischer-Hansen was distinctly interested in this scheme of Captain Christmas, and especially in the possibility that he would be appointed by the Danish Government as its "official attorney." In order to carry on the delicate negotiations necessary to bring about an offer from the American Government for the Danish Islands it was deemed wise to secure the services of Abner McKinley, a brother of President McKinley. Abner, however, was a man of fine sensibilities, and he seemed fearful that because of his relationship to the President it would be improper for him to accept even the office of "associate attorney" in this matter.

At this point, the narratives of Captain Christmas and Fischer-Hansen show a material difference. According to Fischer-Hansen, after Abner McKinley had loftily rejected all offers to be associated with Captain Christmas, advances were then made to a Colonel Brown who was an intimate friend of President McKinley. Brown was commissioned to "sound out" the President with reference to the purchase of the Danish Islands, and he lost no time in talking over the question with both President McKinley and Secretary Hay. He then returned to New York and confided to Fischer-Hansen that the State Department was ready to begin negotiations.

When Fischer-Hansen broke this good news to Captain Christmas, the latter immediately brought up the matter of compensation that would be paid to the "official attorney." Fischer-Hansen, however, at once waved aside all thought of mere money compensation, and assured Christmas that he did not "want a single cent" for his services. All that he desired was to act as the "official attorney" of the Danish Government in any negotiations for the purchase of the Danish West Indies.

Christmas promised Fischer-Hansen that his wishes in this matter would be respected. Then, according to the narrative of Fischer-Hansen, Christmas went to Washington

"where he had an interview with President McKinley, and President McKinley sent him to Secretary Hay, and he had a very lengthy interview with Secretary Hay, the result of which was Secretary Hay sent him to Admiral Bradford and told him to work together with Admiral Bradford in going over the maps and charts etc., and Admiral Bradford was to report to Secretary Hay."[5]

In the Christmas narrative as given in *House Report* no. 2749, there is a distinctly different version of the interview that McKinley granted to Christmas.[6] From this account it would appear that this

[5] *H. Rep.*, 2749, pp. 66-67.

[6] In the Christmas *Report* (No. 2749) there is repeated mention of official letters that passed between Christmas and the Danish Foreign Office. Upon inquiry at the Danish Foreign Office I was informed that "there exist no reports of any kind from Walter Christmas to the Foreign Ministry" with the exception of the long statement contained in *House Report* No. 2749. This general statement of Captain Christmas was not only transmitted "to the Foreign Ministry but also to others, and therefore cannot be regarded as an actual 'report' to the Ministry." The above statement was made by Dr. Hejls, the Keeper of the Archives of the Foreign Ministry.

interview was secured through the agency of the banking firm of Seligman and Company, New York City. It happened that a Mr. Scott, a wealthy shipbuilder of San Francisco, was visiting New York City, and the Seligmans, knowing that Mr. Scott was friendly with President McKinley, asked him to introduce Captain Christmas to the President. Mr. Scott complied with this request, and Captain Christmas was received by President McKinley "most cordially." Christmas promptly adverted to the topic of the purchase of the Danish West Indies, assuring the President that Denmark would consider "with favor a proposition from the Americans for the transfer of the islands on conditions which should prove fair to the inhabitants of the colonies." Christmas also made it clear to the President that he acted entirely on his "own responsibility, had no connection with the Danish Government," and was actuated simply by his "own pecuniary interest in such a sale."

When the President remarked that he had always "considered it natural and right" for America to purchase these islands which had "for a long time been on the market," Captain Christmas was quick to inform the Chief Executive that the King of Denmark would "never allow his colonies 'to be on the market.'" His Majesty found it "out of harmony with the dignity of the country to sell any part of the land, but that it would be of much economic advantage to the islands to get it under the large Republic, and since His Majesty has only the good of his subjects at heart," he would not, therefore, oppose the cession of the islands to the United States.

The President finally advised Captain Christmas to talk the matter over with Secretary Hay. On the following morning Christmas called at the Department of State with a large chart and a descriptive pamphlet on conditions in the West Indies, but he soon discovered that Mr. Hay appeared to know everything regarding the islands. The chart showing the fine harbor on the island of St. John did, however, attract the attention of John Hay. The next day, Captain Christmas had another interview with Secretary Hay, and upon this occasion Admiral Bradford was also present. Both the Secretary of State and Admiral Bradford asked numerous questions about the harbor and the naval facilities on the island of St. John, and Christmas felt certain that their interest was very real.

After the termination of this second interview, Christmas went to New York where he remained until November 20, when he received a letter from the Secretary of State recalling him to Washington. Mr. Hay now informed him that he had made investigations relative to the situation in the Caribbean and also with reference to the harbor on the island of St. John. These investigations had convinced him that all the statements of Captain Christmas "were in accordance with the actual facts," and that therefore he was ready "to take steps to begin negotiations with the Danish Government for securing the Danish colonies."

Captain Christmas was then "fetched downstairs"

for a conversation with Admiral Bradford. The Admiral was astonished

"at the good condition of the harbour and at its value as a war station. On my last visit I had told him that the English Admiralty must possess a harbour chart similar to mine, as the English had measured the harbour in 1807 because they thought at that time of turning it into a naval station. This naval chart had been found by the Naval Attaché in London and it goes without saying that the corroboration which was gained of the correctness of my statements had a particularly favorable effect on my position to Admiral Bradford and Mr. John Hay."

Bradford himself was so enthusiastic about the proposition to acquire the Danish islands that he followed Captain Christmas into the hall of the State, War and Navy Departments building and impulsively assured him as follows:

"I will let you know that I not only wish the islands for the Navy, but I intend to demand them."[7]

When we test the verity of the Christmas narrative with all the available evidence concerning the introduction of the Danish captain to President McKinley, we discover that the story of Christmas is more reliable than that of Mr. Fischer-Hansen, who served for a time as a lawyer for the Christmas project and then, when Christmas became involved in difficulties, strongly denounced his former employer. According to Fischer-Hansen, it was through a Colonel Brown

[7] *Christmas Report,* MS. D. F. O.

that Christmas secured his introduction to President McKinley,[8] while Christmas himself says that the introduction was arranged by the banking firm of J. and W. Seligman and Company, through their friend Mr. Scott, of San Francisco.

In his testimony before the select Committee of the House of Representatives on April 7, 1902, Mr. Isaac N. Seligman corroborates the story of Captain Christmas in this regard,[9] and in the Department of State there is a letter to the same effect. It is from J. and W. Seligman to John Addison Porter, private secretary to President McKinley, and reads as follows:

"We take the liberty of handing this letter to Captain W. v. Christmas Dirckinck-Holmfeld, who desires, if possible, to have an interview with the President on a matter of importance. I trust, dear sir, that we are not taking up the time of the President, and would not address this letter did we not think the subject would interest the President. Thanking you in advance for

[8] See *ante*, pp. 223-24.

[9] *H. Rep.*, 2749, pp. 110-111. In describing his relations with Captain Christmas, Isaac N. Seligman informed the select committee of the House of Representatives that Christmas had come to the office of the firm in October, or November of 1899, and stated that "he was the representative of the Danish Government unofficially, in the matter of the sale of the West Indian islands to be made to the United States, and that he was substantially directed by his Government, also unofficially, to say to it that the sale could take place on a fair basis . . . and that he was desirous of obtaining the instrumentality of reputable bankers to undertake the transmission of the money on commission, etc., and asked us whether we would do it. We told him yes; that we would be very glad to do it."

any courtesy you may extend to Captain Dirckinck-Holmfeld, we are etc."[10]

It would appear, therefore, that the early part of the Christmas narrative is substantially correct. And even in the latter portions of his story, though many statements are certainly fictitious, there are occasional gleams of truth.

Christmas, therefore, had been able to meet both President McKinley and Secretary Hay, and had made a somewhat favorable impression. Hay had informed him that inasmuch as the mission was an informal one without direct authority from the Danish Government, he would highly appreciate it if Captain Christmas "would accompany a trusted diplomat to Copenhagen and secure for him a secret meeting with the chief of the Danish Government."[11] On November 28, 1899, Captain Christmas received two letters from Secretary Hay, one of which informed him that the Secretary of State had written to the American ambassador in London announcing the early arrival of Christmas in that city, and the other one was an introduction to Mr. Henry White, the first secretary of the American embassy in London.[12]   After the receipt

[10] November 8, 1899, MS. Department of State, *Miscellaneous Letters.*

[11] *H. Rep.* 2749, the *narrative* of Captain Christmas, which consists of the reproduction of a report Christmas made to the Danish Government on October 1, 1900, p. 9.

[12] This *narrative* of Captain Christmas is quite faulty with reference to the incidents connected with his meeting with Henry White. He is incorrect in the first place in speaking

of these letters, Christmas took passage for London, where, on December 9, he called at the American embassy to present his letter of introduction to Henry White.

In the meantime, on November 28, Secretary Hay had written to Henry White in regard to the Christmas mission. The pertinent portions of this letter are as follows:

"A Danish gentleman, Captain W. von Christmas Dirckinck-Holmfeld, has been here for some days, and is now about returning to Denmark. He represents that he is authorized by the Danish Government to make known to the Government of the United States that Denmark is no longer able to retain the West India Islands: that it is thought proper, first, to ascertain whether the United States is inclined to enter into negotiations for their cession; and if this is not the case, to offer them in succession to several of the leading European powers. He says that Denmark expects no money payment whatever, but would require that the United States assume the debt of the Islands, St. Thomas, St. John and St. Croix, to the amount more or less of three and a half millions of dollars.

"Mr. Christmas brings no credentials whatever: he is not even introduced by his Minister. He explains this by saying that the Danish Government having sustained a severe rebuff from the United States Senate in Mr. Seward's time, cannot initiate new negotiations

---

of receiving a letter from John Hay to Joseph Choate, the American Minister in London. The letter of introduction was to Henry White. It is also true that Christmas called at the American embassy on December 9, not December 12, and he had his interview at Dover with Henry White on December 9, not December 12.

on this subject without being assured of the reception they are to meet with.

"I have thought the matter of sufficient importance to ask Captain Christmas to call at our Embassy in London and to make himself known to you.

"My purpose is, if it suits your convenience and that of our Ambassador, to ask you to go to Copenhagen, in the strictest privacy, and to have an interview with the Danish Minister of Finance which Mr. v. Christmas professes to be able to arrange for you. Without committing this Government to any definite action, you will, if practicable, ascertain the intentions of the Danish Government in regard to the Islands: the exact terms they will require, in case this Government wishes to take them over: the debt of the Islands, its amount and character, where held and how payable.

"As this proceeding is entirely private and unofficial, it will not be necessary for you to report it to our Minister in Copenhagen. Make your stay there as short as possible. On your return to London, please send me a brief resumé by cable and a fuller report in writing."[13]

When Captain Christmas called at the American Embassy on December 9, he discovered that Henry White had gone to Dover, so he hastened there and had an interview with him during which he assured Mr. White that the Danish Prime Minister would be happy to receive him, and would also acquaint him with the earnest desire of the Danish Government to sell the islands to the United States, It was impossible, however, for Henry White to leave immediately for Copenhagen. Mrs. White was seriously ill, so it would be necessary for her to be removed at once to southern

[13] Hay to White, November 28, 1899, MS. *White Papers*, Library of Congress.

France, after which Mr. White would hasten to the Danish capital.[14]

It was during this interview that Christmas may well have handed to Henry White the following memorandum which is preserved in the *White Papers,* in the Library of Congress:

"The Danish Colonies in the West Indies are: St. Thomas, St. Croix and St. John.

"The colonies are a heavy burden on the Danish budget, indebted as they are from the time of the abolishment of slavery. The debt of the colonies is nearly $3,000,000.

"In time of war Denmark is not able to protect these islands, the Danish navy being too weak, and the warships being only built for the purpose of the coast defense.

"The Danish subjects in the West Indies are all in favor of the idea of becoming American citizens. Under the United States' flag they will be well protected and have far better chances for their trade, the cultivation of sugar, etc.

"These are the reasons why the Danish Government wish to hand over the Islands to the United States, the natural protector and ruler of West Indian lands and waters.

"The United States Government nearly fifty years ago offered to take the Danish islands, but an earthquake, which occurred just before the final transaction was completed, impressed them so unfavorably that the negotiations were stopped.

"Once more the question was taken up, but the outbreak of the American-Spanish War put an end to the negotiations.

[14] Letter of Henry White to Mr. John Dalzell, of the Select Committee of the House of Representatives on the Purchase of the Danish West Indies, April 23, 1902, in *H. Rep.,* 2749, p. 115.

"The Danish Government is perfectly willing to accept any suitable offer from the United States Government.

"For the United States the acquisition of the Danish West Indian Colonies means a practical rounding off of the West Indian possessions with three really valuable islands.

"St. Thomas is well known for its good harbor, important for the trade in these waters. St. Croix is one of the most fertile sugar growing islands in the West Indies. St. John is too, very fertile, rich in minerals and pine forests, and has one of the best harbors in these waters.

"The natural harbor of St. John—Coral Bay—is larger, deeper and better protected than that of St. Thomas. A splendid coaling station may be arranged here. This harbor might become the stronghold of the United States Navy in West Indian waters, the very sally-port to south and east. This harbor is of the greatest strategic importance, easy to defend and large enough to hold the whole of the United States Navy."

W. VON CHRISTMAS DIRCKINCK-HOLMFELD.

October 25, 1899.

There was little in this memorandum that was new to Henry White, and its influence must have been slight. Christmas, however, was not content with the submission of a mere memorandum. He had recently been a visitor to the Danish West Indies, had made a careful study of their strategic features, and could also confide to White the danger from German desires for colonial expansion. Christmas was a charming traveling companion, and he even accompanied White as far as Paris in an endeavor favorably to impress him.

After leaving Henry White *en route* for southern

France, Christmas went to Copenhagen to talk things over with the Danish Foreign Office. Before he arrived there it happened that a friend of his, Dr. F. Hansen, who had accompanied him from New York, but who had not gone on to Dover to meet Henry White, had secured an audience with the Crown Prince of Denmark, at that time acting as Regent during the King's absence. After relating all that had transpired during the stay of Captain Christmas in America, he informed the Crown Prince of the expected visit of Henry White to Copenhagen. His Royal Highness at once expressed his doubt regarding

"the possibility of bringing the matter to an early termination. It had several times failed just as it was almost completed."[15]

On December 16, 1899, Christmas arrived at Copenhagen and at once presented himself to Prime Minister Hörring. When Christmas told him how the negotiations had progressed and that Henry White was shortly to arrive in Copenhagen, the Prime Minister is alleged to have exclaimed:

"Well, thanks to God, that the sale now can be brought about. I must compliment you for what you have accomplished. I had really not believed that it would have been possible for you."[16]

The Prime Minister then inquired about the conditions of the proposed cession to the United States, and Christmas explained how he had guarded the

15 *H. Rep.*, 2749, p. 10.
16 *Ibid.*, p. 11.

honor of the Danish Government by informing President McKinley that the proposed cession was no mere business arrangement. Denmark did not wish to secure any pecuniary advantage but wished merely to provide against any actual loss in the transaction. The Prime Minister then remarked that it would be necessary to receive at least $4,000,000 for the islands in order to liquidate the indebtedness that had been incurred by the Danish Government for the benefit of the inhabitants of the islands and the other expenses attendant upon the cession to the United States. To this figure Christmas made no demur, for he was certain that "the size of the sum would play an unimportant part."[17]

Christmas then adverted to the question of the ten per cent. commission he was to receive for a successful conclusion of the negotiations, and he informed the Prime Minister of the sums he had promised to prominent Americans like Abner McKinley, and to certain press associations in Washington and in New York. He also spoke of his understanding with J. & W. Seligman & Company. The Prime Minister at once expressed his opinion that the political conditions in the United States were "horrible," and that it would be perfectly proper for Captain Christmas to count upon his commission of ten per cent. but "not any more." At this point Captain Christmas voiced some misgivings as to whether the ten per cent. commission would be adequate to cover all the expenses incident to pushing

[17] *H. Rep.*, 2749, p. 11.

the treaty through in the United States. Would it be possible to secure additional funds in Denmark for the purpose of affording a worth while compensation to Christmas himself? To this direct inquiry the Prime Minister could only answer that he would do his best to secure this for Christmas, but it was well to bear in mind how "narrow-minded" the peasant members of the Rigsdag were.[18]

The next move of Captain Christmas was to discuss the situation with some of the leading members of the Danish unofficial committee that had in 1897 commissioned Niels Grön to do what he could to arrange for a cession of the Danish West Indies to the United States. These members, including such well-known Danes as G. A. Hagemann, E. G. Hansen, and General J. J. Bahnson, appeared to be well satisfied with the work that Christmas had accomplished, but they did advise a close co-operation with Niels Grön and H. H. Rogers.

These activities were, of course, quite important to Christmas as a preparation for his return to America, but they did not cause him to overlook the necessity of retaining the respect and good-will of Henry White, who was soon to be expected in Copenhagen. On December 14, 1899, he sent the following telegram to White:

"Prime Minister delighted to receive you. When do you arrive?"[19]

[18] *Ibid.*, p. 11.
[19] Christmas to White, December 14, 1899, MS. *White Papers*, Library of Congress.

White replied at once:

· "Ne peux arriver que mardi soir. Priere arranger entrevue mercredi matin."

A final telegram from White to Christmas was sent from Hamburg:

"Just leaving here, expecting to arrive tonight."[20]

On December 19, White arrived in Copenhagen, and was met by Christmas who has a dubious account in his *narrative* as to how he schooled his American visitor for his audience with the Danish Foreign Minister. It happened that the Prime Minister, Mr. Hörring, was not entirely at ease in carrying on a conversation in English, French, or German, so it was decided that White should have an audience with Admiral Ravn, the Foreign Minister, who was more versatile in this regard. But before Henry White met Admiral Ravn on the morning of December 20, Christmas claims that he instructed White as to just what to say, and that after the conference was over White assured him that "he had used the very words" that had been supplied by Christmas.[21] White, however, afterwards denied that he had asked Christmas for assistance as to the manner in which he should "broach the question to the minister," and stated that he had "never had any doubt" as to the proper procedure.[22]

[20] New York *Herald,* April 11, 1902.

[21] *H. Rep.,* 2749, p. 13.

[22] *Ibid.,* p. 116, letter of Henry White to the chairman of the Select Committee on Purchase of the Danish West Indies. April 23, 1902.

On December 20, White was accompanied to the
Danish Foreign Office by Captain Christmas, and was
"promptly received alone by the Minister." After the
customary courtesies, White stated that the object of
his visit was to "inquire confidentially what the intentions of his Government might be in respect to the
Danish West India Islands of St. Thomas, St. John
and St. Croix—an intimation having reached my Government that Denmark is willing to cede them to
another Power."

Admiral Ravn admitted that the Danish Government was willing to cede the islands for a proper consideration, but he refused to name the sum. However,
if the United States should be disposed to make an
offer for the islands it would be "seriously considered
by the Danish Government." When Henry White
pressed him for further details concerning an approximate figure that would be satisfactory to the Danish
Government, Ravn finally admitted that he thought
that

"between four and five millions of dollars would probably cover the advances made by the Treasury and also
the amount required for the capitalization of certain
pensions which would be necessary in the event of the
cession of the islands to another Power."

White then asked Admiral Ravn about the indebtedness of the islands, whereupon the Admiral turned him
over to two officials from the Ministry of Finance who
furnished White with the budget figures of the governments of the three islands. From these it would appear

that the revenue of St. Thomas and St. John for the current year was estimated at $95,520, and the expenditure at $179,186, thereby showing a deficit of considerable proportions. The revenue of St. Croix was $154,865, while the expenditure was placed at $253,073.64. The deficit for the three islands was $181,874, which was a heavy drain on the Danish treasury. In fact, it was in this manner that the indebtedness of the islands to the Danish Government was created, for again and again loans had been made to enable the island governments to balance their budgets. Altogether, it was estimated that the debt of the islands including loans, accumulated interest, and circulating West Indian credit bills, amounted to some 9,304,762 kroner. To this amount would also have to be added the charge that would arise upon the Danish treasury from the capitalization of existing pensions—4,662,000 kroner, making a total of 13,966,762 kroner.[23]

[23] White to Hay, December 23, 1899, MS. *White Papers,* Library of Congress. In the New York *Herald, April* 11, 1902, the correspondent at Copenhagen claims to have seen a document which contained the following memorandum of Henry White relative to his conversations with Admiral Ravn: "I am to ask, first, the intentions of the Danish Government with regard to the islands; secondly, the exact terms they will require if the United States wishes to take them over; thirdly, the amount of debt of the colonies, where it is held and how it is payable."

In the Danish *Foreign Office* there is an undated memorandum in the handwriting of Chamberlain Krag which deals with this conference between Henry White and Admiral Ravn. The pertinent portion of the memorandum reads as follows: "W. addressed the question to the Foreign Minister whether

On December 22, 1899, we find White back in London writing a long and interesting letter to Secretary Hay concerning the cession of the islands to the · United States. He had

"no doubt that Denmark is most anxious to be rid of the islands; but the coyness of the Government about appearing so to be, is quite comic. The night I arrived a Foreign Office official came late to see Christmas with whom I was dining to inquire in consequence of a telegram from the King, whether I thoroughly understood that the Danish Government was not offering us the islands. It seems also that they had a Cabinet Council on me for days before my arrival and that the Crown Prince had been constantly telegraphing the King, who takes a deep personal interest in the matter and, while very anxious to be rid of the islands, wishes to do the best he can for their welfare and yet will not hear of their being offered to us in view of what he considers the discourteous way he was treated formerly in the same connection by the Senate.

"From your letter I infer that Christmas was entirely mistaken on one point; viz., that no money payment would be required, as the only mode of assuming the debt would be its repayment to the Danish Treasury to which alone it is owing and in the form of

---

Denmark would sell the Islands, and received the answer that an offer from the United States would be taken into conscientious consideration. W. then spoke with the director of the Foreign Ministry who during the conference with the director of the Colonial Office, had brought him the budget of the Danish West Indian Islands. He gave W. a copy of these and wrote down and gave him a list of the State exchequer's claims on the Colonial exchequers and the sugar boileries, the registered value of the State plantations, as well as the approximate amount that the pensions would make when capitalized, in case of the alienation of the Islands."

bonds or tangible securities as I understand the matter. So that the government's only idea of a cession of the islands is on the basis of a money payment. I have reported what the Minister told me and Christmas says that he is absolutely certain that 3½ millions in cash will be accepted. He seems to have a good position in Denmark. I may add that I think they were gratified at your sending me to make the inquiry as I am known to a good many of the leading people there and particularly to the King, who was absent . . . with his daughter but who, when we were last at Copenhagen asked us to dine at Bernstorff Palace and was particularly kind to us. I did not infer that our Minister there is of much account or influence. The Foreign Minister told me however that the latter had asked him recently whether there is anything in the rumored overtures on our part for the purchase of the islands, and that he had replied in the negative. I did not communicate with our Minister in accordance with your suggestion nor did I go to see any of my friends there. . . . If what Christmas says as to Coral Harbor in St. John be true, and he tells me that Admiral Bradford confirms it—there is no doubt that it will make an admirable and admirably situated coaling station for us and would not be dear at 3½ millions."[24]

This visit of Henry White to Copenhagen must have convinced the Danish Government that the United States was ready to commence negotiations, for if we can believe the Christmas *narrative,* preparations were at once made to send Captain Christmas back to Washington. It happened that he had exhausted all the funds at his disposal, so it was arranged that Mr. Hagemann should advance him a letter of credit for 6,000 kroner which should eventually be repaid

[24] White to Hay, December 22, 1899, MS. *White Papers.*

out of the ten per cent. commission Christmas was to receive for effecting the sale of the islands to the United States.[25]

On December 27, 1899, Henry White cabled in cipher to Secretary Hay as follows:

"Christmas tells me to cable you that he leaves in a week for Washington with full instructions, whatever that may mean."[26]

From the text of this cablegram it would seem that Christmas must have had some definite arrangement with the Danish Prime Minister. Indeed, according to the Christmas *narrative,* the Danish Government recognized that it was "necessary" for Christmas to return to America because he had all the "threads" of the negotiations in his hands, and knew "the persons who should agitate during the coming negotiations and acts in Congress." Moreover, says Christmas, Henry White had "urgently advised the foreign minister to let me complete what I had begun, since I, as Mr. White expressed it, was *personae gratissima* in Washington."[27]

Some years later when Henry White read these warm words of approval in the published Christmas report, he vigorously denied that he had ever uttered them. According to his letter to Mr. Dalzell, April 23, 1902, the Christmas *narrative* was entirely untrue

[25] *H. Rep.,* 2749, p. 15.

[26] White to Hay, December 27, 1899, MS. Dept. of State, *Miscellaneous Letters.*

[27] *H. Rep.,* 2749, pp. 14-15.

in this regard. Captain Christmas had never even hinted

"at any idea on his part that it would be necessary for him to return to the United States in order to 'agitate during the coming negotiations and acts of Congress,' and it is untrue that I 'urgently advised the foreign minister to let him complete what he had begun,' as I was wholly unaware that he had done anything but notify our Government privately that Denmark wished to sell the islands and undertake to bring about a meeting between a representative of our Government and a member of that of Denmark. On the contrary, in the course of my interview with the minister I said to him that if my Government should decide to enter into negotiations for the purchase of the islands, which I was not authorized to do, such negotiations would be initiated and conducted through the ordinary diplomatic channels,"[28]

But despite this good advice from Henry White with reference to conducting the negotiations through the "ordinary diplomatic channels," the Danish Prime Minister must have given Christmas some kind of authorization to go to Washington and continue his efforts there, and that is the explanation of Christmas's request to Henry White to cable Washington that he was soon leaving with "full instructions." After sending this cable to John Hay, December 27, 1899, Henry White, on the following day, wrote a letter in which he gave further impressions concerning the situation in Copenhagen. With regard to the cablegram announcing the return of Christmas to Washington, he remarked that it seemed to him that Christmas was

[28] *Ibid.*, p. 116.

"so afraid that we won't offer for the islands that he is going out to poke matters up for fear the iron may cool off. I was not in Copenhagen long enough to find out why he is personally so very keen as he evidently is to unload the islands. It seems hardly credible that patriotism alone would account for it. I have also thought since my report was sent off a week ago that I ought perhaps to have said something in it about the advantages of the islands to us from a naval point of view and also to have alluded to the fact that when they are, if ever, ours, and especially if they enjoy our tariff—that is to say if they were to come under our tariff system as the President has so wisely recommended that Porto Rico shall do, their deficits will disappear in all probability, and doubtless become surpluses. . . . But in the first place I wrote the report in a hurry amid many interruptions during the first day of my return to the Embassy and in the second I thought you must be thoroughly posted by Admiral Bradford as to the advantages of the islands and wanted no advice from me on that point, but only information as to the exact position of the Danish Government in the matter and the status of the debt. If you would like anything further added as a counter-poise to the discouraging statements about the deficits, I shall gladly insert it as I am in favor of our acquiring the islands."[29]

White was too keen to be imposed upon by Christmas, so he quickly realized that there was some economic basis for the patriotic professions of the captain relative to arranging for a sale of the Danish West Indies to the United States. Nevertheless, he was in favor of the acquisition of the islands for strategic reasons even though negotiations so far seemed to be in the hands of a self-seeking adventurer who tried

[29] White to Hay, December 28, 1899, MS. *White Papers.*

to mask his motives. To be successful these negotiations would have to be secret in order to obviate European interference, and for this reason the Department of State had hoped to keep the mission of Henry White to Copenhagen out of the public press, but on January 1, 1900, the following item from their Copenhagen correspondent appeared in the London *Daily Mail* and was copied in American newspapers:

"The sale of the Danish West Indies to the United States bids fair to be accomplished. The Danish Captain Christmas, who has influential connections in the United States, and who has secured the support of President McKinley, Admiral Dewey, and a number of influential American Senators, is acting as intermediary between the two Governments, direct official communication being impossible for Denmark after repeated failures in previous attempts. For several days an attache of one of the principal United States Embassies has been here, having long interviews with the Danish Minister of Finance, Dr. Hörring, and this week Captain Christmas will go to Washington to assist the publication of America's official offer. No opposition is expected from King Christian. The price has been fixed at $4,000,000."[30]

Mr. H. H. Rogers, a prominent official in the Standard Oil Company who had co-operated with Niels Grön in 1897-98 in trying to arrange for a sale of the islands to the United States, became very much interested in this newspaper item, so he at once cabled to Mr. Hagemann, an intimate friend of his on the unofficial Danish Committee, as follows:

[30] Quoted in New York *Times,* January 1, 1900, under the title of *The West India Deal.* See also Washington *Post* for January 1, 1900.

"Danish West India Islands up again, with prospect of success if worked with proper parties. Would like authority to speak."

Hagemann, after a consultation with Christmas, decided to send the following cablegram to Rogers:

"Sale is in official channels: have protected your interests, await arrival Capt. Christmas, *St. Paul*, with instructions to you."

For some reason Mr. Hagemann did not send this cablegram, but substituted for it the following:

"Sale is in official channels; await arrival of Capt. Christmas, *St. Paul*, with introduction to you."[31]

Christmas left Copenhagen on January 3, after a farewell audience with Prime Minister Hörring who concluded the interview by affectionately murmuring: "God be with you, and do not forget to send frequent reports."[32]   But it must have been the God of War that Hörring invoked for the benefit of Christmas, for even before that interesting adventurer set foot in New York there was serious trouble brewing for him.   In the testimony of Carl Fischer-Hansen before the Select Committee of the House of Representatives on April 3, 1902, this lawyer who had been employed by Christmas to assist him in the negotiations for the sale of the Danish West Indies, tells a confused story which impressed the committee, but which is patently false.   According to this account of Fischer-Hansen,

[31] Quoted in New York *Times,* May 1, 1900, and in *House Report* 2749, where wrong date is given.
[32] *H. Rep.,* 2749, p. 17.

Christmas, after employing him to act as his counsel, went to Denmark in December, 1899, and while over there for about a month did not take the trouble to write to Fischer-Hansen and inform him how matters were getting along. This act of discourtesy was distinctly aggravated when Fischer-Hansen learned through a member of the firm of J. and W. Seligman and Company that Christmas had written frequently to one of the Seligmans and had discussed the progress of the negotiations.

Such ingratitude was too much for the sensitive soul of Mr. Fischer-Hansen to bear, so he went to Washington a "couple of days before Christmas," and informed President McKinley that he would not be responsible for Christmas any longer, and that he "would have nothing to do with him." The President expressed his regret that Fischer-Hansen "had been taken in" by Christmas, and after an exchange of commiserations, Fischer-Hansen returned to New York.[33]

This story of Fischer-Hansen is interesting but hardly true. A "couple of days before Christmas" he is supposed to have denounced Captain Christmas to President McKinley as an irresponsible person with whom he would have nothing more to do, but on

[33] *Ibid.*, pp. 68-69. In the New York *World*, January 3, 1900, there is an interview with Fischer-Hansen, who had left on January 2 for Washington to have a conference with President McKinley. In this interview he speaks as though he is still co-operating with Captain Christmas, and tells of the interviews that both he and Christmas had with President McKinley and Secretary Hay.

January 4, he gave an interview to a reporter for the New York *Times* in which he strikes a very different note. Ever since the publication of the news item on January 1, 1900, that negotiations were in progress between the United States and Denmark for the cession of the Danish West Indies, there had been considerable interest displayed in many quarters with regard to this proposed cession. Therefore, in order to satisfy this public curiosity, Mr. Fischer-Hansen gave out an interview in which he tells of his relations with Captain Christmas. Pertinent portions of this interview are given as follows:

"I wish to say first explicitly that I do not represent the Danish Government. If the Danish Government had offered the islands to the United States, it would have been done through the Danish Minister at Washington. However, I am in a position to say that there are on foot negotiations not official as yet looking to the purchase by the United States of the islands. I am interested in that question, and it is true that Capt. Christmas Dirckinck Holmfeld and myself have had several interviews with Secretary Hay and President McKinley. Capt. Holmfeld is a retired officer of the Danish Navy. Secretary Hay assigned Mr. White, Secretary of the American Embassy at London, to accompany Capt. Holmfeld to the Danish capital to bring back assurances that if the United States Government should take up the proposals we have made the Danish Government will agree to them. Capt. Holmfeld left here six weeks ago, after several interviews with the officials in Washington. I expect him back again in two weeks. We have every reason to believe that the islands will in the near future belong to the United States."[34]

[34] New York *Times*, January 4, 1900.

From the tenor of this interview no one would suspect that there had been the slightest difficulty between Christmas and Fischer-Hansen, and it is quite probable that the latter was quite mixed up in his dates when he testified before the Select Committee of the House of Representatives.

But whatever the truth or the lack of it in the testimony of Mr. Fischer-Hansen, it is certain that when Christmas arrived in New York in January, 1900, his troubles became legion. Mr. Hagemann had advised him to see Mr. H. H. Rogers as soon as possible, so on the day after his arrival in New York he called upon Mr. Rogers. The latter seemed distinctly piqued because of the successful activity of Captain Christmas with reference to the sale of the Danish islands, and several times he sharply warned Christmas that he [Rogers] expected to "make money by this, and don't you forget it." When Christmas attempted to discover what sum Mr. Rogers deemed adequate compensation for his services, the Standard Oil magnate refused to commit himself, and finally referred Christmas to Niels Grön, who was to act as the agent of Mr. Rogers. As the interview terminated, Mr. Rogers is supposed to have flung the following words of wisdom straight at Captain Christmas:

"Now Mr. Christmas, I don't know if we can come to an agreement or not; but mind you, this island business will never pass through Congress without my consent. I am able to swing 26 votes in the Senate, and don't you forget it."[35]

[35] *H. Rep.,* 2749, p. 18.

When Christmas sought out Niels Grön and had an interview with him he soon found out that this former Dane was just as hostile as Mr. Rogers. Grön quickly informed Christmas that it would be best for him to turn over his credentials and papers to Mr. Rogers, and retire at once from his mission. After assuring Christmas that Mr. Rogers controlled a large number of Senators, he delivered the following ultimatum:

"The word of the Sandard Oil Company is law, make no mistake about that. They will permit no one but themselves to sell the Danish West Indian Islands. If the deal is not consummated through them, it will not be consummated at all, rest assured of that. You are wasting your time and the time and money of the Danish Government. Turn everything over to Rogers, agree to his terms, or give up hope of ever accomplishing the task for which you have come here."[36]

The difficulties that Christmas was having with Rogers and Grön were soon noised about New York City, and on January 17, he was asked by a reporter of the New York *Times* whether he had been approached

[36] New York *Times,* May 1, 1900. It is possible that one of the reasons for the interest in the Danish West Indies as displayed by Mr. Rogers was the hope of establishing a large fuel oil station for supplying fuel oil to steamers operating between New York and the Pacific coast via the Straits of Magellan. The island of St. Thomas would be ideal for such a station and after the opening of an isthmian canal, its value would be tremendously increased. See letter from the firm of Hopkins and Hopkins, representing the American-Hawaiian S. S. Company to Mr. Hay, MS. Dept. of State, *Miscellaneous Letter* October, 1902, pt. 1.

by a Dane residing in New York City who had admonished him that "if he wanted to consummate a sale he would have to produce $200,000 to be paid to friends close to the Administration at Washington." Captain Christmas admitted that such "overtures had been made," but added that he had said to the man who approached him:

"You are a liar. I do not believe for a moment that you are authorized to make any such overtures."

Captain Christmas was also asked by this reporter whether the negotiations believed to be pending between Denmark and the United States would terminate successfully. Christmas expressed an affirmative opinion, in explanation of which he observed as follows:

"Denmark cannot afford to be on bad terms with the United States. Several of the European powers want the Danish West Indies, but King Christian prefers they should be the property of the United States. In the event of the construction of the Nicaragua or Panama Canal the islands will be of special value to the American people as a coaling station. I am well acquainted with the islands of which my grandfather, Admiral Christmas, was the Governor for many years. I believe the islands will prove valuable property for the United States, and just as soon as matters reach a certain stage I shall disappear, and negotiations will be concluded by Constantine Brun, the Danish Minister at Washington. Henry White, a member of the American Legation at London, has made frequent trips to Copenhagen on this matter, and the affair is about closed."[37]

[37] New York *Times*, January 17, 1900.

After giving out this interview, Captain Christmas went to Washington and informed Secretary Hay of all that had passed between him and Mr. Rogers and Niels Grön. The Secretary of State was quick to express his righteous indignation at such conduct on the part of Mr. Rogers, and he endeavored to relieve the anxieties of Captain Christmas by assuring him that "the Standard Oil Company does not as yet own the United States Government."[38]

Shortly after hearing these wingéd words from John Hay, Christmas was further heartened by receiving on January 18, 1900, a cablegram from the Danish Foreign Office which read:

"Rogers wires give power, must disinterest Christmas. Government answers impossible. Matter official in Christmas's hands.

(Signed) Aagesen,
Secretary."[39]

Christmas could interpret this cablegram only in the sense that the Danish Foreign Office had rejected all advances from Rogers and had placed control of the negotiations in the hands of Christmas himself. He now relates how he talked with Admiral Dewey, with important Senators like Lodge, Depew, and Bacon, and with Representative John J. Gardner of New Jersey. All of them "took a great interest in the acquirement of the islands" and promised him their "very best assistance." So well did things pro-

[38] New York *Times*, May 1, 1900.
[39] New York *Times*, May 1, 1900.

gress that Christmas, in the latter part of January, wrote the following interesting report to his friend Etatsraad Hansen, in Copenhagen:

"Since my last letter nothing official has taken place, but I have accomplished much underhand work. I have been at a couple of secret meetings in Congress, where the plan for future developments was agreed upon. A pair of the leading Senators and some members of the House were present, and the general opinion was that the acquirement of the West Indian Islands would not meet any serious opposition. It was the first intention that some Senators should privately suggest to the President that he should let Secretary Hay apply to the Danish minister here and officially ask if Denmark would sell."[40]

President McKinley, according to Captain Christmas, desired for "political reasons that the affair should not come from the Administration to Congress, but the reverse." For that reason it was finally decided that Mr. Gardner, of New Jersey, should introduce in the House of Representatives a bill providing for the acquisition of the Danish West Indies at a cost not to exceed $4,000,000. On January 31, 1900, Mr. Gardner introduced the proposed bill, but it was quickly shelved in the House of Representatives and nothing came of it. The reason for this legislative inactivity was, according to Christmas, because Mr. H. H. Rogers and Niels Grön were bending all their efforts to make a failure of the Christmas mission. Faced by this predicament, Christmas appealed to

[40] *H. Rep.*, 2749, p. 21.

Senator Lodge, who was the "most respected member of the Senate," and one of the few legislators who could not be bribed. It was Senator Lodge who had discovered

"that Rogers was at work, agitating among his 26 Senators, whose votes he thought to be able to control. Mr. Lodge advised me to seek Mr. Hay, and to inform him of all regarding my antagonistic position to Rogers and Grön. . . . I decided . . . to follow the advice of Mr. Lodge. I worked out a statement, took all my papers, letters, and telegrams, and announced myself to Mr. Hay. Mr. Hay became confused, annoyed, and angry when I told him what was in my mind. He was confused because I, a foreigner had secured such an unfortunate impression of the political conditions in Washington; annoyed because Mr. Lodge had sent me up into the foreign ministry, and angry, or more correctly, enraged, against Rogers and his people. To me he said: 'Well, it may be that these *trust people* are very powerful, but I will show them that they do not yet rule the Administration of this country or its Congress.' "[41]

[41] *H. Rep.*, 2749, pp. 22-23. In an interview published in the New York *Times*, May 3, 1900, Representative Gardner says nothing whatever of the influence of Christmas in securing the introduction of the bill to provide for the acquisition of the Danish West Indies. His account mentions only his fear of German intrigues in the Caribbean, and his desire to forestall them. Later on, April 3, 1902, he gave to the Select Committee of the House of Representatives the following description of his first meeting with Captain Christmas: "When I say I think I met him once I mean this: Somebody, whom I cannot exactly recall now, came to the Labor Committee room one morning and asked to present a lady and her husband. The lady was introduced with a long name, and my recollection is that the gentleman was simply introduced as her husband. He had very gallant manners, however, and

It may have been that Secretary Hay did feel a certain sympathy for Captain Christmas, who like some modern Cnut was trying in vain to stem the fast rising tides that threatened to engulf him. But this sympathy would not blind Hay to the fact that Christmas had finished his rôle of "contact man" between the United States and Denmark, and the time had now come to pursue negotiations along the regular diplomatic channels. Indeed, in his interview given to the newspapers on January 17, 1900, Christmas himself had stated that as "soon as matters reach a certain stage I shall disappear and negotiations will be concluded by Constantine Brun, the Danish Min-

---

seemed like a very fine gentleman." When Mr. Gardner was asked by the committee whether his bill of January 31, 1900, was introduced at the instance of Captain Christmas, he replied: "That was not at the instance of Mr. Christmas, nor could anybody representing him have known anything about it in any way." *H. Rep.*, 2749, pp. 59-60. In a *confidential* despatch from Constantine Brun to Admiral Ravn, the Danish Minister of Foreign Affairs, February 9, 1900, the Danish Minister at Washington observes as follows: "The motion proposed by Mr. Gardner was, as I have been *confidentially* informed, discussed yesterday in the Foreign Affairs Committee of the House. All the members except the chairman were against it, and it must thus be regarded as buried, as might be expected from the observations made by the Secretary of State to me. Indeed, he added that he believed that the motion must probably be due chiefly to the wish of its originator to make himself conspicuous. *As far as I can understand, this motion was the only thing at all that might be ascribed to the endeavors of certain private individuals.*" Brun to Admiral Ravn, February 9, 1900, MS. D. F. O.

ister at Washington."[42]   In the opinion of John Hay
this "certain stage" had now been reached, so on January 29, 1900, the Secretary of State wrote to Mr.
Swenson, the American Minister at Copenhagen, to
inform him that

"the present time appears opportune to approach the
Government of His Majesty the King of Denmark
with a view to reviving the negotiations which in
1867 resulted in the signature of a convention between
the United States and Denmark for the cession to
us of the Danish West India Islands."

The causes which in 1867-70, operated to defeat
the confirmation of the treaty by the United States
Senate no longer existed, while there were many good
reasons to

"favor the approval of such a convention at this juncture. The proximity of the Danish Islands to the recently acquired territory of Puerto Rico of which
they are virtually a geographical offshoot, and the
existence of a harbor in Saint Thomas suitable for
the station and repair of the naval vessels henceforth
necessarily to be maintained in the West Indies are
in point. . . . Bearing these considerations in view,
and cordially mindful of the strong friendship between
the two countries . . . the President desires that you
shall sound the Government of His Majesty touching
its disposition to enter upon negotiations for the acquisition by the United States of the Danish Islands
in the West Indies."[43]

[42] See *ante*, p. 251.
[43] Hay to Swenson, January 29, 1900, MS. Dept. of State,
Denmark, Inst., vol. 16.

On the very day that Hay wrote this instruction to Swenson he also sent an autograph note to Constantine Brun, the Danish Minister at Washington, requesting him to call at the Department of State on January 30, 1900. When the Danish Minister was ushered into the office of the Secretary of State, Mr. Hay informed him that he had been summoned because of a "very important and absolutely confidential matter, viz., the sale of the Danish West Indies." The question of this sale had been the subject of some "unofficial negotiations" in Washington, and therefore he had sent the secretary of the American Embassy in London, Mr. White, to Copenhagen to ascertain the desires of the Danish Government in that regard. From the reports of Mr. White it was evident that the two Governments were "in the main in agreement," so the Secretary of State had given instructions that a draft convention be prepared which provided for the cession of the islands to the United States.

Mr. Hay then urged Mr. Brun to regard this draft convention as final, for the Secretary of State had already found out that at least two-thirds of the Senate would consent to a treaty conforming to the draft provisions. The Administration was

"sure of the votes of the Republican as well as the leading Democratic Senators and knew that there would be no opposition except from one or two Senators, or anyway only from a quite negligible number, that might always be expected to oppose any action."

The Secretary of State then requested Mr. Brun to treat the matter with the greatest secrecy. He himself

"would absolutely deny having mentioned it to me, and he asked me [Brun] to do the same thing, because if the affair came to the knowledge of persons not concerned, it would inevitably be made use of in the discussions of the political parties, and then it would no longer be possible to foresee the consequences."

The Secretary of State concluded his interview with Brun by asking him as to the

"position of Captain Christmas, and especially as to whether he had any authorization from the Danish Government. As a matter of fact, Captain Christmas has denied this in his conversation with the Secretary of State, but he had given other people the opposite impression. The Secretary of State had told Captain Christmas that unofficial negotiators were not needed. I [Brun] therefore explained to the Secretary of State that Captain Christmas possessed no authorization whatever, and that for this reason I had declined his request for an introduction to the Secretary of State, adding that I believed, however, that it had not been Captain Christmas' intention at all to purport to be the representative of the Government. The Secretary of State ended by observing that the whole affair ought to be easily and quickly arranged, to which I remarked that I was able to assure him that the proposal of the United States would be made the subject of the most serious and friendly considerations of the Royal Government, and that I should not fail to communicate immediately with my Government."[44]

It was soon apparent to Captain Christmas that his usefulness in Washington was at an end. His

[44] Brun to Admiral Ravn, January 30, 1900, MS. D. F. O.

services as a "contact man" were no longer needed, and there were many stories afloat concerning his private character and his dismissal from the Danish Navy. Besides, his funds were running low, and if one can place any credence in his narrative, the ways of diplomacy sometimes run parallel with those of high finance. Take for example the following excerpt from his narrative:

"I made the acquaintance of many members of Congress, and had now one, now another, either to dine or to supper at Hotel Raleigh, where I lived. It cost me much money, because Washington is one of the most expensive cities in the world, especially the dinners in the hotels were expensive. It was not alone the members of Congress, but their private secretaries that I had to invite. I had as my especial assistants two men, C. W. Knox, who was an intimate friend of Senator Mark Hanna, and Richard P. Evans, a lawyer in Washington, who represented Mr. Gardner and his friends in the House. . . . I had contacts with them both, according to which they, and through them certain members of Congress, should have a share of the commission if the sale took place."[45]

Faced by ever increasing expenses, Captain Christmas now wrote to his representative in Copenhagen, a lawyer by the name of Salomon, to see the Prime Minister and secure from him some definite guaranty with reference to the commission Christmas was to receive for arranging the sale of the Danish West Indies. Salomon, however, could make no headway whatever with the Prime Minister, and Christmas soon found

[45] H. Rep., 2749, p. 23.

himself repudiated by the Danish Government. This
fact was at first incomprehensible to him, and in his
narrative he tells his reaction to these evil tidings:

"My brain could not contain the idea that the prime
minister who three months ago secured me money
for the journey, gave me instructions, had acceded to
all my plans and propositions, had shown me the confidence of allowing me to administer as large a sum
of money as a tenth of the sum to be paid for the
Danish Islands, who, on my departure had pressed
my hand in a most cordial manner and wished me
'God-speed'—that he now indignantly refused to talk
to anyone who, directly or indirectly, represented
me."[46]

There was nothing for Christmas to do but return
to Denmark and see the Prime Minister. He sailed
for Copenhagen on April 12, and soon after his arrival he had his last audience with the Prime Minister.
His state of mind at this time is graphically related in
his narrative:

"I had not seen the minister since my departure
from Copenhagen in January, and it was in a bitter
frame of mind that I again entered the minister's
reception room in the ministry of finance. I had in
the meantime worked to such a degree that my nerves
were almost ruined and my means entirely exhausted.
I had not saved myself, but thrown my whole energy
into the affair, which the minister had shown such a
lively interest for. In return the minister had done
nothing for me. He had broken his promises and
agreements, even to such a degree that he had proven
untrue to me, and had made it appear that I had made
myself impossible for the minister's confidence. The

[46] *H. Rep.*, 2749, p. 26.

audience terminated for both parties in a very un-
pleasant manner, and my bitterness and anger ran
away with me, and I reproached the minister for his
failure to keep his word and remain loyal to me."[47]

Some three weeks after Christmas had left for
Copenhagen there appeared, on May 1, 1900, a long
article in the New York *Times* which entered into
great detail concerning the Christmas mission to the
United States. This article gives a lengthy digest of
an "unofficial report just submitted to the Danish Government by Capt. W. von Christmas Dirckinck-Holmfeld," and states that the facts in the report of Captain Christmas "are in the possession of the State
Department."[48]

It would be interesting to know just how the New
York *Times* came into possession of the Christmas
report, for Christmas himself claims that he "left no
material behind," and that it was not "clear" to him
"where the article originated and who inspired it."[49]

[47] *Ibid.*, p. 32.

[48] New York *Times*, May 1, 1900.

[49] *H. Rep.*, 2749, p. 31. With regard to the article in the *Times*
concerning the Christmas mission, the Hartford *Post* of May
1, 1900, makes the following comment: "The New York *Times*
scored a beat on its contemporaries by publishing this morning
an exclusive story of recent negotiations for the sale of the
Danish West Indies. The *Times* is always careful and reliable and in this case its article is apparently by the book, as
it quotes official despatches, and its reporter evidently obtained
the details from an inside official source." In the New York
Times for March 18, 1901, the following statement is made
concerning the origin of the articles in the *Times* of May 1,
1900: "Shortly before returning to Denmark last year, Captain

Besides, Christmas did not turn in the report of his mission until May 4, 1900, several days after the article in the New York *Times*. But at any rate, this article must have been based upon "inside information," for it tells practically everything that came out in the published Christmas report of October 1, 1900, which was reproduced in the report of the Select Committee of the House of Representatives (House Report No. 2749).

Of course, this sensational article in the *Times* for May 1, 1900, caused widespread comment, and all the

---

Christmas made an affidavit, which came into the possession of the New York *Times,* and it was made the basis of a publication to the effect that the reason for the failure of Capt. Christmas's efforts to bring about a sale of the islands was the interference of Mr. Grön and his associates."

In the manuscript *report* of Captain Christmas in the Danish Foreign office there is the following statement with reference to this article in the New York *Times* of May 1, 1900: "I had not left a single letter, telegram or any other document belonging to me behind in America. Part of the article is biased fiction which I myself saw for the first time in the article in the *Times.* In the beginning I thought that it was from the foreign minister, to break a possible opposition in the Senate to the island sale. It is not unusuaal that the Government in Washington uses the press in a similar way and it coincided perfectly with the moment—after my departure—when the Minister of War, Root, made some belligerent speeches in which he demanded the acquisition of the Danish Islands to avoid Germany's entering into possession of them. Now, however, I believe that I know better. Anyway, no blame can be addressed to me because of the appearance of the article mentioned above—it would be just as unwarranted as to blame anyone because he had been the victim of thieves and bandits."

public men who were mentioned in it immediately gave
out interviews explaining their attitude. On May 2,
the *Times* ran another long article with reference to
the Christmas mission. Certain "officials" in Washington had been questioned by the correspondent of
the *Times,* and had admitted that the account in the
Times was "substantially correct." One "high official"
in the Department of State

"said that Secretary White's visit to Copenhagen was
made as a result of Christmas's representations. As
was stated in the New York *Times,* Christmas came
here ostensibly as a private citizen and without credentials. He visited the State Department and explained his mission and the grounds on which he considered it advisable for the United States to buy the
islands. His arguments impressed the Administration,
and White was instructed to go to Copenhagen. Christmas, it is declared, acted throughout as a private citizen, although he was a retired officer of the Danish
Navy, and never presented any credentials. Nevertheless, his position was well understood, and it was
known that he was not a broker seeking a commission."[50]

Senator Lodge had read the article in the *Times*
with great interest, and said there were some imper-
fections in it, especially in the section that dealt with
the activities of Mr. H. H. Rogers, of the Standard
Oil Company. "Some time ago," said Mr. Lodge,

"different persons came here to induce this Government to negotiate a purchase of the Danish Islands
by the United States. Messrs. Flint, Eddy & Co., of

[50] New York *Times,* May 2, 1900.

New York, Mr. Rogers, and perhaps some others came over here to ask us to favor a purchase. It was understood that if the purchase was made through them, they were to have a commission. After consultation with the Department of State, it was decided that if any purchase was to be made, and any negotiations to that end were necessary, the proper and regular way would be to conduct the negotiations through the Department of State and the Danish Minister here. . . . When Capt. Christmas arrived, having no official sanction that we knew of, but evidently being at liberty to discuss the matter in an unofficial way, which was all he claimed, it was possible that the purchase might have been arranged with a price at about $3,250,000, but the determination to deal directly with Denmark was adhered to."

With reference to the rôle played by Mr. H. H. Rogers, and his alleged statement that he controlled a large number of Senators, Mr. Lodge remarked:

"All that I know of Mr. Rogers I have told you. It is absurd to talk about his having twenty-six Senators who could hold the Senate. That number of Senators could not hold the Senate. Then from what I have heard, I understand that Mr. Rogers is a man of great wealth, to whom a commission of $300,000 would be regarded as a mere bagatelle."[51]

When questioned about Mr. Rogers and his ability to control twenty-six Senators who would defeat any treaty negotiated by Captain Christmas unless a large commission was paid to him, Senator Chauncey Depew indulged in a hearty laugh. "Why," said he, "Rogers is a man worth $50,000,000. Why should he bother

[51] *Ibid.*, May 2, 1900.

about a deal out of which a commission of $300,000 was to be realized."

On May 1, 1900, persistent efforts were made by a reporter from the New York *Times* to see Mr. Rogers in order to secure his comments concerning the disclosures that had just been printed. Rogers refused to be interviewed, but he did permit his secretary to see the reporter, and the following conversation ensued:

"Mr. Rogers will not see you or any one else. He has nothing to say."

"Will you show Mr. Rogers the copy of this cablegram and ask him whether or not it was sent by him?"

"I will not," said the secretary.

"You are quoted as having said that nine-tenths of the statements made in the New York *Times* this morning concerning Mr. Rogers and his connection with the Danish West Indies are lies. Is that so?"

"I did not say that," retorted the secretary indignantly. "I said that nine-tenths of the statements were not true."

"That seems to be a fine distinction," said the reporter. "Will you kindly point out the one-tenth that you consider truth?"

"I don't know what they are," was the reply. "I only made that assertion off-hand."

"Do you know enough of Mr. Roger's affairs to make that assertion seriously?" was asked.

"I will not say whether I do or not."[52]

Later on in the day, May 1, Mr. Rogers sent the following statement to the press:

[52] New York *Times,* May 2, 1900.

"The article referred to is devoid of truth and common sense. Some three years ago, from an accredited representative of the Danish Government, I was asked to intimate to the United States Government that the Danish West Indies could be purchased. In connection with another merchant of this city, this information was given to the authorities at Washington, and, as I have been informed, was favorably considered at a Cabinet meeting. Later, the subject was presented to the Senate, I think by Senator Lodge of Massachusetts. The Spanish-American war coming on at about this time, I was informed from Denmark that because of the outlook of war with Spain, Denmark would not continue a consideration of the question. Since that time the whole subject has been in abeyance until last Winter, when Capt. Christmas presented himself with a letter of introduction from Denmark. He told me he had the authority of the Danish Government to negotiate a sale, and desired my co-operation. He assured me that if I would render what assistance I could, and the movement was a success, his King would decorate me. In a general way, I was not unmindful of such honor, but did not really know what it meant, because I had never received similar compensation, and I did not accept the proferred terms. I took occasion to give to the Captain a little piece of advice, which in substance, was that it would be impossible to get any such sale consummated during this session of Congress for want of time. The interview ended, and he came to me again a few days later, but I was busy and he was so pressed for time that he did not wait to see me. Since that day I have not laid eyes on the gentleman, and have repeatedly declined to see him. He has telegraphed me, asking for an interview, and has requested interviews repeatedly through a mutual friend. The story he tells as to my claiming the ownership of twenty-six United States Senators is simply falsehood and so absurd on its face that it is hardly worth referring to."[53]

[53] New York *Times*, May 2, 1900.

On this same day, May 2, 1900, Mr. Carl Fischer-Hansen gave out an interview, part of which is as follows:

"It is quite true that I am not, nor have I been, the counsel for Denmark or the Danish Government in this matter. I was Capt. Christmas's counsel, and advised him in all matters upon which he consulted me. As I acted in that capacity, I do not desire to be brought into the matter without the consent of my client, but I can tell you positively that I mean to protect him from assault and aspersion. Capt. Christmas came here first, as the New York *Times* stated, in the capacity of a private citizen acting on his own initiative. As a result of what he told the United States Government, Secretary Hay sent Mr. White to Denmark, whither Capt. Christmas also went. When he came here again it was as the accredited representative of the Danish Government to conduct the terms of the sale of the islands and as such he made his report. If the persons who attack Capt. Christmas persist in their statements that he was not authorized by the Danish Government to act in this matter, I will furnish to the press such matter as will absolutely prove that Capt. Christmas did act as a special envoy under the direction of Prime Minister Hörring of Denmark."[54]

The denial by Mr. Rogers of any claim to control twenty-six Senators, and his sharp attack upon the veracity of the Christmas report which had just been made public by the New York *Times,* did not carry conviction to all minds. The *Times* itself, in an editorial of May 3, 1900, alluded to the doubts that still persisted despite the explicit statement of Mr. Rogers:

[54] New York *Times,* May 2, 1900.

"Mr. Rogers denies that the Standard Oil Company was in any way interested in his public labors as a broker in islands. Mr. Roger's friends may be quite willing to accept this statement as the literal truth, but the general public will not believe it. The gentlemen of the Standard Oil Company must know from their experience that the public is skeptical about statements concerning the affairs of the company. That company has foreign relations of its own. . . . It is hard for people to think of Mr. H. H. Rogers acting in any large matter in a purely personal capacity without regard to his great and active company."[55]

On May 21, 1900, there appeared in the newspapers certain articles critical of Captain Christmas which brought an immediate response from Carl Fischer-Hansen, who had served as counsel for Christmas. The articles had stated that in the event the Danish islands had been sold to the United States through the agency of Christmas, he was to receive the major portion of the purchase price. After making a sweeping denial of all such charges, Mr. Fischer-Hansen observes:

"Capt. Christmas's position and acts in this matter have been honorable, above board, and acquiesced in by the Danish Government. He should not be judged too harshly for having permitted himself to be imposed upon by some irresponsible schemers in Washington."[56]

After this strong statement in behalf of Captain Christmas there was a distinct lull in public interest

[55] New York *Times,* May 3, 1900, editorial entitled "Mr. Rogers and the Danish Islands."
[56] New York *Times,* May 22, 1900.

in the Christmas mission to the United States. The matter was not allowed to drop, however; for the United States continued negotiations for the purchase of the Danish islands, and on January 24, 1902, a treaty was concluded whereby Denmark made a formal cession of her colonial possessions. There were many Danes who believed that such a treaty was tainted because of the Christmas unofficial negotiations that were carried on in 1899-1900, so it was not long before an active propaganda was carried on against the ratification of the convention. One of the most vehement opponents of the treaty was Niels Grön who had been so sharply criticized in the Christmas affidavit that was published in the New York *Times,* May 1, 1900. Grön was able to secure in Denmark a copy of a report that Christmas made to the Danish Government on October 1, 1900, so after translating it into English he hurried back to the United States and showed it to certain members of Congress. Inasmuch as the report contained statements that different Representatives had been open to bribes with regard to their support of the cession of the Danish islands to the United States, a resolution was unanimously passed on March 27, 1902, providing for an investigation of these charges: Speaker Cannon appointed the following members to serve on the Select Committee on Purchase of the Danish West Indies: Mr. Dalzell, Mr. Hitt, Mr. Cousins, Mr. McCall, Mr. Richardson, of Tennessee, Mr. Dinsmore, and Mr. Cowherd.[57]

[57] *Congressional Record,* March 27, 1902, vol. 35, pt. 4, pp. 3330-3344.

On the following day, the Department of State
denied emphatically that Captain Christmas

"acted for this Government in the negotiations for the
purchase of the Danish West Indies, and denied also
that he was recognized in any way by the State Department as the representative of the Danish Government.
Mr. Hay, it was stated, absolutely refused to have
anything to do with go-betweens. There was no occasion for the use of go-betweens. This country wished
to buy, and Denmark wished to sell. Nobody had to
come here to persuade anybody that the United States
ought to own the islands in question, and nobody had
to go to Copenhagen to convince the Government there
that it ought to get rid of the islands. 'Captain Christmas talks of bribery, does he?' commented a State
Department official. 'Why should he bribe anybody?
Usually bribes are offered to overcome opposition, but
in this matter there was no opposition to overcome.
You are safe to assume that if Capt. Christmas said,
as alleged, that he had arranged for the expenditure
of $500,000 in bribes he lied.' . . . It was denied at
the State Department that Christmas was authorized
by Secretary Hay to escort Mr. White from London
to Copenhagen and introduce him there. . . . Mr. White
knew the way from London to Copenhagen, knew
how to proceed when he got to the Danish capital,
and had no occasion at any stage of the negotiations to
use Christmas."[58]

On March 28, 1902, Mr. Carl Fischer-Hansen,
former counsel to Christmas, issued a long statement
to the press. He had just read the excerpts from the
report of Christmas that had been prepared for the
American press by Niels Grön, and he wished to
state that every one of Christmas's allegations regarding obligations

[58] New York *Times,* March 28, 1902.

"to pay money to Abner McKinley, Colonel Brown, members of Congress and other Americans is false. I am glad that there is to be an investigation. I shall certainly do all I can to aid the committee that has been named. . . . The recent negotiations, which have been successful, have been conducted entirely between the American Minister in Copenhagen and the Danish Minister in Washington. As a lawyer, however, I believe that Captain Christmas, having taken the initiative in the matter, is entitled to a commission. Captain Christmas never saw Abner McKinley and Colonel Brown and others whom he names, and if all these men were together in a room with him he could not identify them. Abner McKinley and Colonel Brown are friends of mine, and I know of my own knowledge that Captain Christmas never met them."[59]

After the publication of this statement by Fischer-Hansen, the New York *Times* printed an editorial which attached great importance to such a repudiation of Christmas by his former counsel, and observed that in the light of these disclosures

"Christmas vanishes from the records of serious negotiation and is fitted for the rôle of hero in some tale of romantic and not respectable adventure. Dismissed for cause from the navy of his own country, but retaining influential connections and enjoying certain privileges in the society of the Danish capital, he appears to have laid a plausible plan for extracting money from the Danish Treasury with which to pay imaginary bribes to Americans of alleged influence."[60]

On March 30, 1902, the New York *Times* printed an exclusive statement secured by its Copenhagen cor-

[59] New York *Herald*, March 28, 1902. Compare this statement with that of Abner McKinley, *post.*, p. 274.
[60] New York *Times*, March 29, 1902.

respondent with a "high official" in the Danish Government. According to this Danish official, the Christmas scandal was the result of

"a quarrel between Christmas and Grön. The latter claimed he effected the sale and that, hence, he wanted a commission. Christmas made a similar claim, accompanied by a confidential report to the Danish Government, containing statements regarding bribery and similar practices, as recently published in Washington. Most of the report was printed by the Danish press some time ago. Grön, seeing it was hopeless to expect a commission, started for Washington with Christmas's report in his pocket, boasting to the anti-sale advocates here that he would be revenged by influencing Congress to decline to pass the appropriation for the purchase of the islands. Before the opening of the negotiations Christmas and Grön actually tried to become connected with the matter as agents. The then Premier, Dr. Hörring, gave them some encouragement, and private parties favoring the sale furnished small amounts for their travelling expenses. Dr. Hörring was indiscreet. He discussed a commission, but bribery was not suggested." [61]

A few days later, April 5, 1902, Admiral Ravn, the Minister for Foreign Affairs in the late Hörring Ministry, granted an audience to a reporter for the New York *Herald* in which the Christmas scandal was discussed. He said that when he received Henry White at the Foreign Office he remarked to Captain Christmas:

" 'Mr. Christmas, will you go into the other room, the one to the left? I have nothing to speak about with you.' I saw Mr. White alone and it was through

[61] New York *Times,* March 30, 1902.

that gentleman that the first negotiation was opened. He wanted to know whether Denmark was willing to part with the islands. I own that I was not much in favor of it, but there were reasons which made the sale of the islands desirable. Mr. White never in any way suggested to me that money should be paid for influencing votes. All that passed between us was of a perfectly straightforward nature. . . . Admiral Ravn then said that it was a pity that Minister Hörring, who was president of the council in the government of which he was Minister for Foreign Affairs, had had anything to do with Christmas, but that he did not know any details about the meeting. Mr. Hörring, as Minister of Finance, may have had something to say, but had he appealed to me I would have told him all about Christmas and his reputation. All this confirms what I have previously told you, that M. Hörring acted with much indiscretion in receiving Christmas, but he was probably led into doing so by the plausibility of that gentleman, who also appears to have exercised influence over Mr. Hay."[62]

In the meantime, while all these statements were coming out in the press, the Select Committee on Purchase of the Danish West Indies began on April 1, 1902, to hold its hearings with reference to the Christmas mission to the United States. Niels Grön was the first witness to be called, and he gave a long and detailed account of his relations with Captain Christmas. Needless to say, it was highly unfavorable to the Captain.[63] On April 3, Abner McKinley, a brother to the late President McKinley, was questioned by the committee. In his report to the Danish Government, Oc-

[62] New York *Herald*, April 7, 1902.
[63] *H. Rep.*, 2749, 57 Cong. 1 sess., pp. 33-58.

tober 1, 1900, Christmas had alluded to his acquaintance with Abner McKinley and Colonel Brown, of Ohio, in the following terms:

"These two gentlemen are only very little respected, and their business, which specially consists in securing certain firms' contracts and concessions from the Government, is without question anything but nice, but both Mr. Brown and Mr. Abner McKinley have the entrée to the White House in Washington. They know most accurately all the winding paths through Congress, and are well informed as to what Members of Congress must be paid, as well as to the method which must be used to accomplish it."[64]

When Mr. Abner McKinley was before the committee he stated that he had met Captain Christmas only once, and in the "most casual way" in the lobby of the Manhattan Hotel. He denied having any contract of any kind with Christmas, and had no connection whatever with him relative to the sale of the Danish West Indies to the United States.[65] Colonel Wilbur C. Brown was equally explicit in his denials of any relations with Christmas. He had met Christmas only once when the Danish captain had introduced himself to Brown at the Manhattan Hotel. On this occasion there was no reference whatever to the Danish West Indies, and Colonel Brown had no further relations with Christmas.[66]

Mr. Carl Fischer-Hansen informed the Committee of his intimate relations with Christmas from October,

[64] *Ibid.*, p. 7.
[65] *Ibid.*, pp. 58-59.
[66] *Ibid.*, pp. 62-63.

1899, until Christmas of that year when he denounced Christmas to President McKinley as an "irresponsible" person. He then told of his reconciliation with Christmas and the assistance he had rendered him. It was Mr. Fischer-Hansen's belief that Christmas did have a contract with Prime Minister Hörring to treat for a sale of the Danish West Indies to the United States, with a provision for a ten per cent. commission should the sale be effected. He also informed the committee that if the sale of the islands should result from the visit of Henry White to Copenhagen, then Christmas was "legally entitled to his commission." Christmas did what he was hired to do, and "by coming back to Denmark with Secretary White and by Denmark opening negotiations at that time with White, I give it as my opinion he is absolutely entitled to his commission if the sale about to be consummated is the result of that opening."

The committee finally asked Mr. Fischer-Hansen whether Captain Christmas had ever suggested to him at any time the desirability or the necessity of the use of money to persuade Congressional support. In reply, Mr. Fischer-Hansen said that when Christmas first met him he [Christmas] said that the "general impression in Denmark was that the reason why the islands were not sold in 1867, when both Denmark and America had agreed upon the transaction, was because there had not been bribe money enough to go around and Denmark refused to bribe certain Senators, and therefore when he made overtures to Hörring to go over and try to induce the Americans to take the first step he explained to Hörring it was necessary for him to get a big commission because that was the way they did business in America."[67]

In his report to the Danish Government, Christmas had stated that he had several conversations with Senator Lodge, and had discovered that Lodge was one of the few legislators who could not be bribed. When called before the committee, Senator Lodge told of how Mr. C. W. Knox had come to his committee room one day in 1900, and had introduced himself and then Captain Christmas. In the ensuing conversation, Captain Christmas said

"he had come to talk to me about the Danish Islands. He represented himself as the agent of the Danish Government and I told him I had nothing whatever to do with anything of that sort, that negotiations of that kind were wholly in the hands of the Executive, and the person he ought to see was the Secretary of State. He asked me if I could speak to the Secretary of State in regard to it; and I said I would. I spoke to the Secretary of State, who, I think had either seen him before or heard from him, I am not sure which; but the Secretary of State said what I expected him to say and what I told Captain Christmas he would say—that he could have no dealings whatever with any unaccredited agent from the Danish Government; that if Captain Christmas had credentials from the Danish Government he had simply to produce them or come there with Mr. Brun, who was the Danish Minister, and that if he had no credentials or did not come with Mr. Brun, that the Secretary of State did not wish to see him, and could by no possibility have dealings of any sort. I think the interview with the Secretary of

[67] *H. Rep.*, 2749, pp. 64-83.

State did not occupy three minutes, and he made exactly the statement I expected him to make. I told Captain Christmas that when he came back to my committee room, and I think he came once more to see me at my house and asked me if there was any use in his remaining in Washington, and I told him not the slightest. That is the only knowledge I had of him at all."

The committee then asked Senator Lodge whether he had said to Captain Christmas that the reason the Gardner bill did not go through the House of Representatives was because there were "evil spirits at work —namely Rogers and his friends." To this question Mr. Lodge replied: "No; of course I made no such statement to him."[68]

Senator Chauncey Depew was called before the committee because he was one of the Senators with whom Christmas claimed that he had conversations. Mr. Depew denied ever having met Captain Christmas, and said he was "very much astonished" when he saw his name in the report that Christmas made to the Danish Government.[69]

Senator Bacon was the last of the Senators to be called for questioning before the committee. Christmas had stated in his report that Mr. Bacon had taken a great interest in the "acquirement of the islands" and had promised Christmas his "very best assistance." When the committee brought this statement to the attention of Mr. Bacon, he replied:

[68] H. Rep., 2749, pp. 63-64.
[69] Ibid., p. 100.

"That is absolutely untrue so far as I am concerned. So far from that being the truth I did not desire the Government to acquire the islands and do not desire it now and am very sorry for what appears to be the necessity for that fact."[70]

After the testimony of Mr. Bacon had been concluded, the chairman of the committee read to the other members a letter from Secretary Hay with regard to Captain Christmas. Significant portions of the letter are as follows:

"In the early part of December, 1899, Captain Christmas called upon me at this Department, and informed me that, through private and personal sources in Copenhagen, he had become aware that there was a disposition among some of the leading members of the Danish Government to regard favorably an overture from the Government of the United States looking to the acquisition of the Danish Islands. He said that he had been a naval officer, and spoke at some length in regard to the desirability of the island of St. John as a naval station for the United States. At my suggestion he conveyed what further technical information he had on this subject to Admiral Bradford, of the Navy Department. Although he presented no credentials whatever and expressly declared he had no official character, I thought his story was of sufficient interest to be worth investigation. I told him I would send a confidential and trusted agent of this Government to Copenhagen to ascertain unofficially the true state of affairs, and mentioned to him the name of Mr. Henry White, the first secretary of embassy at London. Captain Christmas said he would like to be in Copenhagen when Mr. White arrived, and bring him into communication with the members of

[70] H. Rep., 2749, pp. 107-109.

the Government whom he mentioned. I gave him a note of introduction to Mr. White, and they met in Copenhagen, where Captain Christmas had arranged for an interview between Mr. White and a member of the Danish Government. Mr. Christmas was not present at this interview, and his connection with the matter ceased entirely at that time. He afterwards returned to Washington, and I saw him once or twice, but told him that there was no need of the services of any private person in any negotiations which might be taken up between the two Governments in regard to the acquisition of the islands."[71]

After hearing all the witnesses and reading the report of Captain Christmas to the Danish Government and the above letter of Secretary Hay to the chairman of the committee, the committee itself came to the conclusion that there was

"not the slightest semblance of evidence that any member of Congress, either directly or indirectly, was offered or received any bribe, or was paid any valuable consideration of any kind or character to vote for or assist in procuring the proposal, adoption, or ratification of a treaty of sale of the Danish West Indian Islands to the United States. There is not the remotest ground from which to draw an inference or on which to base a conclusion that there was any corruption or wrongdoing on the part of the public officials of the United States in connection with the negotiations for the purchase and sale of the Danish West Indian Islands. It is plain beyond peradventure that the bribery alleged in the report could have existed nowhere save in the imagination of Christmas, since the whole burden of his story is that he had no money. It is in evidence that he had to borrow in order to pay his passage home from this country."[72]

[71] *Ibid.,* p. 109.
[72] *Ibid.,* p. li.

In this connection the committee printed a letter from Captain Christmas to the American Minister in Copenhagen in which he denies many of the charges contained in his report of October 1, 1900. Part of his letter is as follows

"By foul means one of these gentlemen an alleged enemy got hold of a confidential report of my doings in America and provided Grön with a copy of the same. I have reason to believe than Grön has falsified my report, and I am already able to state—from newspaper cablegram—falsifications on following points:

"(1) I have never impressed the former prime minister, Hörring, with the idea that bribery was the way of getting the islands sold.

"I never wrote anything like this in my report. The fact is that Grön two years before my taking the matter up invented the whole 10 per cent. commission theory, and declared that without spending this money no sale was possible.

"(2) Nowhere in my report have I given the name of any Congressman in connection with my personal promise of money."[73]

It is interesting to compare the above statement of Captain Christmas with the testimony of Mr. Fischer-Hansen, who informed the select committee of the House of Representatives, that Christmas had told him that in Denmark the general impression concerning the treaty of 1867 was that it failed because there had not been "bribe money enough to go around," and that he, Christmas, had told Prime Minister Hörring that it was necessary to "get a big commission because that was the way they did business in America."[74]

[73] *Ibid.*, p. ii.
[74] See *ante*, pp. 275-76.

It is apparent, of course, that Christmas was trying to take advantage of what he thought was Prime Minister Hörring's ingenuousness with reference to the political atmosphere in America. It would be a simple matter to make out a secret list of legislators that supposedly had been bribed, and Hörring would accept the list without question and Christmas would pocket the money. Such a scheme might well have worked had Hörring been as stupid as Christmas believed him to be, and had Secretary Hay consented to treat with an unaccredited agent of the Danish Government. But at any rate, Hörring does make a distinctly poor showing in this Christmas matter. Even Admiral Ravn, the Minister of Foreign Relations in the Hörring Cabinet, admitted that Hörring had been "indiscreet" in his relations with Christmas,[75] while some Danes agreed with the following remarks of Georg Brandes, the celebrated Danish litterateur:

"There can be no doubt as to the fact that Christmas received a mandate from the Danish Government as its secret agent for the transfer of the islands to the United States, nor to the fact that a considerable sum was promised him after the conclusion of the sale. All too many documents are witnesses of the relations that existed. Those who are old enough to have followed the negotiations in 1867 can testify that the entire political world at that time took it for granted that the treaty failed because a sum of money had not been placed at the disposal of the negotiator. The indignation in Denmark with reference to the report Christmas submitted to the Government, which should

[75] See *ante*, p. 273.

never have been read by foreign eyes, was hypocrisy and nothing else."[76]

On March 19, 1903, Mr. Swenson, the American Minister at Copenhagen, wrote to Secretary Hay concerning this statement by Georg Brandes. In the opinion of Mr. Swenson these remarks by Mr. Brandes "had but little weight. He is not considered competent authority when it comes to discussing subjects of this nature."[77] In this despatch Mr. Swenson enclosed a clipping from the *Berlingske Tidende,* which contained an article by Chamberlain F. Bille, the former Danish chargé at Washington during the years 1868-70, when the treaty of 1867 was before the American Senate for action. Mr. Bille, after reading the article of Mr. Brandes, felt "strongly called upon" to register his protests against the slanders in that statement:

"The 'political world,' is an elastic and obscure phrase—an anonymous tribunal that is subject to no control. But in view of the fact that I have had personal knowledge, at first hand, of the events in question, and have known all the persons connected therewith, especially Senator Sumner—whose integrity was never questioned even by his worst enemies—I feel justified and called upon to protest. If the sentence cited above is understood as indicated—and I think most readers must so understand it—it contains an insinuation which must be considered as a baseless insult against the Senate, as it would be against the

[76] *Politiken,* Copenhagen, February 21, 1903.

[77] Swenson to Hay, March 19, 1903, MS. Dept. of State Denmark, *Desp.,* vol. 24.

Danish Rigsdag, in case that were aimed at. What obscure persons who indulge in idle talk may say is of little consequence; but the attempt of a man of reputation, who is supposed to be conscious of the weight attached to his utterances, is another matter."[78]

It should not be understood, however, that in this article Bille was interested in relieving the Hörring Ministry of any responsibility in the matter of the commission that was to go to Christmas. Quite the contrary! In the previous year Bille had had a conversation with Henry White in London, during which he was

"rather emphatic as to the relations of the previous Ministry with Christmas and says that undoubtedly Mr. Hörring, the late Premier, ought to pay whatever amount Christmas is entitled to—out of his own pocket."[79]

A few weeks after this conversation with Bille, White wrote to President Roosevelt concerning the negotiations with Denmark relative to the cession of the Danish West Indies to the United States. He felt disappointed

"that there is a hitch about the Danish islands sale, but in any case we come out of it all right and are in no way connected with the charges and allegations of Christmas, who however evidently succeeded in making the late Prime Minister of Denmark believe that a large expenditure of money would be necessary to

[78] Swenson to Hay, March 19, 1903, MS. Dept. of State, *Denmark, Desp.,* vol. 23. The letter of Bille in the *Berlingske Tidende* was dated February 24, 1903.

[79] White to Hay, March 1, 1902, MS. *White Papers.*

induce us to buy them and evidently Christmas obtained some sort of a promise out of him. The Danish Minister here tells me that in consequence, all future prospects of public office for the said Minister, Mr. Hörring, are at an end."[80]

In this same connection, there is an interesting letter from John C. Freeman, the American consul at Copenhagen, to David Jayne Hill, the Acting Secretary of State:

"It may be of interest to the Secretary to know that a New York court has sent to Denmark *Letters Rogatory* that the depositions of Captain W. C. Christmas, Mr. Niels Grön, and others may be taken in regard to the negotiations which have taken place in regard to the sale of the Danish West India islands. The hundred and ten pages of interrogatories with the accompanying documents (exhibits) traverse the whole matter of the unofficial negotiations of 1897-1900, and the official negotiations so far as they are understood. The Schested Ministry, the Deuntzer Ministry, and of course the Hay Ministry, come off well, but the Hörring Ministry, a section of the Standard Oil directorate, and various persons of some prominence in Denmark and in the United States, are likely to appear in a somewhat unenviable light when these depositions are made public."[81]

In conclusion, I might advert to the fact that in the appendix of the Report of the Select Committee of the House of Representatives on the *Purchase of the Danish West Indies,* there is a reproduction of the *report* that Captain Christmas made to the Danish Gov-

[80] White to Roosevelt, April 21, 1902, MS. *White Papers.*

[81] Freeman to Hill, January 27, 1902, *Copenhagen, Consular Letters,* vol. 11, MS. Dept. of State.

ernment on October 1, 1900. It is this report that I have designated as the Christmas *narrative,* and from which I have frequently quoted.[82] In the first part of this report there is some authentic evidence of value with reference to the background of the Christmas mission, but the bulk of the narrative is such a mixture of fact and falsehood that it has to be used with great caution. As for Christmas himself, there is ample testimony that he appeared to be a charming and cultivated gentleman with a penchant for fabrication, and one cannot help regretting that Mr. Gamaliel Bradford has confined his sparkling and penetrating studies of "Damaged Souls" to errant Americans.

[82] *H. Rep.,* 2749, pp. 2-32.

CHAPTER V

John Hay Tries His Hand—The Treaty of January 24, 1902

In the previous chapter it has already been related how Secretary Hay, on January 29, 1900, sent a despatch to Mr. Swenson, the American Minister at Copenhagen, in which he indicated a very definite desire to re-open the negotiations for the purchase of the Danish West Indies.[1] In this despatch he enclosed a draft of a treaty which he hoped would be "substantially accepted" by the Danish Government. In the draft treaty it was provided that all three islands of St. Thomas, St. John, and St. Croix, should be ceded to the United States with "all the dominion, rights and powers which Denmark now possesses and can exercise." This cession would convey to the United States the absolute ownership of all public buildings, ports, harbors, fortifications, and all other public property of every kind and description. The Danish subjects inhabiting these islands might remain thereon or might remove therefrom at will, retaining in either event all their rights of property. They would also enjoy all civil and religious liberties, and be permitted to carry on their industry, commerce or professions. In case these Danish subjects remained in the islands they might preserve their allegiance to Denmark by making

[1] See chapter iv.

within two years from the date of the exchange of ratifications of the treaty of cession, a declaration of their intention to preserve such allegiance. Formal delivery of the territory and property was to be made immediately after the payment by the United States of the sum stipulated in the convention. This sum was fixed at three and one-half million dollars in gold, and was to be paid in the city of Washington.

Before Secretary Hay sent this despatch to Swenson with the enclosed draft treaty, he had a conversation with Mr. Brun, the Danish Minister at Washington, in which he discussed the general situation with reference to the cession of the islands to the United Sates. It was important that the treaty be pushed through as rapidly as possible and with few alterations, for the Secretary of State had already ascertained that the requisite two-thirds of the Senate would consent to a treaty in conformity with the enclosed draft.

At this point Mr. Brun interposed

"the question whether the Government could count on the House of Representatives concerning the eventually necessary appropriation, and to this the Secretary of State gave a decidedly affirmative answer, as the Government—as is well known—was in a majority in the House and always followed the Senate in affairs of this kind."

After concluding this interview with Secretary Hay, Mr. Brun wrote a despatch to the Danish Minister of Foreign Affairs in which he analyzed the main points in the treaty as follows:

"It seems in the main to follow the treaty of 1867, with the following modifications—

"1. It comprises all three West Indian Islands.

"2. The purchase money is only three and a half million dollars.

"3. The clause concerning a vote of the inhabitants of the islands is omitted.

"Further, I also venture to call the attention of Your Excellency to the final words of Article 1, viz., 'free and unencumbered by any grants, conditions, privileges or franchises,' and to the words of Article 5, 'free of all encumbrance,' suggesting humbly whether these words might not possibly cause difficulties, e. g. in connection with the telegraphic companies to which a monopoly has been granted."[2]

On February 3, 1900, Secretary Hay sent a cablegram to Swenson in which he urged the American Minister to "impress" upon Minister for Foreign Affairs the desirability of adhering to the terms of the draft convention, inasmuch as it was "extremely unlikely that the Senate would assent to any modification. Time is most important."[3] Some two weeks later, February 19, Hay sent another cablegram to Swenson in which he stressed the importance of having the treaty signed in Washington, for this would enable the Secretary of State to submit it immediately to the Senate.[4]

[2] Brun to Admiral Ravn, January 30, 1900, MS. D. F. O.

[3] Hay to Swenson, February 3, 1900, MS. Dept. of State, *Denmark, Inst.,* vol. 16.

[4] Hay to Swenson, February 19, 1900, MS. Dept. of State, *Denmark, Inst.,* vol. 16.

On February 22, Swenson answered in a long despatch that covered in great detail his interviews with the Danish Minister of Foreign Affairs. He had called upon the Foreign Minister on February 5, and had been informed that a cablegram had been received from Brun stating that he was sending the draft of a treaty of cession, and that the sum offered by the United States was $3,500,000. The Foreign Minister had consulted with the Danish Premier concerning this offer from the American Government, whereupon they had come to the conclusion that it should be at least $4,000,000.

The draft treaty enclosed in Secretary Hay's instruction of January 29, 1900, reached Copenhagen on February 10, and Mr. Swenson lost no time in discussing its provisions with the Prime Minister, the Minister for Foreign Affairs, and the Director General of the Foreign Office. First of all, objection was raised as to the inadequacy of the sum offered by the United States. This, however was not urged "strongly" at that time. Opposition was next voiced with reference to the part of Article 1 which conveyed to the United States the full and entire sovereignty over the islands without any grants or conditions "in any way affecting or limiting the exercise of such sovereignty." Concessions had been granted to certain companies which could not now be revoked at pleasure. A case in point was the grant to the Floating Dock Company at St. Thomas, which on March 12, 1897, had secured the exclusive right to "adopt its own charges, regulations, etc."

A third objection was raised relative to the provisions of Article 3, in regard to the subject of citizenship. In case the inhabitants of the islands desired to retain their Danish citizenship they were required to make a declaration of such intention within two years from the date of the exchange of ratifications of the treaty of cession, and in case they did not, they were then to be regarded as having "elected allegiance to the United States." The Danish officials thought that the inhabitants "ought to be given the opportunity to invest themselves with United States citizenship immediately after the convention takes effect."

Mr. Swenson endeavored to answer these objections by first assuring the Foreign Minister that the American Government would observe the rules of international law with reference to contracts entered into by the Danish Government. It was soon conceded, however, "that the United States could not be expected to assume any obligations as to the concessions in question, especially with regard to the Floating Dock Company." With respect to citizenship, the American Minister pointed out the exclusive right of Congress in that connection, and referred to Article 9, in the treaty of peace with Spain, concluded at Paris, December 10, 1898, in which it was expressly provided that "the civil rights and political status of the native inhabitants of the territories hereby ceded to the United States shall be determined by the Congress."[5]

[5] Swenson to Hay, February 22, 1900, MS. Dept. of State, *Denmark, Desp.*, vol. 22.

On February 17, 1900, a Council of State, composed
of His Majesty the King, His Royal Highness the
Crown Prince, and the Members of the Ministry, was
held at which His Majesty formally gave his consent
to enter upon negotiations for the cession of the Danish West Indies to the United States. Though evinc-
ing "no strong desire" for the transfer of these colonial possessions to another power, His Majesty
expressed the belief that the "best interests of the
islands would be subserved by the cession to the
United States."

After this authorization by His Majesty, the Danish Premier and the Minister for Foreign Affairs had
a formal meeting with the Finance Committees of the
two branches of the Rigsdag, February 21, for the
purpose of apprising them of the proposed negotiations. At this meeting one of the members of the
Government Party was "outspoken" in his antagonism
to the draft treaty, and the Minister for Foreign
Affairs expressed to Mr. Swenson some apprehension
that "public agitation" might prove "disastrous" to
the negotiations.[6]

For some weeks the matter of the cession of the
islands remained in abeyance, and on March 17, Mr.
Swenson wrote that the political conflicts in the Rigsdag had prevented any further action relative to the
proposed treaty. Indeed, the disagreement between
the Government and the Folkething had actually cul-

[6] Swenson to Hay, February 22, 1900, MS. Dept. of State,
Denmark, Desp., vol. 22.

minated in the resignation of the Ministry. Mr. Swenson did not believe that the proposed cession of the Danish West Indies had in any way contributed to the fall of the Ministry, for there appeared to be a strong sentiment in both branches of the Rigsdag in favor of the cession. The Premier and the Minister for Foreign Affairs had expressed the opinion that the change of Ministry would merely delay the negotiations, but Mr. Swenson had noted that there was some public agitation against the cession of the islands, and that meetings of protests were being held.[7]

The change of Ministry caused a definite delay in the negotiations, so it was not until May 3, 1900, that Mr. Swenson was able to discuss the question of the cession of the islands with Mr. Schested, the new Minister for Foreign Affairs. Mr. Schested confided to Mr. Swenson that he had at first been opposed to the sale of the islands on "lyrical grounds," but that a closer study of the conditions prevailing in those possessions had modified his views. The agitation against the sale had made more of an impression in Denmark than had been anticipated by the Foregin Minister, but he regarded it largely as the result of misapprehension, and a great deal of it would disappear when the facts in the case were generally known.

The public had already learned something of the scandals connected with the Christmas mission to the United States, and the public press had "aired the fact

[7] Swenson to Hay, March 17, 1900, MS. Dept. of State, *Denmark, Desp.*, vol. 22.

that certain adventurers who posed as official agents in this matter have been actuated only by selfish motives of pecuniary gain." In consequence, expressions were frequently heard to the effect that "the honor and good name of the Danish Government and people have been compromised by disreputable persons."

Finally, Mr. Swenson advised the Secretary of State that he had heard from a reliable source that

"the Empress Dowager of Russia on her recent visit at this court endeavored to prevail upon the King to withdraw his sanction to further negotiations. Though His Majesty has been adversely influenced by his illustrious daughter, as well as by the Crown Prince and other prominent persons opposed to the sale, the Minister of Foreign Affairs does not think that he will interpose any obstacles to the conclusion of the proposed convention."[8]

The hesitation felt by the King of Denmark relative to the sale of the islands to the United States after the publication of the Christmas scandals, was regarded with distinct concern in some quarters in the United States. On May 5, 1900, the New York *Times* published an editorial which first quoted a London despatch to the effect that the Danish King was opposed to the sale, and then commented as follows:

"Very good. We shall be well content to let Denmark keep the islands if public sentiment and her King oppose their sale. . . . But we hope King Christian and his advisers are sufficiently familiar with our traditional policy to understand well that the transfer

[8] Swenson to Hay, May 4, 1900, MS. Dept. of State, *Denmark, Desp.*, vol. 23.

of title and possession to any of the great powers of Europe would not be countenanced by the Government of the United States. . . . The islands must be and remain Denmark's or ours. If Denmark understands this she may be spared the embarrassment of impracticable commitments."[9]

A few weeks later, May 26, 1900, Henry White wrote to Hay with reference to a recent conversation with Mr. Bille, the Danish representative in London:

"Bye the bye, Bille tells me that he thinks the Danish islands matter will have to rest a while. A party in Denmark has got it into their heads that they will get up a huge bank and develop the islands and keep them—an idea which is doomed to failure in his opinion but it will take some little time to discover it. He said that he does not know how the new ministry feels on the subject, but the foregoing opinion is merely his own."[10]

From all indications it would seem that the new Danish Ministry had rapidly swung round in favor of the treaty. At first some of the members were opposed to a transfer of the islands, but after a thorough examination of the question the Ministry was "unanimous in its opinion that a sale is desirable." Mr. Swenson believed that popular agitation against the sale was at an end, and that negotiations could now be conducted "under more favorable conditions than a few months ago."[11]

[9] New York *Times*, May 5, 1900.
[10] White to Hay, May 26, 1900, MS. *White Papers.*
[11] Swenson to Hay, June 20, 1900, MS. Dept. of State, *Denmark, Desp.,* vol. 23.

In his despatch of June 20, 1900, Mr. Swenson had enclosed a note that the Danish Foreign Minister had written him relative to the draft treaty that Secretary Hay had desired to serve as the basis of the negotiations for the cession of the Danish West Indies. In this note Mr. Schested first called the attention of the American Minister to the ardent desire of His Majesty to cede the islands only on condition that thereby the welfare of the inhabitants should be materially improved. In view of the fact that the draft treaty did not contain any provision for a plebiscite of the inhabitants relative to the proposed change of sovereignty, the Danish King thought it imperative that the following points be clearly understood. First of all, His Majesty wished the draft treaty to be so amended that the inhabitants of the islands who might not wish to retain their status as Danish citizens, shall obtain, as soon as the cession shall have been effected, the rights enjoyed by American citizens. Secondly, His Majesty desired that, simultaneously with the cession, these inhabitants should be exempted from all customs duties in their relations with the United States, or obtain in this respect at least the same advantages recently accorded to the inhabitants of Porto Rico. And moreover, inasmuch as His Majesty could not consider the cession of the islands as "a mere commercial transaction," the Royal Government wished as compensation

"only an amount sufficient to reimburse the Danish

Treasury for sums, with accrued interest, advanced to the colonial treasury of the islands, to the commune of St. Croix, and to the stock-company, the Sugar Factories of St. Croix; also by capitalization, for pensions which in consequence of the cession, would have to be paid to the functionaries of the islands."

This reimbursement would require a compensation of at least four millions of dollars, the sum of three and a half millions of dollars as provided in the draft treaty being insufficient. But in any case the consent of the Danish Rigsdag could not be secured unless "an absolute guarantee can be given that the Danish Treasury will be liable for no obligations after the cession has been made."

Finally, in the draft treaty, provision is made that the islands "shall be free from all encumbrances limiting the exercise of sovereignty." The difficulty in this case is that there are in existence "a number of such encumbrances in the islands." such as the monopoly granted to the St. Thomas Floating Dock Company, and the concession enjoyed by the English West India and Panama Telegraph Company. Of such rights the Royal Government can not divest the possessors, as that would be a violation of the laws at present in force in the islands. The Government of the United States will, therefore, have to pledge itself

"to indemnify the Danish Treasury for claims that might be made against it by parties considering themselves damaged in consequence of the cession, in their rights of monopoly, privileges, concessions . . . or similar claims."[12]

As soon as this note from the Danish Minister of Foreign Affairs reached the Department of State it received careful study and a formal "memorandum" upon it was prepared. In this memorandum notice is first given to the attempt that had been made in the draft treaty to base it upon the Treaty of Peace with Spain. Such a treaty, however, was not a good precedent, for the United States was

"not proposing to make with Denmark a Treaty of Peace. We are not dealing with a defeated adversary. Hence we are not in a position to demand, nor is Denmark in a position to concede points which Spain, as a conquered nation might be required to yield. When we propose that Denmark shall give us an 'unencumbered' sovereignty, and she replies that she cannot do it unless we guarantee her against the claims of those to whom she has contracted obligations, her situation is wholly unlike that of Spain. We never demanded, nor does the Treaty of Peace contain, any agreement or stipulation that the sovereignty ceded or relinquished by Spain should be 'free and unencumbered by any grants, conditions, privileges or franchises.' The controversy on that subject at Paris related solely to the refusal of the United States to agree to an express stipulation for the wholesale assumption of Spain's encumbrances.' "[13]

[12] Schested to Swenson, June 18, 1900, MS. Dept. of State, inclosed in Swenson to Hay, June 20, 1900, *Denmark, Desp.*, ol. 23.

[13] Memorandum on the Confidential Note of the Danish Minister of Foreign Affairs of June 18, 1900, MS. Dept. of State, *Miscellaneous Letters* (unbound).

After these introductory remarks, the *memorandum* then discusses the modifications desired by the Danish Government in the draft treaty. With reference to those Danish subjects who do not file any declaration of their intention to retain their Danish citizenship within two years from the date of the exchange of ratifications of the treaty, the Danish Government asked that these former subjects "shall obtain, as soon as the cession shall have been effected, the rights enjoyed by American citizens."

In this regard the *memorandum* did not view such a request as unreasonable, for "all our treaties of annexation, except the late treaty with Spain, admit the inhabitants of the annexed territory of the 'rights' of 'citizens' of the United States." Therefore, it was recommended that the draft treaty be amended so as to include in Article 3 a clause to the effect that these former Danish subjects "may at any time after the cession of the islands definitively elect such citizenship by making a declaration" of this change in status.

The second modification desired by the Danish Government was that the islands should be exempt from customs duties in their relations with the United States, or that they shall have "at least the same advantages recently accorded to Porto Rico." The author of the *memorandum* considered this modification to be "a reasonable stipulation," and recommended that it be met by a clause which should read that "the United States, in extending its customs administration to the islands ceded by this convention, will give the as favorable treatment as had been accorded by recent legislation to Porto Rico."

The memorandum then proceeds to discuss in great detail the modification desired by the Danish Government relative to raising the compensation from $3,500,-000 to $4,000,000. The basis for this larger compensation was the claim that the Danish Treasury would have to be reimbursed for the sums advanced to the colonial treasury of the islands, to the commune of St. Croix, and to the stock company called "The Sugar Factories of St. Croix." Also, provision would have to be made for the capitalization of certain pensions which, in consequence of the cession, would have to be paid to the functionaries of the islands.

With special reference to the sums advanced to the colonial treasury, to the commune of St. Croix, and to the stock company called The Sugar Factories of St. Croix, the author of the *memorandum* did not believe that they constituted valid criteria of any kind. They really represented nothing "but the sums which Denmark, as the sovereign of the islands, has been compelled to spend in their government." The colonial revenues being insufficient for the governmental upkeep, it was obvious that the longer Denmark held the islands the greater the indebtedness would become. These items, therefore, "instead of being an index as to what would be a proper price for a cession of the islands, would appear to bear an inverse ratio to their value."

The fourth modification desired by the Danish Government was in regard to the clause in the draft treaty which provided that the islands when ceded to the United States should be "free from all encumbrances limiting the exercise of the sovereignty." The Danish note of June 18, 1900, had referred to the concessions that had been granted to certain corporations, and contended that either these concessions would have to be respected or indemnities be paid for the liquidation of the claims of these corporations.

With respect to this contention of the Danish Government the author of the *memorandum* professed to be in complete accord:

"In maintaining that her successor in sovereignty must either recognize the obligations embraced in the fourth modification or else enable her to satisfy the claims of those whose rights may be ignored, Denmark takes a position the justice and validity of which the United States has never contested."

This being true, it was suggested that the American Government could take either of two courses. As its offer of $3,500,000,

"presupposed the conveyance of an 'unencumbered' sovereignty, it may cut down that amount to $3,000,-000 or $3,250,000, and offer to fulfil the obligations contracted toward the St. Thomas Floating Dock Company, the West India and Panama Telegraph Company, Limited, and the Sugar Factories of St. Croix, provided that those obligations do not upon fuller examination prove to be more onerous than they now appear to be; or it may offer $3,750,000 (or, if that should seem preferable, even $4,000,000) for an unencumbered sovereignty, i. e. unencumbered by pecuniary obligations, permitting Denmark to settle with those whose rights are effected."[14]

After receiving this *memorandum,* which was prepared by John Bassett Moore, Secretary Hay made it the basis of an instruction to Mr. Swenson, November 16, 1900. In regard to the request of the Danish Government that Danish subjects "shall obtain, as soon as the cession shall have been effected, the rights enjoyed by American citizens," Secretary Hay was influenced by the suggestion in the *memorandum* and offered the following amendment to Article 3 of the draft treaty:

"In case they remain in the islands, they may preserve their allegiance to the Crown of Denmark by making within two years from the date of the exchange of the ratifications of this convention a declaration of their intention to preserve such allegiance, in default of which declaration they shall be held to have re-

[14] From a letter addressed to Secretary Hay by John Bassett Moore, September 20, 1900, it would appear that Mr. Moore was the author of this State Department *memorandum* from which we have liberally quoted. Mr. Moore had recently served as Assistant Secretary of State, and as secretary and counsellor to the American Peace Commission at Paris. In his letter of September 20, Mr. Moore remarks as follows: "Nearly a fortnight ago, Adee, acting, as he informed me, on your request, handed me two envelopes containing papers in relation to the Danish West Indies. Those papers I have just returned to him, and I herewith enclose: 1. A memorandum on the note of the Danish Minister of Foreign Relations of June 18, 1900. 2. A draft of instructions to Mr. Swenson. 3. A new draft of a convention." See Department of State, *Miscellaneous Letters* (unbound).

nounced it, and to have elected allegiance to the United States."[15]

The second modification desired by the Danish Government in the draft treaty was the insertion of a provision that the islands should be exempt from customs duties in their relations with the United States, or that they should have at least the same advantages as were recently accorded to Porto Rico.   In his *memorandum* Mr. Moore had recommended that this request of the Danish Government be acceded to, and stated that he regarded such a modification as a "reasonable stipulation."   Secretary Hay, however, did not adopt this suggestion of Mr. Moore, and in his instruction of November 16, 1900, he observed as follows:

"This modification if embodied in the treaty would limit and direct the legislative discretion of the Congress, which it is not practical to do.   In point of fact, the ceded Danish islands would necessarily share in the administrative scheme of Porto Rico, to which they are adjacent, and it is not supposable that the Congress in legislating for their governance would impose unfavorable conditions upon them.   Another rea-

[15] Although Secretary Hay was influenced by Mr. Moore's memorandum with reference to the wording of the amendment to Article 3 of the draft treaty, he did not accept Mr. Moore's suggestion to insert in the draft treaty a modification which would permit the former Danish subjects in the islands elect American citizenship "at any time after the cession of the islands" by merely making a declaration to that effect. This knotty problem of citizenship for the islanders was soon to be determined by the Supreme Court in the so-called *Insular Cases,* and Secretary Hay would await this decision.

son for omitting a conventional stipulation in this regard is that the question of the commercial relations of our lately acquired islands to the Union as well as the citizenship of their inhabitants remains to be passed upon by the Supreme Court of the United States."

The third modification which the Danish Government had suggested related to an increase in compensation for the islands from $3,500,000 to $4,000,000. The basis for this request for a larger compensation was the claim that the Danish Treasury would need to be reimbursed for the sums advanced to the colonial treasury of the islands, to the commune of St. Croix, and to the stock company called The Sugar Factories of St. Croix. Mr. Moore had stated in his *memorandum* that he did not believe that these claims could be considered as valid criteria for fixing the amount of compensation for the cession. These debts really represented the sums which Denmark, as the sovereign of the islands, had been compelled to advance for their effective administration. Therefore, instead of being an index as to what would be a proper price for a cession of the islands, they would appear to bear "an inverse ratio to their value."

In this connection Secretary Hay precisely followed the reasoning in Mr. Moore's *memorandum*. In his instruction to Mr. Swenson he discusses these claims advanced by Denmark, and then comes to the conclusion that such items seemed

for the most part to bear no relation to the amount of compensation to be paid, unless as an argument for reducing it, for the cause of their existence being a deficiency of colonial revenue, it is obvious that they denote an apparent decrease in the value of the islands, and that, if adopted as the basis of compensation, they must, while steadily draining the Danish Treasury, soon render a cession of the islands impossible."

The final modification of the draft treaty which had been adverted to by the Danish Government referred to that clause which provided that the islands when ceded to the United States should be "free from all encumbrances limiting the exercise of sovereignty." The difficulty was that concessions had been granted to certain corporations, so it was contended that either these grants would have to be respected or indemnities be paid for their cancellation.

Mr. Moore had readily recognized the justice of this position, and he had recommended that the United States offer $3,000,000 or $3,250,000 for the islands and agree to respect these concessions, or to offer $3,750,000 or $4,000,000 for an "unencumbered sovereignty." Secretary Hay had no difficulty in accepting this viewpoint of Mr. Moore, and in his instruction to Mr. Swenson he states that it is his opinion that if the American Government should

"assume the obligations which the Danish Government has specified, it should not pay that Government more than $3,250,000 in cash, and . . . if it should expressly assume those obligations, which, as they are the only ones that Denmark has mentioned, presumably are all that exist, it should not suggest the setting up of groundless demands, to the annoyance of both Governments by inserting in the treaty a general and indefinite engagement to indemnify Denmark against the claims of those who may imagine themselves to have been damaged by the cession. . . . On the other hand the United States would undertake to pay, for a cession unencumbered by pecuniary obligations the sum of $3,750,000."[16]

After Secretary Hay despatched this instruction to Mr. Swenson, negotiations were to lag for some time. Of course, the usual rumors were rife, and on December 30, 1900, the New York *Times* reported that negotiations for the islands were in progress, the United States offering $3,240,000 for them.[17] Two weeks later there was another rumor that the negotiations were approaching a settlement. The King and Ministry were reported to be in favor of the sale, but strong opposition was anticipated in Denmark.[18] On February 1, 1901, a Danish merchant in New York City announced that he had received a cable from Copenhagen advising him that a committee of the Rigsdag had reported favorably on the question of the cession of the islands to the United States. The committee, however, had imposed the condition that a plebiscite be held in the islands to ascertain the desires of the inhabitants.[19] Shortly after this announcement, the Copenhagen correspondent of the London *Daily Mail* reported that "with only one dissenting voice the Financial Committee of the Landsthing has approved the sale of the Danish West Indies."[20]

[16] Hay to Swenson, November 16, 1900, MS. Dept. of State, *Denmark, Inst.*, vol. 16.
[17] New York *Times*, December 30, 1900.
[18] New York *Times*, January 12, 1901.
[19] New York *Times*, February 1, 1901.
[20] Quoted in the New York *Times*, February 13, 1901.

These rumors must have excited the curiosity of Secretary Hay, who, on February 16, sent the following cablegram to Swenson:

"What progress, if any, in negotiations for islands? The papers report contradictory statements, but nothing heard from you or the Danish Minister."[21]

A week later Mr. Swenson replied with a despatch enclosing a note from the Danish Minister of Foreign Affairs to the American Minister. In this formal note the Foreign Minister outlined his objections to the draft treaty which had not been met by the modifications proposed by Secretary Hay in his instruction to Mr. Swenson of November 16, 1900. After a most careful examination of the modifications proposed by Secretary Hay, the Danish Government was still

"unable to consider as satisfactory the stipulations contained in the projects regarding the rights guaranteed to the inhabitants of the islands as well as the amount of the consideration offered; and in consequence it does not dare to hope that it would be able to obtain the consent of the Rigsdag to the amended draft of the convention."

With regard to the question of the inhabitants of the islands acquiring United States citizenship, the Danish Government was not in favor of the slight change in wording proposed by Secretary Hay. It will be remembered that Mr. Moore had anticipated this firm stand on the part of the Danish Government,

21 Hay to Swenson, February 16, 1901, MS. Dept. of State, *Denmark, Inst.,* vol. 16.

and had recommended that a provision be inserted whereby the former Danish subjects could "at any time after the cession of the islands" elect American citizenship merely by making a declaration to that effect. The Danish Government would probably have accepted this modification proposed by Mr. Moore, but Secretary Hay had refused to adopt it and had adhered to the position that such a modification encroached on the legislative discretion of Congress. In support of their contention the Danish Government referred to Article 3 of the convention of October 24, 1867, whereby these former Danish subjects were to be given the right of retaining their Danish allegiance or acquiring the rights of citizens of the United States.

The Danish Government also insisted

"on securing for the islands free trade with the United States; as it seems natural that in this respect they ought to be given a position identical with that secured to Porto Rico after March 1 next year."

With reference to the compensation offered by the United States the Danish Government wished to observe that this was not to be considered as

"a purchasing sum for which the United States would eventually acquire the claims and demands which the Danish Government at present possesses the right to enforce against the colonial treasuries; inasmuch as it is the desire to rid the islands of this debt and their consequent cramped condition, without necessitating a loss on the part of the Danish Treasury of the sums that it has loaned or advanced to the colonial treasuries, and thereby make a better financial and economic future for the islands possible, that after all should induce Denmark to transfer these islands to a foreign Government. The Government must therefore expressly guard against the possibility of eventually construing the wording of Article 1, . . . to import that the financial claims now held by Denmark against the colonial treasures had been transferred to the United States. Though the Government of the King believes itself in full accord with the Government of the United States on this point, . . . it nevertheless considers it desirable in order to avoid possible misunderstanding and to reassure the inhabitants of the islands, that this view should be expressly embodied in the text of the convention, so that it should be stipulated that in the event of the transfer of the islands the colonial treasuries were to be considered released from their debts and obligations to the Danish Government Treasury."

With respect to the compensation to be offered by the United States for the islands the Danish Government insisted that it should receive at least four millions of dollars in gold, and even this large sum would not give the islands to the United States in a condition of "unencumbered sovereignty," for the American Government would still have to bind itself to respect the concession to the Floating Dock-Company of St. Thomas, in accordance with the terms of which no other floating dock could be built in that harbor within twenty-one years from March 12, 1897.

The Danish Government also wished to add to Article 3, a provision that Danish subjects not living in the islands but owning property there shall not in any way be effected in their property rights by a cession, and to Article 4 it was desired to add the following words: "Their arms as well as the military stores existing in the said territory or islands are not included in the cession."[22]

On March 11, 1901, Mr. Swenson wrote to Secretary Hay to inform him of the political conditions in Denmark that made it requisite for the Ministry to insist upon the modifications to the draft treaty proposed by Secretary Hay. The present Ministry was weak,

"being opposed by a large and aggressive majority in the lower house of the Rigsdag, and being supported only in a half-hearted way, by a faction within its own party sufficiently large to reduce its majority to one or two votes in the upper house whenever important differences in political policy arise."

As a result of this condition the Ministry was lacking in self-confidence and in courage to take the initiative in important matters. It was natural therefore that it should manifest a strong tendency to defer to the Rigsdag even on what might seem non-essential points relative to negotiations with the United States. In this way it was hoped that opposition to the treaty might be obviated, and thus prepare for its speedy approval by both the Landsthing and the Folkething.

The modifications considered most important by the Rigsdag were those concerning the rights and political status of the inhabitants of the islands, and the future customs relations between the islands and the United

[22] Schested to Swenson, February 21, 1901, enclosed in the despatch of Swenson to Hay, February 23, 1901, MS. Dept. of State, *Denmark, Desp.*, vol. 23.

States. The Danish Foreign Office realized the delicate nature of negotiations towards those ends, and the reluctance of Secretary Hay to give way on those points. It was necessary, however, in order to anticipate opposition in the Rigsdag, to press these points strongly, and to insist that satisfactory modifications be inserted in the draft treaty.

The King was personally opposed to the sale of the islands, but he felt that he should not stand in the way of superior advantages being bestowed upon the islanders. The Ministry also favored the sale, but prominent business men were

"quietly trying to induce the Government to break off the negotiations; and are proposing plans whereby, with the cooperation of the Rigsdag, they would make an effort to improve the economic and commercial conditions of the islands."

The general manager of the East Asiatic Steamship Company, Mr. Anderson, Admiral Richelieu, who was expected soon to return from Spain, Director Gluckstadt of Landmandsbanken, and other prominent Danes were strongly in favor of retaining the islands in order to develop them with Danish capital. These leaders had considerable influence in Denmark, and were shrewd enough to base their opposition to the sale on grounds of patriotism.[23]

It was now obvious to Secretary Hay that further concessions would have to be granted in order that

<hr />

[23] Swenson to Hay, March 11, 1901, MS. Dept. of State, *Denmark, Desp.*, vol. 23.

a satisfactory treaty could be negotiated with the Danish Ministry, so on March 26, 1901, he sent a lengthy instruction to Swenson in which he endeavored to conciliate the Danish opposition and yet withhold some of the concessions they most strongly demanded. In the new draft treaty which he enclosed with this instruction there were contained several of the changes desired by the Danish Government. In Article 1 it was provided that the cession should convey to the United States the islands in "entire and unencumbered sovereignty," and this is followed by the modification asked for by the Danish Government in Mr. Schested's note of February 21:

"It being however understood and agreed that the consummation of said cession does not import the transference to the United States of the financial claims now held by Denmark against the colonial treasuries of the islands, but that the colonial treasuries are to be considered released from their debts and obligations to the Treasury of the Danish Government."[24]

In Article 2, Secretary Hay had again inserted the desired amendment which exempted from American ownership the "arms and military stores existing in the islands at the time of the cession and belonging to the Government of Denmark." He also incorporated in Article 2, a further amendment to the effect that

[24] Article 1 also contained the pledge that the United States would "assume and continue to discharge from the time of the cession the current obligations heretofore contracted by the Danish Government towards the St. Thomas Floating Dock Company, and the West India and Panama Telegraph Company."

"where the Danish Government shall at the time of the cession hold property taken over by the Danish Treasury for sums due by individuals, property shall not pass by this cession, but the Danish Government shall sell or dispose of such property and remove its proceeds within .. months from the date of the exchange of ratifications of this convention."

In Article 3, Secretary Hay incorporated the amendment requested by the Danish Government to the effect that

"Danish subjects not residing in the islands but owning property therein at the time of the cession shall retain their rights of property, including the right to sell or dispose of such property, being placed in this regard on the same basis as the Danish subjects residing in the islands."

After making these concessions, Secretary Hay refused to give way with reference to Danish desires concerning the political status of the inhabitants of the islands and their future customs relations with the United States. In this new draft treaty of March 26, he had paragraph two of Article 3, read as follows: "The civil rights and the political status of the native inhabitants of the islands shall be determined by the Congress." In defense of this position he argues that it was a firmly established fact under our Constitution that

"the Congress alone has the power to prescribe rules of naturalization, therefore it is found impracticable to embody an express provision to that end in a treaty, the making of which is an executive, not a legislative function."

With regard to Mr. Schested's insistent request that the islands be put on a basis of free trade with the United States, in this way approximating the position of Porto Rico after March 1 of the following year, Secretary Hay assured the Danish Foreign Minister that it was the "belief of this Government, amounting to a certainty, that . . . it will soon be practicable to give to the Danish islands all the privileges of Puerto Rico."[25]

Finally, it was provided that in consideration of the cession of the islands in full, entire and unencumbered sovereignty, the United States would pay within ninety days from the date of the exchange of ratifications of the treaty, in the City of Washington, the sum of four millions of dollars in gold.

A few days after Secretary Hay sent his instruction of March 26 with the enclosed draft treaty, the New York *Times* reported a statement of its Washington correspondent to the effect that the State Department had done nothing towards "acquiring the islands since last Spring, when the negotiations fell through. According to a high officer of the Department, the United States Government is not now seeking outlying islands and people."[26] On April 1, 1901, the *Times* then published an editorial which discussed

[25] Hay to Swenson, March 26, 1901, MS. Dept. of State, *Denmark, Inst.,* vol. 16. The new draft treaty enclosed in this instruction of March 26 may be found in *Miscellaneous Letters* (unbound) in the Department of State.

[26] New York *Times,* March 29, 1901.

the rumors of negotiations and concluded with the statement that

"Denmark is eager to sell the islands, the expenses of which she is tired of paying, but . . . nobody in the United States is clamoring for the Danish islands, nobody shows the slightest interest in the progress of the negotiations, if any negotiations are in progress, and nobody would personally—and knowingly—contribute 10 cents either to promote or to prevent the acquisition."[27]

While these sparkling bits of misinformation were going the rounds, Mr. Swenson, in a note of April 8, 1901, communicated to the Danish Minister of Foreign Affairs the instruction of Secretary Hay of March 26, and the enclosed draft treaty. This new draft treaty appeared to make a "most favorable impression" upon the Danish Ministry," but there were additional modifications still to be inserted in certain articles.[28] With reference to Articles 5 and 6 the Danish Government professed to be satisfied with them as they stood, but Article 3 still left much to be desired. The Danish Government especially regretted that

"the Government of the United States did not see its way clear to accede to the proposal to embody in the convention provisions regarding the customs relations of the islands and the rights of the inhabitants after

[27] New York *Times,* April 1, 1901.

[28] Swenson to Hay, April 16, 1901, MS. Dept. of State, *Denmark, Desp.,* vol. 23. The modifications desired by the Danish Government in the draft treaty of March 26, 1901, with respect to Articles 1 and 2, were comparatively unimportant and dealt largely with phraseology.

an eventual cession. . . . One of the principal advantages expected from a union between the islands and the United States was that their principal products, especially sugar, would be admitted to the markets of the United States free of duty or, in any event, with a considerable reduction of duty. How to surmount this difficulty and how to arrange the customs relations in a manner satisfactory to both parties is one of the question that is giving concern to His Majesty's Government; and it would be grateful if the Government of the United States likewise would consider how this matter might be best arranged, and submit a proposition to His Majesty's Government on this subject."[29]

With respect to the civil status of the inhabitants, the Danish Government first invited the attention of the United States to the fact that the organic law in force in the islands insured to these inhabitants a large measure of autonomy in the administration of local affairs. Next, it was pointed out that not only did the convention of October 24, 1867, "assure to the inhabitants of the islands in the event of a cession United States citizenship," but that Article 2 of the Treaty of April 26, 1826, between Denmark and the United States specifically provided that Danish subjects in the United States shall "enjoy all the rights, privileges, and exemptions in navigation and commerce which native citizens or subjects do or shall enjoy, submitting themselves to the laws, decrees, and usages there established to which native citizens or subjects

[29] Schested to Swenson, June 29, 1901, enclosed in the despatch of Swenson to Hay, August 8, 1901, MS. Dept. of State, *Denmark, Desp.*, vol. 23.

are submitted." In the draft treaty of March 26, however, it was provided that "the Danish subjects born in the islands or permanently residing there" shall be "subject to such laws as are applicable to other foreigners." This provision would, without doubt,

"be regarded with much disfavor in the islands; inasmuch as the inhabitants that acquired domicile in the United States would be less favorably situated than they now are, under the provisions of the above named treaty (1826); while those remaining in the islands would not obtain United States citizenship."

At all events His Majesty's Government did not wish

"to omit pointing out that the project of the convention will have to be modified in the sense indicated; so that the inhabitants would continue, after the cession . . . to enjoy the private as well as the municipal and religious rights accorded them under the laws now in force in the islands; and that if these laws should be changed they would, with respect to these rights, be treated as citizens and subjects of the United States."[30]

This question of arranging satisfactory treaty terms was not, however, to be completed by the Schested Ministry, for in July, 1901, a new Ministry came into power with Dr. Deuntzer as Premier, and with Alfred Hage as the Minister of Foreign Affairs.[31] And it was to this new Ministry that Alvey A. Adee, the Acting Secretary of State, was to submit a new draft

[30] Schested to Swenson, June 29, 1901, enclosed in Swenson to the Secretary of State, August 8, 1901, MS. Dept. of State, *Denmark, Desp.,* vol. 23.

[31] New York *Times,* July 20, 1901.

treaty which was enclosed in an instruction to Mr. Swenson, September 10, 1901.[32] In this third draft treaty the suggestions of the Danish Government relative to the wording of Articles 1 and 2 were adopted, but the American Government still held firm with reference to conferring upon the islanders the rights of free trade with the United States or granting them United States citizenship.

It would be a difficult matter to persuade the Danish Government to give way on these two points, so on August 1, 1901, Secretary Hay wrote to Henry White a long personal letter in which he carefully canvassed the whole situation regarding the negotiations. He understood that

"the new Ministry in Denmark—and particularly the Premier and Minister of Foreign Affairs—are favorable to our Treaty. Swenson is at home on leave of absence, and the man left there in charge, Professor Freeman, Consul, is entirely unfit for any diplomatic business. It is evident that the Danish Government have very little confidence in Brun, so that I am shut up to two courses of action; either to do nothing till late autumn and then try to hurry things through for December; or to attempt, in some extra-official manner, to get the Danish Government to take up the question now, and if possible decide it before another parliamentary crisis comes on.

"From all I have heard from Brun and from Swenson I infer that the Danish Cabinet has been several times on the point of accepting our propositions—but some flurry in Danish politics, or possibly some action of interested parties who do not want the islands

[32] Adee to Swenson, September 10, 1901, MS. Dept. of State, *Denmark, Inst.,* vol. 16.

ceded to us unless they can make something by it—
has always prevented the final agreement.

"...

"I have concluded to submit this suggestion to your
consideration and beg you will discuss it with Mr.
Choate and then cable me in a word or two, your idea
of its practicability. It is that you go to Copenhagen,
whenever convenient to you, and put yourself in personal communication with the Minister of Foreign
Affairs either through the intervention of acquaint-
ances in Denmark — e. g. Frijs or Ravn — or by the
presentation of the enclosed note, if the other course
should prove inconvenient; tell him that by reason of
the absence of Mr. Swenson from his post, and my
own temporary retirement from Washington, it seemed
expedient to this Government to resort to this somewhat irregular means of communication: that the
President desires to be informed whether it is probable that a convention for the cession of the islands
can be signed in time for submission to Congress the
first days of December; if not, that we would be
grateful for some intimation of the reasons that stand
in the way of such an agreement. We have been led
to understand that the last draft of a treaty sent to
Denmark through Mr. Swenson, in which the President had gone to the limits of his power to meet the
suggestions of the Danish Government, was on the
whole acceptable to His Majesty. If that is the case
we would be glad if instructions might be sent to
Mr. Brun to conclude a treaty in accordance with
that draft.

"... If the Minister should show a disposition to
open a discussion of the whole matter upon its merits,
you will of course listen with attention to anything
he may say, but it might be as well for you to say in
reply that your Government was of the opinion that
we had substantially agreed upon the draft of a convention, and that you would regret to have to inform
me that so little progress had been made; and that, in

your opinion, the present draft embodied the views of the President in the most favorable form he could give them, adopting, as we have done, nearly all the suggestions of the Danish Government.

"If, in the course of conversation, an opportunity should present itself you might refer to the stories current in the European and American newspapers, about the interest that private parties have in these negotiations, and say that so far as we are concerned, there is not a word of truth in them; that we have refused to listen to any such suggestions from any quarter. . . .

"You will understand that this is in no sense an instruction. I suggest these things to you, only in case they commend themselves to your judgment, and you find it convenient to carry them out. I hope if you go, you will move with the same celerity and discretion you showed before. . . .

"You will not give the Danish Minister to understand that we are over-anxious in the matter. We simply wish to know why there is so much delay in a negotiation which seemed acceptable to both parties. You might let him understand that there will be some opposition in Congress, which as the matter stands, we hope to overcome—but that this opposition will constantly increase if the negotiations are unduly protracted."[33]

As a postscript to this letter of August 1, Hay wrote as follows to White:

"If they are still haggling over the status of the inhabitants after cession you might refer to Porto Rico and the immense advantage they have gained by their annexation, including at last absolute free trade with the United States, at the same time letting them understand that this is not a matter for Executive

[33] Hay to White, August 1, 1901, MS. *White Papers.*

action in a treaty, but must be left for Congress to determine."

Hay took care to send as an enclosure in this letter to White a copy of the third draft treaty which he hoped that White would be able to persuade the Danish Government to accept. On August 15, he sent another letter to White in which he explained at length the impossibility of yielding in the matter of customs relations and citizenship, and pressed for a speedy settlement of the whole matter. In answer, Henry White cabled from London that he was starting for Copenhagen on August 28, and would stop one day in Jutland with Count Frijs in order "to ascertain the political situation."[34]

As soon as White reached Copenhagen he cabled to Hay that Mr. Swenson had written to the Danish Minister of Foreign Affairs announcing his return to his post. In view of this fact it was very possible that the Danish Government would not agree to sign any treaty until Swenson's arrival.[35] On September 5, 1901, White sent a second cablegram from Copenhagen in which he recounted the conversation he had had with the Danish Premier and the Minister of Foreign Affairs. When he submitted the third draft of a treaty for the cession of the Danish West Indies to the United States, he explained the "impossibility of further concessions on nationality or commercial

[34] White to Hay, August 27, 1901, MS. Dept. of State, *Miscellaneous Letters* (unbound).
[35] White to Hay, *White Papers.*

questions but added that President would recommend free trade after Porto Rico precedent." The Prime Minister "seemed to appreciate situation and finally intimated those questions no probable obstacle to agreement." Indeed, the Prime Minister appeared much more anxious as to the possible defeat of the treaty by the American Senate, which action he feared would cause the downfall of his Ministry. He then inquired whether it would be possible to get the Senate "committed in advance." Mr. White thought such a procedure impossible, but assured the Premier that he regarded ratification as a "practical certainty." The Premier also objected to the inadequacy of the proposed compensation for the three islands, and asked Mr. White whether the United States would not be satisfied with the island of St. John alone, for that had a splendid harbor. Mr. White, however, quickly informed him that the United States wished to purchase all three islands, and that really the American Government was showing great kindness in this matter because Denmark while anxious to be rid of the islands, would for political reasons, be permitted to sell only to the United States.

The "real obstacle and probable cause of delay" was the refusal of the Sugar Factories of St. Croix to agree to cancel the claim to the 5% interest guaranteed it by the colonial treasury of St. Croix. The island government had been applied to by the Danish Government in order that pressure might be brought to bear upon the recalcitrant company, but it was doubted whether that government would accede to such a request, and in that case it would be necessary for the matter to be settled by the Danish Rigsdag.[36]

On September 10, White sent a cipher cablegram to Secretary Hay with reference to an interview he had had with the Prime Minister on the 6th. Dr. Deuntzer was still worried about the rejection of the treaty by the American Senate, and the difficulty of coming to terms with the St. Croix Sugar Factories, which he thought could best be done by the American Government. The situation in Denmark was very delicate and he could not agree to the draft treaty unless the following modifications were inserted. First of all it would be necessary that the United States "take over the claims of Danish Government as creditor against Saint Cross Sugar Factories Company with all rights resulting from hypothecation to Danish Treasury of companies properties there, our Government paying Danish Government in liquidation of debt due latter by Company, three million Danish crowns, also that we take steps to release Saint Cross Treasury from guarantee assumed in 1876 of five per cent."

The next modification referred to the rights of the Danish subjects in the islands. The Danish Government had strongly objected to the following clause in Article 3 of the draft treaty: "And in case they remain in the islands they shall enjoy all civil and religious liberties and be allowed to carry on their in-

[36] White to Hay, September 5, 1901, MS. Dept. of State, *Miscellaneous Letters* (unbound).

dustry, commerce and professions, being subject to
such laws as are applicable to other foreigners." This
placing of Danish subjects on the same level as "other
foreigners" grated on the sensibilities of the Danish
Ministry, and they insisted that the clause be amended
to read as follows:

"And in case they remain in the islands, they shall
continue until otherwise regulated to enjoy all private
i. e. non-political rights, municipal and religious liberties granted them by legislation now in force, and if
this legislation is changed they are to be treated in
the same manner as American citizens or subjects."

In his interview that he granted to Mr. White, the
Prime Minister stated that these modifications were
the result of a meeting of the Cabinet Council, and
of a subsequent conversation with the King, and that
they would have to be inserted in the draft treaty or
negotiations would have to lapse. Mr. White, however could "hold out no hope of their acceptance" by
the American Government, and endeavored to convince the Prime Minister that the modification proposed in Article 3 relative to the civil rights of the
Danish subjects in the islands would be an encroachment upon the exclusive rights of the American Congress. The Prime Minister then observed that inasmuch as his chief object in drafting the modification
was to "eliminate the word 'foreigners,' to which the
King is irrevocably opposed, any phraseology attain-
ing to that end probably acceptable."[37]

[37] White to Hay, September 10, 1901, MS. *White Papers.*

On this same day, September 10, 1901, White sent a second cablegram to Secretary Hay in which he expressed the opinion that the

"Danish Government think they must justify public enthusiasm on their accession by making better terms than predecessors. I fear increased amount inevitable if Treaty is to be signed promptly, which is very desirable, there being considerable adverse sentimental feeling, besides that of parties otherwise interested, but Danish Government do not expect to get all they ask, and I think another quarter or half million and elimination, if possible, of the word 'Foreigners,' sufficient. Would suggest any such offer if made be on condition that Treaty is signed before November fifteenth, threatening otherwise to drop negotiations."[38]

Three days later, Hay answered these cablegrams by sending one to White in which he expressed his fear that negotiations

"will fail by reason of the new demands of the Danish Government, in reference to the St. Croix Sugar Company. The final propositions we made were the result of careful inquiries among the leading Senators as to the best terms we should be justified in offering with any hope of their acceptance by the Senate and they were made with an earnest desire to meet the expressed wishes of the Danish Government and a sincere conviction that we had done so. I have the gravest doubt whether we could induce the Senate to accept any further increase of our offer, direct or indirect."[39]

[38] White to Hay, Private and Confidential, September 10, 1901, MS. *White Papers.*

[39] Hay to White, September 13, 1901, MS. Dept. of State, *Miscellaneous Letters* (unbound).

White was back in London by the time this cable-gram reached Copenhagen, and the first thing he did upon reaching the American embassy was to scratch off a short, informal note to Secretary Hay, whom he dubbed as usual, "Dear Chief." He expressed his regret that the Danish Prime Minister refused to sign the draft treaty sent by the Secretary of State, and it was his belief that any

"future negotiations had better be by cable. It wakes them up and keeps their minds, which are very dila-tory, up to a decision—Swenson being a Dane is, I fancy, a good deal like other Danes in the working of his mind. . . . It is important to have got Deuntzer to say that he will sell and I don't suppose half a million one way or the other is of real consequence to us, though of course I did not let him know this."[40]

On September 13, 1901, White wrote two important letters relative to the progress of the negotiations. The first was addressed to Mr. Swenson, the American Minister at Copenhagen. After explaining that, be-cause of the absence of Mr. Swenson in America, Mr. Hay had thought it expedient to hasten the negotia-tions by sending a confidential agent to Copenhagen, Mr. White disclosed to Swenson the details of his mission and of his failure to persuade the Danish Ministry to accept the draft treaty sent by Mr. Hay.[41]

The second letter Mr. White wrote on September 13, was to Secretary Hay in which he discussed at

[40] White to Hay, no date, MS. Dept. of State, *Miscellaneous Letters* (unbound).
[41] White to Swenson, September 13, 1901, MS. *White Papers.*

length his recent visit to Copenhagen. In his conversation with Dr. Deuntzer he at first thought that the Prime Minister was suggesting that

"we should take over the liability for the unpaid 5% interest on the Company's shares only, which seemed to me, although I did not say so of course, a possibility, if nothing more were asked, and that is why I inquired about the relations between the Company and the Danish Government. But the moment I discovered the complicated arrangements of that company I saw the utter impossibiltiy of it.

"He evidently intended when I left him the first time to let the matter rest until Swenson should arrive and I imagine that it was perhaps owing to Krag [the Director General of the Danish Foreign Office] who is genuinely desirous of selling the islands and to whom I expressed regret that his Chief should not have been willing to take the matter up while I was there and to close it, that he reconsidered his determination. I explained to him the various objections and dangers of delay which Krag fully saw and it was the next day when I went to get the figures about the Sugar Company which he promised to get for me, that he gave me to understand that Deuntzer had changed his mind and meant to consult his colleagues and the King on the subject at once and wished again to see me.

"I gathered from Frijs with whom I stayed on my way to Copenhagen for a day, that Deuntzer is not so sure of the popularity of selling the islands just now and consequently is not so keen as his predecessor was for the sale. It seems that Hörring the late Prime Minister evidently promised Christmas something handsome if he should bring about a sale, which accounts for the latter's activity and Krag confided to me that the Government will also have to reckon with him. The King seems to feel really very deeply about the word 'Foreigners' and if that can be in some way got over, I think he will assent to anything else.

"Of course there is little doubt that Deuntzer and his cabinet are 'trying it on,' and it is for that reason that I recommend prompt action by cable and a plain intimation from you that we cannot go on indefinitely. I gathered from Jusserand that the Danish Government has a rooted objection to making up its mind on any matter which can possibly be postponed, and I fancy Swenson, being of that nationality, does not know how to hustle them and quite understands their dilatory tactics. . . . I think your telegram to Swenson admirable and just calculated to stir up the Ministry and our Minister. I quite understand the feelings you express in the confidential telegram as to the offer of another quarter of a million, and it has occurred to me that if you approve, I might write Krag with whom I am now on excellent terms, privately, that I have ascertained from you that there is no chance, as I told him and Mr. D., of the acceptance of the terms proposed in Mr. Deuntzer's memorandum and in my opinion the best chance Denmark will have for a long time of selling the islands will be lost unless something is promptly done to save the situation; that I believe the only concession which might possibly be made would be another quarter of a million more. . . . If you think favorably of this project perhaps you would send me a private cablegram."[42]

As soon as Secretary Hay received this letter from Henry White he responded with the following cablegram:

"We will eliminate the phrase containing the word 'foreigners' and add a quarter million dollars to purchase price if that will insure unencumbered conclusion. You may write Krag as you propose, mentioning full amount."[43]

[42] White to Hay, September 13, 1901, MS. *White Papers.*
[43] Hay to White, no date, MS. *White Papers.*

In accordance with this instruction, White, on October 3, 1901, wrote to Krag, the Director General of the Danish Foreign Office, and laid the matter before him:

"As I felt sure, and made every effort not to disguise from Mr. Deuntzer, and as I think he and you must have since been informed by Mr. Swenson, it is quite impossible for my Government to accept the proposal contained in the first paragraph—headed 'to add to Article 1'—of the memorandum which Mr. Deuntzer handed to me on the 6th ultimo for transmission to Mr. Hay; not only because of the large increase thereby involved in the amount to be paid by us, but still more on account of the impossibility of ascertaining in advance the exact amount of such payment, to say nothing of the complicated relations existing between the St. Croix Sugar Company and the Danish Government, the Treasury of the Island, and the Shareholders. Nor was it possible for me to recommend to my Government the acceptance of a proposal involving such complicated negotiations with private individuals. But I did venture to suggest, in view of what Mr. Deuntzer said to me as to the inadequacy, in his opinion, of the amount which the late Danish Ministry had agreed to accept for the Islands, that, if my Government should deem it possible to secure the ratification by the Senate of a Treaty providing for a slight increase in the amount in question, it would be advisable to do so, and I furthermore suggested that the word 'foreigners,' which Mr. Deuntzer explained to me is particularly objectionable to the King, should if possible be dropped from Article 3 of the proposed Treaty.

"I am now in a position—am authorized in fact—to enquire whether your Government will accept, instead of the proposals contained in Mr. Deuntzer's memorandum aforesaid, an increase in the amount to be

paid for the *unencumbered* cession of the Islands from
4,000,000 (four millions)—the sum agreed upon by the
late Danish Ministry—to four and one-quarter millions (4,250,000) of dollars, together with the elimination of the phrase containing the word 'foreigners'
from the Treaty, which would in all other respects be
similar to the draft which I laid before Mr. Deuntzer
on the 3rd of last month.

"If you can assure me that these terms will be
accepted by your Government and will insure a prompt
conclusion of the matter—i. e. the signature of the
Treaty in ample time to be submitted to the Senate
when that body meets the first week in December, I
may say to you confidentially that they will be thereupon officially conveyed through the usual channel to
Mr. Deuntzer."[44]

Mr. White also urged upon Mr. Krag to speed the
negotiations as much as possible lest a suspicion

"should . . . arise that the present Danish Government
is endeavouring to obtain a higher price for the Islands
than their predecessors believed them to be worth, or
more than they were willing to accept; and I am quite
sure that the President, whom I know well, is not
likely, particularly at the commencement of his administration, to risk a rebuff on the part of the Senate
by making any further concessions. It is in the hope
of saving the situation that I write this to you."[45]

[44] White to Krag, October 3, 1901, MS. *White Papers.* In
an editorial in the New York *Times,* September 16, 1901, reference is made to the renewed negotiations for the Danish
islands, and the following comment is made: "The transaction would prove an eminently fitting feature of the first
few months of Mr. Roosevelt's Administration, which, as
regards the principle of judicious expansion, has so much to
confirm and so very little to create."

[45] White to Krag, October 3, 1901, MS. *White Papers.*

Two days later, White wrote to Secretary Hay with regard to the letter to Krag. He had submitted it to Ambassador Choate before sending it to Copenhagen, and while it seemed a little long, neither he nor the Ambassador could see just where it could be "advantageously curtailed." The main difficulty was to have Krag understand clearly that the offer was "bona fide and official if accepted, and no offer at all if they won't agree to it."

With reference to increasing the compensation to be paid to Denmark for the islands, White had talked the matter over with Senator Henry Cabot Lodge, then visiting London, but "without telling him exactly what we are doing." Lodge thought that a million one way or the other would make no difference whatever to the Senate, for they "don't care about the money part of it." Any serious opposition to the treaty would probably be based upon the fact that "the islanders have not been consulted by a plebiscite as they were before and that we are consequently annexing foreigners against their consent."[46]

[46] White to Hay, October 5, 1901, MS. Dept. of State, *Miscellaneous Letters* (unbound). As this letter indicates, White had some suspicion of the reaction of Lodge to this matter of the purchase of the Danish West Indies, and he sounded him out without "telling him exactly what we are doing." Although Lodge was an important member of the Senate and a personal friend of President Roosevelt who had lately come into office, Secretary Hay trusted him very little and at times warned White against him. These suspicions are well illustrated in the following excerpt from a letter from Hay to White, February 10, 1901: "I return Lodge's letter as

On October 11, Mr. Krag wrote to White in answer to the letter of October 3, 1901. He had submitted the matter to the Prime Minister, Mr. Deuntzer, who expressed his disinclination

"to enter upon a discussion of new proposals which were to be withheld from the United States accredited Minister, deeming it unnecessary to interrupt negotiations through the usual, regular channel."

It was also true that not only Mr. Deuntzer, but the entire Danish Cabinet, held the opinion that it was impossible for them to regard as a reasonable price for the islands

"an amount which, resting upon a computation of expenses already made or sure to arise from the cession, would have been acceptable to the late Ministry, provided they could have attained their principal aim, which was the insertion in the treaty of stipulations in favor of the rights of the inhabitants and the future prosperity of the islands."[47]

---

you request. It proves anew his selfish treachery. He knew I wished you named for Italy when Roger Walcott was chosen, and afterwards when he was pressing Meyer. He pretends the National Committee wanted Meyer. This is not true. . . . He is equally false about me. He is not unfriendly to me personally, in the abstract, nor is he to you. But neither you nor I would weigh a feather's weight with him, as against any selfish advantage. He would cut my throat or yours for a favorable notice in a newspaper." MS. *White Papers.*

[47] R. Krag to White, Private and confidential, October 11, 1901, MS. *White Papers.*

When Henry White received this letter from Mr. Krag, he forwarded it to Secretary Hay with some pertinent comments. He was

"rather disappointed not to have got more out of him, but while he is very keen to arrive at a settlement for the sale of the islands he is also a permanent official, and whatever he might say privately, he could evidently say only what Deuntzer practically dictated to him. I am afraid there is nothing more that I can do for you in the matter at present. It was unfortunate that Swenson should have been returning so soon, otherwise I might have stayed on and gone back and arranged the thing personally by constantly telegraphing you. It is very evident that Deuntzer is not averse to selling, but whether Swenson can bring him to terms in time for the meeting of Congress, I don't know. I suggested in the telegram which I sent you on receipt of Krag's letter, that it might be well, as you indicated in your last letter, to renew the offer I made him privately through Swenson to the Danish Government; as Krag does not absolutely decline it, and it occurred to me that at least it might be a means of getting them to say what they will take. Mr. Choate rather thinks that the best way will be to let the matter drop; otherwise they will go on raising their terms and never coming to a decision. No doubt that would be the cheapest way of getting the islands but, I fear, not the quickest, as in due time they must come to us, for they are more and more a care and expense to Denmark. But I should like to get them at once. How would it do if Deuntzer declines the four and a quarter million to offer four and one-half through S. and *then* break off negotiations for a time? I think the President is quite safe in offering four and one-half as far as the Senate is concerned or even five, from what Cabot said to me. The King is quite will-

ing to sell provided he gets the word 'foreigners' out;
so that it is really Deuntzer who is 'trying it on.' "[48]

Hay evidently thought well of White's advice, for
on October 18, he cabled to Swenson to

"represent to Danish Government the great desirability of deciding at once whether they will make the
treaty. We cannot continue negotiations after Congress meets. Ascertain whether offer of a quarter
million dollars more will conclude matter."[49]

On October 23, Swenson cabled back that

"a quarter million dollars more would not satisfy
Danish Government. Convention will not be concluded without concession on points difference and an
increase of compensation."[50]

The following day Swenson wrote an explanatory
despatch to Secretary Hay in which he indicated a
distinct stiffening in the attitude of the Danish Cabinet. There was a general impression in Denmark that
the United States was very eager to buy, and that if

[48] White to Hay, October 15, 1901, *White Papers*. On the
previous day White cabled in cipher to Hay the decision of
the Danish Prime Minister not to interrupt negotiations
"through usual regular channel." He also indicated that the
compensation offered was not satisfactory to Danish Cabinet,
and concluded with the following question: "Would it not be
advisable for you to telegraph Swenson and make same offer
officially and to reply by telegraph?" White to Hay, October
14, 1901, *White Papers*.

[49] Hay to Swenson, October 18, 1901, MS. Dept. of State,
Denmark, Inst., vol. 16.

[50] Swenson to Hay, October 23, 1901, MS. Dept. of State,
Denmark, Desp., vol. 23.

the Danish Government would continue to delay the negotiations it would secure a considerably higher offer for the islands. Moreover, the Minister of Foreign Affairs had assured Swenson that until

"within the last three weeks he would have assumed the responsibility of signing a treaty conforming substantially to the draft last submitted by the Government of the United States, except as to the amount of compensation; but that now he would feel constrained to insist on embodying in such convention provisions expressly conferring citizenship upon the inhabitants and granting the islands free trade, in the event of a cession. . . . Then also, the King considers the question of citizenship as the most important."

The position of Prime Minister Deuntzer, therefore, was quite strong, and he could easily continue his policy of procrastination, for

"the King and other members of the royal family would personally rather see the islands remain in the possession of Denmark; and inasmuch as there are no strong influences systematically agitating, or even advocating, the sale."[51]

The obstinate attitude of Dr. Deuntzer must have been very vexatious to Secretary Hay. The demands of the Danish Cabinet were daily growing more exacting, for not only were they now demanding a larger compensation for the islands, but were also resurrecting old conditions about conferring citizenship upon the islanders and granting them the commercial privi-

[51] Swenson to Hay, October 24, 1901, MS. Dept. of State, *Denmark, Desp.*, vol. 23.

lege of free trade with the United States. Something
would have to be done at once to save the treaty, so
Hay wrote to President Roosevelt to seek advice:

"I have a mingling of sweet and sour in my correspondence this morning. The Isthmian canal treaty
is all right. . . . My crumpled rose leaf is that Swenson
says the Danes will not negotiate unless we raise the
price. Please think a little about it and tell me to
morrow what I shall do."[52]

Hay also wrote to the leading Democratic Senator
on the Senate Foreign Relations Committee to ascertain whether the opposition in that body would raise
a strong protest against a more liberal compensation to
Denmark for the islands:

"I had succeeded in bringing pretty nearly to a close
our negotiations for the Danish Islands when the
recent crisis in the Danish Ministry occurred. The
new Minstry pretend that they will suffer a great loss
of popularity, and perhaps, a parliamentary defeat
unless they are able to obtain a considerable increase
of the price which was virtually agreed upon. I write
now, in strict confidence, to ask your opinion whether
if we should make a further concession to them, raising the price, say from four millions to not more than
five, it would endanger the acceptance of the treaty
by the Senate. Of course I am asking your opinion
for my own guidance, and the expression of your
views will be very gratefully received."[53]

[52] Hay to Roosevelt, October 25, 1901, MS. *Roosevelt Papers,*
Library of Congress.

[53] Hay to Morgan, October 26, 1901, MS. *John T. Morgan
Papers,* Library of Congress.

Although Senator Morgan's reply is not available, it was probably favorable, for subsequently he raised no objection to the finished treaty. Then, having received this assurance from the leader of the opposition party on the Foreign Relations Committee, Hay again turned to Roosevelt, and on November 8, made the following inquiry:

"The Danish Minister informs me that his Government authorizes him to say that if we will offer Five Million Dollars, 'we may expect the Treaty to be signed as drawn up by us, with very slight modifications.' May I say we will give that amount provided the slight modifications referred to are satisfactory to the President and provided also, that the Treaty is ready for signature before the end of this month?"[54]

The President was willing to authorize the payment of the five millions if necessary, so Hay began to feel as though the signature of the treaty would not long be delayed. On November 11, Swenson wrote that the advance in the compensation from four to five millions had produced a most favorable effect and that the "psychological moment" for concluding the negotiations had been reached. The Danish Government still insisted on the insertion of a clause to the effect that no responsibility of any kind would be incumbent upon it with reference to the guaranty that the colonial treasury of St. Croix had assumed with regard to the payment of five per cent. interest annually to the holders of the shares of the St. Croix Sugar Fac-

[54] Hay to Roosevelt, November 8, 1901, MS. *Roosevelt Papers*, Library of Congress.

tories. Also, the King was still greatly concerned over the civil status of the inhabitants of the islands and would like to have Article 3 amended so as to provide that those inhabitants who remain in the islands

"shall continue, until otherwise provided, to enjoy all the private, municipal, and religious rights and liberties secured to them by the laws now in force. If the present laws are altered, the said inhabitants shall not thereby be placed in a less favorable position in respect to the above mentioned rights and liberties than they now enjoy."[55]

Secretary Hay was willing to accept the modification of Article 3, relative to the civil status of the inhabitants of the islands, but he was at first opposed to any clause in the treaty which would relieve the Danish Government from any responsibility in regard to interest payments that were due from the colonial treasury to the St. Croix Sugar Factories. Swenson, however, strongly urged that the United States concede this point of non-responsibility for these interest payments, so Hay finally gave in.[56]

In the meantime Hay had talked the situation over with many of the Republican and Democratic Senators, and was very optimistic concerning the fate of the treaty in the Senate. It was in this vein that on November 18, 1901, he wrote as follows to Henry White:

[55] Swenson to Hay, November 11, 1901, MS. Dept. of State, *Denmark, Desp.,* vol. 23.

[56] Swenson to Hay, November 26 and 27, 1901, MS. Dept. of State, *Denmark, Desp.,* vol. 23.

"The Danish matter promises well though we shall have to pay five millions—but I think I have got the Senate solid in advance."[57]

In this same connection Senator Lodge wrote to Henry White that Secretary Hay

"has assurances from all the leading Democrats that they will suport the treaty for the Danish Islands, and I am hoping earnestly that that treaty will soon be signed and sent to the Senate."[58]

But Henry White was not satisfied with assurances from "leading Democrats" as to the probable ratification of the treaty by the Senate. He wanted to be certain that the more important Republican Senators were equally friendly, so on December 13, 1901, he wrote to Senator John C. Spooner, of Wisconsin, as follows:

"It is possible that I may soon ask your assistance in behalf of the Danish Islands Treaty which I hear is on the point of signature. I initiated the negotiations originally and have been again to Denmark this summer pushing it on, and I earnestly hope if a Treaty is made and is sent to the Senate that you will do your best to move its ratification. They [the Danes] have a terrible dread of another rebuff from the Senate which will cause promptly, the Prime Minister told me, the downfall of the Ministry which is the first Liberal Ministry the King has ever called into Power."[59]

[57] Hay to White, November 18, 1901, MS. *White Papers.*
[58] Lodge to White, November 21, 1901, MS. *White Papers.*
[59] White to Spooner, December 13, 1901, MS. *Spooner Papers,* Library of Congress.

On January 6, 1902, Spooner replied with the following reassurance:

"I note what you say about the Danish Islands treaty. I think it will go through all right, if such a treaty is made."[60]

On the basis of these promises of support, Secretary Hay went ahead and endeavored to bring the negotiations to a speedy conclusion. The Danish Government, however, seemed desirous to postpone matters for a while, and the necessary authorization to Mr. Brun to sign the treaty was withheld. This procedure made Secretary Hay so impatient that he cabled to Mr. Swenson to

"remind Minister of Foreign Affairs that the Senate adjourns for the holidays on Thursday and that it would be quite desirable to have the treaty signed before that day if possible."[61]

The Danish Ministry, however, was not to be hurried in this matter, and it was intimated to Mr. Swenson that it was very likely that the United States would have to consent to the holding of a plebiscite in the islands. Mr. Swenson, however, would give the Danish Foreign Minister no hope in this regard. Instead, he informed him

"politely, that the treaty had been agreed upon by the two Governments; that the Danish Foreign Office had desired to examine the text as accepted by the Secre-

---

[60] Spooner to White, January 6, 1902, MS. *Spooner Papers.*
[61] Hay to Swenson, December 17, 1901, MS. Dept. of State, *Denmark, Inst.,* vol. 16.

tary of State, pledging itself to cable Mr. Brun full power to sign the document as soon as it had been verified, and that Mr. Hay, in consequence, considered the negotiations ended, and nothing wanting but the formality of signing."

The Minister of Foreign Affairs agreed that Mr. Swenson was entirely correct in his statements, but he indicated the strong feeling throughout Denmark in favor of a plebiscite, and the difficulty of ignoring such a mandate. As for himself, the Minister was "tired of the whole business," and "did not know what to do."[62]

Mr. Swenson, however, was not to be bluffed by this sudden stand of the Danish Ministry. He was confident that the treaty would be signed without a plebiscite, so on January 2, 1902, he cabled to Secretary Hay to hold firm against such a demand.[63] Five days later, the Danish Minister at Washington addressed a note to Secretary Hay in which he stated that the Danish Government found itself confronted with a situation that rendered it

"absolutely necessary that some arrangement should be made in regard to the taking of a popular vote in the islands with a view to ascertaining the wishes of the inhabitants concerning a transfer to the sovereignty of the United States."[64]

[62] Swenson to Hay, December 21, 1901, MS. Dept. of State, *Denmark, Desp.,* vol. 23.

[63] Swenson to Hay, January 2, 1902, MS. Dept. of State, *Denmark, Desp.,* vol. 23.

[64] Brun to Hay, January 7, 1902, MS. Dept. of State, *Danish Legation, Notes from,* vol. 8.

To this final request of the Danish Government Secretary Hay was firmly opposed, and in his answering note to the Danish Minister he pointed out that

"during the period of two years in which the question of this cession has been under consideration by the two Governments, the Government of the United States has negotiated with successive Ministries of Denmark and always with an evident and sincere desire to conform in every possible way to the views and wishes of the Danish Government in the matter. Step by step, the draft treaty has been advanced to its present shape, nearly all the proposals of the Danish Ministry having been accepted by us, even to the extent of setting aside agreements reached with one Ministry and substituting therefore amendments brought forward by its successor. . . . At no time in the course of our prolonged discussion of the subject has the condition of a popular vote in the islands as a precedent to the cession been seriously advanced. . . . It is deeply regretted that at this late day . . . an obstacle should be discerned in the path of Denmark, and it is sincerely to be hoped that it may not prove a barrier to the realization of a project which appears to be so mutually advantageous."[65]

On January 15, 1902, Swenson cabled to Hay to "press for immediate signature protesting against such delay and plebiscite as contrary to agreement,"[66] and on the same day the Secretary of State cabled the attitude of the American Government with reference to the insertion in the treaty of a clause providing for

[65] Hay to Brun, January 9, 1902, MS. Dept. of State, *Denmark, Notes to,* vol. 7.

[66] Swenson to Hay, January 15, 1902, MS. Dept. of State, *Denmark, Desp.,* vol. 23.

a popular vote in the islands on the question of the cession to the United States. Such a clause had no proper place in the treaty that had been negotiated. If the Danish Government thought it necessary to hold a plebiscite in the islands before transferring them to the United States, such action would be regarded by the American Government merely as a part of the treaty procedure in Denmark. Each party to the treaty would sign "subject to ratification according to its own domestic procedure, the form and manner of which is not subject to the consent or question of the other party."[67]

This cablegram removed the last objection that could be raised against the treaty, which was finally signed at Washington on January 24, 1902.[68] In accordance with its terms the cession conveyed to the United States the Danish West Indies in full sovereignty, entire and unencumbered, except that the

[67] Hay to Swenson, January 15, 1902, MS. Dept. of State, *Denmark, Inst.*, vol. 16. In a despatch to Hay, January 15, 1902, Swenson told of a recent interview that he had had with Prince Hans of Glucksburg, the King's brother, in which he "ridiculed the demand for a plebiscite. He also expressed himself as being strongly in favor of the sale of the islands. His advice is generally sought by the King; and his influence carries much weight in all official circles." *Denmark, Desp.*, vol. 23.

[68] On January 22, 1902, White sent a cipher telegram to Secretary Hay to inform him that he had "just received private letter from well informed quarter at Copenhagen stating East Asiatic Company not obtained all money promised for development of Islands and Cabinet has forced Prime Minister to assent to sale." MS. *White Papers*.

American Government agreed to asume the obligations relative to the St. Thomas Floating Dock Company and the West India and Panama Telegraph Company. With reference to the claims of the St. Croix Sugar Factories it was provided that no responsibility of any kind whatever was incumbent upon either the Danish or the American Governments for their settlement. In regard to the civil status of the islanders Secretary Hay won his contention. These inhabitants were to continue to enjoy all the private, municipal and religious rights and liberties secured to them by the laws then in force, and if the present laws were altered the said inhabitants were not thereby to be placed in a less favorable position. In this way the objectionable word "foreigners" was eliminated, but it was specifically provided that "the civil rights and the political status of the inhabitants of the islands shall be determined by the Congress" of the United States. This disposed of the request of the Danish Government that United States citizenship be bestowed upon the inhabitants by treaty, and it was a distinct victory for Secretary Hay. In the matter of free trade between the islands and the United States Secretary Hay was equally victorious, for such a provision was conspicuous by its absence. The compensation for the cession was fixed at the sum of five millions of dollars in gold coin of the United States.[69]

[69] The text of the treaty of January 24, 1902, was published in U. S. Foreign Relations, 1917, pp. 514-17. On January 25, 1902, the New York *Times* published an interesting account

of the treaty and its provisions, and with reference to the victory of Mr. Hay it remarked as follows: "It is known that Denmark has abandoned the position she was inclined to occupy in regard to the conservation of the political rights of the inhabitants of the islands, and that she leaves the United States a free hand with them, without pledge of American citizenship or of free trade. It is assumed that the status of the islands, politically and commercially, should the treaty be ratified, will be similar to that of Porto Rico. Having gained these points in the negotiations, the State Department officials believe that the treaty is certain to receive the approval of the Senate."

CHAPTER VI

Denmark Calls a Halt—The Defeat of the Treaty

As soon as the Department of State announced the signature of the treaty with Denmark, varying opinions as to the value of the islands began to be reflected in the press. The New York *Times* thought they were of little value to the United States as a naval station since the acquisition of Porto Rico. The sole reason that justified their purchase was the fact that they might be transferred to some European power unfriendly to the United States, and thus constitute a menace to the maintenance of the Monroe Doctrine.[1] The Philadelphia *Record* was of the opinion that the "strategic value of the islands, of which Mr. Seward was convinced in 1867 by an impressive experience a few years before, has not been diminished by lapse of time. A naval force of sufficient strength with St. Thomas for its base would command every passage from the Atlantic into the Pacific."[2] The Philadelphia *Times* was equally in favor of the purchase:

"To ask us to annex the Danish West Indies, which is the proposition put up to the nation by the State Department, is after all, no very great request. We are

[1] New York *Times*, January 25, 1902.
[2] Quoted in the New York *Herald*, January 26, 1902.

not adding very materially to our responsibilities. All three islands taken together have a smaller area than the city of Philadelphia."[3]

Among these favorable comments concerning the purchase of the islands is a letter to the editor of the New York *Times* from Gertrude Atherton, a distinguished American novelist. Mrs. Atherton had paid an extended visit to the islands during the winter of 1901, and therefore could speak from first-hand information. She could vouch for the fact that

"not only—with the exception of a clergyman who holds his living under crown appointment—were the Americans, creoles, and resident Danes, for the sale to a man, but more than one official ingenuously remarked that he would like nothing better, as he would be retired on a pension amounting to two-thirds of his large salary. The petty officials who could expect no pension, the druggists, the doctors, who also are appointed by the crown, and this clergyman I have men-

[3] Quoted in the New York *Herald*, January 27, 1902. The Philadelphia *Inquirer* believed that the purchase of the islands would "remove all possible temptation to call the integrity of the Monroe Doctrine into question. We could not stand idly by and see a foreign Power encroach upon our territory even by purchase," while the Cincinnati *Enquirer* considered the purchase as "a strengthening of the Monroe Doctrine." Quoted in the New York *Herald*, February 10 and 15. The Springfield *Republican* did not believe that any "insuperable objection to the annexation of the islands is apparent, provided: 1. That the inhabitants of the islands express a willingness to come. 2. That the islands be treated on the old-fashioned American plan, . . . with American citizenship and free trade." Jan. 25, 1902.

tioned, are the only opponents and the only agitators."[4]

These favorable opinions reported in the press were shared by the members of the Senate Committee on Foreign Relations which had the treaty under consideration. As early as January 25, 1902, Senator Cullom, the chairman of the committee, wrote to Secretary Hay that there were "one or two things" that he did not "quite understand" about the treaty, and he would be greatly obliged if the Secretary would send him all the information available with respect to the liabilities of the United States under the treaty.[5] The Secretary promptly responded by transmitting a long memorandum relative to such encumbrances as the obligations due the St. Thomas Floating Dock Company and the West India and Panama Telegraph Company.[6]

[4] New York *Times,* January 27, 1902. In contrast to this favorable picture by Mrs. Atherton relative to the desire of the islanders to come under the sovereignty of the United States, one should read the Danish newspaper *Aftenposten* of June 11, 1901, which contains an interview with Dr. John Fejlberg, who had returned to Denmark after an extended sojourn in the Danish West Indies. Fejlberg states that "among the inhabitants of St. Croix, the Danes, the Americans, the Irish and the Creoles, the sentiment at the present time is in favor of remaining under Denmark."

[5] Cullom to Hay, January 25, 1902. MS. Dept. of State, *Miscellaneous Letters* (unbound).

[6] *Memorandum* of Dept. of State, January 28, 1902, MS. *Miscellaneous Letters* (unbound). On January 25, the Washington correspondent of the New York *Herald* reported that the "treaty will be sent to the Senate on Monday next. It will be referred to the Committee on Foreign Relations and

In regard to the attitude of the Senate committee towards the treaty, Secretary Hay wrote to Henry White that most of the difficulties were being raised by the Republican members:

"You will have seen by the newspapers that we signed the convention the other day, and the Senate Committee is now exercising its keenest wits upon it trying to pick some flaws in it. The mortgage which the Danish Government holds on the sugar company is worrying one member, who thinks that in that way the Danish Government is going to retain possession of some of the land. Another member kicks at our allowing the half dozen or so pensions which still have a few years to run. . . . But there seems to be no doubt that the treaty will go through. There appears to be no opposition on the part of the other side. The most of the worry comes from the perfectionists on our own side, who always treat a diplomatic negotiation as if it were an entirely new subject with which they were qualified to deal *in vacuo*, without any regard to actual circumstances."[7]

On February 5, the Senate Foreign Relations Committee brought in a favorable report on the treaty

---

will be immediately reported by that body. Senator Cullom, chairman of the committee, enjoys friendly relations with the administration and has always advocated the acquisition of the islands. Confidence is expressed in the State Department that the treaty will be ratified without difficulty."

[7] Hay to White, January 31, 1902, MS. *White Papers*. In reply to this letter, White wrote as follows to Hay, February 12, 1902: "Many thanks for your interesting letter about the Danish Islands. I am thankful that the Treaty has been signed and imagine that it cannot fail to weather the 'keenest wits' of its Senatorial critics." MS. *White Papers*.

which was partly based on the memorandum that had
been received from the Department of State. In regard to the value of the islands to the United States,
the report observed as follows:

"These islands, together with Porto Rico, are of
great importance in a strategic way, whether the
strategy be military or commercial. St. Thomas is
the natural point of call for all European trade bound
to the West Indies, Central America, or northern
South America. These islands, together with Porto
Rico, form the northeastern corner of the Caribbean
Sea and are of great importance in connection with
the American isthmus, where a canal will be constructed between the Atlantic and Pacific. They are
of first importance in connection with our relations
to the region of the Orinoco and the Amazon and
with our control of the Windward Passage."[8]

On February 17, the Senate consented to the ratification of the treaty after a little more than an hour's
consideration. Even Senators Bacon and McLaurin
who objected to certain provisions in the convention,
were careful to state that these objections were not
serious enough to cause them to vote against it.[9]

On February 19, 1902, Secretary Hay gave formal
notice to Mr. Swenson of the favorable action taken
by the American Senate with reference to the treaty,
and in a despatch of March 5, Mr. Swenson tells of
his communication of this news to the Danish Minister of Foreign Affairs. The Minister had few doubts
about the attitude of the Folkething towards the con-

[8] *Sen. Ex. Report* no. 1, *Confidential,* 57 Cong., 1 sess., p. 11.
[9] New York *Times,* February 18, 1902.

vention, but seemed to be "still in the dark" concerning the probable action of the Landsthing. For his own part, Mr. Swenson believed that the Rigsdag would ratify the treaty "in its present form."[10] This was also the opinion of Senator Henry Cabot Lodge, who wrote to White, March 10, that he thought

"the Danish Treaty will probably pass the Danish Parliament, and the latest news seems to be favorable to it. At all events we have taken an important step by showing our readiness to accept the treaty which makes it impossible for them to say, if they reject it, that we would not buy and would not let anyone else buy."[11]

On March 13, the treaty was considered in the Folkething in an open session, and Premier Deuntzer made a strong speech in favor of ratification. On the following day, by a vote of 88 yeas against 7 nays, the Folkething gave its formal consent to the treaty without amendment.[12]

This favorable attitude on the part of the Folkething caused President Roosevelt to look around for a governor of the Danish West Indies when they were formally transferred to the United States. To his mind the best appointee would be his friend Jacob A Riis, a native Dane and a naturalized American who had long stood high in Roosevelt's regard. Riis,

[10] Swenson to Hay, March 5, 1902, MS. Dept. of State, *Denmark, Desp.,* vol. 23.

[11] Lodge to White, March 10, 1902, MS. *White Papers.*

[12] Swenson to Hay, March 22, 1902, MS. Dept. of State, *Denmark, Desp.,* vol. 23. New York *Times,* March 14, 1902.

however, did not wish the appointment, so he wrote
to the President to suggest that such a high office
would require a "man of affairs" and not a "dunder-
head."[13]

Roosevelt, of course, would not accept such absurd
self-depreciation, so he promptly wrote to Riis the
following note:

"Before I decide in the Danish Islands business of
course I shall consult with you at length. I thought
that if I could get you down there, even though you
only intended to stay a few months, and give you some
good fellow whom you could trust underneath, it would
be a good thing all around. I would like to be able
to call you Governor hereafter and I should be awfully
proud at being able to give you the appointment."[14]

In the meantime, in Denmark things seemed to be
moving very smoothly. On March 19, the Landsthing,
in executive session and in Committee of the Whole,
voted to ratify the treaty. This was merely a preliminary step, and the treaty would have to be formally
voted upon at a subsequent meeting. On March 25,
and on April 3, 4, 5, 7, and 9, other meetings were
held during which the treaty was discussed from every
angle. The opposition was led by the President of the
Landsthing, Professor Matzen, Mr. Estrup, former
premier, and Mr. Holger Pedersen, a wealthy manufacturer. Part of the opposition was based upon the
claim that the treaty was tainted because negotiations
had been initiated by Captain Christmas, and Niels

[13] Riis to Roosevelt, March 17, 1902, MS. *Roosevelt Papers.*
[14] Roosevelt to Riis, March 18, 1902, MS. *Roosevelt Papers.*

Grön and his friends strove in every way to discredit the convention. On April 1, 1902, the Select Committee of the House of Representatives started its inquiry into whether members of Congress or Senators had been guilty of accepting bribes in order to facilitate treaty negotiations in the United States, and this investigation caused further criticism in Denmark of the treaty.[15]

On March 25, it was reported from Copenhagen that both the Dowager Czarina of Russia and Queen Alexandra of England were soon to visit Denmark, where they would use their efforts to defeat the treaty.[16] On April 5, it was stated in the European edition of the New York *Herald* that not only was King Christian of Denmark personally opposed to the cession of the islands, but also Crown Prince Frederick and his son, Prince Christian were bending their efforts to defeat the transfer of the islands. The most

[15] Swenson to Hay, April 14, 1902, MS. Dept. of State, *Denmark, Desp.*, vol. 23. Also New York *Times,* March 20, and New York *Herald,* April 1, 1902. At the same time that the Christmas scandal was arousing opposition in Denmark to the treaty, another factor appeared which should have helped to calm some of this opposition. On March 22, it was reported in the press that the Secretary of the Treasury had written to the Danish Minister in Washington to inform him that "in harmony with the decisions of the United States Supreme Court in the insular cases, sugar shipped to this country from St. Croix after the exchange of ratifications of the treaty of cession would be delivered free of duty in the absence of any provision in the treaty to the contrary." New York *Times,* March 23, 1902.

[16] New York *Times,* March 26, 1902.

conspicuous opponent of the treaty in court circles was the Princess Marie, wife of Prince Waldemar, who never lost an opportunity "of expressing her disapproval and doing her utmost to influence all those she can reach against the sale." The King, however, though personally opposed to the cession, had decided to subordinate his personal feelings to the decisions of the Deuntzer Ministry. His support of the Ministry was clearly indicated by a little incident that occurred during one of his general receptions. Professor Matzen, President of the Landsthing and a strong anti-sale leader, openly expressed at the reception his regret "that his party should be called upon to ratify so antipathetic a treaty." The King was distinctly annoyed at such an indiscretion, and served a reprimand upon Professor Matzen by asking Dr. Deuntzer "to almost unheard of honor of dining as a single guest at the private royal dinner table."[17]

On April 22, the Landsthing considered in open session the treaty of cession, and the Prime Minister created a sensation by quoting from the publications of the American State Department certain excerpts that indicated that Mr. Estrup, now such a bitter opponent of the treaty, was perfectly ready in 1892 to open negotiations for their sale. In the report of the New York *Herald's* Copenhagen correspondent for April 23, there is an interesting account of the verbal exchanges between the Prime Minister, Dr. Deuntzer, and the former premier, Mr. Estrup:

[17] New York *Herald,* April 10, 1902.

"Dr. Deuntzer yesterday said, referring to Mr. Estrup, 'You appear to have been in favor of the sale as late as 1892.'

" 'It is an untruth,' replied Mr. Estrup, his long mustachios quivering and the papers in his hands trembling distressingly.

"Dr. Deuntzer, however, held in his hand the Washington State Department's record of a report of the American Minister, Mr. Carr, telling how Mr. Estrup had approached him, urging the sale.

"But in spite of this, Mr. Estrup desperately repeated his denial.

"But from that moment he was lost. Dr. Deuntzer pounded him with terse, hard facts and ready replies."[18]

In the course of his speech on April 22, Dr. Deuntzer also gave a survey of conditions when he became Prime Minister:

"This is the situation—I assumed the post of Foreign Minister at a time when negotiations were in progress and were well under way. I continued these negotiations; I sought advice of those who should bear responsibility because it would never occur to me to seek counsel from irresponsible people—and from all sides I received the information that the transfer was desired. There was a difference of opinion as to the conditions but the transfer itself was desired. As to this there was no doubt before January 22d of this year, yes even until January 24, and for this reason the treaty was concluded.

"It can only be regarded as unfortunate that a new sentiment has developed during these last two months after the treaty has been concluded. It is unfortunate: but better late than never. If it is a sound and sensible sentiment, then one must respect it; but I ask: Why should anyone oppose the treaty under any conditions? It is because . . . a canal is to be built at Panama or some other place. Furthermore, there is some talk of a sugar convention; and finally because there has been aroused in the Danish business world a strong spirit of enterprise; finances have become available which will insure the energetic utilization of the opportunities opened by the preservation of the islands as Danish possessions. . . . Can anyone guarantee that the results will amount to anything?"[19]

On this same day, April 22, the former Prime Minister, Mr. Schested, made a speech in which he strongly opposed the treaty, and endeavored to explain how his Ministry had conducted the negotiations in a very different spirit:

"I wish to call attention to the fact that as we of the preceding Ministry considered the case, negotiations were conducted in such a manner that special emphasis was placed upon the fact that the object of the transfer of the islands was not a matter of business, but was primarily out of consideration for the inhabitants and for their future. If it were possible to insure them a better future through a transfer, the Government was prepared to carry the matter through. We regarded it as vital to the future welfare of the inhabitants that they be granted the rights of citizenship and free trade. Also, that the colonial treasury be relieved of the burden it had borne since 1876. We have now heard how His Excellency the Prime Minister has endeavored to show that these considerations are of minor importance. In the last note we sent to the United States this point was expressly

[19] *Rigsdagstidende, Forhandlinger paa Landstinget,* 54 de Ordentlige Samling, 1901-02.

set forth, and we concluded by requesting the American Government to find some means by which a guarantee could be provided for these three conditions. The answer which was received after we had left office, stated that 'these conditions cannot be included in the treaty.'

"When so categorical a reply to this question has been received there remain but two alternatives—either we are willing to give up those conditions and accept the convention, or since we are unable to obtain guarantees for them . . . we cannot consider such a transfer. The present administration has chosen the first alternative. I presume that if we had received this reply to our question, we would have gone in the other direction, and would have informed the United States that, since we could not obtain these guarantees, we could no longer discuss the transfer."[20]

But these were not the only conditions which the Conservatives thought should be granted by the United States. The question now arose as to whether it was necessary to hold a plebiscite in the islands in order to ascertain the attitude of the inhabitants in regard to the change of sovereignty. On March 14, the Folkething had ratified the treaty without any amendment, but the Landsthing regarded a plebiscite as an essential preliminary to the cession of the islands. On April 29, the Folkething, by a vote of 98 yeas against 7 nays, voted in favor of a plebiscite "similar to that of 1867, arranged by the Danish Government."[21] This was regarded as the extreme limit of concession on the part of the majority in the Folkething, but argu-

[20] *Rigsdagstidende, Forhandlinger paa Landstinget,* 54 de Ordentlige Samling, 1901-02.

[21] New York *Times,* April 30, 1902.

ments immediately arose as to the rules governing the holding of such a plebiscite. The majority desired that the "right to vote be granted to every person of good character, who has attained the age of 25, who has the right of a native, or who has resided in the islands for a period of at least five years; unless, having no household of his own, he is employed as a private servant, and provided that he has at no time been a public charge, and that he has the disposal of his own estate."

The opponents of the treaty objected to holding a plebiscite under such a liberal rule. It was their belief that the "differences between the inhabitants of this country and those of the islands are so great that it would be very questionable to permit the bulk of the inhabitants of the islands to exert a decisive influence in so important a question . . . by giving them a right to vote for or aganist the treaty of January 24, 1902." These inhabitants are generally

"unmoneyed, and have heretofore been excluded from all influence on or participation in the public affairs of the islands. To give these persons a right to vote, the minority finds so much the less defensible in view of the fact that, in its opinion, the only consideration that would speak in favor of a cession of the islands is their present and future economic welfare. Consequently, only that part of the population which has real economic interests in the islands ought to have an influence in deciding the question under consideration."[22]

[22] Swenson to Hay, April 14, 1902, May 6, 1902, MS. Dept. of State, *Denmark, Desp.*, vol. 23.

As a result of this deadlock between the majority in the Folkething, representing the views of the Ministry, and the views of the majority in the Landsthing, representing the party of opposition, the Rigsdag was prorogued, the next elections taking place in September.[23]

Dr. Deuntzer, the Danish Premier, had high hopes that the fall elections would indicate popular approval of the Ministerial program for the sale of the islands, and it was certainly true that an important part of the Danish press had come out in favor of this project. On January 2, 1902, the Copenhagen newspaper *Politiken,* published a list of excerpts from important Danish newspapers in the provinces in order to indicate the tide of public sentiment. The *Frederiksborgs Amtsavis* was distinctly to the point: "Our position is that both for the good of the islands and for Denmark we desire that they [the islands] be sold." The *Horsens Avis* inquired: "Why shall we retain these islands which only have caused us loss of money and trouble. All talk about the inhabitants being our fellow-countrymen is beside the point. The majority of the inhabitants are English-speaking Negroes and this same Negro population, moreover, at one time voted in favor of coming under American rule." The *Bornholms Tidende* was equally favorable to the sale, while both the *Koldings Folkeblad* and the *Ringkobing Amts Avis* urged the sale because of

[23] Swenson to Hay, May 22, 1902, MS. Dept. of State, *Denmark, Desp.,* vol. 23.

heavy financial loss to Denmark should the islands be
retained.

In the United States the failure of the Landsthing
to ratify the treaty was not taken as a definitive rejection of the Deuntzer program to sell the islands,
and judgment was reserved until the meeting of the
Rigsdag in the autumn. Secretary Hay apparently
thought well of the prospects of the treaty, for he
went ahead and on June 7, 1902, signed a supplementary convention which extended for twelve months
from July 24, 1902, the time within which the ratifications might be exchanged.[24]

As the summer of 1902 wore on it seemed more
and more probable that the Landsthing would finally
ratify the treaty when it met in October. On September 5, it was reported in the American newspapers
that the recent elections in Denmark had resulted in
"large Ministerial gains, insuring the Government a
majority in the Landsthing and the ratification of the
treaty."[25] Two weeks later the election returns were
officially issued in Copenhagen, and were commented
upon by a member of the Deuntzer Government as
follows:

[24] Hay to Swenson, June 12, 1902, MS. Dept. of State,
Denmark, Inst., vol. 16. For an interesting and informing
article on the situation in Denmark, see Harold C. Peterson,
"Anomalies of Danish Politics," *Gunton's Magazine,* June,
1902, pp. 527-534.

[25] New York *Times,* September 5, 1902. See also New York
Herald for September 5, 20, 1902.

"The sale of the islands is now absolutely certain, and the matter will be settled next month, or at the latest in November. The Landsthing will be composed of thirty-seven members of the Ministerial party, as against twenty-nine of the opposition."[26]

On October 6, the Rigsdag formally convened, and in the Landsthing the sixty-six members were divided into the following political groups: twenty-nine ultra-Conservatives, eight Independent Conservatives, three Conservatives not belonging to any faction, and twenty-six Radicals, including one Socialist. The former President of the Landsthing, Dr. Matzen, was defeated for this office by Mr. H. N. Hansen, a member of the Independent Conservatives. Inasmuch as Dr. Matzen was a bitter opponent of the sale of the islands, his defeat was considered highly significant and a promising augury for the ratification of the treaty.[27]

On October 15, discussion began on the bill to ratify the cession of the islands,[28] and Dr. Deuntzer assured

[26] New York *Times*, September 20, 1902.

[27] London *Times*, October 7, 1902.

[28] In his speech on October 15, 1902, Dr. Deuntzer gave the following picture of the situation when he became Prime Minister: "When I became Foreign Minister a year ago I found a draft of a treaty—and I observed that an agreement had been reached with regard to the majority of the articles. The United States had conducted these negotiations for two years with increasing impatience and wished to bring them to a close. . . . I believed then, and I still believe that it would be detrimental to Denmark's prestige not to assume a definite position." See *Rigsdagstidende, Forhandlinger paa Landstinget*, 55 de Ordentlige Samling, 1902-03.

the members of the Landsthing that he had received from the United States a written promise that "after the cession free imports from the islands into the United States would be granted."[29] But despite this assurance it appeared that more than the anticipated opposition to the sale of the islands was developing in the Landsthing, so much so that the Copenhagen correspondent of the London *Times* felt that the fate of the treaty was decidedly doubtful.[30]

On October 19, the New York *Times* admitted that the bill for the cession would have a "hard time" passing the Landsthing, but nevertheless it was felt that the measure would be adopted by a slender majority, but on October 22, the Copenhagen correspondent of the *Times* cabled that the "probabilities" were against the adoption of the bill. He had sensed the situation correctly, for on that day the vote was taken in the Landsthing and the bill was defeated by a tie vote, 32 yeas to 32 nays. The tactics pursued by the Conservatives in effecting the defeat of the cession bill are interestingly described in the report of the Copenhagen correspondent of the New York *Times:*

[29] New York *Herald*, October 16, 1902.

[30] London *Times*, October 16, 1902. With reference to Deuntzer's statement that he had a written promise from the United States relative to free trade for the islands after the cession was completed, the New York *Times*, in an editorial of October 18, observed as follows: "The plain fact is that nobody is authorized to make such a promise. Under the law and the decisions, the islands would be completely, after annexation, at the disposition of Congress."

"The result of the vote was doubtful until the last moment. One member had not taken a definite stand, and it was uncertain whether two sick members would be able to attend. The ages of these men, Thygeson and Raben, are ninety-seven and eighty-seven years, respectively. The death of both of them has been expected for several weeks. They were bedridden at their homes, 150 miles from Copenhagen, but were brought to the city, prominent anti-sale leaders being sent to transport them here. The sufferers, who were accompanied by physicians, were carried into a saloon car, which was rolled on to a ferryboat, on which it crossed from Jutland. On their arrival at Copenhagen they were met by leading anti-sale politicians, and were driven in carriages to a hotel. There the two old men were guarded and nursed overnight, and were eventually carried to their chairs in the Landsthing Hall an hour before the meeting began. A prompter was on hand to assist them in voting."[31]

In the Danish press opinions varied in accordance with the political affiliations of the editors. *Vort Land,* one of the leading opposition newspapers, was jubilant at the result:

"At last we have been delivered from the fear of disgrace which like a nightmare has weighed on large numbers of the Danish people, not by any means the most insignificant. There was after all a sufficient number of men in the Upper House to prevent the declaration of national bankruptcy which the short-sightedness and obstinacy of the Left had prepared. . . .The promise which the Landsthing gave yesterday of the nation's vitality, of its desire and ability to exert itself lest it be overlooked and forgotten, such promise it now rests with the people to redeem."[32]

[31] New York *Times,* October 23, 1902.
[32] October 23, 1902.

The *Nationaltidende* expressed itself in similar vein:

"We greet with the deepest satisfaction the great event that has taken place today. We believe that abroad it will redound to the honor and profit of our country; and that at home it will usher in a cooperation between His Majesty's Government and the legislative branch."[33]

The *Samfundet* had only words of praise for the action of the opposition in blocking the treaty:

"Danish possessions remained undiminished, the Danish flag had won; it was decided once and for all that the red and white colors were still to fly over the islands, which we had come so near yielding up, to the shame and injury of our national self-respect."[34]

The Ministerial papers regarded the rejection of the treaty with outspoken dissatisfaction:

"What Danish ministries of different parties, what practically the whole Folkething and the public have agreed upon, what the dignity of the country demanded, what the inhabitants of the islands wished, and what common sense told every sensible man;— all this was destroyed by the old Right in the Landsthing; by men like Estrup, Nellemann, Matzen, Goos, all the most reliable troops of the embittered reactionary party."[35]

In the *Dannebrog* there is not only an editorial condemning the policy of the opposition in bringing about the rejection of the treaty, but there is also a very

[33] October 23, 1902.
[34] October 23, 1902.
[35] *Politiken*, October 23, 1902.

interesting account of the scene in the Rigsdag when the vote was announced. Thus:

"An hour and a half before the time set for the meeting, people began to arrive. At the entrance a regular fight ensued between the crowd, which tried to force its way in, and the messengers of the Landsthing. The latter were being gradually pushed back, when the President of the Landsthing, Mr. Hansen, arrived on the scene and took a hand in the fray, with the result that the Rigsdag forces remained in possession of the field. . . . The spectators followed the roll call with intense excitement, many keeping tab on the vote. . . . A few times the silence was broken by manifestations of approval or disapproval. When Gustav Hansen, formerly member of the pro-sale committee, voted no, there were cries of 'Shame!' When the result was announced, 32 yeas, 32 nays, the spectators gave vent to their feelings with such demonstrations that the like of it has seldom, if ever, been witnessed in the dignified Landsthing. Applause, cries of 'bravo,' 'shame,' filled the air. The President rang the bell energetically; but it was some time before he succeeded in quieting the galleries."[86]

In America there was a feeling that in spite of the rejection of the treaty by the Danish Landsthing, it was only a matter of time before the islands became a possession of the United States. One thing, however, was very certain, and that was that the Danes would never be permitted to sell the islands to any other power. In this regard the New York *Times* thought that we could afford

"to possess our souls in patience, in view of the loss in the Danish Legislature by a tie vote of the treaty

[86] October 23, 1902.

in accordance with which Denmark would have un-
loaded what to her is and always will be a liability,
but what in our hands would be an asset. . . . We have
made it clear to Denmark that while, in the words of
the original promulgation of the Monroe doctrine,
with her posession 'we have not interfered and shall
not interfere,' we have no notion whatever of her disposing of her holdings to any other Power which may
seek to extend its political system to this side of the
Atlantic."[37]

The Pittsburg *Gazette* was equally vehement about
asserting the importance of maintaining the Monroe
Doctrine, and the following excerpt is typical of the
American press at this time:

"What the future of the islands may be no one is
now able to say, but the United States must be strong
enough to insure that neither these nor any other
islands in the West Indies be transferred to a foreign
Power."[38]

At the same time the *Gazette* thought that "the
United States has worried along without the Danish
islands until this time, and can continue to do so,"
while the Brooklyn *Eagle* thought that the defeat of
the treaty "merely postpones the inevitable." The
Boston *Transcript* expressed the opinion that there
was scarcely any doubt but that "the islands will come
to us eventually," and this view was repeated in a

[37] October 25, 1902.
[38] For digests of public opinion relative to the rejection of
the treaty see *Literary Digest*, November 1, 1902, p. 543, and
the New York *Herald*, October 26, 1902.

statement issued to the press by Senator Cullom, chairman of the Senate Committee on Foreign Relations.[39]

Some voices of protest were raised against the treaty, however, and the most effective of these opponents and certainly the most vociferous, was a famous American author, Mrs. Gertrude Atherton. In January, 1902, Mrs. Atherton had come out in favor of the sale, but by the autumn of that year her views underwent a complete change. In the October issue of the *North American Review*, Mrs. Atherton launched a bitter attack upon the treaty. In her opinion,

"even although every one of the charges of the adventurer, Christmas, against reputable American citizens was proved to be false, and although his broad assertion that Senator Lodge was the only American official who could not be bribed sank of its own weight, even in disgusted Denmark, still the fact remains that he has discredited us in Europe. . . . It is all very well for the Prime Minister of Denmark and the American Secretary of State to repudiate Christmas, to have flung him overboard with contumely at a certain stage of the game; the cold truth is, the negotiations he set on foot have never been interrupted, that the present situation is on his wheels, awkward and blocked as they may be. . . . Many of the strongest men in the United States government are dissatisfied with the treaty. The truth is, we do not want any more colonies. Our explosive imperialism has subsided."[40]

In the New York *Times,* October 19, 1902, Mrs. Atherton published a long statement which took on a

[39] The statement of Senator Cullom was published in the New York *Times,* October 25, 1902.

[40] *North American Review,* October, 1902, pp. 500-505.

far sharper tone than her article in the *North American Review*. Her criticisms of Secretary Hay were distinctly acrid when she discussed the supplementary convention of June 7, 1902. Thus:

"Last May the Landsthing practically disposed of the treaty. The feeling against the sale of the islands has been enhanced by the 'report' of Capt. Christmas, which placed the whole affair in too disgraceful a light for any honorable man to countenance. As the last vote was about to be taken the Prime Minister, who had some difficulty in appreciating their sentiments, uttered this warning: 'Remember that if you sustain this position it means the death of the treaty.' They sustained the position. Every newspaper in Copenhagen, Conservative and Liberal, came out that evening and the next morning announcing that the matter was closed; that the treaty was killed. What happened? Mr. Hay cabled asking for the extension of one year's time for the settlement of the matter; in other words, that the sitting Landsthing, whose majority was Conservative, should not be admitted to have decided the matter, but that it should be held over to the next session, when, after the pending elections, it was probable that the majority might swing to the Liberals.

"It was an extraordinary request, and Denmark was well aware that it would never have been made to one of the great powers of Europe. It was, indeed, practically a command, the command of a big nation to a little one. For some days no answer was given. Then the diplomatically worded request was agreed to. Denmark dared not antagonize so mighty a power as the United States.

"It can hardly fail to strike the most casual observer of affairs that this is an extraordinary position in which to place a nation which aspires to convince the world that it is the ideal republic. . . . The word coercion is not supposed to occur in the national dictionary. And yet no other word can be applied to Mr. Hay's methods in dealing with a small and weak country like Denmark. It may be imagined what effect this unusual performance had upon the ignorant classes of Denmark. . . . Mr. Hay's veiled command frightened them thoroughly. It was, indeed, all that might be expected of a nation which only awaited an excuse to grab three islands and pay nothing. That evil at least could be prevented by speedy ratification, and the new liberal members of the Landsthing, who have been elected by peasant votes, know what is expected of them. It is on the wisdom, patriotism, and independence of two or three of them that hope at present is centred."

In the New York *Herald*, October 25, 1902, Mrs. Atherton came out with another statement in which she attacked the American press for its mis-statements concerning the defeat of the treaty of cession by the Danish Landsthing. After redressing this lack of balance in American newspapers, she then gave a very sympathetic interpretation of the action of the two aged members of the Landsthing, Thygeson and Raben, in making a forced journey to Copenhagen in order to vote against the treaty. She could well understand how such an episode might seem ridiculous to Americans, who

"are patriotic, but in a different way; therefore it is difficult to be sympathetic with the ways of older and simpler nations. Our complex and strenuous life compels us to live on the surface of our natures. Of the deep introspective natures of Northern lands, with their long nights and uneventful days—uneventful from our standpoint—their absolutely simple, almost

primal codes and standards, we, as a race, know
nothing. They may have humor, but it is not our
humor; therefore it seems to the Scandinavian mind
quite a natural thing that two aged patriots should
be thankful to crown a long life of devotion to Denmark by making their last journey but one to save
the islands for which it is not too much to say that
the Danes cherish a passion second only to that which
they gave for the nation itself.

"The United States will never get the three islands.
That danger is passed for Denmark. But it is possible that we can have one. That is a different matter."

These sharp attacks of Mr. Atherton upon the
policy of Secretary Hay were deeply resented by the
Secretary himself, and the following letter he addressed to Henry White gives us a little insight into
the ways that American officials have of striking back
at those who offend their sensibilities. It also gives us
a fuller understanding of the character of John Hay:

"Following the bad custom of the State Department, I signed the other day a note I found on my
table introducing Mrs. Gertrude Atherton, at the request of Senator Hale. As I do much of the stuff
that comes under my hand, I signed it without especial consideration, and, after it was gone, I felt that
I owed an apology at least to you and Swenson for
signing such a letter.

"The woman, you know, is the author of a somewhat pornographic novel called 'Senator North,' of
which Eugene Hale is the hero; but I am not a censor
of novels, and would not object to that or any other
of her works, if it were not that she had been black-
guarding the Administraiton right and left, paying
particular attention to you and me in connection with
the Danish Islands business. You will, therefore, be

careful to put no facilities in her way which may help her to fling further filth in that direction. If she resents your coolness, and tells you she will have you removed, as she probably will if you do not introduce her to the King, you can keep your soul in patience and tell her that I am the chief offender and she had better go for me first."[41]

After receiving this somewhat hysterical letter, White replied as follows:

"I note and have told Carter what you say about the treatment to be accorded to Gertrude Atherton when she comes to us. She has not appeared nor has O'Laughlin."[42]

I was very much interested in this little episode involving a former literary man of great ability and a literary woman of distinct genius, so in order to get her viewpoint I wrote to her and inquired just why she took the stand she did in the matter of the treaty with Denmark. Her reply is illuminating:

"This was the way of it. I happened to be in Copenhagen at the time the purchase of the West Indies by the United States was agitating the Danes. A lot of those Landsthingmen got at me and begged me to help them to prevent it. Although their ownership of the islands was a heavy burden, costing them something like a hundred thousand dollars a year, yet they feared a loss of prestige if they relinquished them. I didn't know a thing about the matter and cared less, but they had been very hospitable to me and gave me no

[41] Hay to White, May 18, 1903, MS. *White Papers.* Along the top of this letter Hay wrote the significant warning: "Delenda."

[42] White to Hay, June 13, 1903, MS. *White Papers.*

peace. I cabled to the editor of the *North American Review,* asking him if he would publish an article on the subject. He replied that he would, and then from the notes they gave me I wrote the article—and found myself in hot water when I got home.

"I must add that Harry White forgave me, and if I had heard his side of the story first I probably should not have written the article."[43]

I am very much inclined to think that if John Hay had ever read this letter he too would have promptly forgiven her.

[43] Atherton to Tansill, New York, July 21, 1930.

[44] Owing to the courtesy of Mr. R. L. Luthin and to Mrs. Gertrude Atherton, a galleyproof of Mrs. Atherton's latest book, *The Adventures of a Novelist,* has been submitted to me. The following excerpts from this autobiography confirm the above account of how the Danish opponents of the treaty of January 24, 1902, secured the services of Mrs. Atherton. On a visit to Copenhagen she was warmly welcomed; the reason was obvious: "I soon discovered why those statesmen were paying me such assiduous court. They were deeply disturbed because of a project to sell the Virgin Islands to the United States. . . . A powerful group in the government was negotiating with the United States and the party with which I happened to be associated was in a condition of patriotic despair and begged me to help them. Could I not write for some prominent American publication that would persuade the citizens of the United States of the elephant they would have on their hands if they bought those islands? . . . I cabled to the editor of the *North American Review,* Mr. Rice, asking him if he would care for an article on the subject, and as he replied with some enthusiasm, I set to work with the aid of Captain Ramsing, who, with his wife, were the closest friends I made in Denmark. It may be imagined how much I knew of the ins and outs of such a subject: Captain Ramsing dictated the greater part of the article and I put it into as interesting a form as I could compass. . . .

I cannot recall a word of that article, but I do remember that it was designed even more for home consumption than for what influence it might have on the tax-payers of the United States; it was to be translated after publication and a copy put into the hands of every voter in Denmark. . . . Well! that article did play its part in delaying the purchase of the islands for something like fourteen years."

CHAPTER VII

GERMANY AND THE DANISH WEST INDIES

Ever since the defeat of the treaty of January 24, 1902, in the Danish Landsthing, it has been assumed by many people in the United States that German intrigue was really responsible for this check to American aspirations in the Caribbean. Indeed, so strong has been this suspicion and so widely has it been accepted that it is necessary to devote an entire chapter to German policy with reference to the Danish West Indies. Such a chapter implies a discussion of German-Amercian relations in the decades prior to the close of the nineteenth century, for it is obvious that any alleged ambitions that Germany might nourish in regard to expansion in the Caribbean would run directly counter to the Monroe Doctrine, and thus lead to a possible conflict with the United States.

German-American relations since the American Civil War afford an interesting illustration of the rapidity with which public sentiment in certain countries can undergo a fundamental change. At the outbreak of the Franco-Prussian war, public opinion in the United States was overwhelmingly in favor of a decisive German victory over the armies of imperial France. During the recent American Civil War, Napoleon III had been actively hostile to the Lincoln administration, and his malodorous Mexican expedition had left bitter memories throughout the North. Prussia, on the other hand, had not only lent its moral support to the North, but in addition, many of its citizens had readily purchased American bonds and thus extended much-needed financial support to the Northern cause.[1]

After the formation of the German Empire there were many reasons why friendly relations with the United States should continue to develop. It flattered many people in the United States to believe that the German statesmen had consciously copied the American frame of government when they erected the German federal state.[2] In 1872, Emperor William I, acting as arbitrator between Great Britain and the United States relative to the Northwest boundary, returned a verdict in favor of the American claim.[3] While undoubtedly this decision was based on an impartial

[1] For a discussion in the Senate with reference to German assistance during the American Civil War, see *Congressional Globe,* February 4, 1871, 41 Cong., 3 sess., pt. 2, pp. 954 ff. On the general subject of German-American relations since 1870, there is a monograph by Dr. Jeannette Keim, *Forty Years of German-American Political Relations* (Phila. 1919) ; and Dr. Clara E. Schieber, *American Sentiment Toward Germany* (Boston, 1923). For definitive studies of German-American relations since 1870, American scholars are looking forward to the publication of the volumes of two brilliant German publicists, Dr. Alfred Vagts, and Count zu Stolberg-Wernigerode.

[2] See the message of President Grant to Congress, February 7, 1871, Jas. D. Richardson, *Messages and Papers of the Presidents,* vol. 9, pp. 4074-75.

[3] J. B. Moore, *History and Digest of the International Arbitrations to which the U. S. has been a Party* (Wash., 1898), vol. 1, pp. 227-231.

survey of the evidence in the case, yet many regarded it as a gesture of good-will. Also, the great statesman who guided the destinies of the new German Empire was on the most friendly terms with the American Minister at Berlin, George Bancroft, and there were few observers in Europe who would have discounted in any way the value of Bismarck's friendship.[4]

In the first decade after the establishment of the German Empire, there was little chance for any friction to develop between the two countries. Bismarck, at first, was opposed to any movement for the acquisition of German colonies, and this fact led him to give the warmest assurances to the United States that no fear need be entertained concerning German expansion in the Caribbean.[5] By 1880, however, Bismarck had altered his viewpoint and was giving German expansionists his "whole-hearted, if secret, support,"[6] but this did not lead to any friction with America because the German colonial empire was to be located in Africa and not in South America.

[4] On the relations between Bancroft and Bismarck, see M. A. D. Howe, *Life and Letters of George Bancroft* (N. Y., 1908), vol. 2, pp. 166 ff. Also, the interesting article by Count zu Stolberg-Wernigerode, "Bismarck and His American Friends," in the *Virginia Quarterly Review*, July, 1929, pp. 397 ff.

[5] See *ante*, chap. iii.

[6] M. E. Townsend, *Origins of Modern German Colonialism* (N. Y., 1921), p. 195; Maximilian von Hagen, *Bismarck's Kolonialpolitik* (Stuttgart, 1923), pp. 42-69, 118-293, 332 ff; K. Herrfurth, *Fürst Bismarck und die Kolonialpolitik* (Berlin, 1917), chaps. iv, v. vi, vii, viii, ix, x.

Later on, when German colonial expansion pene-
trated into the Pacific, there were serious difficulties
in regard to the control of the Samoan Islands. In
March, 1889, it appeared that open conflict between
American and German squadrons in the harbor of
Apia was averted only by the timely visitation of a
typhoon which destroyed all the ships of both the
nations involved, and for another decade the Samoan
tangle remained a constant source of irritation.[7] As
a result of this friction, American sentiment toward
Germany became at times sharply hostile, and the
attitude of Vice-Admiral von Diederichs at Manila
Bay made many Americans feel that Germany only
awaited a favorable opportunity to strike at the United
States.[8]

Moreover, it was soon evident that German colonial
ambitions were more far-reaching than they had been
in the eighties, so American statesmen began to view
Germany as a menace to the maintenance of the Monroe Doctrine. In Latin America the political influence

[7] Jeannette Keim, *Forty Years of German-American Political Relations,* chap. v; C. E. Schieber, *American Sentiment
Toward Germany,* chap. ii; Robert Louis Stevenson, *A Foot-
note to History* (N. Y., 1897).

[8] For the attitude of Germany towards the United States
during the Spanish-American War, see Fred. Rippy, *Latin
America in World Politics* (N. Y., 1928), chap. x; and Lester
B. Shippee, "Germany and the Spanish-American War," in
American Historical Review, vol. 30, pp. 754-777. On the
Manila Bay incident see George Dewey, *Autobiography*
(N. Y., 1913), pp. 252-267; and Vice-Admiral von Diederichs,
in the *Royal United Service Institution, Journal,* vol. 59, pp.
421-446.

of the United States was paramount, and it was feared that German emigration and German investments might be the means of bringing about a fundamental change in this status. By 1896 there were some 400,-000 persons of German descent in Latin America, while German trade with those countries reached the goodly total of $146,000,000, and German investments had amounted to a half of a billion dollars.[9] Perhaps it was time for Uncle Sam to bestir himself!

It was significant, also, that the German press appeared to be adopting a belligerent attitude toward America. In 1896, Great Britain acceded to the American demand for arbitration in the Venezuela Boundary Controversy. In some quarters in Germany this action was regarded as indicating distinct weakness on the part of Great Britain, and the *Kölnische Zeitung* formally served notice that Germany could not be treated in such a manner:

"England has not come out of the affair with much honor. The bluff of the Americans was in the first place a success, as it caused England to submit to the appointment of the Venezuelan commission. And now England willingly acknowledges the Monroe Doctrine. The American papers are therefore not in the wrong if they talk of a complete back-down on the part of England. We wish, however, to state right here that England stands perfectly isolated in the establishment of this precedent. Germany at least will never permit a foreign power to interfere if she finds it necessary to defend German interests in South or Central America."[10]

[9] J. Fred. Rippy, *Latin America in World Politics,* chap. ix.
[10] Quoted in the *Literary Digest,* December 5, 1896, p. 152.

Bismarck, himself, felt called upon to criticize the Monroe Doctrine as interpreted by Secretary Olney and President Cleveland:

"The idea which people in America have of the Monroe Doctrine is a proof of extraordinary insolence. It is just the same as if a European state, say France or Russia, were to assert that no change of frontier may take place on the European continent without its consent, or if Russia or England were to dictate in a similar manner in Asia. The immense wealth with which the United States, owing to its extent, provides its comparatively sparse population, has evidently created an overestimate of their own power and an underestimate of the strength and rights of other American as well as European nations."[11]

This statement of Bismarck took on an added significance when it coincided with an effective show of German force in Haiti. This German naval demonstration grew out of the so-called "Lueders case" in December, 1897, the very month that Bismarck aired his

[11] *Ibid.*, December 4, 1897, p. 952. In a conversation with Herr Wolf von Schierbrand, shortly after the outbreak of the Spanish-American War, Bismarck expressed himself in a very similar vein. After denouncing the American Government for making war upon Spain, Bismarck then paid his respects to the Monroe Doctrine as follows: "That is a species of arrogance peculiarly American and inexcusable." See Schierbrand's volume entitled, *Germany, The Welding of a World Power* (N. Y. 1902), p. 352. The eminent German publicist, Maximilian Harden was equally explicit in his condemnation of the Monroe Doctrine. It was his opinion that "the doctrine should be buried, and if the United States are unwilling to acquiesce in the interment, they may expect to have a war upon their hands sooner or later." See *Harper's Weekly*, January 3, 1903, p. 19.

views on the Monroe Doctrine. It happened that a certain Emile Lueders, a German national, became involved in a dispute with a Haytian policeman, for which he was thrown into prison and afterwards sentenced to imprisonment for one month. He appealed, and was tried under another Haytian law which denied the right of appeal to defendants. The result of the second trial was that he was fined $500, and sentenced to prison for one year. The German representative in Hayti protested against such a mutilation of justice, but to no avail. He then cabled to the German Foreign Office and was instructed to demand the release of Lueders, the removal from office of the justices who convicted him, the imprisonment of the policeman who made the charge, an indemnity of $1,000 a day for each day's imprisonment under the first judgment, and $5,000 a day for every day thereafter. These demands were presented to President Simon Sam, not by a note from the German representative, but at a public reception. The President feeling deeply outraged at such a disregard of diplomatic procedure, refused to receive such a verbal communication, whereupon, on December 6, 1897, two German warships made their appearance at Port au Prince and delivered the following ultimatum: an indemnity of $30,000; permission for Lueders to resume his business with an avowal of responsibility for his future safety; an apology for the treatment accorded the German representative; the renewal of diplomatic relations, and the prompt acceptance of a German representative.

Faced by superior force, President Simon Sam quickly yielded compliance with all these demands and diplomatic relations were resumed.[12]

In the United States a great deal of indignation was voiced in the press at this summary action on the part of Germany. The Springfield *Republican* regarded the conduct of Germany in the Lueders case as the "most flagrant piece of international bullying that has occurred in this part of the world for many years."[13] The Chicago *Tribune* thought that the position taken by Germany was "utterly unjustifiable," and pronounced a solemn warning that "the bullying of feeble American republics by European powers will not be tolerated by this country."[14] The Boston *Transcript* expressed the opinion that Germany had acted as an "international highwayman,"[15] while the New York *Times* reminded the German Government that "in dealing with a little republic a big empire cannot too scrupulously observe the obligations of courtesy and the rules of law."[16]

[12] For the Lueders incident see the instructions of Secretary of State Sherman to Mr. Powell, American Minister at Port au Prince, December 22, 1897, and January 11, 1898, MS. Dept. of State, *Hayti, Inst.,* vol. 3. Also, J. B. Moore, *Digest of International Law,* vol. 6, pp. 474-76; Jeannette Keim, *Forty Years of German-American Political Relations,* pp. 276-78.

[13] December 8, 1897.

[14] December 1, 1897.

[15] December 10, 1897.

[16] December 4, 1897.

This public indignation was by no means quieted when it was reported that the *Deutsche Zeitung* had remarked that after the tirade of abuse in the United States for German "intermeddling in Haiti," it sincerely hoped that von Buelow "will draw appropriate conclusions for his future policy in regard to America, whose interfering insolence needs taking down." It was also stated in the press that Kaiser Wilhelm had recently remarked that "this American meddlesome policy must cease or we will be obliged to teach them manners."[17] Whatever the truth of this dubious quotation, it was patent that in certain circles in America the Kaiser was growing increasingly unpopular, and many would have agreed with the opinion expressed in the Providence *Journal* that he was a "hare-brained individual." [18]

That this opinion was becoming widespread in the United States was clearly understood by the American ambassador at Berlin, Mr. Andrew D. White, who

[17] Quoted in the New York *Times,* December 12, 1897.

[18] November 27, 1897. For a summary of the criticisms of the Kaiser in the American press see Dr. Clara E. Schieber, *American Sentiment Toward Germany,* pp. 209 ff. Even before the "Lueders incident," Theodore Roosevelt, serving as Assistant Secretary of the Navy, wrote a letter to Capt. B. H. McCalla, U. S. N., August 2, 1897, which distinctly reveals his suspicions of German policy in general: "I entirely agree with you that Germany is the power with which we may very possibly have ultimately to come into hostile contact. How I wish our people would wake up to the need for a big navy." See *Theodore Roosevelt and His Time* (ed. by J. B. Bishop, N. Y., 1920), vol. I, p. 78.

protested to Secretary Hay that it was incorrect for
Americans to regard the German Emperor as

"merely a fitful and versatile man, 'everything by
turns and nothing long.' He is, indeed, a man of remarkably varied abilities—an orator, a poet, an artist,
and much else, but, with this, a man of convictions,
of ideas, of real force of character, successful in devising plans and managing men, and deeply impressed
with the inherited Hohenzollern ambition of extending
the power of Prussia and Germany. . . . Probably no
sovereign in recent times has put himself into direct
relations with so many of his subjects and in so many
ways. . . . It would be a serious mistake to suppose that
he has not the respect or love of his subjects. On
the contrary I feel sure that he has been growing
steadily and rapidly in both, and especially for two
or three years past."[19]

In his despatches to the Department of State, Ambassador White also indicated how public sentiment in
Germany had become increasingly hostile to the United
States. The contrast between the German cordiality
so evident in the seventies and early eighties, and the
open dislike of everything American that was being
voiced in the German press in the nineties, was very
striking. Mr. White also believed that

"beyond a doubt, too, envy of American success is
very general in this Empire; but envy, in so far as it
takes the form of hatred, is, I think, mainly confined
to a small part of the German nation. . . . I believe
that the former feeling of Germany towards the United
States, as a great kindred power naturally friendly

[19] White to Hay, June 18, 1898, MS. Dept. of State, *Germany Desp.*, vol. 66.

and tied to the older country by innumerable links of interest and sentiment, is increasing throughout the nation. In spite of all this filthy froth on the surface of the city press, I do not despair of seeing a restoration of the old, hearty relations between the two countries which I knew during my former official residence here."[20]

But despite this tone of optimism expressed by Mr. White, the American ambassador well recognized the fact that there were certain economic factors that promised continued friction between Germany and the United States. The rapid industrial development of Germany after 1870, had wrought a fundamental change in the economic structure of the German state. The growth of manufactures brought about a concentration of population in the cities, with the consequent effect of making Germany a food-importing nation. At the same time, the American northwest had become one of the great grain producing areas of the world, and as a result, American grain threatened to supplant German grain, even in the German home market. This led to warm protests from the German agrarian interests, and resulted in the tariff of 1879. Protection for German manufactures was also extended under this new policy, but it was realized that this protective policy could not be applied indiscriminately, for German manufacturing interests needed cheap food for their workers and cheap raw materials for their fac-

[20] White to Hay, December 10, 1901, MS. Dept. of State, *Germany, Desp.*, vol. 75. See also the interesting passages on German-American relations in the *Autobiography* of Andrew D. White, vol. 2, pp. 131 ff.

tories. Many of these raw materials could best be obtained from the United States, which was so fortunate as to be largely self-sufficient from an economic point of view. Germany, therefore, was distinctly handicapped in any trade war with the United States, for America could shut out with impunity German manufactures while at the same time her raw materials like cotton could enter Germany at very low rates because of world competition in cotton manufactured goods.

In face of certain American restrictions on German products, the German government retaliated by excluding American pork on the ground that it was contaminated and therefore dangerous to the health of German workers. American fruits were also banned because of alleged defects. Controversies affecting American pork, fruits, and fruit trees, extended through many years, and helped to sharpen the differences between the two countries.[21] There was also the difficulty concerning varying interpretations of the most-favored-nation clause in German-American treaties.[22]

[21] For an informing discussion of the pork controversy during the periods when Mr. Blaine was Secretary of State, see Alice F. Tyler, *The Foreign Policy of James G. Blaine* (Minneapolis, 1927), chap xii.

[22] For a discussion of the economic factors that produced German-American friction, see Dr. George M. Fisk, "Continental Opinion Regarding a Proposed Middle European Tariff Union," *Johns Hopkins University Studies,* vol. 20 (1902); and the same author's article entitled "Most-favored nation relations, German-American," in the *Journal of Political*

Another important cause of friction between the two countries was the rising tide of imperialism that became so manifest in Europe after the Franco-Prussian War. In Germany, the industrial evolution that marked the period subsequent to 1871, together with the general commercial "boom" in part created by the large war-indemnity received from France, resulted in an extraordinary over-development and over-production. This, in turn, led to the industrial crisis of 1873, which brought nation-wide disaster, and confirmed the beliefs of the expansionists that the domestic market had proved too narrow for German capital and labor. Some colonial outlet for surplus German production was considered imperatively necessary.[23]

The dynamics of German imperialism are lucidly summarized by Miss Mary Townsend as follows:

"An enhanced national consciousness expressed by Germans both at home and abroad; a swollen purse requiring objects for expenditure, and then a depleted purse in need of large dividends regardless of risk; and abnormally inflated production demanding outlet markets; mushroom industries clamoring for raw materials; an overstocked labor market using emigration as a safety-valve; and finally an ever growing navy promising protection to oversea ventures and investments. Assuredly, such influence would seem to

Economy, March, 1903, pp. 220 ff. Also, Dr. Richard Calwer, *Die Meistbeguenstigung der Vereinigten Staaten von Nordamerika* (Berlin, 1902), and Dr. Jeannette Keim, *Forty Years of German-American Political Relations,* chap. iv.

[23] A. Cheradame, *La Colonisation et les Colonies Allemandes* (Paris, 1905), pp. 24-45; A. Zimmerman, *Geschichte der Deutschen Kolonialpolitik* (Berlin, 1914), pp. 1-44.

have produced a mental atmosphere most propitious for the growth of any idea of colonialism."[24]

In the United States a spirit of imperialism—a desire to expand at the expense of other nations and a disregard for the rights of backward peoples—had existed since the beginning of the nineteenth century. America, however, had been faced with the great problem of developing a vast hinterland which until the close of the nineteenth century had absorbed all her energies and her surplus capital. By 1898 a strong feeling had arisen in many circles that the United States had come to man's estate, politically speaking, and was now ready to take on new responsibilities. The Spanish-American War was one of the results of this consciousness of national strength, and to President McKinley the gospel of imperialism came as a divine afflatus which counselled him to keep the distant Philippines as a sort of Christian task or "white man's burden."[25]   And in McKinley's case the voice of God

[24] M. E. Townsend, *Origins of Modern German Colonialism, op. cit.*, pp. 16-17; M. von Hagen, *Bismarck's Kolonialpolitik* (Stuttgart, 1923), pp. 1-41; P. Decharme, *Compagnies et Sociétés Coloniales Allemandes* (Paris, 1903), pp. 24-40.

[25] C. S. Olcott, *Life of William McKinley* (N. Y. 1916), vol. 2, pp. 109. For an acrid estimate of American policy before, during, and after the Spanish-American War see the recent study by Walter Millis entitled *The Martial Spirit* (Boston, 1931). Mr. Millis not only points out how journalists like Hearst and Pulitzer soon discovered how jingoism accelerated circulation figures, but also that many Americans cloaked their greed and love of adventure with a transparent enthusiasm for "Cuba Libre." See also Leland H. Jenks, *Our Cuban Colony* (N. Y. 1928).

was also the voice of the American people : the United States was ready to avow as well as practice the doctrine of economic imperialism.

For the practice of economic imperialism America was amply ready. Controlling an immense land area with a central river valley of unrivalled fertility, the United States had a natural economic position without comparison. Moreover, her political isolation had been of great advantage in an economic sense, for while Europe had been spending a large portion of her surplus capital in the preparation of great armaments for national protection or as a safeguard for her colonial empires, the United States was using her surplus capital to develop the mechanical equipment so necessary to the modern industrial state. In her intensive cultivation of the arts of peace, America was building blast furnaces instead of dreadnaughts, great factories instead of battle cruisers.[26] The machine age had come to America and surplus capital was ready for investment in backward countries where the rate of interest was high.

There were many spokesmen to welcome this new era. President McKinley soon discovered that imperialism was a corollary of Christianity, while John Hay became so enthusiastic over the general prospect that at times he soared to lyric heights. The Spanish-American War was a prelude to Imperialism, therefor it was:

[26] Scott Nearing and Joseph Freeman, *Dollar Diplomacy* (N. Y. 1925), chaps. i-ii; Parker T. Moon, *Imperialism and World Politics* (N. Y. 1927), chaps. i-iv.

"A splendid little war; begun with the highest motives, carried on with magnificent intelligence and spirit, favored by that Fortune which loves the brave." [27]

Such a "splendid little war" brought fruits that Hay would not disdain. If certain far-flung islands should become ours by right of conquest, we should by all means keep them, and he professed to be unable to understand the viewpoint of the anti-imperialists who wished America to give the Philippines to some other nation. To him this attitude seemed much like that of the old maid who having come to the belief that "her jewels were dragging her down to Hell, she immediately gave them to her sister." [28]

This warm espousal of imperialism found a ready echo in the utterances of President Roosevelt after his accession to office in September, 1901. His creed of imperialism, however, was tinged with a definite idealism as is revealed in his first message to Congress, December 3, 1901, in which he referred as follows to the task that confronted America in regard to the Philippines:

"Our aim is high. We do not desire to do for the islanders merely what has elsewhere been done for tropic peoples by even the best foreign governments. We hope to do for them what has never been done for any peoples of the tropics—to make them fit for self-government after the fashion of the really free nations." [29]

[27] Hay to Roosevelt, July 27, 1898, MS. *Roosevelt Papers.*
[28] Joseph B. Bishop, *Notes and Anecdotes of Many Years* (N. Y. 1925), pp. 64-65.
[29] Theodore Roosevelt, *Addresses and Presidential Messages* (N. Y. 1904), p. 316.

Armed with the righteousness of a just cause, Roosevelt was contemptuous of those who disagreed with him on the question of imperialism. As early as July 30, 1900, while Governor of New York, he had written to Secretary Hay and expressed the low opinion that he had for anti-imperialists:

"The attitude of Carl Schurz, Godkin and the rest of that group down to the smaller vermin of the Jack Chapman, Garrison, Atkinson and Winslow type, is even more discreditable because of the element of hypocrisy in these men."[30]

To Bishop H. C. Potter he was equally explicit:

"I do not care a rap for the ordinary anti-imperialist creature or his requests, but when you make a request I want to pay all possible heed to it."[31]

[30] Roosevelt to Hay, July 30, 1900, MS. *Roosevelt Papers.*

[31] Roosevelt to Potter, January 2, 1902, MS. *Roosevelt Papers.* Roosevelt's sharp denunciation of the anti-imperialists can only be understood when we realize that it was a counterblast against the unrestrained attacks of the anti-imperialists. Thus we have Louis R. Ehrich, of Colorado Springs, writing as follows to Carl Schurz, May 16, 1901: "You ask as to the present condition of public sentiment here with regard to Imperialism and also what our people think of the attitude of the Administration towards Cuba. I have been home only a few days but my judgment is that here, as elsewhere throughout the country, the public is not bothering its head about Imperialism or Cuba or anything else outside of the making of money. The whole Nation is wallowing in a slough of selfishness. . . . My heart is heavy when I see the public honors showered upon McKinley whom I cannot but regard as the greatest criminal of this age." *Schurz Papers,* Library of Congress. Another typical letter is one from John B. Henderson to Schurz, August 24, 1900: "It

The ardent acceptance of imperialism and vehement dislike of those who opposed his viewpoint made it inevitable that President Roosevelt would pay particular heed to the advice of naval officers concerning the acquisition of certain islands for naval stations, and made him disregard the opinions of those who would sharply limit expenditures for this purpose. Ever since the close of the Civil War important officers in the American navy had pointed out the value of the Danish West Indies from a strategic point of view. Admiral Mahan had repeatedly indicated their importance with reference to defending an isthmian canal, and in 1898, Admiral Bradford sent a personal memorandum to Secretary Hay in which he emphasized the following points:

"1. I beg to call attention to the importance of purchasing the Danish West Indies.

"2. Their possession as a coaling station is not now as important as it was before the war, since we have other ports nearby that can be utilized for that purpose.

"3. It is known, however, that their possession is coveted by Germany and that they are for sale.

"4. They can be purchased, as I am informed by Mr. Chas. R. Flint, of New York for $5,000,000 or less.

---

really seems that but little is left except an earnest and open support of Bryan. -McKinley is clearly in for the partition of China and for American participation in the dirty business. I honestly believe that he is in a deliberate scheme to change the form of our government." *Schurz Papers*, Library of Congress.

"5. They are the only islands in the West Indies that are in the market or likely to be.

"6. The proposition to purchase is made in order to prevent them from falling into the hands of Germany.

"7. In accordance with the principles of the Monroe Doctrine this country would be forced to object to their acquisition by Germany.

"8. It appears to be a good business proposition to buy rather than risk a war on their account."[32]

This memorandum is important for two reasons. First of all, it indicates the opinion of leading naval officers relative to the need of acquiring certain islands in the Caribbean, and secondly, it shows that these same officers were regarding Germany as the European nation most likely to create difficulties in Latin-American waters. Whether Germany actually desired to

[32] Bradford to Hay, September 28, 1898, quoted in A. L. P. Dennis, *Adventures in American Diplomacy* (N. Y. 1928), p. 271. It is needless to point out that one phase of the growing spirit of imperialism in both the United States and Germany was the demand for naval expansion. The connection between naval needs, and colonial empire is clearly indicated by Admiral A. von Tirpitz in his volumes, *My Memoirs* (N. Y. 1919). It was the opinion of Tirpitz that "without a sea-power to protect our industry, we should have ceased to be a European Great Power," vol. 1, p. 144. See also Archibald Hurd and Henry Castle, *German Sea-Power* (London, 1913). The growing sentiment in the United States in favor of a larger and more efficient navy is admirably treated by that distinguished American naval historian, Dr. Charles O. Paullin, in his articles in the *U. S. Naval Institute, Proceedings,* vol. 40, pp. 1469-1508, and vol. 41, pp. 111 ff. See also, John D. Long, the *New American Navy* (N. Y. 1903), 2 vols., and Lawrence S. Mayo, *America of Yesterday as Reflected in the Journal of John Davis Long* (Boston, 1923).

challenge American hegemony in the Caribbean, or whether she really endeavored to thwart American attempts to secure the Danish West Indies can best be answered by examining the unpublished materials in the German Foreign Office.

As early as January 18, 1896, we find in the correspondence of Alfred von Kiderlen-Waechter, the German Minister at Copenhagen, scattered references to the Danish Islands in the Caribbean. On this date he writes to the Imperial Chancellor that "recently there has been revived in the press the question of the sale of the Danish West Indies to the United States." The Danish Government has a strong desire to sell these islands which "instead of producing the surpluses of happier years, now imposed an annual charge of the Danish budget of some 600,000 kronen." For this reason the Danish Ministry would willingly cede the islands if the United States would make a worth while offer, but the Americans apparently believed that if they would wait long enough the islands would "fall into their lap for practically nothing."[33]

On February 20, Kiderlen again wrote to recount a conversation he had had with the Danish Minister of

[33] Kiderlen-Waechter to the Imperial Chancellor, Prince Hohenlohe-Schillingsfürst, January 18, 1896, MS. *Auswärtiges Amt* (German Foreign Office, hereafter cited as G. F. O.), *Copenhagen, Desp.*, no. 6. In securing access to the manuscript correspondence in the German Foreign Office, I am deeply indebted to my distinguished German friend, Dr. Alfred von Wegerer, of Berlin. I wish also to express my indebtedness to another German friend, Dr. Alfred Vagts, one of Germany's most able young historians.

Foreign Relations relative to the Danish West Indies:

"Baron Reedtz-Thott confirmed what I already stated on a former occasion that this government recently had made no move in the matter, and that it knew of no earnest intentions on the part of North America to again discuss the question of the purchase of the Danish Antilles. The Minister further remarked that because of the fact that Denmark had almost been insulted during the progress of the negotiations in 1867, it would now be impossible for her to take the initiative in this matter. The Minister then gave a brief survey of the course of the negotiations at that time which led to the conclusion of a treaty which was never even brought before the American Congress for a vote, but was simply buried in committee.

"In summarizing the situation, the Minister casually remarked: 'We had made provision in the treaty for a plebiscite, and *at that time* (he laid emphasis on this) we hoped also to settle other questions by a popular vote.' Finally, he remarked as though in a half-monologue: 'I do not find it fitting to sell those islands for money. I rather thought that some day we could exchange those islands for which we no longer care, for some other possession, which in turn, others do not care for. Those Americans, however, are opposed to any transfer of posessions.'

"The idea of selling the islands to Germany has been expressed more than once, and statements to that effect appear occasionally in the press. Up to this time I considered that as something intended to bring pressure upon the United States. The remark of the Minister, however, suggests that they are thinking here of entering into the possession of the districts of North Schleswig by some friendly agreement despite the assurance which His Majesty gave to King Christian in 1890."[34]

[34] Kiderlen to Prince Hohenlohe-Schillingsfürst, February 20, 1896, MS. G. F. O., *Copenhagen, Desp.*, no. 22.

In January, 1898, the question of the sale of the Danish West Indies to the United States is again adverted to in Kiderlen's correspondence. The introduction in the American Senate of a bill by Senator Lodge authorizing the purchase of these islands had revived interest in Copenhagen in this matter. There was, however, very little hope of effecting the sale because Mr. Swenson, the New American Minister at Copenhagen, had assured Danish newspaper reporters, that the United States was so deeply concerned over the situation in Cuba, Hawaii, and China, that it could give little consideration to the Danish islands. The chief interest that the American Government had in the Danish West Indies was with reference to their possible transference to another power. This, of course, could not be permitted. Mr. Swenson had also modestly admitted that he was at least partly responsible for the "mention of the purchase of the Danish West Indies in the Republican platform." This particular plank was, however, in the nature of an election bait, and now that the elections were over the President would be guided not by the voice of the people but by actual national needs. But if it should happen that these islands became really valuable from the viewpoint of expansion in the Caribbean, then they would most surely "come under the starry banner." Finally, as a sort of explanation of this very confident statement of eventual American acquisition, Mr. Swenson observed that "come what may, the United States would never act in so harsh a manner towards smaller states, as for example, Germany did against Haiti."[35]

Some months later, after the outbreak of the Spanish-American War, Kiderlen had a long conversation with Admiral Ravn, the Danish Minister of Foreign Affairs with regard to the action of the Danish Government in sending a small warship to Danish West Indies. Ravn confided to him that

"after ripe reflection the Danish Government had sent out this small warship on purpose. In view of the increasing lack of consideration shown by the Americans, it was feared that some day they would declare that their interests demanded a 'provisional' occupation of the harbor of St. Thomas. If that step was actually taken, Denmark would not and could not oppose force by force, for that would be useless. Therefore the smaller the ship that Denmark stationed in the islands the less would be the reflection on her honor in such a contingency. The 'St. Thomas' could declare without shame that under the circumstances it could not oppose in an active manner the move of the American warships against the Danish West Indies. Denmark, of course, would protest very emphatically, but only on paper. I cannot judge at this moment whether any such moves on the part of the United States are to be expected. But these confidential words of Admiral Ravn left me under the impression that after all they would be quite glad to get rid of their expensive possessions in the West Indies by just such an act of 'douce violence.' "[36]

It happened however, that the Spanish-American War proved to be little more than a summer excursion

[35] Kiderlen to Prince Hohenlohe-Schillingsfürst, January 20, 1898, MS. G. F. O., *Copenhagen, Desp.*, no. 5.

[36] Kiderlen to Prince Hohenlohe-Schillingsfürst, May 3, 1898, MS. G. F. O., *Copenhagen, Desp.*, no. 34, *Confidential.*

for the armed forces of the United States, so there was no necessity for seizing the island of St. Thomas by an act of "douce violence." But the very ease with which the Americans achieved their ends in the island of Cuba, awakened apprehension in certain quarters of the Caribbean, so we find President Ulisses Heureaux, of the Dominican Republic, applying to the German Minister resident for German intervention. If the German Government should desire it, the Dominican President would arrange for the lease of an island or for a portion of the Dominican mainland to be used as a German naval station. Buelow, the German Foreign Secretary, was undecided as to the course to pursue, so he cabled to the German Minister at Washington to learn what would be the American attitude with reference to such a German acquisition.[37]

The German Minister promptly cabled back that any acceptance by Germany of an offer of a naval station in Santo Domingo would make the "worst conceivable impression" upon the American public, and that if such a consummation were really desired, it would be expedient to consider the inevitable consequences.[38] On September 2, 1898, von Buelow wrote to the Kaiser at Hanover to ascertain his views on the subject, and on the following day His Imperial Majesty sent word that the

[37]Buelow to von Holleben, August 30, 1898, in *Die Grosse Politik der Europäischen Kabinette*, 1871-1914 (Berlin, 1924), vol. 15, p. 109.

[38] Holleben to Buelow, August, 1898, *op. cit.*, pp. 109-110.

offer should be declined for he "did not wish to be at logger-heads with the United States."[39]

After this Dominican interlude had passed off the stage, German interest in the Caribbean was centered for a while upon the Danish West Indies. The chief actor in this new scene was none other than the versatile Captain Walter von Christmas Dirckinck-Holmfeld, whose winning ways and dubious conduct we have discussed in a previous chapter. In the late autumn of 1898, as related in the well-known Christmas *narrative*, Christmas went to Germany for the express purpose of persuading the German Government, by direct or indirect means, to secure control over the Danish island of St. John in the Danish West Indies. On December 11, 1898, in a letter addressed to an important German official, Christmas outlines a plan by which Germany can obtain a foothold in the Caribbean:

"Regarding my plan to obtain for Germany a suitable port and naval base in the West Indies you must have been already informed by the Imperial Ministry of the Navy which took the matter under advisement. I beg to be permitted to express in the following lines

[39] Buelow to Kaiser Wilhelm, September 2, 1898, and Graf Metternich to Buelow, September 3, 1898, *op. cit.*, pp. 110-111. On the margin of Buelow's letter of September 2, 1898, the Kaiser made the following characteristic notation: "O die liebe Unschuld! Auf solchem Leim krieche ich nicht." With reference to this offer on the part of Ulisses Heuřeaux of a naval station for Germany it is informing to read chapter 8, of Sumner Welles's *Naboth's Vineyard*, in order to understand how this offer from the Dominican President was motivated not by any love for Germany but from a desire to seek some support for his own shaky and dubious administration.

my own ideas as to how the island shall be acquired by Germany: The Danish Government earnestly desires to get rid of her possessions in the West Indies which require the expenditure of large sums of money and are of no interest to the country. A direct public sale of one or several of the Danish islands to different nations would meet with difficulties inasmuch as the United States would probably oppose such transactions. The situation, however, would be quite different if the island of St. John should get into the possession of Germany by some private channel after German citizens will have stayed there for some time. This course would make it much easier for Denmark to transfer the island to Germany and the Americans would not oppose it so strongly if the German flag were raised in a place which to all appearances belongs to German capital. Furthermore, St. John, despite her unquestionable advantages over the island of St. Thomas, is almost unknown and the Americans would hardly notice the transfer of this island.

"Herr A. Ballin, Director of the Hamburg-America Line, has promised to the best of his ability to further my project. As soon as the Government of his Imperial Majesty will have expressed the desire to acquire the island for Germany and will have approved my plan— according to which the island must be secured first by German capital through a private transaction before any diplomatic steps shall be taken—the necessary sums of money will be placed at my disposal."[40]

[40] Christmas to W. L. R. Klehmet, December 11, 1898, MS. G. F. O. In the archives of the German Foreign Office there is an interesting memorandum by Captain Christmas relative to the island of St. John. It stresses the importance of the harbor of Coral Bay, which "is three times as large as the harbor of St. Thomas. It is deep, well protected and free from obstructions. The bay toward the north, ends in two ports. . . . These two natural harbors are in places so deep that even the largest steamers may come close to the coast which would facilitate the erection of quays."

Klehmet, who was a member of the German Privy Council, was so impressed with this letter from Captain Christmas that he wrote to Buelow, the Foreign Secretary, and put the matter squarely before him. He was particularly interested in that part of the plan of Christmas whereby the island of St. John could be purchased

"by buying up through private channels the entire property now owned by the private owners which will in this manner pass into German hands. He [Christmas] claims that Mr. Ballin, of Hamburg, has declared his readiness to lend a helping hand in this. In this manner any difficulties which would be created by the United States would be avoided.

"He [Christmas] would like to make some money out of this deal. He claims to have been several times on the Island of St. John where his father owned large tracts of land. He has connections there which will enable him to buy up the entire property for about half a million marks. He also knows that the Danish Government is willing to cede the island to Germany because of the large expenditures it entails and for the reason that it will not be able to hold it indefinitely. Moreover, Russia has approached Denmark in regard to the purchase of the neighboring island of St. Thomas. If Germany and Russia could agree upon the steps which they wish to take in common, the American Government will not dare to oppose the move. He claims, therefore, that the matter must be pushed for otherwise Russia will cast an eye upon the island of St. John. He knows that Admiral Tirpitz and Admiral Freiherr (Baron) von Senden attach great importance to the purchase of the island. He declares that he was informed at the Ministry of the Navy that they would present the matter to the Ministry of Foreign

Affairs, and that he was requested to help in the matter."[41]

Admiral Tirpitz was as good as his word, for on January 7, 1899, he sent a secret communication to the Foreign Office in which he discussed the plan of Christmas to secure control over the island of St. John. Christmas had informed Admiral Tirpitz that

"Germany would be welcome as a buyer, but the present time would be rather unfavorable for entering into diplomatic negotiations because of the dissatisfaction that was created by the evictions and also because it must be apprehended that at the present time the United States would oppose the sale of the island to another power. These reflections brought Holmfeld to favor a plan to bring the island of St. John into the possession of Germany gradually and through private channels. He claims that he disposes already of four-fifths of the entire acreage and that he has already secured in Copenhagen a part of the money required for the purchase and that he could easily secure the rest in Germany. For this purpose he approached a director of the Hamburg-America Line, who is said to have shown a lively interest in the plan, and to have promised financial assistance for its fulfillment.

"Holmfeld, who is quite frank about his intention to make as much money as possible out of his plan, is ready to form a company which will purchase the island *as soon as the Imperial Government will show its interest in acquiring it, and as soon as it will inform him of this interest in some manner.* He reasons that when the island will be in the hands of German capitalists, the ground will be prepared for the actual possession of it, and that then it would be just a matter of a formal announcement during a favorable turn of political affairs.

[41] Klehmet to Buelow, December 13, 1898, MS. G. F. O.

" . . . While I have the honor of informing Your Excellency of this, I may suppose that the great importance which attaches to the possession of naval bases abroad, from the political, economic, and military standpoints is well known to you, and may merely remark that the acquisition of a naval base in the West Indies in view of the proposed resumption of work on the Panama Canal is now of greater interest for us. If we may draw conclusions from the existing literature and maps of the island of St. John, it would seem that this island has all the requirements necessary for a naval base." [42]

Some weeks later, Buelow wrote a carefully worded letter to Tirpitz in which he canvasses the situation:

"The Ministry of Foreign Affairs has not been informed whether the Hamburg-America Line is really in on the proposed plan as is claimed by Mr. von Holmfeld. If such a partnership were actually a fact, or in the case where the interests of German citizens were involved, we could in this, as in other similar cases, reckon on the protection of the rights of German citizens by their own Government. But in this particular case the demand has been made that even before private rights shall have been acquired by German citizens, the Imperial Government shall make known that it has an interest in the project of Mr. von Holmfeld. By taking such action the Imperial Government would assume a responsibility which, in my opinion, would be justified only in the event of compelling reasons. The present political situation is such, however, that any step towards the acquisition of territory in the West Indies by the German Government is not advisable. Under the existing circumstances, the Ministry of Foreign Affairs can adopt only an encouraging

[42] Tirpitz to Buelow, January 7, 1899, MS. G. F. O. The italics are those of Admiral Tirpitz.

attitude towards the undertaking of Mr. von Holmfeld, which means that the matter will be brought to the attention of His Majesty the Emperor only in the event that Your Excellency and the commanding Admiral believe that in the interest of the Imperial Navy it is urgent that the plan of Mr. von Holmfeld should now be promoted."[43]

In order to overcome this hesitancy on the part of Buelow, Admiral Zirzow, at that time retired, wrote to Baron von Richthofen, the Imperial Undersecretary in the Ministry of Foreign Affairs, and strongly argued the case in favor of securing possession of the island of St. John. To his mind it was fundamentally important,

"in the interest of the German Empire and of the Imperial Navy to possess naval bases in the trans-oceanic waters, in order that a foreign power may not, when it chooses, confiscate all coal supplies in foreign waters, as for example, England did recently in the waters of Eastern Asia from Singapore to Shanghai, which would create an awkward situation for both the war and commercial fleets. . . . Similar conditions exist for Germany in the West Indies, where the acquisition of a coaling station is of increasing importance the nearer the completion of a canal which will connect the Atlantic with the Pacific ocean.

"Although for the present, on account of political reasons, such an acquisition could not be made officially, yet there is an extraordinarily good opportunity to secure without any complications with the United States a very suitable location through indirect means. The location referred to is the Danish island of St. John which is situated close to the island of St. Thomas

[43] Buelow to Tirpitz, February 3, 1899, MS. G. F. O.

" . . . Mr. Dirckinck von Holmfeld . . . is so convinced of the importance of possessing the harbor, that he . . . has conceived the plan of bringing the entire acreage of the island into private ownership, that is, into the possession of a corporation which is to be formed and which in some future period could make good use of it. The agent for the Hamburg-America Line in St. Thomas told Mr. von Dirckinck-Holmfeld, when he was there, on his recent visit, that the packet boat line would transfer its seat to St. John from St. Thomas if a private corporation would do some work on the harbor, because the harbor of St. Thomas is small, and because it is not more than 23 feet deep in the deepest part, while in St. John even those ships which have a displacement of 28 feet could easily cast anchor, and this would apply to our largest ironclads.

" . . . The undersigned, whose family comes from the Danish island of St. Thomas, recently made . . . the acquaintance of Captain von Dirckinck-Holmfeld, and because the interests of Germany demand that the matter be handled with despatch and discretion, he went to Hamburg in order to obtain information as to the extent that the Hamburg-America Packet Boat Line was interested in this plan of Captain Holmfeld. The director of that line, Herr Ballin, informed the undersigned, that the above-mentioned remark of their agent in St. Thomas was based on a misunderstanding, and that the harbor conditions in St. Thomas were sufficient for their purposes, and that the company as such had no special interest in promoting the plan regarding St. John. He declared, however, that because of the far-reaching political importance, he was willing, along with Captain Dirckinck-Holmfeld, secretly to bring the entire island into German possession . . . if the Ministry of Foreign Affairs and the Ministry of the Navy were interested in its acquisition, and if he could at some future date count upon the support of these authorities in a discreet manner.

"Though it would be possible, even without Herr Ballin, to procure the funds necessary for the acquisition of the islands, yet it is undoubtedly advantageous and important if the name of Herr Ballin were connected with the corporation making the purchase, for in that case, neither England nor the United States, according to international law, could oppose the transfer to the island of St. John of the dockyards of the Hamburg-America Packet Line. Such a step would be considered as natural and wise in view of future business expansion, while the purchase of the land could be explained on such grounds.

"The assistance of Herr Ballin would be necessary also for the purchase of St. John in order that it may be made with despatch and discretion. The form and manner of some possible reservations which would have to be granted by the competent authorities to Herr Ballin could easily be arranged in a private interview which probably would satisfy all parties. This could be effected if the Ministry of the Navy would reach an agreement with the Hamburg-America Packet Line (which would not have to be made public) whereby the company would obligate itself to keep a certain amount of coal in her coaling station for German war ships . . . in reward for which service they would receive a certain annual rental from the Ministry of the Navy."[44]

While Buelow was obviously interested in this communication of Admiral Zirzow to the Foreign Office, he was still somewhat uncertain as to the exact attitude of Herr Ballin in regard to this project for acquiring in an indirect manner the island of St. John. In a letter to Count Metternich, at Hamburg, he discusses

[44] Admiral Zirzow to Baron Richthofen, the Imperial Undersecretary in the Ministry of Foreign Affairs, February 19, 1899, MS. G. F. O.

the communication that had been received from
Admiral Zirzow. It would seem from the statements
made in that letter,

"that Herr Zirzow in his conversation with Herr
Ballin laid stress upon the political side of the question, and he also claimed that the Imperial Government was interested in the matter. One gets the impression from that communication that Herr Ballin
was won over mainly because so much stress had been
laid on the political side of the plan. Herr Zirzow's
communication does not show there exists on the part
of the Director of the Hamburg-America Line any
spontaneous, personal or economical interest in the
matter."

In view of this fact, Buelow instructed Count
Metternich

"to gather oral information as to just how much Herr
Ballin is interested in the project. While securing this
information, please refrain from any remarks which
Herr Ballin could interpret as a support of the idea
by the Imperial Government. The Ministry of Foreign
Affairs has declined to act in this matter."[45]

The Prussian ambassador at Hamburg replied
almost immediately to this instruction from Buelow.
He had sought out Herr Ballin and had had a long
conversation with him in which he admitted that for
all practical purposes the island of St. Thomas
belonged to the Hamburg-America Line. All the
harbor frontage along with the wharves and coal

[45] Buelow to Count Metternich, Prussian Ambassador in
Mecklenburg and the Hansa Cities, February 27, 1899, MS.
G. F. O.

depots belonged to the company. These facilities were entirely sufficient to satisfy all the needs of the company, which therefore, saw no necessity "of extending its influence to the island of St. John." Recently, however, Admiral Zirzow and Mr. Dirckinck von Holmfeld had used every possible means of persuasion to induce Herr Ballin to purchase a controlling interest in the island of St. John, Mr. von Holmfeld being quite frank about the fact that he was anxious to realize a profit of about $100,000 from such a transaction. Herr Ballin had rejected the propositions of Zirzow and Holmfeld until Zirzow claimed that

"the purchase of St. John involved the interests of the Empire, and that such a project was supported by the Ministry of the Navy and the Ministry of Foreign Affairs. The island was needed by the Imperial Navy for a coaling station. Only after the admiral had thus entreated him, did Herr Ballin yield. Otherwise, as he jokingly remarked, he would appear even to himself as an unpatriotic scoundrel had he resisted any longer. But he declared to Admiral Zirzow that he would be solely responsible if he should advance the $100,000, and that eventually such an action might cost him his position in the Hamburg-America Line. He further remarked that he would take action only if the Ministry of Foreign Affairs and the Ministry of the Navy would demand the purchase of St. John.

"After Herr Ballin found out that his statements to Messrs. Zirzow and von Holmfeld had not been faithfully repeated to the State's Secretary of the Ministry of the Navy, he acquainted the latter of it by mail and explained the situation to him.

" . . . Herr Ballin would naturally prefer to see, in case that one of the two islands should come into the possession of Germany, that this choice should fall on the island of St. Thomas because of the wide interests of his company on that island, but he is content with matters as they now stand.

"I should like to mention another statement of Herr Ballin. Inasmuch as Admiral Zirzow kept on pointing to the necessity of coal depots in St. John for the Imperial Navy, Herr Ballin sent a wire to the Governor of St. Thomas, where the situation is similar to what it would be in St. John, if it should be owned privately by the Hamburg-America Line, and requested the information whether he would have any objections if the company should want to sell coal to warships. The governor replied that the furnishing of coal would be permitted except in time of war to ships of the countries involved in the war. Herr Ballin drew the right conclusion from this information — that the private ownership of St. John without violation of the neutrality of Denmark—would be of no more value to us than the private possession of St. Thomas is at present."[46]

During these conversations between Admiral Zirzow, Captain Christmas Dirckinck-Holmfeld, and Herr Ballin, mention had been made of the possibility that the Russian Government would purchase the island of St. Thomas from Denmark. Herr Ballin did not discount entirely this statement of Capt. Christmas, but he regarded such a transaction with indifference as far as the Hamburg-America Line was concerned. When this same story came to the ears of Buelow he placed very little credence in it, but nevertheless he instructed the German ambassador in Copenhagen to make inquiries as to whether any negotiations were being con-

[46] Metternich to Prince Hohenlohe-Schillingsfürst, March 1, 1899, MS. G. F. O.

ducted between Russia and Denmark in this regard.
And then by way of conclusion, he further instructed
the German ambassador, in order that the Danish
Government would not think that the German Gov-
ernment wished to purchase one of the Danish West
Indies, to state expressly

"that we know that the Hamburg-America Line is
fully satisfied under the Danish Government in St.
Thomas, and that the Imperial Government is interested only in knowing that the present status quo will
remain unchanged."[47]

It was now apparent to Captain Christmas that the
German Government was not disposed to adopt his
plan for securing the island of St. John, and that the
Hamburg-America Line as represented by Herr Ballin
was not inclined to transfer its harbor facilities from
St. Thomas to St. John merely in order that Captain
Christmas should thereby be made $100,000 richer.
Rebuffed in this attempt to gain easy riches, Christmas
turned to certain German individuals for assistance in
promoting his schemes. On March 2, 1899, he entered
into a formal contract with Colonel Meisner, Lieutenant-Colonel Triepeke, and Lieutenant-Colonel Knak,
to form an association

"for the acquisition of the right of preemption, and
of such privileges and concessions as may be obtainable, for the lands lying adjacent to the port of the
island of St. John: Coral Bay, Hurricane Hole,
Princess Bay, etc., which lands surround said port."

[47] Buelow to German Ambassador in Copenhagen, March
8, 1899, MS. G. F. O.

In order to promote this partnership or association, Colonel Meisner was to advance the sum of 2,000 marks, Lt.-Colonel Triepeke the sum of 3,000 marks, and Lt.-Colonel Knak the sum of 2,000 marks. These three officers then formally authorized Captain Christmas to go to the island of St. John and

"there to set on foot and conclude all negotiations and legal arrangements that may be necessary to secure to his constituents the rights of preemption and the privileges and concessions named in Article 1."

If the purchases referred to in this agreement should

"lead to the formation of a company, or if the rights acquired shall be ceded to another person or company, each member of the association shall receive the sum paid in by him, with interest, at the rate of 5 per cent. from the day on which such payment was made, and also three times the amount of said sum in cash or shares."[48]

After the signature of this contract, Captain Christmas went on a hurried visit to the Danish West Indies in order to secure the rights of preemption to a large portion of the land on the island of St. John. During his absence, Lt.-Colonel Knak, Lt.-Colonel Triepeke, E. Martini, a manufacturer living in Berlin, and Admiral Zirzow, whom we have met before, formed a syndicate called *Die Kolonial und Handelsgesell-schaft St. Jun,* or the St. John Colonial and Trading Company. On May 20, 1899, these four individuals

[48] A copy of this contract may be found in the Department of State, MS. *Miscellaneous Letters,* March, 1899 (unbound).

met and authorized Captain Christmas "to lay the petition of the company for the aid of its enterprise, verbally before the Royal Danish Ministry of Finance." Christmas immediately carried out this authorization, and journeyed to Copenhagen to present the petition. The Danish Government refused to grant the extensive concessions for which the company petitioned, so the scheme fell through and Christmas, in the autumn of 1899, paid a visit to the United States in order to ascertain whether he could arrange for the sale of the Danish West Indies to the American Government.[49]

In his secret report to the Danish Government, October 1, 1900, Captain Christmas gives the following account of his relations with this syndicate which was called the St. John Colonial and Trading Company:

"In the fall of 1898 I went to the West Indies and examined the conditions on St. Johns. . . . I got a large amount of the island's land upon my hands, and returned to Copenhagen to secure money for my project of buying the land and using it and for putting the harbor in order for receiving ships. I worked upon that for several months; secured also a loan of money from different persons interested in my undertaking, but failed to secure enough capital to carry my

[49] The articles of association of the St. John Colonial and Trading Company enumerate in detail the concessions desired on the island of St. John. Captain Christmas deposited the original copy of these "Articles of Association" in the Danish Foreign Office, from which I was fortunate enough to obtain a copy. See also Dept. of State, MS. *Miscellaneous Letters,* May, 1899. There is also in the Danish Foreign Office another document dated September 9, 1899, which deals with the plans of this St. John Colonial and Trading Company.

plan through. I was then advised to seek capital in Germany, and that in a short time I succeeded in doing in Berlin. A syndicate was formed, and I went again to the West Indies, this time in order to study the conditions on the English and French islands and for the purpose of measuring and making a chart of the harbor on St. John's. This I accomplished in the spring of 1899 and returned to Berlin with chart and plans.

"The German syndicate that in the meantime had established itself was 'Die Kolonial und Handels-gesellschaft St. Jun,' and had laid large plans for bringing the island in under the German sphere of interest by first buying up all the land and afterwards to put the harbor in order for German commercial ships and men-of-war. The plan had been presented to authorities of the German navy, who seemed to look upon it with favor, for just as desirable as it was for Germany to secure a foothold in the West Indies, so impossible did it seem if they should proceed openly by offering Denmark to buy the islands, for it was known that America would never allow another European power to establish itself in the West Indies. On the other hand it seemed possible that Germany, through the indirect way, as proposed by the Company St. Jun, could make use of the newly made harbor, and gradually, as time would pass, secure control over the harbor and over the whole island.

". . . The plan was, as already stated, adherence (?) at the highest places, and it was attempted to get the Hamburg-America Line, which has about 60 steamers running in the West Indies, to take up the affair. That company's director, Mr. Ballin, had several conferences with the St. Jun Company director, Admiral Zirzon (Zirzow?). Herr Ballin requested certain guaranties of the Government, which it hesitated to give, and the negotiations proceeded very slowly. On my return from the West Indies the directors of the 'Company St. Jun' asked me to go to Denmark to seek the Danish Minister of Finance, with a view of securing such concessions as to make the establishment of the new harbor possible.

"In June, 1899, I sought Herr Schlichtkrull, department chief in the ministry of finance, and later the minister of finance, Hörring, and presented to them both the plan, and at the same time explained to them how the situation had evolved itself. The minister was not disposed to give concessions or permission to establish a new harbor, and he expressed as his opinion that the only thing which could be done for the West Indian Islands, was to transfer them to America. Such a transfer would, in the opinion of the minister, be the final outcome. I informed the German syndicate of the result of my interview with the minister of fianance, and secured an agreement whereby I would be able to do as I might think best in the project of establishing the harbor in return for paying the syndicate a sum of money."[50]

It was evident to Christmas that the Danish Government believed that the only practicable solution of the colonial question was to sell the islands to the American Government. It was futile to endeavor to develop the island of St. John with the aid of German capital so as gradually to prepare the way for the extension of German sovereignty over it. This would never be permitted by the United States because it would directly conflict with the Monroe Doctrine. Such being the case, the only course open to Christmas was to try to sell the Danish West Indies to the United States on the basis of a commission, and it was for this purpose that he visited the United States in the autumn of 1899. We have already seen how this

[50] H. Rep., 2749, op. cit., pp. 4-5.

unofficial visit resulted in the journey of Henry White to Copenhagen in December, 1899, to confirm the report of Captain Christmas that Denmark was ready to consider an offer from the United States for the Danish islands.[51]

These unofficial negotiations did not escape the notice of the German ambassador in Washington, who was informed by Secretary Hay that while the American Government was not considering an actual offer from Denmark relative to the Danish West Indies, yet "certain private individuals without official character" were trying privately to arrange the transfer. The Secretary thought that in a few weeks he would hear something more definite with reference to the desire of the Danish Government in this regard, and this additional information would enable him to view the matter in a more serious light.[52]

On the day following this despatch from the German Minister at Washington, Kiderlen reported as follows from Copenhagen:

"It is doubtless true that while Denmark herself will make no new offer, yet she would accept with joy any halfway acceptable offer from America."[53]

In the early part of January, 1900, the Danish press was filled with rumors of Danish-American negotiations, and the new German ambassador at Copenhagen, Baron von Schoen, wrote to the Chancellor that

[51] See *ante,* pp. 230 ff.

[52] Holleben to the German Minister of Foreign Affairs, December 11, 1899, *Washington, Desp.,* no. 291, G. F. O.

[53] Kiderlen to Prince Hohenlohe-Schillingsfürst, December 12, 1899, MS. G. F. O. *Copenhagen, Desp.,* no. 78.

"a certain Captain Christmas-Holmfeld is mentioned in that connection, who, it is said, arrived recently in Washington where he claims to be a fully empowered agent for Denmark. It may be assumed that these press reports may be traced to the same person, and they are just like the man himself, a regular humbug. Captain Christmas-Holmfeld is nothing but a clever adventurer, who repeatedly, as for example in Siam and in Central America, claimed to be on 'missions,' and who was discharged from the Danish navy dishonorably.

"Admiral Ravn and the American Minister to this country have assured me that no negotiations between the two governments are now being conducted, either in an official or semi-official manner."[54]

By the first week in February Schoen had discovered that as early as December, 1899, there had been certain unofficial attempts on the part of Henry White "to sound out" the Danish Government concerning its desire to sell the islands, and this led von Schoen to comment upon the unusual manner in which the American Government conducts its foreign relations.[55]

[54] Von Schoen to Prince Hohenlohe-Schillingsfürst, January 22, 1900, MS. G. F. O., *Copenhagen, Desp.*

[55] Von Schoen to Prince Hohenlohe-Schillingsfürst, February 5, 1900, MS. G. F. O., *Copenhagen, Desp.*, no. 14. These comments deal with the manner in which Henry White was sent to Copenhagen without the knowledge of the American Minister resident there. This "backstairs diplomacy" was not to the liking of Schoen. With reference to Schoen's service in Copenhagen as the German ambassador, it would appear that he was distinctly popular with the Danes. Dr. Egan, the American Minister to Copenhagen from 1907 to 1917, in his very readable volume entitled *Ten Years near the German Frontier,* observes that von Schoen "gave so many parties that all the young Danish people loved him." p. 73.

At the end of February, Schoen was adopting a skeptical attitude with reference to Danish assurances that no negotiations were in progress relative to the sale of the Danish West Indies to the United States. Thus:

"Local papers, and to the same effect foreign newspapers, have reported recently in a confident tone that the sale of the Danish Antilles to the United States is now an accomplished fact, and that the Parliament will, within a short time, receive notice that the purchase price has been fixed at twelve million kroner. In the face of such rumors the Government has given out an official statement which firmly declares that the questions of the sale has not been advanced in any form, and that it is taking a passive attitude in the matter.

"With reference to this situation I was confidentially informed that the Government had an estimate made of all the liabilities in the form of cash advances and guaranteed loans with reference to the Antilles, which indicated that the sum amounted to twelve and one-half million kroner, which is about the same amount as that which was offered by America, or four and one-half million dollars. It seems that after all the Government earnestly considers the question of a sale.

"In the meantime the question of the sale of the islands in the West Indies is discussed both *pro* and *con* in the local press and in meetings. In general the organs of the liberal and moderate parties are for it, while the nationalistic and orthodox conservatives are against it. . . .

"The truth probably is, as it now and then comes out, that the opponents will not surrender the hope that it would be better business to exchange the Danish West Indies for northern Schleswig. In the main the number of those that favor a sale is greater than those who oppose it."

As a postscript, von Schoen adds:

"I have just learned from an authentic source that the Government of the United States had made a confidential inquiry whether there is a willingness to sell the islands. The Government here has reserved for the time being any answer."[56]

On March 13, Schoen writes to inform the Chancellor that the

"campaign for and against the sale of the Danish West Indies, which, considering local conditions, has been conducted with unusual heat, has died down as quickly as it began. This suggests that the fire was kindled by somebody, and in fact there are many signs to show that unofficial agents who have been active during the whole affair, have also been busy here. To these unauthorized agents belongs above all that Captain Christmas, concerning whom I was able on January 22, of this year, to tell you what the local newspapers now relate, that he has been representing himself in Washington as a Danish plenipotentiary, without, finally being able to show in any way his authority. The news which was spread in America that Germany was trying to purchase the island and that I had been entrusted with that mission may probably be traced back to him.

". . . The leader of the opponents of the sale is Scavenius . . . who represents those die-hard Danish politicians who cannot get rid of the idea of exchanging the Danish West Indies, or one of the islands, for northern Schleswig. When they admonish the Parliament to proceed with caution it may be interpreted to mean that it should wait for a last-minute offer from Germany."[57]

[56] Schoen to Prince Hohenlohe-Schillingsfürst, February 28, 1900, MS. G. F. O., *Copenhagen, Desp.*

[57] Schoen to Prince Hohenlohe-Schillingsfürst, March 13, 1900, MS. G. F. O., *Copenhagen, Desp.*

Some weeks later, Schoen informed Prince Hohen-lohe-Schillingsfürst that the negotiations between Denmark and the United States suddenly "came to a halt towards the middle of last month." Even the King was now opposed to the sale, and the Danish Minister of Foreign Affairs had confided to Schoen that

"this change of mind of His Majesty came about after the visit of the Empress Dowager of Russia, and must be ascribed to the national sentiment that she stirred up. Vice-Admiral Ravn was quite upset over this matter, and gave me to understand that this disappointment was a determining factor with reference to his acceptance of a portfolio in the future cabinet. Under the circumstances this proposition, [of a sale of the islands] if not wholly abandoned, will certainly be postponed. It appears quite questionable whether this affair will again be taken up during the life of King Christian. The Crown Prince is a strong supporter of the cession of the islands to the United States."[58]

In the meantime, in the United States Captain Christmas had been busy sowing suspicions in the minds of American officials concerning the desire of Germany to secure the island of St. John. This course was taken with the idea that such suspicions would accelerate the interest of the American Government in the purchase of the entire group of the Danish West Indies. According to the Christmas *narrative,* Secretary Hay

"became actually very excited when he learned that a German company had contemplated making use of

[58] Schoen to Prince Hohenlohe-Schillingsfürst, April 5, 1900, MS. G. F. O., *Copenhagen, Desp.*

the harbor and of buying the whole island. Once he exclaimed: 'They are trying to sneak into the West Indies, are they?' "[59]

These suspicions were also fanned by Mr. Carl Fischer-Hansen, the attorney for Captain Christmas, who gave out an interview on January 3, 1900, which distinctly called attention to the danger of possible German intervention in the Caribbean. After discussing the background of the Danish-American negotiations for the purchase of the islands, he observed as follows:

"Although they are not so much needed now, it is of prime importance for the United States to keep European powers from acquiring territory in the Western Hemisphere, or bringing up the question of the Monroe Doctrine at least. A syndicate of Berlin and Hamburg business men secured options last year on the harbor at St. John, and the entire river front. This syndicate was duly incorporated in Germany. It had been rumored that Germany intended to acquire the Danish West Indies, but the German Ambassador denied it."[60]

These warnings had a distinct effect, for on April 27, 1900, at a dinner given in New York City in memory of President Grant, the Secretary of War, Elihu Root, sounded a note of defiance to any European power which might have designs upon any territory in the Caribbean. Thus:

"No man who carefully watches the signs of the times can fail to see that the American people will

[59] H. Rep., no. 2749, pp. 8-9.
[60] New York World, January, 3, 1900.

within a few years have to either abandon the Monroe doctrine or fight for it, and we are not going to abandon it. (Cries of 'hear! hear!'). If necessary, we will fight for it, but unless there is a greater diligence in legislation in the future than in the past, when the time comes it may find us unprepared. We will never give up the Monroe doctrine, and if the time comes when we have to fight for it, then if we are not prepared, how we will cry out for one hour of Ulysses S. Grant, for one hour of that indomitable will."[61]

On May 1, 1900, the New York *Times* published a long article which endeavored to show that the above declaration of Secretary Root was inspired by the belief that German intrigues constituted a real danger to the maintenance of the Monroe Doctrine. To prove this contention, the *Times* published an affidavit of Captain Christmas which dealt with his relations with the German syndicate, The St. John Colonial and Trading Company. It also went into detail concerning the tactics alleged to have been employed by Mr. H. H. Rogers, of the Standard Oil Company, and of his associate, Mr. Niels Grön.

The New York *Herald* made light of this affidavit of Captain Christmas and the consequent implications. For some weeks

---

[61] New York *Times*, May 1, 1900. Root was not alone in harboring suspicions of German desires in the Western Hemisphere, with the consequent danger to the maintenance of the Monroe Doctrine. On February 5, 1898, Roosevelt wrote to Mr. F. C. Moore as follows: "Of all the nations of Europe it seems to me Germany is by far the most hostile to us. With Germany under the Kaiser we may at any time have trouble if she seeks to acquire territory in South America." *Theodore Roosevelt and His Time, op. cit.,* vol. I, p. 79.

"this story has been kicking around Washington, seeking a purchaser, at space rates. At least four New York papers had it investigated, and proved its absurdity." [62]

The *Times,* however, stuck to its story, and on May 2, it published a statement to the effect that "certain officials" in Washington had admitted that the account in the *Times* of May 1, had been substantially correct." On the following day it published an interview with Representative John J. Gardner, who, on January 31, 1900, had introduced a bill providing for the purchase of the Danish islands. In this interview Mr. Gardner explained as follows the reasons why he introduced his measure:

"I live in a district where many refugee Germans and their descendants reside. They read German papers from the other side, and they get ideas from them that sometimes do not reach our papers until much later. From some of them I obtained the impression that Germany was looking enviously upon the Danish Islands, and would seize any excuse for occupying them, and later on making them colonies of the empire. After inquiry, I learned that nothing was being done about the matter by us, and without suggestion from anybody, and after consulting only one of the Senators from New Jersey, I drew up the bill which I introduced. That bill was sent to the Foreign Affairs Committee. Soon after that I learned from Mr. Hitt that he considered it an inadvisable measure, as it might interfere with the success of the negotiations, if any were undertaken, for the purchase of the islands. With that explanation I abandoned the bill, did not go before the committee to make any argu-

[62] New York *Herald,* May 3, 1900.

ment in behalf of it, and have had no more interest
in it, although I still hope the islands . . . should be
ours."[63]

It was soon apparent that many people thought
there must be some truth in these statements published
in the *Times,* and this belief persisted in spite of denials on the part of the Department of State and of
Secretary Root. In this regard the attitude of the
Springfield *Republican* is typical:

"Secretary Root's remarkable deliverance concerning the probability of war over the maintenance of
the Monroe doctrine affords the New York *Times* an
opportunity to exploit a yellowish story regarding the
attempted sale of the Danish West Indian islands to
the United States the past winter. The story leaves
us confronting Germany, of course, and it follows that
Secretary Root in his speech was warning the Kaiser
not to buy islands that Denmark would never be
permitted to deliver. The state department says the
story is nonsense, which is distinctly reassuring, yet
the documentary evidence presented by the *Times*
seems to furnish a substantial basis for what is really
an entertaining tale. . . . As for Secretary Root, he
denies that he indirectly referred to Germany and
these islands in his speech last week. His speech and
this yarn go well together, however. One is no more
yellowish than the other."[64]

And the New York *Herald,* in its issue of May 12,
interpreted a speech of Senator Lodge on the previous
day, as a distinct "warning to Germany." Mr. Lodge's
speech was in favor of a strict maintenance of the

[63] New York *Times,* May 3, 1900.
[64] Springfield *Republican,* May 2, 1900.

Monroe Doctrine, and while no nation was specifically named, yet he "made it clear that Germany was threatening to encroach upon the Western Hemisphere by attempting to secure the Danish islands and a foothold in Brazil. Senator Lodge more than emphasized the veiled allusions which Secretary Root made to the danger threatened from Germany in a recent speech in New York. He left no room for doubt that Germany was the country the United States had to fear in upholding the Monroe doctrine."

The German Minister at Washington did not fail to see the implications in Secretary Root's speech which he termed "bellicose," and which he believed called the attention of many persons in the United States to "the dreaded competition by Germany" in Caribbean waters.[65]

The German Foreign Secretary, however, did not appreciate the real significance of Secretary Root's speech, for on June 16, he wrote to von Holleben at Washington to inquire as to the attitude of the American Government relative to the acquisition by Germany of the Jungfern and Galapagos islands for "cable stations and for other purposes." He was to avoid "direct inquiry" in this regard, and could base his answer upon what he knew of the situation.[66]

---

[65] Von Holleben to Prince Hohenlohe-Schillingsfürst, May 5, 1900, MS. G. F. O., *Washington, Desp.*

[66] Buelow to von Holleben, June 16, 1900, MS. G. F. O., no. A. 93.

In his reply, von Holleben did not mince matters:

"The truly hysterical irritation which has been displayed here recently with reference to the interpretation of the Monroe doctrine, would lead to incalculable consequences in case a foreign power should attempt any action that could be viewed as a violation of that doctrine. And this feeling will remain not only as long as the excitement attending the elections endures, but it will also continue under any administration like that of Mr. McKinley. It is also true that no Democratic administration would risk its popularity by showing a greater willingness in this matter.

"More than twenty years ago I called attention to the value of the Galapagos islands, and since that time I have again done so. At that time we could have obtained both those islands and also many other privileges in South America, but this could now occur only after some great catastrophes. Anything that relates to the Danish islands causes the greatest excitement here. Both political parties consider it as immaterial whether it will be a question of annexation or purchase. The latter mode, however, could possibly be used for agreements with some of the stronger South American republics. The establishment of coaling stations is, naturally enough, something different. No opposition would be made here against agreements of that sort with Denmark or Ecuador, although they would be viewed with displeasure." [67]

The question of the sale of the Danish West Indies to the United States remained quiescent for the rest of the summer of 1900, but in October of that year the German chargé d'affaires at Washington wrote to Chancellor Buelow that the matter was again being discussed as a result of the receipt

[67] Von Holleben to Prince Hohenlohe-Schillingsfürst, June 30, 1900, MS., G. F. O., *Washington, Desp.*

"of a telegram regarding a statement by the Danish Prime Minister in the Folkething in which he mentioned that he was hopeful of being able soon to make a declaration in that regard. I did not wish personally to inquire at the Department of State with reference to this affair, for I did not wish to evince an interest in the matter that could easily lead to false conclusions. However, I heard from a diplomat-friend who discussed the matter with the Secretary of State, that the latter had declared that no discussions had been held with the Danish Government since April of this year. A number of go-betweens who were hoping to make some money out of this matter, seem to have made it their business to see that the question does not fail to appear in the daily newspapers. The Government here, seems desirous of purchasing the islands because the harbor of St. Thomas is particularly suitable as a naval base, but it is opposed to the employment of go-betweens in such a matter. On the other hand, the Government of Denmark is aware of the intentions of this country, but is forced to deal with all sorts of opinions in Denmark and therefore is not entirely free to act as it would like."[68]

After the easy victory of the Republican Party in the elections of 1900, the question of the purchase of the Danish islands was revived and certain activities were apparent. Baron von Schoen, in Copenhagen, was soon aware of this continued interest on the part of the American Government in this matter, and it did not surprise him. Indeed, he had always been certain that the question would come up sooner or later, and

[68] A. Quadt to Chancellor Buelow, October 26, 1900, MS. G. F. O., *Washington, Desp.*

"not even a refusal of the King, or adverse national sentiment in Denmark would keep American politicians from making a new attempt at bargaining and buying. Of course, as long as the presidential elections absorbed all political interests the question of the Antilles remained undiscussed, but after this political battle had ended and was decided in favor of Imperialism, then new steps could be expected in the direction of the West Indies. These soon took place and were prefaced by a press propaganda, the tactics of which we are familiar to the point where they become disgusting, wherein we are pictured as intriguing competitors. It is true that the Danish Government and the American minister, remembering the evil consequences of the indiscretions of last year, are silent in this regard, but it may be assumed with certainty that America has cautiously inquired whether there is a willingness to resume the negotiations. At the same time, the Americans, in true merchant fashion, purposely show little interest and seem to be inclined to reduce the amount of their offer. . . . Although, just like last spring, a certain opposition is being raised against the sale, and great projects of improvement are advanced by certain mercantile organizations, yet it is probable that the final decision will be in favor of selling the islands for the simple reason that the Danish state finances are no longer able to support the expensive luxury of the possession of the Antilles."[69]

Schoen was wise enough to realize that imperialism is a tremendous motive force in the direction of colonial acquisition, and he also realized that imperialists are always eager for naval expansion in order to protect these colonial holdings. Therefore, neither he

[69] Schoen to Chancellor Buelow, January 19, 1901, MS. G. F. O., *Copenhagen, Desp.*

nor other members of the German diplomatic corps
were surprised to learn that on November 8, 1901,
the American Secretary of the Navy had requested the
General Board, with Admiral Dewey at its head, to
prepare a memorandum with reference to the purchase
of the Danish West Indies. Of course, such an inquiry had reference only to the purchase of the islands
from the viewpoint of naval strategy, and the answer
of the Naval Board was lengthy and informing. In
view of the proposed construction of an isthmian
canal, and taking into consideration the European
settlements in South America, the Board believed that

"every additional acquisition by the United States in
the West Indies is of value. The further east the
acquisition, the greater the value as against aggression
from European bases; the further south the acquisition, the greater the value for aggressive action on our
part against localities in South America.
"Under ordinary conditions of probable war with
European powers, we must possess a place of arms,
a naval stronghold, in the northeastern Caribbean, or
we must risk the loss of our isolated territory of Porto
Rico. Against any one of the naval powers of Europe,
or a coalition of two or more of these powers, our
navy will not be strong enough to maintain itself in
Porto Rican waters, isolated twelve or fifteen hundred miles from home ports, without a well fortified
naval base in that vicinity. A campaign based upon
the Windward Passage, at a stronghold such as Guantanamo, would be the most reasonable and logical
method of combating a powerful enemy coming from
continental Europe and having as his objective our
isthmian canal or the occupation of South America.
But with our main force based upon Guantanamo we
could not expect to preserve Porto Rico from capture,

under the conditions likely to exist, and it is believed that no government would approve of any plan that included the voluntary surrender of, or withdrawal from, Porto Rico. Hence we must, during peace, provide a well equipped naval base for our fleet in the vicinity of Porto Rico, capable of holding out for several months in case of temporary withdrawal of our fleet, and of preserving for it, at all times, a shelter when it shall return.

"St. John, in the Danish group, offers, as far as we know, a most excellent position, but our knowledge of it is limited, as it has been but little visited by our officers.

"St. Thomas had much to recommend it. It has a small interior harbor, completely sheltered, which, with moderate dredging, would accommodate many vessels. . . . The island would make an excellent base of operations and would be a formidable menace to any line of communications if in our possession, or conversely, an even greater danger to us if in other hands.

"Careful investigation into the radius of coal endurance of foreign men-of-war, based upon the actual performance of our own vessels and allowing equality of foreign vessels with our own, shows that virtually the uttermost reach of European men-of-war from their own ports, on a single supply of coal, in the direction of the proposed isthmian canal, is in the neighborhood of Haiti or St. Thomas. Therefore, we find Germany deeply interested in Haiti, and undoubtedly she would be equally interested in the acquisition of St. Thomas if opportunity were ripe. Were Germany to own St. Thomas or Santa Cruz, she would interpose between our ports or bases and the German settlements in South America.

"Finally, the General Board is of the opinion that, in addition to such points in Porto Rico as we already possess and can utilize, both St. Thomas and St. John would be valuable possessions, while their occupation by any foreign power would be a decided menace to us. Their acquisition (Santa Cruz being regarded as unimportant) is therefore strongly recommended by the General Board."[70]

Some two weeks after the General Board sent in its recommendations to the Secretary of the Navy, the German Minister at Washington wrote to Chancellor Buelow and gave him the gist of the whole report. Not only were the islands of St. Thomas and St. John of great value as potential naval bases, but the proposed construction of an isthmian canal at Nicaragua made them doubly important as a barrier of defense against the attack of any European power.[71]

The favorable report of the General Board of the United States Navy relative to the purchase of the Danish West Indies, merely confirmed the desire of Secretary Hay to conclude a treaty of cession as soon as possible. By December, 1901, most of the difficulties in the way of a treaty had been smoothed away, but there still remained the question of the holding of a plebiscite in the islands. The Conservatives in Denmark were strongly opposed to ceding the islands without a specific provision in the treaty whereby this popular vote would be held. Such opposition, of course, was not based upon any high regard for popular rights, but upon the feeling that if they should

[70] Admiral George Dewey, President of the General Board, to the Secretary of the Navy, November 12, 1901, MS. Department of State, *Miscellaneous Letters* (unbound).

[71] Holleben to Chancellor Buelow, November 25, 1901, MS. G. F. O., *Washington, Desp.*

ignore the plebiscite principle they would thereby sanction the policy of Bismarck.

The basis of this Conservative opposition to the treaty of cession was clearly understood by the German representative at Copenhagen, who wrote to Chancellor Buelow that

"this manner of reasoning is not illogical . . . but incomplete, for it conceals the fact that the chauvinists dislike the sale of the Antilles to America, whether that should take place with or without a popular vote, mainly for the reason that that would put an end to their dreams of regaining North Schleswig by exchanging it for the Antilles. In this, of course, there is an advantage for us that should not be undervalued, since the hopes on which the Danish agitation have been based, would thereby lose a great deal of ground. It would be better yet if this loss could be increased by the non-observance of the plebiscite principle."[72]

On January 24, 1902, the treaty of cession was formally signed,[73] and the next steps would be the ratification of that instrument by the American Senate

[72] Von Schoen to Chancellor Buelow, December 21, 1901, MS. G. F. O., *Copenhagen, Desp.*

[73] On January 26, 1902, Count Speck von Sternburg wrote to President Roosevelt from Calcutta as follows: "The purchase of the Danish West Indies has caused considerable comment here, though the press says that their acquisition does not materially affect the strategic situation. In spite of that though, the leading papers give a warning to England to cling to every islet she possesses in the Lesser Antilles and to consolidate her waning influence. It is a big stroke of your government to have gained all the territorial possessions you require to safeguard the great highway you are going to build." MS. *Roosevelt Papers,* Library of Congress.

and the Danish Rigsdag. With reference to the sentiment in Denmark regarding the treaty, Schoen wrote to Buelow that

"the cession of the Danish Antilles to the United States of America has not caused the least noticeable excitement in this country in spite of the fact that because of it many a cherished hope has been defeated and the Danish national pride has been put to a new hard test. . . . Public opinion is as yet in the dark concerning the question of a popular vote by the inhabitants of the islands. . . . This question, however, must arise in the near future, for the treaty must be submitted to the Danish Rigsdag as soon as it has been ratified by the Senate in Washington. I have been confidentially informed that when the Danish Government refers the treaty to the Rigsdag it will refrain from touching upon this point, and will not bring about any discussion of the question.

"The Government is opposed to a plebiscite of the inhabitants of the Antilles because it is convinced that it would result in a farce in which the rum and the dollar would play the principal parts, and also because it realizes that the Americans could now win over the Danes more easily than thirty-five years ago when the plebiscite was in favor of the United States by an overwhelming majority. The hint to North Schleswig which the advocates of the plebiscite let drop more or less openly fails to attract a government which deals with real facts, and which, apart from this, must consider the enormous difference between the English-speaking negroes of the Antilles and the Danish-speaking inhabitants of North Schleswig.

"The Government is convinced that the Folkething will accept the cession of the Antilles without a plebiscite, but with reference to the fate of the measure in the Landsthing it is not so sure. Some opposition is being levelled not against the sale as such but against it without the mention of a plebiscite. This opposition seems to look to the crown for support, and will claim that the King sanctioned in principle the holding of a plebiscite in the negotiations during the sixties. It would also seem that there are tactical rather than objective reasons for this opposition, and this occasion is to be used to let the radical ministry of Mr. Deuntzer feel somewhat the counter-balance of the conservative Landsthing, and to warn it against a too rapid stride towards democracy."[74]

On February 17, 1902, the American Senate gave its formal consent to the ratification of the treaty with Denmark, but the opposition in Denmark to the cession of the islands became more and more manifest in conservative circles, and was finally able to defeat the treaty in the Landsthing. With reference to the tactics employed by the Conservatives, Schoen wrote to Buelow as follows:

"Those who opposed the sale of the Antilles have again stirred up matters after the excitement had died down by securing statements from the unofficial go-betweens who were active in this matter. Such strategy has been successful, for the agents themselves, after the publication of these statements, have become engaged in personal strife, and have tried to excel one another in revealing scandalous facts. In this manner a surprised public has been informed in detail how the negotiations have not been conducted through the usual diplomatic channels, but through the agency of more or less questionable characters, and principally by the Danish-American journalist, Niels Grön, and by a Captain Walter Christmas, who was discharged from the Danish Navy. These agents conducted the

[74] Schoen to Chancellor Buelow, February 3, 1902, MS. G. F. O., *Copenhagen, Desp.*

negotiations partly upon their own initiative and partly upon the order of certain organizations, with the connivance and approval of the Danish Government. They had been promised a commission of ten per cent. of the amount of the purchase price.

"These statements have been accompanied by numerous proofs. The two agents, the public has been told, defend their rights to a commission by stating that influential Americans could not be 'induced' to consider the question of the purchase.

"Among other things that these revelations have brought to light is the fact that Christmas was not successful in his attempts to interest the Hamburg-America Line or the Imperial Admiralty in the purchase of the island of St. John or of the harbor of St. Thomas. They further indicate that Christmas fabricated certain statements that Germany had designs in America, which statements the Secretary of State accepted in all seriousness, and which caused him to send the secretary of the American embassy in London, Mr. White, with Christmas to Copenhagen where they were to plan the first move toward a purchase treaty.

". . . As regards ourselves, these revelations, which only confirm the reports which you have received from here and from other posts, are after all of value in showing the source of the *lie that we were planning to acquire the Danish West Indies.*" [75]

Along the margin of this last paragraph the Kaiser wrote the following marginal comment: *"The main thing."*

On October 22, 1902, the treaty of cession was defeated in the Danish Landsthing by a tie vote, and

[75] Von Schoen to Buelow, February 21, 1902, MS. G. F. O., *Copenhagen, Desp.* The italics are the author's.

[76] London *Times*, October 27, 1902.

all of Secretary Hay's efforts came to naught. Immediately after this action by the Landsthing, both in America and in Europe, it was rumored that the defeat of the treaty was really due to German intrigues in Denmark, and this view was given additional credence by the fact that on October 26, the Crown Prince of Denmark left on a visit to the Prussian Court.[76] On October 28, the Copenhagen correspondent of the London *Times* wired that the Danish press noted

"with great satisfaction the hearty reception of the Crown Prince of Denmark in Berlin. The general opinion is that the visit is a political event and a clever move on the part of the Danish Government. Even the Socialist newspapers agree in praising the Court's standpoint towards Germany."[77]

In America the newspapers accepted the defeat of the treaty with perfect good temper, for it was the general belief that the islands would eventually become American possessions, and that Denmark would soon reverse her policy. In some of the papers, however, there was a note of warning to Germany to keep her hands off any of the islands in the Caribbean, which, in turn, led a portion of the German press to claim that Great Britain was busy sowing seeds of suspicion against Germany. In this regard the following paragraph from the Berlin *Kreuz Zeitung* is typical:

"In palliation of the American suspicions it can only be alleged that English machinations are mostly

[77] London *Times*, October 29, 1902.

to blame. They find a fruitful field in Jingoism. It is well understood in England that America is preparing for great things in the future, and there is anxiety in consequence, especially on account of Canada. Hence England plays the part of 'the best friend' in Washington, and in that capacity makes herself 'solid' by brotherly warnings against wicked Germany and her vast plans of conquest. This must not be lost sight of in Germany. When we grasp this fact we will also know how to arm ourselves against it."[78]

In this connection, it should not be forgotten that in November and December, 1902, the British and German Governments applied pressure upon Venezuela with reference to the satisfaction of certain claims. When the German blockading squadron resorted to aggressive tactics along the coast of Venezuela, the American press sharply denounced such actions, and public opinion in Germany soon realized that American goodwill had largely vanished.[79] This fact had been obvious to the Kaiser even before the Venezuelan imbroglio, and had led him, early in 1902, to send his brother, Prince Henry, to America in order to "win the Americans with manner and appearance," and to convince them of the "sympathy of His Majesty for the great and rapidly growing American people."[80]

Although at the close of this visit President Roosevelt appeared to believe that the American irritation

[78] Quoted in the *Literary Digest,* December 13, 1902, p. 805.

[79] For the Venezuela episode see *Die Grosse Politik, op. cit.,* vol. 17, pp. 242 ff. Also, J. Fred Rippy, *Latin America in World Politics,* chap. xi; and Howard C. Hill, *Roosevelt and the Caribbean* (Chicago, 1927), chap. v.

[80] *Die Grosse Politik,* vol. 16, p. 243, note.

against Germany had been greatly allayed, yet the American press had not been very enthusiastic about the royal visitor or about the restoration of friendly feeling between the two countries.[81]

Buelow, himself, was keenly aware of this unfriendly spirit that was rapidly developing in America against Germany, and he believed that it might have been aided by the impression that the German Government had actually worked against the ratification, by the Danish Landsthing, of the treaty for the cession of the Danish West Indies to the United States. So impressed was he with the importance of correcting this false impression that, on December 29, 1902, he wrote the following memorandum in his own handwriting for immediate action thereon:

[81] For a survey of press comments concerning the visit of Prince Henry to the United States, see Clara E. Schieber, *American Sentiment Toward Germany*, chap. vi. On March 11, 1902, Roosevelt wrote to Prince Henry the following letter: "Not only have I enjoyed your visit personally, but on behalf of my countryment I wish to express to you the pleasure it has been to see you and the real good I think your visit has done in promoting a feeling of friendship between Germany and the United States. It is my most earnest wish that this feeling may strengthen steadily." On the following day, March 12, 1902, he also wrote as follows to the German Emperor: "Your brother's visit to this country has accomplished much in showing the depth of kindly feeling which exists between the two nations. It has been most fortunate in every way, and I trust you will permit me to congratulate you on the admirable manner in which he has borne himself. He has won the genuine and hearty sympathy and regard of all with whom he has been brought in contact." Both these letters are in the *Roosevelt Papers,* Library of Congress.

"Seine Majestat hat aus guter Quelle gehört, dass dem Präsidenten Roosevelt und Staatsekretär Hay gesagt worden ist, wir hätten Dänemark von einem Verkauf seiner westindischen Insel und die V. St. abgeraten. Ich bitte baldmöglichst dem amerikanischen Botschafter anzudeuten, hieran sei kein wahres Wort. Wir hätten garnichts dagegen, dass jene Inseln in amerikanischen Besitz übergingen und würden es ganz naturlich finden, wenn dies geschähe. Der Verkauf sei durch die anti-deutschen dänischen Chauvinisten, die Prinzess Waldemar von Dänemark und die französische Diplomatie verhindert worden. Dasselbe soll Speck von Sternburg an seine amerikanischen Freunde schreiben [Roosevelt]."[82]

In the United States, however, this false impression of German activity against the treaty of cession continued to persist, and it was widely believed that Germany was intriguing for a foothold in the Caribbean. On October 23, 1902, the day after the Danish Landsthing rejected the American treaty, the German chargé at Washington had a conversation with Secretary Hay in which the action of the upper house of the Danish Rigsdag was discussed. After some comments on the situation in Denmark, Secretary Hay

"suddenly remarked that of course the United States would never permit Denmark to sell the islands to another power. . . . He said that the United States did not greatly care to purchase the islands, but that it seemed only right, when the Danish Government had offered the islands for sale, for the American Government not to refuse them and at the same time forbid their sale to another power."[83]

[82] Memorandum of Chancellor Buelow, December 29, 1902, MS. G. F. O.

[83] A. Quadt to Chancellor Buelow, October 23, 1902, MS. G. F. O., *Washington, Desp.*

John Hay, however, was not the only prominent American who cherished suspicions against Germany with reference to the defeat of the treaty of cession. Henry White, usually well-informed and certainly a diplomat of exceptional ability, could never rid himself of the belief that Germany had a hand in the defeat of the treaty of cession in the Danish Landsthing. In a letter of November 4, 1902, he unburdens his feelings to John Hay:

"Of course I was much disappointed at the upshot of all our efforts in respect to the Danish islands and especially as it was owing to the devices resorted to in bringing two dotards with nurses into the Landsthing and getting them to vote. I have little doubt that the result is largely due to German intrigue and G. Bertie agrees with me (he says that they are at it everywhere, all the time against England as well as us, and that they are chiefly responsible for preventing Russia from getting on better terms with England; which I believe). I have not yet been able to see Bille, who is away at the Hague presenting his credentials to the Queen of Holland, to whom he is also now accredited, but I understand that the member of the Landsthing for the district adjoining Schleswig was induced to change his vote at the last moment which of course decided the question. You may also have observed that the very morning after the rejection a company was started for promoting trade between the islands and German Baltic ports, and shortly afterwards the Crown Prince paid his state visit to Germany where he now is. Of course we can afford to wait and for us it is a mere question of time and Denmark will be the loser in the end. The islands must eventually come to us, for with our tariff against them they cannot be made to pay nor will the line of steamers pay either. But it is nevertheless annoying that with the vast majority in Denmark and the islands in favor of the sale a few persons for motives of self interest should have stopped it for a time."[84]

Some months later White wrote an even lengthier letter to Hay on the subject of German intrigues in the matter of the defeat of the American treaty:

"I wrote you at such length so recently that I hesitate to inflict another letter upon you but the German Emperor's visit and the cordiality of his reception at Copenhagen recall to my mind certain features of the Danish islands question in connection with that Potentate which I have always meant to communicate to you.
"When I chanced to meet the King and Queen (of England) at luncheon some time ago at the Carrington's, . . . the latter . . . said she could not help being delighted that they ('the Danish islands') had been preserved to her country, and that we do not really want them, etc., and in reply to my suggestion that we had only come into the matter at all in order to relieve Denmark of a burden upon the Treasury, the Queen said: 'It was all bad management; with the new management you will see how the islands will flourish and be made to pay,' to which I replied that I feared that she was mistaken but hoped she might not be as we have not the least desire to dispossess Denmark of them. She then added: 'But I hope you will never let Germany have the islands, that's what we (the Danes) would dread above all things,' to which I replied that Her Majesty might make herself quite easy on that point as it would be the grossest infringement of the Monroe Doctrine which our country would spare no expense to put a stop to. Curiously enough,

[84] White to Hay, November 4, 1902, MS. *White Papers.* There is an excellent life of *Henry White* by Professor Allan Nevins (N. Y. 1930), which, however, gives scant space to the Danish islands question.

her brother, the Crown Prince, as I think I wrote you at the time, had asked me the very same question last year when he was here for the Coronation. The king hearing the conversation between the Queen and me across the table (we were only about 8 or 9) broke in saying: 'I hope you know my dear White that I have always been in favor of your having the islands and you'll have them yet. It was a great mistake in Denmark to reject the Treaty and she will soon see it.

"On the following Saturday we went to Windsor (January 31) to stay two nights, and on the second evening Prince Charles of Denmark and I got into conversation—introduced by him—on the subject of the islands. He said he heard I had been talking to the Queen about them and he wanted me to know that he differed from most of his family in wanting us to have the islands which could be nothing but a financial drain on Denmark and which that country is powerless to protect against any Power 'such as Germany.' Prince Charles, after some further conversation said that he would like to be informed on one point, viz., if the Germans should take or buy the islands from Denmark and the United States should have to 'take them' from Germany, would they be restored by our country to Denmark again. I replied that such a contingency had probably never occurred to any American statesman as Germany knows perfectly well that the United States would never allow her to obtain possession of the Danish islands, but certainly if such a state of things could be imagined as our having to turn out Germany I could not believe it probable that we should return the islands after having had to fight for them.

"You will remember that immediately after the rejection of the Treaty by the Danish Upper House, the Crown Prince paid an official visit to Berlin (within a week, I think, if not the very next day or two) and now the German Emperor has been received with great cordiality at Copenhagen and has been especially thick with Princess Waldemar who was the chief agent in stirring up the agitation against our purchase. You know that she is a great agitator and a thorough woman of business when it is worth her while.

"In view of what Mr. Choate wrote you recently as to the German Emperor's designs upon two harbors in Southern California and of the mention made to you by several members of the Danish Royal family of his possible intention with regard to the Danish islands, I don't think it requires a great stretch of the imagination to realize that he had a hand in the defeat of our purchase scheme and that he is fairly lying awake at nights wondering how he can possibly get hold of them."[85]

Secretary Hay promptly communicated the substance of this letter to President Roosevelt, who was at that time visiting Montana. In reply the President wrote:

"That is very interesting what you say about the conversations anent the Danish islands with Harry White. Both the Dutch and the Danish possessions in America will be constant temptation to Germany unless, or until, we take them. The way to deliver Germany from the temptation is to keep on with the upbuilding of our navy."[86]

Two years later, this suspicion of German intrigues was again kindled by reports that the Hamburg-American Line was securing, in an indirect manner, the entire control of the shipping facilities on the island of St. Thomas. On June 5, 1905, the Ameri-

[85] White to Hay, April 7, 1903, MS. *White Papers.*
[86] Roosevelt to Hay, April 22, 1903, MS. *Roosevelt Papers,* Library of Congress.

can consul at St. Thomas, Mr. Christopher H. Payne, wrote to the Third Assistant Secretary of State that the Hamburg-American Line had recently absorbed the Danish West India Company and was rapidly extending its influence in the island.[87]

It was three months before the Acting Secretary of State, Mr. Alvey A. Adee, answered this despatch from Consul Payne. When he did, however, he informed the American consul that

"the Department is in receipt of advices from its representatives in Copenhagen tending to confirm this report as well as the rumor respecting the purchase of Water Island, which it appears was acquired by the Danish West India Company by purchase from private ownership, although it is not stated whether the ownership of this island passed to the Hamburg-American Line with the control of the steamship interests of the Danish West India Company. It is desired that you make discreet inquiry respecting these reports and furnish the Department with as full information as may be thus obtained."[88]

The scene now shifts to Copenhagen where the American Minister was able to secure the information desired by the Department of State. As early as June 30, 1905, Mr. T. J. O'Brien, the American Minister at Copenhagen, reported a conversation with Count Raben-Levetzau, the Danish Minister for Foreign

[87] Payne to Third Assistant Secretary of State, June 5, 1905, MS. Department of State, *St. Thomas, Consular Desp.*, vol. 17.

[88] Adee to Payne, September 2, 1905, MS. Dept. of State, *Instructions to Consuls*, vol. 197.

Affairs, in which the latter admitted that the failure of Denmark to ratify the treaty of cession was a "mistake," especially so in view of the fact that the islands were "a continual financial burden to Denmark." The Minister also inquired as to the verity of a report that the question of the unratified treaty would be discussed in the next meeting of the American Congress.[89]

On July 15, 1905, Mr. Adee instructed Mr. O'Brien that the matter of the unratified treaty with Denmark could not come again before the American Congress because the Senate, which alone dealt with treaties, had already taken final action when it consented to the ratification of the treaty of cession.[90]   Four days later, Mr. Adee then wrote a second instruction which directed Mr. O'Brien to "ascertain, in an informal manner, whether or not the Danish Government is now inclined to ratify a treaty for the cession of these islands."[91]

In accordance with this instruction, Mr. O'Brien called to see the Danish Minister for Foreign Affairs, and was advised that while the Minister's own views on the subject had not changed, yet he "did not believe the time opportune to bring forward the subject—that it was too soon after the defeat of a treaty con-

[89] O'Brien to the Secretary of State, June 30, 1905, MS. Dept. of State, *Denmark, Desp.,* vol. 25.

[90] Adee to O'Brien, July 15, 1905, MS. Dept. of State, *Denmark, Inst.,* vol. 16.

[91] Adee to O'Brien, July 19, 1905, MS. Dept. of State, *Denmark, Inst.,* vol. 16.

cerning the same matter." Also, the Minister in a recent conversation with the Danish Crown Prince, had discovered that even this member of the Royal family was now opposed "to the plan."

There was one particularly "disquieting" rumor that Mr. O'Brien wished to call to the attention of Secretary of State, and this dealt with the consolidation of the Danish West India Company with the Hamburg-Amercian Line, and the consequent control of Water Island which lies in the harbor of St. Thomas. Mr. O'Brien had been informed that on the occasion of the German Emperor's late visit to Copenhagen he sent for "and conversed for some time with Mr. Andersen, one of the Managers of the West India Company." It was also well-known that the Emperor was a personal friend of Albert Ballin, the chief directing spirit in the Hamburg-American Line.[92]

President Roosevelt was greatly interested in these despatches from Copenhagen and from the island of St. Thomas, and as a result of the death of John Hay, July 1, 1905, he assumed more than his usual burden in the conduct of American foreign relations. After reading these communications from Minister O'Brien and Consul Payne, he had his personal secretary return them with the following note:

"The President wishes these despatches brought to the attention of Mr. Root when he returns; and mean-

[92] O'Brien to the Secretary of State, August 11, 1905, MS. Dept. of State, *Denmark, Desp.,* vol. 25.

while he desires a report from our Consul at St. Thomas about the matter."[93]

While the President was waiting for a definitive report on the question of the expansion of the Hamburg-American Line in the island of St. Thomas, the Chicago *Daily Tribune,* on October 4, 1905, published a long article by John Callan O'Laughlin with sensational headlines: "Germany in Coup against America? U. S. Naval Experts Aroused Because of Strategic Value of Position in Case of War with the Kaiser." After a short review of the recent negotiations between the United States and Denmark relative to the acquisition of the Danish West Indies, Mr. O'Laughlin then observed as follows:

"It would not be surprising should Admiral Dewey, who undoubtedly will be consulted as president of the general board, call the attention of the state department to the necessity of making representations either to Germany or Denmark contemplating a cancellation of the sale of causing the abandonment of the plan to

[93] William Loeb, Jr., to F. B. Loomis, Acting Secretary of State, August 30, 1905, MS. Dept. of State, *Denmark, Desp.,* vol. 25. See also note from William Loeb to A. A. Adee, September 4, 1905, in same volume of *Denmark, Despatches.* On June 12, 1905, Captain Christian Cold, the Danis Governor-General of St. Thomas, issued a statement in which he stated that "the reports to the effect that a foreign power has acquired rights at St. Thomas or at any other place in the Danish West Indies are devoid of any truth. . . . Water Island, where a coaling station is said to have been established by the Hamburg-American Steamship Company, is owned by a private individual." New York *Times,* June 13, 1905.

make Water Island a coaling station. The naval authorities point out that in case of acquisition of the Danish West Indies by this country it would be highly objectionable for a foreign steamship company whose vessels may be impressed into the service as auxiliary cruisers to have possession of one of the small keys which command the entrance to St. Thomas harbor, where a secondary naval station might be established by the American navy. It was further said that the navy had had its eye upon Water Island with a view to its use for coaling purposes, so that if it remains under control of the Hamburg-American company this will not be possible."

When this article was brought to the attention of Minister O'Brien, at Copenhagen, he decided to have an interview with Admiral Richelieu, president of the West India Company, in order to test the truth of these rumors. When he inquired whether "there was any community of interest or ownership between the West India Company and the Hamburg-American Line, the admiral replied that there "was none." He then added that

"when the West India Company began its service two or three years ago the Hamburg Line reduced its rates with the intention of driving the West India Company out of business. Finding that this could not be accomplished the two companies made an arrangement in respect to freight and passenger rates, but that otherwise they are wholly independent of each other."

With respect to Water Island, Admiral Richelieu informed Mr. O'Brien that "it was purchased from private hands, and that it is now owned by the West India Company."[94]

These assurances of Admiral Richelieu quieted the apprehensions of the Department of State, but they did not allay the suspicions of prominent Americans like Henry White and Senator Henry Cabot Lodge. White wrote to President Roosevelt, August 10, 1905, that the Kaiser's recent

"intimacy with Denmark . . . is interesting and dates from our failure to obtain the Danish West India islands in which I have always believed he had a hand. He has just paid a second visit there."[95]

Even as late as September, 1914, Henry White still harbored his suspicions of Germany, and in a letter to Rear-Admiral F. E. Chadwick, he remarks as follows:

"Of course I hope Germany will not be crushed, much less dismembered, but that does not imply a desire that she should be entirely triumphant; as I cannot but fear in that event she might assume much the same position towards us and the world at large which you predict for England in case the Allies be completely victorious. I cannot forget that Germany's interference with Denmark prevented our getting the Danish West Indian islands which I had practically

[94] O'Brien to the Secretary of State, October 20, 1905, MS. Dept. of State, *Denmark, Desp.*, vol. 25. The interesting life of *Albert Ballin,* who was largely responsible for the rapid development of the Hamburg-American Line, by Bernhard Hüldermann (London, 1922), does not contain any data on these alleged German intrigues in the Danish West Indies.

[95] White to Roosevelt, August 10, 1905, MS. *White Papers.*

obtained for John Hay; that she has lately been trying to insist upon becoming a party to any customs arrangement we make with Hayti, and has frequently shown a disposition to be diplomatically 'irritating'!"[96]

Senator Lodge's attitude was much the same. Early in May, 1905, he wrote to President Roosevelt, from Rome, that it would be very advisable to buy Greenland from Denmark:

"We ought to have done it long ago. I urged including Greenland with the Danish Islands and the idea was looked on as a joke. As the treaty failed it made no difference. . . . I believe we could buy it if it was done quietly and quickly, and the German Emperor, whose intrigues defeated the island treaty, would probably now make Denmark sell to us."[97]

On June 10, he wrote the President a second letter with reference to the Danish islands, this second communication being inspired by press despatches relative to the expansion of the activities of the Hamburg-American Line in the island of St. Thomas. Lodge thought that these activities indicated that the

"Kaiser is still hankering after those islands and under cover of a commercial company is establishing a coaling station which may be used for other than commercial purposes. It is the thin end of the wedge and I do not like the move at all. A coaling station is what Germany most lacks in our waters and the Kaiser

[96] White to F. E. Chadwick, September 19, 1914, MS. *White Papers.*

[97] Lodge to Roosevelt, May 12, 1905, *Selections from the Correspondence of Theodore Roosevelt and Henry Cabot Lodge* (N. Y. 1925), vol. 2, p. 120.

could use this commercial station for warships. He is restless and tricky and this ought to be looked after. It is and always has been a danger point. It means too, that he would prevent Denmark from selling the Islands as he did before. I think a broad hint to him and to Denmark would be well."[98]

In the American press, and in the writings of American publicists, this same suspicion of German motives has been echoed, and it has helped even down to the present time to color our judgments of German policy with regard to the Danish West Indies. In the *Forum* for January-March, 1903, A. Maurice Low, an English journalist of high standing in the United States, contributed an article which directly asserted that German influence had defeated the treaty providing for the cession of the Danish islands to the United States. Thus:

"Germany's political intrigues have more than a passing interest for the United States at the present time. If the secret history of the Danish West Indies treaty negotiations were ever published, it would probably be discovered that Germany had a very large finger in that pie. One is inclined to ask why Denmark, after having apparently welcomed the thought of ridding herself of the incubus of the Danish West Indies, should suddenly discover that they were of value to her and defeat the treaty. The answer might be that Germany was possessed of sufficient influence at Copenhagen to bring about a reversal of sentiment."[99]

[98] *Selections from the Correspondence of Theodore Roosevelt and Henry Cabot Lodge*, vol. 2, pp. 135-36.
[99] p. 346.

In 1913, Stephen Bonsal brought out a colorful volume entitled *The American Mediterranean,* which discusses in a breezy fashion the situation in the Caribbean. With reference to the defeat of the treaty of cession, Mr. Bonsal observes:

"The treaty was rejected in the Landsthing or Upper House of the Danish parliament by a tie vote after unusual measures had been adopted by both sides in the hope of gaining the day. At first this change of front on the part of the Danes was quite generally explained and interpreted as the exhibition of a childish desire on their part to reciprocate the discourtesy with which the treaty with a similar object had been treated in our Senate as long ago as 1867. An examination of the facts, however, tells quite a different story and reveals a more novel and certainly a more interesting situation. The treaty was clearly defeated by the pro-German members of the Danish royal family, with Prince Waldemar at their head, and the campaign which resulted in such narrow but yet decisive success was directed from Potsdam or from Berlin, wherever the German Emperor happened to be. Prince Waldemar and his friends celebrated the victory with a banquet, which, if not public, was certainly not concealed."[100]

This statement of Mr. Bonsal was confirmed by a distinguished authority on international relations, Mr. Willis Fletcher Johnson, who wrote an article in the *North American Review* entitled *The Story of the Danish Islands.* After reviewing the history of the negotiations from 1865 to 1902, Mr. Johnson then discusses the defeat of the treaty of cession in the Danish Landsthing:

[100] pp. 22-23.

"The lower House, or Folkething, of the Danish Parliament, also ratified it without delay, in accordance with the undoubted will of the people. But then an obstacle was encountered. The treaty had also to be acted upon by the upper House, or Landsthing, and there German influence was active, potent and hostile. Two motives chiefly animated Germany to compass the defeat of the treaty. One was the enmity toward the United States which it had manifested all through the Spanish War, and which had been intensified by our annexation of the Philippines and our consequent blocking of Germany's designs for the partition of China. The other was Germany's purpose to make itself a Caribbean Power, through the acquisition of the Dutch West Indies, the spoliation of Venezuela, or the acquisition of land grants from Colombia at Panama, including the Panama Canal. . . . There were in the Landsthing many members who were susceptible to German influence. Some were half German, or were closely related by marriage to German families. Others owned estates in Schleswig and Holstein, the Danish provinces now held by Prussia. Others were deeply interested in trade with Prussia. So, after many weeks of intriguing, thirty-three members of the Landsthing, making exactly one-half of that body, were prevailed upon to vote against ratification."[101]

It is not true, however, that all American publicists set forth the view that the American treaty of cession was defeated in the Landsthing through German intrigues. In 1919, Dr. Maurice Francis Egan, an eminent American man of letters, and an able diplomat, brought out an interesting volume which he termed, *Ten Years Near the German Frontier*. In a chapter devoted to the question of the "purchase of the Danish

[101] July-December, 1916. pp. 381-90.

Antilles," he treats of the defeat of the American treaty as follows:

"In 1902 the project for the sale had been defeated in the Danish Upper House by one vote. Mr. John Hay attributed this to German influence, though the Princess Marie, wife of Prince Valdemar, a remarkably clever woman, had much to do with it, and she could not be reasonably accused of being under German domination. The East-Asiatic Company was against the sale and likewise a great number of Danes whose association with the islands had been traditional. Herr Ballin denied that the German opposition existed; he seemed to think that both France and England looked on the proposition coldly. At any rate, he said that Denmark gave no concessions to German maritime trade that the United States would not give, and that the property of the Hamburg-American Line would be quite as safe in the hands of the United States as in those of Denmark. . . . At that time Germany might have preferred to see the Islands in the hands of the United States rather than in those of any other European power. . . . I have never had reason to believe that Germany prevented the sale of the Danish Antilles in 1902."[102]

After a careful canvass of all the evidence available, it would seem that this last sentence by Dr. Egan is very close to the truth. It also indicates how shrewdly Dr. Egan was able to size up the situation, for not only does the manuscript material from the German Foreign Office that I have already quoted in this chapter fail to disclose any sign of German intrigue, but I had Dr. Hejls, of the Danish Foreign Office, search

[102] (N. Y. 1919), pp. 236-38.

the correspondence that passed between Copenhagen and Berlin for the years 1900-1903, and his report is distinctly negative. In his letter of October 7, 1931, Dr. Hejls remarks as follows concerning the alleged German influence that was exerted upon the Danish Landsthing in order to defeat the American treaty:

"In spite of the fact that this rumor seems quite absurd inasmuch as the movement that was raised in Denmark against the sale of the Islands was solely dictated by consideration for Danish interests, the political reports from the Danish Minister in Berlin for these years (1900-1903) have been examined, and this search revealed that the projected sale of the islands is not mentioned in any of the reports of the Minister."[103]

[103] Dr. Hejls has the official title of Keeper of the Danish Foreign Archives. I am deeply indebted to him for this unusual courtesy. In the Copenhagen *Social-Demokraten* of August 6, 1911, there is an article which repeats the old version of the German intrigue in the Danish Landsthing in 1902. The following paragraph indicates its general tenor: "In 1902 it was of vital importance to German shipping interests in the West Indies that Denmark should keep St. Thomas. At that time the German trade had a widely spread field of action in the West Indies and in South America, but there was a feeling of uneasiness due to not possessing a harbor of its own, belonging to a Power whose trade would not compete with its own. St. Thomas was just the base needed by the German ships, particularly the Hamburg-American Line. It was for this reason that this line exercised itself to the utmost to the end that St. Thomas should remain a Danish possession. It was in reality the influence of the German ship owners that prohibited the sale, a result which the patriots of Denmark naively imagined they had accomplished."

In the face of the proofs that I have adduced from the foreign office archives of both Denmark and Germany, it will be difficult for any future historian to conjure up again the old bogey of "perfidious Allemagne."

CHAPTER VIII

MR. LANSING CONCLUDES A LONG CHAPTER—
THE TREATY OF AUGUST 4, 1916

In the late summer of 1907, President Roosevelt sent a new American Minister to Copenhagen, Dr. Maurice Francis Egan. Dr. Egan was an eminent scholar in the field of English literature, and possessed great personal charm. For some years he had been an intimate friend of the President, who warmly admired his wide but unobtrusive scholarship, and his unfailing tact that enabled him to handle personal equations with rare facility. If a diplomat was really needed at Copenhagen, there was little doubt that Dr. Egan could rise to the occasion.[1]

[1] The present author was fortunate enough to have met Dr. Egan when he was Professor in English Literature in the Catholic University of America, Washington, D. C., and to have heard him lecture many times. In a delightful volume entitled *Recollections of a Happy Life* (N. Y. 1924), pp. 216ff., Dr. Egan tells of the circumstances that led to his appointment as Minister to Denmark: "Neither President Roosevelt nor Senator Lodge believed that these islands [the Danish West Indies] could be bought, but they both seemed to think that I was the best man to pave the way! . . . The question of details faded into the background before the chance of being useful in Denmark, and President Roosevelt made it clear that I could be useful. . . . Mr. Loeb approved of what he called my 'plasticity,' and President Roosevelt said suddenly one day: 'That defect of your qualities will help you very much as a diplomat—you will soon be sufficiently Danish to make them understand you, and still sufficiently American to keep that steel rod which answers for a backbone in a perpendicular position.'"

From the current expressions in Danish newspapers relative to the United States, it was apparent that an American Minister of unusual ability was very badly needed in the Danish capital, for public opinion was none too friendly to Americans. There were some Danes who regarded Americans as blatant imperialists who had few of the graces but many of the failings of Europeans. Others could not forget that in 1870 the American Senate had rejected a treaty which embodied every desire expressed by the American Government, and which had been ratified by the Danish Rigsdag and approved by the King. American good faith could not be relied upon. Also, in almost every circle in Denmark there was a deep-seated belief that Americans were in mad pursuit of material things, with very little appreciation of art or literature. The Danish press was "either contemptuous or condescending," and was filled with lurid accounts of the rapid descent of American morals.

The practice of lynching negroes was especially revolting to the Danes, who feared that if the United States should acquire the Virgin Islands the black inhabitants might fall victims to American violence. When Dr. Egan labored to correct such a false impression, the knowing Danes would silence his arguments with the crushing rejoinder: "We have all read

2 In Dr. Egan's book, *Ten Years Near the German Frontier*, chap. xii, there is an interesting account of the attitude of the Danish public towards the United States in the early years of the twentieth century.

'Uncle Tom's Cabin'."[2] Even the Danish Queen felt
very deeply on this matter of humane treatment of
negroes, and as soon as Dr. Egan arrived in Denmark
and presented his credentials, Her Majesty promptly
engaged him in conversation on this topic. Thus:

"Her Majesty alluded to the Islands. I felt it my
duty to assume that she meant the Philippines, and
asked whether Denmark was inclined to buy them.
She laughed and said: 'No, Denmark would not take
them as a gift.' I regretted this politely, at which she
laughed very much. She returned to the Islands, this
time there was no mistaking them—she mentioned the
West India Islands, and said that she loved her work
in them. I took the hint of course, while wondering
how I was to get these Islands out of the conversation.
'Are there many blacks there,' I asked. 'I am glad,'
Her Majesty said energetically, 'that your President
treats the niggers (Her Majesty used this term quite
seriously and respectfully) as human beings; it is
much to his credit; I admire your President's sentiments; he will settle the negro problem in a very
Christian way.'
". . . Her Majesty shook hands with me again, and
hoped that we might have other conversations on the
work going on for the improvement of the people in
the West India Islands. She was most gracious and
evidently intended to compliment the United States
through its representative, very cordially."[3]

As a result of this state of public opinion it was
impossible for Dr. Egan to make much headway in
the matter of the cession of the Danish islands to the

[3] Egan to Roosevelt, September 12, 1907, MS. *Roosevelt
Papers.* See also M. F. Egan, *Recollections of a Happy Life,*
pp. 230-31.

United States until he had given personal proof that he was far different from what the Danes imagined his countrymen to be. This took many months, and in March, 1909, the Roosevelt administration came to an end. Dr. Egan was prepared to send in his resignation, but President Taft was well pleased with the progress that had been made in winning over Danish public opinion, so he wrote to Dr. Egan the following assurance: "You shall remain in your post as long as I remain in mine."[4]

At length, on April 17, 1909, Dr. Egan wrote to Secretary Root that financial affairs in Denmark were in a "deplorable condition," and that this fact might lead the Danish Government to consider the sale of the Virgin Islands. The great obstacle in the way of such an arrangement was the "touchiness of some of the conservatives" who regarded the United States as a great and arrogant power that might even resort to force to compel a sale of the islands. Also, there was the inevitable opposition arising from the fact that the political party out of power would be bound to oppose the program of the party holding the reins of government.[5]

Three months later, Dr. Egan was "quite sure that a time will come when it will be expedient, if our Government continues to hold it advisable, to open the question of the Danish Antilles." If it would be

[4] M. F. Egan, *Ten Years Near the German Frontier*, p. 111.
[5] Egan to the Secretary of State, April 17, 1909, *U. S. Foreign Relations*, 1917, p. 557.

possible for him to receive a leave of absence in September, he could accompany to the United States a certain Captain Cold, late Governor of the Virgin Islands, and now Superintendent and Director of the Scandinavian-American Line. Any visit of Captain Cold to the United States was of special significance because of the fact that he was the "principle aide of Admiral de Richelieu, who is, by all odds, the most important man in Denmark at present."[6]

In August, 1909, Dr. Egan informed Secretary Knox that, "owing to the change of secretaries here," it would not be possible for him to return to the United States at that particular time. However, this would not affect the visit of Captain Cold to the United States, and Dr. Egan was very anxious that this distinguished Danish visitor should meet the Secretary of State, who could dissipate any impression that the United States "is an arrogant Power, determined because of that power to acquire some of the few remaining possessions of this little country."

In Denmark, political conditions were in a disturbed state, and it looked as though Admiral de Richelieu might be asked to form a government. In the event that the Admiral became the Prime Minister it would augur well for the future sale of the islands to the United States, for he "is very progressive and . . . has no prejudices whatever against the sale." The time, however, was not ripe for any negotiations look-

[6] Egan to Assistant Secretary of State Adee, July 19, 1909, *For. Rel.*, 1917, p. 557.

ing towards that end: "In this time of crisis it would fall dead; people have other things to think about; but the press is becoming more and more favorable to the United States."[7]

It was nearly a year before Dr. Egan again adverted to the question of the sale of the Danish islands to the United States. In July, 1910, the Danish Treasury was none too overflowing, and the Radicals and the Socialists would be glad to get rid of the islands which were a source of constant expense. The Conservatives and some of the Moderates, however, still cherished the hope that in some way an exchange could be effected whereby Germany would secure possession of the Danish West Indies, and North Schleswig would be returned to Denmark. Moreover, the Conservatives regarded any sale of the islands as a "national disgrace."

It was true that the United States was now held in "high esteem" in many Danish circles, but the moment was not propitious for any conversations looking toward the cession of the Danish islands. Yet, as soon as the Panama Canal should be completed, this question was certain to rise again. Until that time, however, Dr. Egan thought it best to maintain a discreet silence.[8]

On September 20, 1910, Dr. Egan finally sent to the Assistant Secretary of State a "very important and

[7] Egan to the Secretary of State, August 9, 1909, *For. Rel.*, 1917, pp. 557-9.

[8] Egan to the Secretary of State, July 15, 1910, *ibid.*, pp. 559-61.

very audacious suggestion." It was really a resumé
of propositions that had been made to him by persons
of importance in Denmark, and it set forth the following scheme:

"1. Denmark should surrender to the United States
of America all her enormous possessions in Greenland,
estimated to be more than 800,000 English square miles
in area.

"2. The United States of America should in return
give over to Denmark the southern group of the Philippines, consisting of the Islands of Mindanao, Pala-
uan and the small islands south of these.

"3. Denmark should then surrender to Germany all
her rights to the southern group of the Philippines as
she received them from America.

"4. Germany should then in return for the southern
group of the Philippines, give back to Denmark that
part of the province of Schleswig which lies north of
a line along the middle of 'Slien,' along Dannevirke
to 'Trenen,' following that river to where it joins
"Eideren' and then following that river to the point
where it flows into the North Sea."

One of the reasons that should impel the American
Government to support such a scheme was the fact
that the "Yellow Peril" spectre that had been con-
jured up from time to time by the German Kaiser was
now becoming a real peril to the *status quo* in the Far
East. Japan had risen to the position of a great power,
and if she should aspire to the rôle of leader of the
yellow races it would not be difficult to foresee what
revolutionary changes would take place in eastern
Asia. Japanese hegemony would place in peril the
trade of other nations in the Far East, and the Anglo-

Japanese Alliance would prevent Great Britain from making any effective protest. It seemed obvious, therefore, that there was

"only one great European Power whose interest in east Asia runs parallel with those of America, and that is Germany. America and Germany are both great industrial countries with a rapidly increasing population, and for both countries it is of the utmost importance that the immense market of eastern Asia shall not be closed to their manufactures, or in any way interfered with, and neither of them could for a moment tolerate a policy which eventually would exclude them from the market of Korea and Manchuria, and weaken them in the other markets of east Asia."

One important step in the way of circumventing Japanese control in the Far East would be for Germany to return Kiao-Chou to China, thereby winning the good will of the Chinese Government. Then, in order to compensate Germany for this sacrifice, the American Government should cede the southern group of the Philippines to Denmark, which in turn would cede them to Germany. In this way Germany would secure a point of vantage in the Far East that would enable her to protect her large commercial interests and to co-operate effectively with the United States in the preservation of the Open Door.

In this interesting resumé there is no mention of the acquisition by the United States of the Danish West Indies, but Dr. Egan thought that in the event that the President accepted this program of German-American co-operation in the Far East, it would not be difficult to prevail upon Denmark to cede the Islands.[9]

With reference to the authorship of this resumé Dr. Egan admitted that he himself was "responsible for the analysis of the German Far East condition." And in this connection it should be noted that Dr. Egan probably believed that the policy he had outlined was in substantial accord with the views of the Secretary of State. In the previous year, November 6, 1909, Secretary Knox had submitted to the British, German, Russian, Japanese and Chinese Governments a proposal for the neutralization of the Manchurian railways. It was his belief that the most effective way

"to preserve the undisturbed enjoyment by China of all political rights in Manchuria and to promote the development of those Provinces under a practical application of the policy of the open door and equal commercial opportunity would be to bring the Manchurian highways and the railroad under an economic and scientific and impartial administration."[10]

On January 21, 1910, both Japan and Russia rejected Secretary Knox's proposal, and in order further to extend their control over Manchuria they entered into the well-known treaty of July 4, 1910.[11] It was at

[9] Egan to the Assistant Secretary of State, September 20, 1910, *For. Rel.,* 1917, pp. 561-64.

[10] *For. Rel.,* 1909, p. 211.

[11] *For. Rel.,* 1910, pp. 251 ff. See also J. O. P. Bland, *Recent Events and Present Policies in China* (London, 1912), pp. 317-19; Dr. Herbert Wright, "Philander C. Knox," in *The American Secretaries of State and Their Diplomacy,* vol. 9 (N. Y. 1929), pp. 327 ff; P. Leroy-Beaulieu, "Les

once apparent to every student of the situation in the Far East that these two nations had divided Manchuria into "spheres of interest," and that the so-called Open Door policy in that province might be hardly more than a fiction. It was for this reason that Dr. Egan took the trouble to forward the resumé enclosed in his despatch of September 20, 1910, with the belief that it would awaken the interest of the Secretary of State. There was, however, little chance for its acceptance by the Taft administration.

But despite the fact that Secretary Knox did not see fit to adopt the scheme proposed by Dr. Egan relative to the acquisition of the Danish islands through an exchange of certain islands in the Philippine archipelago, yet the Secretary did continue to evince a lively interest in the matter of eventually securing those islands. And Dr. Egan himself, lost no opportunity to keep the Secretary well informed. Thus, on December 6, 1910, he wrote to report "that the tendency towards the sale of the Danish West Indies is growing here." He had recently, through a third party, sounded out the Danish Minister of Finance on this subject and had received the following reply:

"1. To offer to sell the islands now might injure Denmark's chances of getting a loan of about 90,000,-

---

États-Unis, Le Japon et la Russe dans le Nord du Celeste-Empire," *L'Economiste Francaise,* March, 1910. In the *Knox Papers* in the Library of Congress there is some significant material on the policy of Secretary Knox in the Far East. See also M. F. Egan, *Recollections of a Happy Life,* p. 240.

ooo kroner, which is badly needed. 2. The King is against the sale. 3. If a proposition were made to the United States, a breakdown in the negotiations would ruin the present Government."

After receiving this memorandum, Dr. Egan concluded that "it would be useless to approach the subject at the Foreign Office here until public opinion is more formed."[12] Therefore, it was nearly eight months before he again recurred to this topic in the despatches he forwarded to Secretary Knox. On July 21, 1911, he discussed from several viewpoints the possible sale of the islands to the United States. There was in Denmark, particularly among the business men, a growing number in favor of the sale. But there were certain conservative landowners who would "not consent even at the last resort to the sale, unless on our part we would offer some salve to the pride of the Danes." Also, there were some distinguished Danes like Admiral de Richelieu, who still clung to the hope that the Danish islands might be made the basis of a bargain for the restoration of North Schleswig. The

[12] Egan to the Secretary of State, December 6, 1910, *For. Rel.*, 1917, pp. 564-65. In regard to the exchange of Mindanao for North Schleswig, Dr. Egan, in his *Ten Years Near the German Frontier*, remarks as follows: "Admiral de Richelieu, who will never die content until Slesvig is returned to Denmark, looked on the arrangement as possible. 'Germany wants peace with you; she could help you police the Philippines; Greenland would be more valuable to you than to us, —and Slesvig would be again Danish.' 'But suppose we should propose to take the Danish Antilles for Mindanao?' I asked. 'Out of the question,' he said firmly. 'You will never induce us to part with the West Indies,'" p. 257.

majority of voters were quite indifferent to the whole question of the sale, and nothing but an increase in the taxes would stimulate their interest in that regard.

It was apparent, therefore, that no proposition would be made by the Government of Denmark with reference to the islands unless "public sentiment is expressed very strongly." As for the price that might be asked for the cession, the sum of $15,000,000 had been hinted to Dr. Egan as a reasonable consideration, but the American Minister himself questioned whether the islands were worth that much. It was certainly true that the harbor of St. Thomas "would by no means be so very useful to us either as a strategic point or as a coaling station."[13]

In November, 1911, Dr. Egan had further conversations with the Danish Foreign Minister on the subject of the possible sale of the islands, during which the Minister confided to Dr. Egan that "he had once been in favor of selling the islands to the United States for the reason that they were of no profit to Denmark, and in case of war it was difficult to defend

[13] Egan to the Secretary of State, July 21, 1911, *For. Rel.*, 1917, pp. 566-67. In his book *Ten Years Near the German Frontier*, Dr. Egan observes as follows regarding the attitude of the Danish conservatives with reference to the sale: "Many of my friends among the more conservative of the Danes scorned the idea of the sale on any terms. Among these was Admiral de Richelieu, whose father is buried in St. Thomas, and who is the most intense of Danish patriots. If objections to the sale on the part of my best friends in Denmark had governed me, I should have despaired of it." p. 242.

colonies so far distant. His view had changed of late, however, as conditions in the islands were improving."[14]

After this rebuff, Dr. Egan had to wait nearly four years before he saw any possibility of accomplishing the purchase of the islands. On March 8, 1915, he wrote to Secretary Bryan a detailed despatch in which he discussed the situation in Denmark. But first of all, Dr. Egan commented on the lack of interest shown by the Department of State in the matter of the purchase:

"For seven years I have hoped that the Department might instruct me to make such suggestions to the Danish Government as would lead to an offer of these islands to the United States at a reasonable price. For good reason, I am sure, I received little encouragement; it was necessary to soften the suspicion of our arrogance and imperialisitc tendencies which had arisen here and seemed fixed."

Only once during the administration of President Taft had there "seemed some hope that the matter of the purchase of these islands might be considered as probable in the near future." This was "sometime after a number of distinguished Danes" had sent him a memorial proposing that the American Government accept Greenland in exchange for Mindanao, the Danish Government having the right to surrender Mindanao to Germany in exchange for Northern Schleswig. The President, however, had not been greatly

[14] Egan to the Secretary of State, November 14, 1911, *For. Rel.*, 1917, p. 577.

interested in the matter and merely inquired whether the Danish islands could be placed under the same jurisdiction as Porto Rico, and what price might be asked for them.

After the outbreak of the World War, Dr. Egan believed there was a definite danger that in the event Germany should prove victorious, Denmark would be absorbed. In that case, the Danish West Indies would then become "the property of Germany, as Heligoland, under very different circumstances, became her property."[15]

[15] Egan to the Secretary of State, March 8, 1915, *For. Rel.,* 1917, pp. 588-90. In an article by Secretary Lansing, "Drama of the Virgin Islands Purchase," published in the New York *Times Magazine,* July 19, 1931, pp. 4-5, there is the following comment on the negotiations for the Danish islands that were carried on during the Taft administration: "Another abortive attempt at negotiation was made in 1911-1912, but it seems to have been very badly handled in Washington and came to nothing." Secretary Lansing also refers to certain discussions of the question during the period when Mr. Bryan was Secretary of State. Thus: "While the question of attempting to purchase the islands had been considered by Secretary Bryan in 1913 and was discussed in a general way when I was Secretary *ad interim,* and while the President expressed his interest in the matter from the naval standpoint, the inclusion of the purchase in my outline of foreign policies of July, 1915, rested upon a different ground." It is significant to note that in the *Taft Papers* and in the *Philander C. Knox Papers* in the Library of Congress there is no mention of the negotiations of 1911-12. A careful search through the *Bryan Papers,* and the *Lansing Papers,* in the same institution, failed to reveal any material on the discussions in 1913.

In the latter part of May, 1915, Dr. Egan reported
to the Secretary of State the burden of some recent
conversations he had had with the Danish Minister for
Foreign Affairs.   In regard to the financial conditions
in the islands the Minister had agreed that the situation was growing worse every year, and that the best
citizens were migrating to the United States. After
this admission had been extracted from the Minister,
Dr. Egan then asked him point-blank as to "his personal attitude towards the sale of the islands" to the
United States. The Minister replied that personally
he thought that the islands "ought to be sold, and that
they eventually would be sold to the United States."
The present time, however, was "a time hardly ripe
for any proposal on the part of Denmark, but, if the
United States gave any encouragement to the consideration of the possibility of such a sale, it might be
possible."[16]

It was difficult for Dr. Egan to extract much hope
from this conversation, and in his book, *Ten Years
Near the German Frontier,* he gives an interesting picture of conditions in Denmark in the summer of 1915:

"If the islands were to be ours, now was the acceptable time.   In Denmark, the prospect looked like a
landscape set for a forlorn hope. Erik de Scavenius,
democrat, even radical, though of one of the most aris-
tocratic families in Denmark, would consider only the
good of his own country. He was neither pro-German,
pro-English, nor pro-American. Young as he was, his

[16] Egan to the Secretary of State, May 24, 1915, *For. Rel.,*
1917, pp. 590-91.

diplomatic experience had led him to look with a certain cynicism on the altruistic professions of any great European nation. . . . The Radicals, like Edward Brandes, despaired of righteously ruling their Islands on the broad, humanitarian principles they had established in Denmark. The position of the Government was so precarious that to raise the question might have serious consequences. This we all knew, and none better than Erik de Scavenius.

" . . . In June, 1915, my wife and I were at Aalholm, the principal castle of Count Raben-Levetzau. I was hoping for a favorable answer to my latest despatch as to the purchase of the Islands. . . . During this visit, there was one care that rode behind me in all the pleasant excursions about the estate. It constantly asked me: What is your Government thinking about? Will the President's preoccupations prevent him from considering the question of the purchase? . . .

"One day at Aalholm, the telephone rang; it was a message from the Clerk of the Legation, Mr. Joseph G. Groeninger, of Baltimore. . . . The message, discreetly voiced in symbols we had agreed upon, told me that the way was clear. Our Government was willing—secrecy and discretion were paramount necessities in the transaction.

"Returning to Copenhagen, I saw the Foreign Minister. The most direct way was the best. I said, 'Excellency, will you sell your West Indian Islands?'

" 'You know I am for the sale, Mr. Minister,' he said, 'but—' he paused, 'it will require some courage.'

" 'Nobody doubts your courage.'

" 'The susceptibilities of our neighbor to the South—'

" 'Let us risk offending any susceptibilities. France had rights?'

" 'France gave up her rights in Santa Cruz long ago; but I was not thinking of France. Besides the price would have to be dazzling. Otherwise the project could never be carried.'

" 'Not only dazzling,' I said, 'but you should have more than money,— our rights in Greenland.'

" '. . . You would never pay the price.'

" 'Excellency,' I said, 'this is not a commercial transaction. If it were a commercial transaction, a matter of material profit, my Government would not have entrusted the matter to me, nor would I have accepted the task, without the counsel of men of business. . . . Unless the price is preposterous, as there is no ordinary way of gauging the military value of these Islands to us, I shall not object. My Government does not wish to haggle.' . . .

"He will ask $50,000,000, I thought; he knows better than anybody that we shall be at war with Germany in less than a year. I felt dizzy at the thought of losing the Gibraltar of the Caribbean ! . . .

"He pushed the slip towards me, and I read:

" '$30,000,000 dollars, expressed in Danish crowns.'

"I said, 'There will be little difficulty about that; I consider it not unreasonable; but naturally it may frighten some of my compatriots, who have not felt the necessity of considering international questions. You will give me a day or two?'

" 'The price is dazzling, I know,' he said.

" 'My country is more generous even than she is rich. The transaction must be completed before—.'

"Mr. de Scavenius understood. My country was neutral *then;* it was never necessary to over-explain to him; he knew that I understood the difficulties in the way."[17]

As one looks through the diplomatic correspondence preserved in the Department of State, one looks in vain for anything as highly-colored as the above recital. It is true that on June 16, 1915, Secretary Lansing did send to Dr. Egan the following instruction:

[17] Maurice Francis Egan, *Ten Years Near the German Frontier,* pp. 263-66.

"Department is of the opinion that plan suggested in your despatch No. 833, March 8, is desirable and may be feasible and you may very discreetly approach the proper officials with a view to ascertaining whether a proposal such as contemplated would be received not unfavorably."[18]

It is interesting in this connection to note that the above instruction of Secretary Lansing refers to a "plan" suggested in the despatch from Dr. Egan of March 8, 1915, and the Danish Foreign Office is to be approached with a view of ascertaining whether this proposal would be favorably received. This plan or proposal was nothing less than the suggestion that had been made to Dr. Egan in September, 1910, with reference to an exchange of Mindanao for Greenland. Some prominent Danes had at that time believed that it would be feasible to arrange such an exchange, the sequel of which was a further exchange of Mindanao for North Schleswig. Dr. Egan still coddled this idea as late as March of 1915, and in his despatch of March 8, he enclosed a copy of this Danish suggestion which had been previously sent to the Department of State in his despatch of September 20, 1910.[19]

In his book from which we have several times quoted, Dr. Egan makes no mention of the context of this instruction from Secretary Lansing, and it would appear from his narrative that he simply received from Washington specific authority to commence negotiations for the purchase of the Danish

[18] Lansing to Egan, June 16, 1915, *For. Rel.,* 1917, p. 591.
[19] See *ante,* pp. 459-63.

islands. It would also seem evident from Dr. Egan's account given in his book, that he promptly returned to Copenhagen after this instruction of June 16, 1915, and opened negotiations with the Danish Minister for Foreign Relations. As a matter of fact, Dr. Egan did not have an audience with the Danish Foreign Minister until more than two months after the instruction of June 16, and this audience resulted from a second instruction from Secretary Lansing, dated August 10, 1915. From the diplomatic correspondence in the Department of State it is evident that after Dr. Egan returned to Copenhagen from his visit at Aalholm, some time in the latter part of June, or the first weeks in July, 1915, he first saw Mr. Christian Helweg-Larsen, Governor of the Danish West Indies. In the interview he had with the Governor it was quite manifest that this Danish official would strongly oppose the sale of the islands. Moreover, the Governor seemed strongly to doubt that the American Government really wanted them, and expressed the opinion that Dr. Egan was "alone" in his belief that they would be a valuable acquisition for the United States.[20]

As soon as the Department of State received this despatch of July 17, Secretary Lansing sent a second instruction of August 10, 1915, in which he suggested that Dr. Egan should

"discreetly and confidentially speak to Minister for Foreign Affairs with the view of ascertaining whether

[20] Egan to the Secretary of State, July 17, 1915, *For. Rel.,* 1917, pp. 592-3.

the Government of Denmark would be willing to approach subject of sale of islands at this time."[21]

It was after the receipt of this second instruction that Dr. Egan finally made arrangements for an interview with Mr. Scavenius on August 18. In his official report of this interview, Dr. Egan does not give the dramatic version contained in his book. There was no mention of the price of the islands, and no sum was agreed upon. The Danish Foreign Minister did admit that he had always believed it would be advisable to sell the islands to the United States, but he made it clear that this was merely his personal opinion, and did not in any way bind his Cabinet colleagues. He then stated that

"the previous experience of Denmark in her relations with the United States in regard to the sale of the islands had been so unfortunate, owing, he thought to a misunderstanding on both sides, that the prestige of both countries demanded that the United States should not propose pecuniary terms which would lead to haggling or fail to give guarantees which would effect the kind treatment of the present inhabitants, principally negroes."

When Dr. Egan assured him that the United States was not in the habit of buying anything because it was cheap, and that the Americans were so well acquainted with the true character of the negroes that they could make them more content than the Europeans, the Danish Foreign Minister remained "very polite" but hesitated to agree with these views. Finally he reiterated the statement that in view of the

[21] Lansing to Egan, August 10, 1915, *For. Rel.,* 1917, p. 593.

"past negotiations for the islands, which had not reflected credit on either country, Denmark could not
make an offer of the islands to us, but that he was
reasonably certain, though he spoke only personally,
that if a suitable offer was made it would be seriously
considered."[22]

When Secretary Lansing received this despatch of
August 18, he decided that the time had arrived when
negotiations for the Danish islands would have to be
opened and vigorously pushed. The German submarine
campaign, with the attendant loss of American lives,
had greatly shocked Mr. Lansing, and had led him as
early as July 11, 1915, to come to the conclusion that
"there existed a deep-seated opposition between the
German system and democracy; that America's task

[22] Egan to the Secretary of State, August 18, 1915, *ibid.*,
pp. 593-95. In his *Recollections of a Happy Life,* pp. 286 ff.,
Dr. Egan gives the following account of the situation in Denmark in 1915-1916: "I had long known that one of the dreams
of President Wilson was the acquisition of the islands. I do
not think that either President Wilson or Senator Lodge
looked on the prospect of their becoming our property with
much hope. . . . I knew very well that if I could strike
President Wilson at the psychological moment with precision
and directness, he would trust me to do the job. I must say
the chance, until 1916, seemed rather remote. . . . I knew
very well that for the Minister of a great country like the
United States to hint at any bargain for the islands that might
irritate the national pride of the Danes would be fatal. . . .
It was the Princess Marie, however, who gave the last *coup*
to our hopes; she was quite frank about it and she once said
to me, 'If any American Minister ever succeeds in helping to
secure the islands for his Government, I should wish it to be
you; but no American Minister will ever do it! Those islands
must remain Danish!'"

was to save democracy, and that she must eventually take part in the war if that course was necessary to prevent a Germany victory."[23]

President Wilson was much of the same opinion. The sinking of the *Lusitania* had left an impression of German brutality that could not be easily erased, and Mr. T. W. Gregory, Wilson's Attorney-General in the pre-war period, has told in a very interesting manner how the President at a Cabinet meeting likened the struggle of the Allies against Germany to a fight against "wild beasts."[24] Indeed, so strong were the President's anti-German sentiments that in September, 1915, he confided to Colonel E. M. House that

"he had never been sure that we ought not to take part in the conflict and, if it seemed evident that Germany and her militaristic ideas were to win, the obligation upon us was greater than ever."[25]

In regard to Secretary Lansing's anti-German feeling in the summer of 1915, it is evident that a goodly portion of it sprang from a fear of German expansion in the Caribbean. Prominent American publicists like Admiral Mahan[26] and Lewis Einstein[27] had indicated how Germany's naval program was a growing menace

[23] Quoted in *American Secretaries of State and Their Diplomacy*, vol. 10, p. 55.

[24] See letter of Mr. Gregory to the New York *Times*, January 29, 1925.

[25] Charles Seymour, *The Intimate Papers of Colonel House* (N. Y. 1926-28), vol. 2, p. 84.

[26] *Collier's Weekly*, April 24, 1909, pp. 12 ff.

[27] *American Foreign Policy* (N. Y. 1909), p. 67.

to the maintenance of the Monroe Doctrine, while American diplomatic and consular representatives in Haiti and in the Dominican Republic, sent repeated warnings against German intrigue. In 1913 and again in 1914, the Department of State was advised through "official and unofficial sources," that a German commercial firm was active in an attempt

"to secure extensive concessions from Haiti containing grants sufficiently broad to permit the building of coaling stations at Mole St. Nicholas, the concessions to be combined with a loan secured by control of the Haitian customs by the concessionaire."[28]

According to Mr. Lansing, "there was good reason to believe that in the years 1913 and 1914 Germany was ready to go to great lengths to secure the exclusive customs control of Haiti, and also to secure a coaling station at Mole St. Nicholas."[29] This fear of German designs in the Caribbean led not only to American intervention in Haiti, but also inclined Mr. Lansing to favor the immediate purchase of the Danish West Indies, which would be of great value to Germany as a submarine base.

In October, 1915, Secretary Lansing had a conversation with Mr. Constantine Brun, the Danish Minister at Washington, in which he spoke of the desire of the American Government to initiate negotiations looking toward the purchase of the Danish islands. In con-

[28] Letter from Mr. Lansing to Senator Medill McCormick, May 4, 1922, published in *Cong. Record*, December 30, 1922, vol. 64, pt. 2, p. 1129.

[29] *Ibid.*, p. 1129.

clusion he requested the Danish Minister to regard for the present this avowal of a desire to open negotiations as "entirely informal."

Some days later, Mr. Brun called at the Department of State to inform Secretary Lansing that the Danish Government

"at the present time would not negotiate upon the subject as they had very large commercial interests which were vastly increasing by the construction of the Panama Canal."

Mr. Lansing then suggested that, in the event of the sale of the islands to the United States, the American Government "might incorporate certain commercial privileges in favor of Danish subjects." Next, he told Mr. Brun

"very bluntly that there was danger that Germany, taking advantage of the upheaval in Europe, might absorb Denmark and that she might do so in order to obtain a legal title to the Danish West Indies, which the German Government coveted for naval uses. The continued possession of the islands by Denmark might, therefore, become a menace to Danish independence."

Mr. Lansing then advised Mr. Brun that

"in the event of an evident intention on the part of Germany to take possession of his country or to compel Denmark to cede the islands to her, the United States would be under the necessity of seizing and annexing them, and, though it would be done with the greatest reluctance, it would be necessary to do it in order to avoid a serious dispute with the German Government over the sovereignty of and title to the islands, as we would never permit the group to become German."[30]

It was plain to Mr. Lansing that "this plain-spoken threat of what might occur under certain conditions had the desired effect," for it caused the Danish Government "to reconsider its decision not to engage in a negotiation for a cession of the islands."[31] This change of heart was soon noted by Dr. Egan, who, on November 8, 1915, cabled to the Secretary of State that "the sentiment in favor selling islands to the United States growing very fast."[32]

In reply, Mr. Lansing instructed Dr. Egan to give the question of the sale of the Danish islands his "close attention," and to attempt to secure "some tentative offer from the Danish Government, as it is necessary to have some proposal from it upon which to base any suggestions which the President might care to make to Congress."[33]

On November 15, the Danish Minister paid a visit to the Department of State in order to present to Mr.

[30] Robert Lansing, "Drama of the Virgin Islands Purchase," New York *Times Magazine,* July 19, 1931, p. 4.

[31] *Ibid.,* p. 4.

[32] Egan to the Secretary of State, November 8, 1915, *For. Rel.,* 1917, p. 595. On November 6, 1915, Mr. Hagemann, a Danish Councillor of State, gave out the following statement: "If the question of selling the Danish West Indies should arise again, I am sure that the proposal would receive favorable consideration, as it is useless to continue spending large sums from which no improvement results." New York *Times,* November 7, 1915.

[33] Lansing to Egan, November 9, 1915, *For. Rel.,* 1917, p. 597.

Lansing an "embarrassing question" that had been propounded to him by his government. Upon inquiry, Mr. Lansing discovered that the question from the Danish government was as follows: "Whether he [Mr. Brun] thought in case the Danish Government did not agree to a sale of the islands the United States would feel it necessary to take possession of them."

Secretary Lansing was prompt to express the opinion that although he had not believed such drastic action would be necessary, yet he "could conceive of circumstances which would compel such an act." When Mr. Brun asked what these circumstances were, Mr. Lansing referred to the possible absorption of Denmark by "one of the great Powers of Europe." Such a loss of sovereignty

"would create a situation which it would be difficult to meet other than by occupation of the islands, in view of the fact that Danish possessions would come under a different sovereignty in Europe and in case it did, the result might be very serious. The other circumstance was that if Denmark voluntarily, or under coercion, transferred title to the islands to another European power, which would seek to convert them into a naval base."[34]

Four days later, November 19, Dr. Egan wrote to the Department of State concerning a recent conversation he had had with Sir Henry Lowther, the British Minister at Copenhagen. Sir Henry had confided to him that he had always advised his Government to make "no opposition" to the sale of the Danish islands

[34] Robert Lansing, *op. cit.*, p. 4.

to the United States, and that personally, he considered it "very much to the interest of England that we should possess these islands." As Sir Henry was a "very cautious man, not given to expressing opinion of his own," Dr. Egan believed that there was little doubt that he had been instructed by the British Foreign Office to convey this message.[34a]

With reference to public opinion in Denmark, Dr. Egan reported that the Danes no longer regarded the United States as "imperialistic and desirous of acquiring territory by superior force."[35]

This last phrase must have caused Mr. Lansing some little amusement, when, on December 1, the Danish Minister called to inform the Secretary of State that the

"Danish Minister of Foreign Affairs had instructed him that only the pressure of necessity would compel Denmark to consider the cession of the islands to the United States. He said that his government appreciated the friendliness of the American Government

[34a] In this connection it is interesting to note the following remarks in Dr. Egan's *Recollections of a Happy Life,* p. 238, with reference to the attitude of Great Britain: "British diplomacy, while unchanging in its object and absolutely sure of what it wants, is far-sighted only as regards that object. It pursues its way very often by a series of blunders. . . . This struck me during our negotiations for the purchase of the West Indian Islands. A careful study of what might be called 'unedited documents' had taught me that neither England nor France was desirous that we should possess those islands; but England especially disliked the idea."

[35] Egan to the Secretary of State, November 19, 1915, *For. Rel.,* 1917, pp. 596-97.

in so frankly stating the possible circumstances which might compel it to occupy the islands, and that if Denmark declined to negotiate, there would be the constant fear of being drawn into the European war."

In view of this pressure from the United States, Mr. Brun confided to Secretary Lansing that "his country would be unable to refuse to consider a proposition for the sale of the islands to the United States."

Shortly after the conclusion of this interview, Secretary Lansing informed President Wilson of the status of the negotiations, and on December 5, the President not only expressed "gratification" that the Secretary of State had been "so frank with the Danish Minister," but he also requested that Mr. Lansing continue with the negotiations.[36]

Armed with this instruction, the Secretary of State requested the Secretary of the Navy to furnish him with the opinion of the General Board as to the advisability of the purchase of the Danish islands. On December 10, Admiral Dewey sent a letter to the Secretary of the Navy, pertinent portions of which are as follows:

"The General Board does not consider that there is any military reason for acquiring the Danish West Indies connected with preparations by the United States itself for a campaign in the Caribbean. The harbors and waters of Porto Rico and the adjacent islands now under our flag afford as good facilities for an advanced base as do those of any of the Danish West Indies, and they are so near that the acquisition of the Danish Islands for the mere purpose of establishing a

[36] Robert Lansing, *op. cit.*, p. 4.

base upon which the United States fleet could rest would not be worth while.

"The Danish Islands, however, do afford several harbors and anchorages more or less protected from prevailing winds and seas, and more or less capable of artificial defense, that would be very useful to a foreign nation conducting a campaign in the Caribbean. If that nation were an enemy of the United States the resulting situation would be exceedingly embarrassing in the conduct of a campaign by the United States. Denmark is a small nation with limited sea power, and would not be able to prevent the seizure of the Danish Islands by a strong military power desirous of using them as a base. It might not even be able to withstand an attempt by such a Power to purchase the islands.

"In a military sense, that of forestalling a possible enemy rather than that of endeavoring to gain a favorable position for ourselves, it is advisable that the Danish Islands should come under our flag by peaceful measures before war. The Caribbean is within the peculiar sphere of influence of the United States, and if any of the islands now under foreign jurisdiction should change their nationality, the General Board believes that for military reasons the United States should not tolerate any change other than to the United States itself.

"The General Board believes that the political aspect reinforces the military argument which has just been advanced. The Monroe Doctrine is probably the most fixed external policy held by the United States. The United States raises no objection to the continued possession by European nations of territory in the Western Hemisphere already under their jurisdiction, but there can be no doubt that the Monroe Doctrine would cause the United States to oppose the transfer of sovereignty of any territory in the Western Hemisphere to a European nation. For this political reason, therefore, if the acquisition of all the Danish West Indian

Islands can now be peacefully brought about, the General Board believes it is highly desirable that it should be done."[37]

Before proceeding any farther, Secretary Lansing next turned to Mr. Lester H. Woolsey, at that time the Assistant Solicitor of the Department of State, and requested him to prepare memoranda relative to the historical background of the negotiations of 1867 and 1902. After numerous conversations with Mr. Woolsey, and as a result of a careful examination of the manuscripts in his possession, the present author is able to follow in a very complete fashion the successive steps in the negotiation of the treaty of August 4, 1916. It has also been made apparent what a very important share Mr. Woolsey had in these negotiations, and how largely Secretary Lansing relied upon his judgment, not only in questions of a general nature, but in all the technical aspects of the drafting of the treaty itself.

In the first memorandum that Mr. Woolsey prepared for Secretary Lansing, he dealt in detail with the proposed purchase price of the Danish islands. After discussing the amounts offered in the treaties of 1867 and 1902, Mr. Woolsey then remarked as follows:

"it must be borne in mind that the United States is purchasing not only land and water of Denmark, but is taking away from Denmark her last colonial possession except Iceland, Greenland and the Faroe Islands.

[37] Admiral George Dewey to the Secretary of the Navy, December 10, 1915, *Confidential, Woolsey MSS*.

Moreover, Denmark in parting with the Danish West
Indies is parting with a piece of territory known the
world over as containing some of the best harbors in
the Western Hemisphere, which other naval nations
have no doubt been desirous of possessing for many
years. On this account these islands have a peculiar
significance to the United States, particularly so at
the present time, in view of the obligation of the
United States to operate and defend the Panama
Canal. They are strategically most important and it
is difficult to estimate the pecuniary value of such portions of territory in the tropics." [38]

After having received assurances from both Admiral
Dewey and Mr. Woolsey, Secretary Lansing went on
with the negotiations, and on December 27, he was
advised by the Danish Minister that his government
"made an offer to negotiate for the sale of the Danish
West Indies on the basis of a hundred million kroner,"
that is, for $27,000,000. Secretary Lansing thought
that such a price was "excessive," and that $20,000,000
might serve as a basis for negotiation. The Danish
Minister, however, was doubtful about any reduction
in the purchase price, and on January 5, he informed
Mr. Lansing that his government "insisted on the
original sum which it had asked."

Mr. Lansing at once consulted President Wilson
who replied that he considered the acquisition of the
islands

"of sufficient importance to justify a negotiation on
the basis of $27,000,000, and that it would be a mis-

[38] *Woolsey MSS.*

take to break off negotiations 'on a question of money'."[39]

On January 10, 1916, Secretary Lansing cabled to Dr. Egan that the American Government "would consider an offer of the sale of the Danish West Indies for the sum of twenty-five million dollars, although not agreeing to pay that amount, which seems excessive."[40]   Twelve days later, Mr. Brun called at the Department of State to acquaint Secretary Lansing that the Danish Government had agreed to negotiate on the basis of a payment of $25,000,000.   In commenting on the question of the purchase price of the islands, Mr. Lansing later observed in part as follows:

"There is no doubt in my mind that we could have driven a better bargain and might have succeeded in cutting down the price to $20,000,000, which was our original offer, but to do so would probably have prolonged the negotiations for months and might have in the end jeopardized the acceptance of the treaty by Denmark. . . . Expediency demanded that in the circumstances the United States should be generous."[41]

[39] Robert Lansing, *op. cit.*, p. 5.

[40] Lansing to Egan, January 10, 1916, *For. Rel.*, 1917, p. 598.

[41] Robert Lansing, *op. cit.*, p. 5. The comments in the manuscript *Diary* of Secretary Lansing are very brief with reference to the progress of the negotiations. Thus: "Jan. 5, 1916. Danish Min. handed me telegram from his Govt, as to 27 mill. Jan. 10: W. W. Smith on Danish offer to sell Danish W. Indies. Jan. 19: Danish Min. in regard to sale of Danish W. Indies. Jan. 22: Danish Min. stating his Govt will accept 25 mill. for D. W. Indies. Jan. 25: W. W. Smith on Danish West Indies. Jan. 28: Saw Prest. at W. H. (7-7.40 P. M.). Went over Danish W. Indies Treaty draft. Thurs-

On January 29, Secretary Lansing wrote to Mr. Brun requesting that the Danish Government furnish the Department of State with the following data:

"(1) The character and extent of the public property of every kind and description now belonging to the Danish Government or the Governments of the Danish West Indies, together with all appurtenances thereto, in these islands, including all public, Government or Crown lands, public buildings, etc." . . .

"(2) The nature and extent of all grants, concessions, franchises and privileges which have been dispensed by the Danish Government or by the Governments of the Danish West Indies, or in any way relating to these islands and which are now in existence.

"(3) The nature and extent of any Government obligations resulting from or connected with the matters mentioned in paragraphs (1) and (2)."[42]

In response to this request, Mr. Brun cabled the Danish Government on February 1, and on February 7, he informed Secretary Lansing that he had been advised that a "definite statement" of the character and extent of Danish obligations and rights in the Danish West Indies had been prepared by the Danish Foreign Office and had left Copenhagen on February

day, Feb. 3: Danish Minister on proposed treaty.   Feb. 24: Danish Min. with documents in re Dan. W. Indies.   May 1: Woolsey on Danish counterdraft by cable.   May 4: Danish Min. on purchase of D. W. Indies.   August 4: Met Danish Minister at 9:30 A. M. at Biltmore and signed treaty for purchase of Danish West Indies at 10:30. L. H. Woolsey present."

[42] Lansing to Constantine Brun, January 29, 1916, *For. Rel.,* 1917, pp. 595-99.

6, on the Steamer Frederik VIII.[43]   The stage was now set for the commencement of the treaty negotiations, but before we consider the successive steps that led to the signature of the treaty of August 4, 1916, it is worth while to give some cursory notice to one of the important reasons that impelled President Wilson to push for the cession of the Danish islands. We come now to the imminence of war with Germany.

In the early months of 1916, President Wilson was looking forward to a war between Germany and the United States, and his policy with reference to the Danish West Indies was shaped by that contingency. Although from the beginning of the World War he had endeavored to be impartial in his attitude towards the belligerent powers, yet his intellectual background was so thoroughly British that it was soon evident where his sympathies lay.   Despite the fact that Great Britain adopted war measures that ran directly counter to what ·Americans had long considered as basic principles of international law, the President could never bring himself to view these violations in the same light that he regarded violations on the part of Germany.   It was for this reason that Secretary Bryan severed his connection with the Department of State on June 8, 1915.   His successor, Mr. Robert Lansing, was not disposed to spend his energies in a fruitless attempt to correct this English bias of President Wilson, and although at times, like in his note of October 21, 1915, he voiced sharp protest against Brit-

[43] Brun to Lansing, February 7, 1916, *ibid.*, p. 599.

ish practices, it was soon recognized that this was merely an empty challenge meant to impress American voters of anti-British tendencies. As Professor Pratt tells us, the "uncourteous" tone of this state paper was "in the main for home consumption."[44]

Towards the close of the year 1915, President Wilson was becoming more and more convinced that war between Germany and the United States was inevitable. There was, of course, a possibility that a peace mission conducted by the ubiquitous Colonel House might induce the belligerents to abandon war, so rather than neglect this remote chance, he sent the cautious colonel to Europe with a peace plan whose terms he knew would not be acceptable to Germany. The chances were all against any acceptance by the German Government of this dubious olive branch, and the President was prepared in that event to endeavor to lead America to embrace the cause of the Allies.[45]

It behooved him, therefore, to sound out the feeling in Congress with reference to war with Germany, with what surprising results the following entry in the manuscript *Diary* of Secretary Lansing clearly shows:

[44] Julius W. Pratt, "Robert Lansing," in *The American Secretaries of State and Their Diplomacy,* vol. 10 (N. Y. 1929), p. 68. See also the admirable sketch of "William Jennings Bryan" in the same volume of this series, pp. 23 ff.

[45] For a critical discussion of the House mission and of the policy of President Wilson in 1915-16, see C. Hartley Grattan, *Why We Fought* (N. Y. 1929), chap. xii, and Harry E Barnes, *World Politics in Modern Civilization* (N. Y. 1930), pp. 352 ff. Colonel House's account of his mission is contained in *The Intimate Papers of Colonel House,* vol. 2, pp. 136 ff.

"February 25, 1916: Monday night many members of the House were informed that the President desired war with Germany. This followed an interview between the President, Senators Stone & Kern & Representative Flood. On Tuesday the House was seething. Wednesday and Thursday it was the same. Opposition to war developed considerable strength. Thursday night the President sent a letter to Senator Stone. Friday the conditions were less hysterical."[46]

This "hysterical" opposition on the part of Congress to any policy of war with Germany greatly upset the calculations of the administration with regard to the prompt entry of the United States into the World War on the side of the Allies, but nevertheless Secretary Lansing thought it best to push the negotiations for the Danish islands as vigorously as possible. Mr. Woolsey had prepared with great care a draft of a treaty with Denmark for the cession of the Danish islands to the United States, and this draft was sent to Dr. Egan in an instruction of March 14, 1916. Article 1 conveyed the three islands to the United States with the rights of property in all public, Government, or Crown lands, public buildings, etc. Under the terms of Article 3, the United States specifically recognized a long list of concessions that had been granted to certain corporations and individuals. Article 4, with reference to the formal delivery of the islands to the United States, was practically a repetition of Article 4 in the rejected Treaty of January 24,

[46] MS. *Diary*, January 3, 1915-December 31, 1916, Library of Congress.

1902. Article 5 differed from Article 5 of the Treaty of January 24, in that the sum offered for the islands was $25,000,000 instead of $5,000,000. Article 6 was largely a reproduction of Article 3 of the first draft treaty that Secretary Hay had endeavored to induce the Danish Government to accept in January, 1900, and it would not have as clearly safeguarded the rights of Danish residents in the islands as did Article 3 in the Treaty of January 24, 1902. In particular, it repeated the following clause which had been so objectionable to the Danish Government in 1902, and which had been deleted from the Treaty of January 24:

"Danish subjects residing in the territory may remain in such territory or may remove therefrom, retaining in either event, all their rights of property . . . and their right to carry on their industry, commerce and professions, being subject . . . to such laws as are applicable to other foreigners."

Article 6 of the new draft treaty also included the paragraph in Article 3 of the Treaty of January 24, to the effect that "the civil rights and political status of the native inhabitants of the territories hereby ceded to the United States shall be determined by the Congress of the United States." In 1902 the Danish Government had objected to this paragraph because it did not specifically provide that United States citizenship be conferred upon the Danish inhabitants of the islands, and because it failed to arrange free trade between the United States and the islands. This objection was again to be pressed by the Danish Government in 1916.

After Dr. Egan presented to the Danish Government the draft treaty enclosed in his instruction of March 14, the negotiations failed to proceed with the rapidity that was earnestly desired by the Department of State. Dr. Egan believed that the "sole cause of the delay" was the fact of strained relations between the United States and Germany, and as this tension slackened, the negotiations once more made headway. On April 27, 1916, Dr. Egan forwarded to the Department of State a *contre-projet* drawn by the Danish Foreign Office. In explaining the Danish attitude towards the cession of the islands, he indicated how sensitive was the feeling relative to conferring upon the inhabitants of the islands the benefits of American citizenship. While the Danish Government did not insist upon a paragraph that would specifically confer this privilege, yet they were earnestly in favor of such a provision. Moreover, they deeply desired some arrangement that would bring about a condition of free trade between the islands and the continent of the United States. Finally, a wish had been expressed for the holding of a plebiscite in the islands.[47]

In response to this despatch of Dr. Egan, Secretary Lansing wrote that it would be impossible to include in the treaty a

[47] Egan to the Secretary of State, April 27, 1916, *For. Rel.*, 1917, pp. 617-21.

"guarantee that the inhabitants of the islands shall immediately have all the rights of American citizens. Full citizenship has not been accorded as yet to Porto Ricans, though the present Congress has the matter under consideration. Danish West Indians, however, will be regarded as nationals of the United States and entitled to its full protection, and will receive every possible political liberty."

As to the question of exempting the inhabitants of the islands from customs duties, this right was entirely within the province of Congress. Mr. Lansing, however, had no doubt

"that every facility for the rejuvenation of the commerce of the islands will be accorded them, as has been the case with the present insular possessions of the United States."[48]

Along with this instruction of June 9, Secretary Lansing sent a new draft treaty which embodied some of the suggestions of the Danish *contre-projet*. But even this new draft was not acceptable to the Danish Government, especially in regard to the legal status of the inhabitants of the islands after the change of sovereignty, so on June 30, 1916, Dr. Egan cabled to the Department of State a new Danish *contre-projet*.[49]

[48] Lansing to Egan, June 9, 1916, *ibid.*, p. 622. With reference to the holding of a plebiscite in the islands, Secretary Lansing wrote that the American Government could not favor submitting "the question of transfer of the islands to a vote of the inhabitants."

[49] Egan to the Secretary of State, June 30, 1916, *For. Rel.*, 1917, pp. 625 ff.

Mr. Lansing turned over this new Danish *contre-projet* to Mr. Woolsey for examination, and the latter, on July 22, sent in his report. First of all he adverted to the desire of the Danish Government for a sweeping declaration from the United States respecting the rights of Denmark in Greenland. This declaration, Mr. Woolsey believed, was too broad in its phraseology. He also objected to the wording of Article VI in the new Danish *contre-projet:*

"The Danish Government retains the objectionable provision: 'If the present laws are altered, the said Danish inhabitants shall not thereby be placed in a less favorable position in respect to the above-mentioned rights and liberties than they now enjoy.' This provision refers to general rights of property, religion, liberty, etc. . . . On principle I do not think the objectionable provisions should be included, as it creates a preferred class of aliens in the islands."[50]

Secretary Lansing was in entire agreement with the views of Mr. Woolsey on these two points, and in his reply of July 24, he observed as follows:

"I am not at all disposed to accede to the wish of the Danish Government as to the declaration which they desire from the United States. I feel that we should secure the principle of equal opportunity for all nations in the matter of commerce and industry on the same theory that we have always insisted in regard to China. Possibly we could go so far as to agree to a declaration reading as follows: 'In view of the development of the political and economic interests of Denmark in Greenland, the Government of the United States of America will not object to the Dan-

[50] Woolsey to Lansing, July 22, 1916, *Woolsey MSS.*

ish Government's adoption of such measures of control and protection in Greenland as may be necessary to safeguard and extend these interests, provided that such measures and their administration are based upon the principle of equal opportunity in commerce and industry to all nations.'

"I think we should insist upon this point and I believe that an exchange of notes is the best way to admit the Danish rights in Greenland.

". . . In regard to the preferential treatment of Danish subjects in the Islands, I do not think we can go further than we did in our last proposal, which you quote on page two of your letter. I believe that our laws sufficiently guarantee personal rights and that the Danish Government should not seek to have treatment for their subjects other than that which is accorded to all aliens. To draw this distinction would invite, I fear, controversy, and it is even possible that the most favored nation clause might be invoked by other governments."[51]

On July 22, before receiving Mr. Woolsey's letter, Secretary Lansing, at Henderson Harbor, New York, had already written as follows to Mr. Polk, the Acting Secretary of State:

"In regard to the Danish treaty I think that the President should call Senator Stone to the White House and explain the terms of the treaty before it is signed. I have an indistinct remembrance of having said something to the Senator about the negotiations, but if I did it was very vague. Before the President speaks to the Senator, however, I would suggest that Woolsey look over the terms of the treaty to see if the Danish amendments are satisfactory. I would also consult with the President as to the advis-

[51] Lansing to Woolsey, July 24, 1916, *Confidential, Woolsey MSS.*

ability of speaking to Senator Lodge upon the question."[52]

In his reply of July 26, Mr. Polk informed Secretary Lansing that the

"President most anxious that treaty should be signed at once without waiting to examine original documents[52a] relating to concessions or attempting to modify provision in regard to special rights of Danish subjects. He thinks that you should meet their representative at once in New York and close matter, otherwise it may fail."[53]

In spite of the President's fear that unless the treaty were soon signed it might be defeated through some intrigue, Secretary Lansing still clung to the idea that the treaty should be amended so as to eliminate the objectionable clauses he had indicated. In a letter to Mr. Polk, July 28, he adverted to his previous stand as follows:

"I understood from what you telegraphed me that the President was disposed to waive the objection which we had raised as to the treaty, especially as you informed me that the treaty was being engrossed. As you perceive from my letter to Woolsey, two of the objections I consider of especial importance. One only affects the terms of the treaty and that is the preferential treatment of Danish subjects. The other objec-

[52] Lansing to Polk, July 22, 1916, *Strictly confidential, Woolsey MSS.*

[52a] The Department had, of course, examined official copies of these documents and was waiting for the receipt of the originals.

[53] Mr. Polk to Secretary Lansing, July 26, 1916, *Strictly confidential, Woolsey MSS.*

tion relates to the declaration affecting Greenland. My suggestion is that you submit these two objections to the President and if he does not think them sufficiently important to delay the signature of the treaty I am willing to waive them. I fear that the opposition in the Senate may . . . obtain a certain measure of support from their use. I would not myself waive these two objections unless it was entirely satisfactory to the President, nor would I urge changing the text unless he felt it advisable to do so." [54]

The President thought it best to waive these objections, so preparations were made for an immediate signature of the treaty. On August 4, 1916, at the Hotel Biltmore in New York City, the treaty of cession was finally signed by Secretary Lansing and Mr. Constantine Brun, the Danish Minister. As had already been provided in the draft treaties, the American Government paid for the islands the sum of twenty-five millions of dollars in gold coin of the United States. In return the United States was to receive, in addition to the three islands, the adjacent islands and rocks, and the rights of property in all public, government, or Crown lands, public buildings, etc. [55] This cession was limited, however, by a lengthy list of concessions which were recognized by the United States. The most important change in the final treaty, as com-

[54] Secretary Lansing to Mr. Polk, July 28, 1916, *Strictly confidential, Woolsey MSS*.

[55] In one of the memoranda submitted by Mr. Woolsey to Secretary Lansing it is estimated that the Government-owned property in the Danish West Indies amounted to some 805,-255 francs.

pared with the successive drafts, was with reference
to Article 6. We have already noticed how Secretary
Lansing had been very anxious to secure the acceptance of an article which strictly controlled the rights
of the islanders after the cession had been completed,
and to this end he had adopted the wording of Article
III of Secretary Hay's first draft treaty. The Danish
Government had objected to this wording in 1902,
and had compelled the Secretary of State to modify
it when it was incorporated as Article III in the Treaty
of January 24, 1902. And now in 1916, thanks to the
President's anxiety to get the treaty signed, the Danish Government had again won their point and under
the terms of Article VI the Danish nationals in the
islands were made "a preferred class of aliens."

In regard to a recognition of Danish rights in Greenland, Secretary Lansing, on August 4, handed to
Mr. Brun a declaration to the effect that "the Government of the United States of America will not
object to the Danish Government extending their political and economic interests to the whole of Greenland."[56] Once again the insistence of the President
upon an early signature of the treaty prevented Secretary Lansing from expressly stipulating for a recognition of the Open Door principle.

On August 8, 1916, President Wilson transmitted
the treaty to the Senate for its advice as to ratification,
with a request that the details be kept secret.[57] On

[56] *For. Rel.*, 1917, p. 700.
[57] *For. Rel.*, 1917, p. 646.

August 10, however, the Washington *Post* published
an outline of the treaty, with literal quotations from
the various articles. This Senatorial "leak" caused
quite a row in the Senate, and Senator Stone grew so
indignant that he "boiled over" in his wrathful denunciation of the unknown individual who gave this
secret information to the press. He was extremely
sorry

"to believe that any Senator has been guilty of such
infinite, unspeakable disregard of the decencies and
proprieties that should be observed in international intercourse as that here indicated. . . . It is hard for me
to believe that any Senate official could be guilty of
this offense."[58]

Senator Borah rose to inform the Senator from
Missouri that such "leaks" were quite common in the
history of American foreign relations, and only illustrated the futility of secret diplomacy. As for the
treaty itself it was merely a

"real-estate deal. We are going to pay a very large
sum of money. The people who will have to pay may
well claim the right to know all about it before the
obligation to pay is incurred. . . . There is nothing
connected with this treaty, so far as the Government of the United States is concerned, which the
people of the United States might not well know in
advance of their entering into an obligation to pay
$25,000,000 for the lands which we are to get. How
much better it would be that the facts be put out in

[58] *Congressional Record*, August 10, 1916, vol. 53, pt. 12,
pp. 12413-14.

full and with frankness rather than have them go out by connivance."[59]

Of course this "leak" was not discovered and the matter soon ceased to attract any attention. On August 18, Secretary Lansing appeared before the Senate Foreign Relations Committee for the purpose of explaining the necessity for the purchase of the Danish islands at this time. His principal defence of the treaty was that it was "desirable to get the islands out of the market to prevent foreign complications." This statement did not greatly impress some of the members of the committee, who inquired "if the Monroe Doctrine would not be a bar to any foreign nation obtaining the Danish West Indies by colonization or purchase?" Mr. Lansing seemed to acquiesce in this viewpoint, but insisted that it was "necessary for the United States to have the islands, and created the impression among some committeemen that he had undivulged reasons for thinking so."[60]

On September 5, Senator Stone, Chairman of the Senate Committee on Foreign Relations, submitted a

[59] *Congressional Record,* August 10, 1916, vol. 53, pt. 12, p. 12414. On August 5, 1916, Acting Secretary of State Frank L. Polk, wrote a memorandum relative to the publicity that had attended the negotiations of the treaty. Already the London papers had, on July 22, published a complete story of the outlines of the treaty about to be signed, and this had later been copied by the American press. After these publications appeared it was evident that the secret was out through no fault of the Department of State. See *For. Rel.,* 1917, p. 644.

[60] New York *Times,* August 19, 1916.

report recommending the ratification of the treaty
for the purchase of the Danish islands. On the following day the treaty was discussed in executive session, and on September 7, it was agreed to by a large
affirmative vote. The opposition was led by Progres-
sives like Clapp, Norris, and Kenyon, while many of
the old-line Republicans like Penrose supported the
administration.[61] Senator Lodge, who had long been
an advocate of the purchase, remained consistent and
voted in the affirmative. Indeed, from the moment
the treaty was signed, Senator Lodge worked in favor
of its ratification, and in a statement issued in the
press he stressed the importance of early favorable
action :

"In the interests of peace it is of great importance
that these islands should pass into the hands of the
United States. From a military point of view their
value can hardly be overestimated. The fine harbor
of St. Thomas fulfills all the required naval and military conditions. As had been pointed out by the late
Admiral Mahan, it is one of the great strategic points
in the West Indies."[62]

[61] *Ibid.,* September 7, 1916.

[62] New York *Times,* August 5, 1916. In a cablegram from
Secretary Lansing to Mr. Brun, it is stated that the treaty
was ratified in the Senate "by a majority of about six to
one." *For. Rel.,* 1917, p. 674. It is significant to note that
while Progressive leaders in the Senate were opposed to the
treaty, the great Progressive leader in the country at large,
ex-President Roosevelt, was decidedly in favor of the convention. In the Lansing manuscript *Diary* for August 18,
1916, there is the following entry: "Cal O'Laughlin in to say
that T. Roosevelt strong for Danish Treaty."

The report of the Senate Foreign Relations Committee on September 5, was largely based upon a lengthy memorandum of Mr. Woolsey, which was sent to Senator Stone by Secretary Lansing on August 22, 1916. Moreover, so carefully did Mr. Woolsey draft the terms of the treaty of August 4, that the Senate accepted it with but a single reservation. This reservation dealt with the Danish National Church in the islands, and it distinctly asserted that the advice and consent of the Senate should not be

"taken and construed by the High Contracting Parties as imposing any trust upon the United States with respect to any funds belonging to the Danish National Church in the Danish West Indian Islands, or in which the said Church may have an interest, nor as imposing upon the United States any duty or responsibility with respect to the management of the property belonging to said Church, beyond protecting said Church in the possession and use of church property as stated in said Convention, in the same manner and to the same extent only as other churches shall be protected in the possession and use of their several properties."[63]

If a review is made of press opinions of the treaty it will be discovered that a majority of the editors favored the purchase of the Danish islands. It will also be apparent that there was a great deal of public interest in this acquisition, for scarcely a week went by in 1916 without some notice of the importance of the islands to the United States. On February 21, 1916, the New York *Times,* discussed the possibility

[63] *For. Rel.,* 1916, pp. 699-700.

of the purchase of the islands as a means of thwarting German ambitions in the Caribbean, and there were many variations of this theme.[64] Another favorite argument in favor of the purchase was the value of the islands as affording naval bases which could protect the approaches to the Panama Canal. Thus, Rear-Admiral Caspar F. Goodrich, in a long article in the New York *Times* of July 25, treats in detail the defensive advantages that would accrue from the purchase of the islands, and comes to the following conclusion:

"The harbor of St. Thomas is by no means ideal, but it can be made to serve. . . . The need of such a base for operations against us or for our defense, should the ratifications of the present treaty with Denmark be exchanged, is manifest. Nowhere else can

[64] In this regard it should be noted that on August 16, Dr. Gottlieb von Jagow, the German Foreign Minister, made a statement in response to an inquiry by a representative of the *Overseas News Agency* with reference to rumors that in connection with the proposed transfer of the islands apprehension was felt in the United States because "a certain foreign power had adopted an underhanded, antagonistic attitude towards the change in ownership." Dr. Jagow stated that he only knew of the matter from what he had read in the newspapers, but that one thing was absolutely certain: "Germany is antagonistic to nobody's intention as to the distribution of sovereign rights in those parts of the world. The German policy was plainly stated by the Imperial Chancellor in his speech in the Reichstag on April 4, when he made known to every one that Germany harbors no plans of aggression or annexation toward Canada, Brazil, or any portion of America whatever." See New York *Times,* August 17, 1916.

its like be found. . . . Thus, it appears, north, east, south, and west, these islands are a most valuable *point d'appui* for any European Government wishing to quarrel with us. It is, therefore, in the highest degree essential that we spare no effort to prevent them falling into unfriendly hands."

When the signature of the treaty was announced in the first week of August, 1916, the New York *World* thought that the price seemed large, "but as an insurance against the menace of an inimical Power it is cheap enough." The New York Evening *Sun* was of the opinion that "if the Monroe Doctrine is to mean anything the United States must be the purchaser, and the present is the golden opportunity," while the New York *Tribune* was equally favorable: "We need the Danish islands. Their people would benefit economically from a transfer to our sovereignty. . . . It is a transaction through which all parties will reap an advantage." It was the belief of the Washington correspondent of the New York *Evening Post* that "the plain truth of the matter seems to be that the Administration is seeking the new base as a measure of naval preparedness, certainly not against Great Britain, which has so many strategic points in the Atlantic, but against Germany herself."[65]

On August 3, 1916, the New York *Nation* published an editorial which was frankly skeptical of the wisdom of the purchase, and two days later the New York *Times* ventured the opinion that $25,000,000 was "en-

[65] *Literary Digest,* August 5, 1916, pp. 290-91.

tirely too large a sum" to pay for the islands.[66]   *The Independent,* however, rejoiced "that the Administration has seized the opportunity to negotiate for the purchase of the Danish West Indies, for we have urged their annexation for fifty years."[67]

Important publicists like T. Lothrop Stoddard and Edwin E. Slosson quickly came to the support of the treaty.   Stoddard believed that the Danish West Indies were "the keys to the Caribbean," and therefore most essential to American hegemony in those waters.[68] Mr. Slosson had long been an advocate for the annexation of the islands, which advocacy had recently led him to make a special trip to the Caribbean for the purpose of personal observation.   He had returned more enthusiastic than ever.[69]

These favorable press comments which appeared not only in the newspapers and periodicals in the East but also in a majority of the journals throughout the country,[70] only confirmed the disposition of the Senate

[66] This unfavorable opinion on the part of the New York *Times* was quickly modified, and on August 19, we find an editorial in the *Times* to the following effect: "We do not want the islands to become the property of any other European Power. The price is high, and it might be trimmed a little.   But we must not let slip this opportunity to possess St. Thomas, St. John, and St. Croix."

[67] August 7, 1916, pp. 175-76.

[68] *Review of Reviews,* September, 1916, pp. 292-98.

[69] *The Independent,* September 4, 1916, pp. 333-335.

[70] There is an interesting analysis of public opinion in regard to the treaty in the *Literary Digest,* December 30, 1916, pp. 1697-98.   Also *Current Opinion,* September, 1916, pp. 151-52, in which it is stated that "hardly a paper of influence opposes the purchase."

to advise the ratification of the treaty. This action was formally taken on September 7, 1916, so thereafter the fate of the treaty was in the hands of the Danish Rigsdag.

In Denmark the course of the treaty was much like that of true love; certainly it was far from smooth. Some of this friction was due to Danish newspaper reporters who thought they had been tricked by Minister Egan, and lied to by two members of the Danish Cabinet, Erik de Scavenius and Edward Brandes. When Mr. Egan was asked whether he had ever spoken to Mr. Brandes on the subject of the sale of the islands, he could honestly answer NO, for he had conducted all the negotiations with Mr. Scavenius, the Danish Minister for Foreign Relations. When the inquiries were pushed further and Mr. Egan was asked whether he had discussed the question of the sale with Mr. Scavenius himself, his reply had always been merely an expression of hope that such a sale could really be effected. These evasions were not regarded by Mr. Egan as a lie, for in his opinion a lie was the "denying of the truth to those who have a moral right to know it. The press had no right whatever to know the truth, but even the direct diplomatic denial of a fact to persons who have no right to know it, is bound to be—uncomfortable." In this regard both Mr. Scavenius and Mr. Brandes were soon made decidedly uncomfortable by the Opposition press which looked upon their direct denials as downright lies, and failed to absolve them because of diplomatic necessity.[71]

On August 4, the Rigsdag went into "executive session" for the purpose of discussing the treaty for the sale of the islands. Mr. Scavenius made a strong speech in favor of ratification in which he attempted to show that the convention furthered all Danish interests, and provided a handsome equivalent for islands that were nothing but a source of expense.[72] It was soon apparent, however, that the Conservatives would oppose the treaty as warmly as they did in 1902. On August 10, the first reading of the bill providing for the sale of the islands was taken up in the Folkething, and during the discussion there was a great deal of excitement manifested, some of the women spectators shouting loudly, "We will not sell."

Edward Brandes, the Minister of Finance, aroused great interest by his assertion that the treaty would have to be approved because of pressure that was being exerted by the United States. Those who opposed the sale

"had an easy task because the Government was unable to unveil its chief arguments in favor of the sale. What should be done, for instance, if the United States took possession of the islands? Should Denmark declare war against the United States or appeal to Europe? The Government felt bound to submit to the desire of a great State."

[71] Maurice Francis Egan, *Ten Years Near the German Frontier*, pp. 268-72.
[72] New York *Times*, August 5, 1916.

Mr. J. C. Christensen, ex-Premier and leader of the Opposition, refused to believe that

"Denmark was forced to sell or that there was any international danger, as such belief would be an insult to the United States. The proposal to sell the islands was not only a surprise, but had come as a *coup de main,* and in the opinion of his party nothing should be decided during the war or until after the elections."[73]

With reference to this statement by Edward Brandes that the United States was exerting pressure upon Denmark to ratify the treaty, Dr. Egan has the following comment:

"Suddenly, a crashing blow struck us; Edward Brandes, in the midst of a hot debate, in which he and de Scavenius were fiercely attacked, announced that the United States was prepared to exert 'friendly pressure.' Brandes is too clever a man to be driven into such a statement through inadvertence; he must have had some object in making it! What the object was I did not know—nobody seemed to know. Even de Scavenius appeared to think he had gone too far, for whatever were the contents of Minister Brun's despatches, it was quite certain that neither he nor our Government would have allowed a threat made to Denmark involving the possession of her legitimately held territory to become public! Something had to be done to avoid the assumption that we were no more democratic than Germany. . . . 'We, the most democratic of nations, prepared to pay for certain

[73] New York *Times,* August 11, 1916. In this debate Mr. de Scavenius denied that the Government "was forced to sell," but he did indicate that "it would be a serious matter" if the sale were postponed.

Islands; but if it was not convenient for a friendly power to sell her territory, we would take it.' This was the inference drawn from Mr. Edward Brandes' words in Parliament. I could not contradict a member of the Government, and yet I was called on, especially by Danes who had lived in the United States, to explain what this 'pressure' meant."[74]

It required all of Dr. Egan's facility as a diplomat to counteract the effects of this impolitic but correct statement of Mr. Brandes,[75] and this was all the more so when German newspapers like the *Neueste Nachrichten* of Munich declared that Denmark would be forced to yield to American compulsion: President Wilson had "put the pistol on the chest of little Denmark."[76]

[74] M. F. Egan, *Ten Years Near the German Frontier*, pp. 275 ff.

[75] It would appear that Dr. Egan was not aware of the pressure that Secretary Lansing had brought to bear upon the Danish Government. Neither in the published materials relating to the treaty, nor in the unpublished letters, despatches and instructions which passed between Dr. Egan and Secretary Lansing, is there any mention of friendly pressure being exerted.

[76] New York *Times*, August 15, 1916. The statement of Mr. Brandes was made in the Danish Folkething, on August 10, 1916, and is substantially as follows: "When the wish again met us in 1915, the World War had already been in progress a year, and was passing into the next, and this time it was presented on a different basis by America. It was not presented on the same grounds as in the two previous negotiations for the transfer of the islands. It was presented to us in such a manner as to indicate a desire, as I would call it to round out American territory; a desire to bind American soil to the United States. It was not what one could call

the geopolitical (geopolitiske) view that was the deciding factor as had been in the earlier negotiations. I might mention in this connection that there is something called the 'Monroe Doctrine!' which was pronounced many years ago. Its underlying principle is that American soil cannot pass into the hands of a European power upon being released from the jurisdiction of another sovereignty.

"This, therefore, is the government's impression and background for reopening the negotiations. We felt that for us it was a compelling reason to accede to the desire for negotiation, which we had refused two years previous—in such a manner as a little and weak state must accede to the wishes of a large and powerful state when living in a world where justice is abolished or enforced by might, yes, where might not so seldom forms and molds justice. We believed that we acted in the nation's best interests, that we acted to protect the country's independence by entering upon these negotiations and endeavoring to conduct them to a most favorable conclusion. Naturally, we can also express the words which now are found in all the newspapers, at all meetings, and which are set forth with so much suffering, with so much pathos, and naturally with so much agitation—we can express the words with complete truthfulness, that it is bitter for a small country to reduce its territory, to transfer its possessions. We can deplore and express sorrow over the fact that the flag must be struck. But when a hurricane rages, which causes the mountains to sway, is it so strange to one who will consider the matter that the storm will blow away a flag from a West Indian hut?—

"While we opened the negotiations with—according to our belief, which we intend to be able to prove (som vi mener at kunne dokumentere)—pressure from the outside, a friendly pressure from the United States, there was also a pressure from within, which became the prevailing factor (som gjorde sig gaeldende), the purely historical pressure (historisk tryk), arising from the fact that on two previous occasions Denmark had—if one shall use the word—sold the islands. On the one occasion it was America that rejected the sale, while we agreed to it; and the second time, while all parties

On August 14, the Folkething voted in favor of selling the Danish islands to the United States after a
favorable plebiscite had been held. The vote was by
no means unanimous in favor of the sale, there being
sixty-two yeas, and forty-four nays.[77]   In the Landsthing on August 25, the following order of the day
was approved by a vote of forty-two yeas to eight
nays:

"If the sale of the islands cannot be postponed until
after the war, it is moved that the question be decided
by a Parliament elected in accordance with the new
Constitution."[78]

The question of the sale of the islands was again
brought up in the Folkething on September 26, when
a bill providing for the transfer was once more approved. This bill was then referred to a joint committee of fifteen members from each House of the
Rigsdag.[79]   Three days later, Mr. de Scavenius cabled
to Washington as follows:

---

here in the Rigsdag were agreed on the transfer, it stranded
in the exalted 'Landsting' by accident (tilfaeldighed).   A
single man's vote—a very old man, who perhaps did not
have a very clear understanding of what he was voting for
—decided in reality the fate of the motion."   See *Rigsdagstidende Forhandlinger paa Folketinget 68 de ordentlige Samling* 1915-1916. III, No. 273-351, Sp. 4349-5608.

[77] New York *Times,* August 15, 1916.

[78] Egan to the Secretary of State, August 25, 1916, *For.
Rel.,* 1917, pp. 667-68.

[79] New York *Times,* September 27, 1916.

"The crisis has now been solved through an understanding among the three political parties that one representative of each of the three parties be included in the Cabinet as Ministers without portfolios and further that the proposal of the Government as to the proceedings of the Committee in the West Indian question with a referendum to follow has been accepted. The time limits set for the work of the possible committee is six weeks and the referendum shall take place within fourteen days after the committee has submitted its resolution. However in the present circumstances I do not consider it out of the question that the time limit for the work of the committee be shortened."[80]

On September 30, both Houses of the Rigsdag passed a bill providing for a plebiscite on the question of the sale of the Danish West Indies to the United States. This plebiscite was to include the Faroe Islands, but not Iceland nor Greenland.[81] A week later the joint committee of the Rigsdag on the question of the sale of the islands reached "a series of conclusions relative to its course of procedure," one of which was to call for the entire diplomatic correspondence relative to the treaty negotiations.[82]

On October 19, Mr. Brun, the Danish Minister at Washington, wrote to the Secretary of State to inform him that the task of the joint committee was so onerous that it had been found necessary to extend the

[80] Egan to the Secretary of State, September 29, 1916, *For. Rel.*, 1917, pp. 680-81.

[81] New York *Times*, October 1, 1916.

[82] Egan to the Secretary of State, October 5, 1916, *For. Rel.*, 1917, p. 682.

period required for its labors until November 25. In view of this fact it would not be possible to hold the proposed plebiscite until either December 13th or 14th.[83]

The joint committee finished its work on November 25, and on that day distributed copies of its decision. This decision was divided into three parts, section one being drawn up by twenty-two of the thirty members of the committee, section two represented the views of seven members, while section three contained the opinion of only one member. Section one, the work of the majority of the joint committee, strongly urged the sale of the islands; section two argued against the sale, while section three, containing the opinion of only one Conservative, was favorable to the sale. Thus, twenty-three of the thirty members of the joint committee went on record as supporting the Ministry in negotiating the treaty of cession.[84]

The next step was to hold the plebiscite in Denmark relative to the transfer of the islands, and this was set for December 14. In this national referendum, women were to be allowed to vote, so it was extremely

[83] Brun to the Secretary of State, October 19, 1916, *For. Rel.*, 1917, p. 685. In *Politiken* for November 11, 1916, there is printed an interesting review of the opinions of the delegates from the Danish West Indies who appeared before the joint committee of the Rigsdag. All these delegates favored the sale of the islands to the United States. See also *Politiken* for November 15, 1916.

[84] Egan to the Secretary of State, November 25, 1916, *For. Rel.*, 1917, p. 686.

necessary to conciliate the leaders of the Women's Party. The way that this was accomplished is told by Dr. Egan in his own inimitable way:

"On all sides I was told that the women's votes would be against the sale. It was not unreasonable to believe that ladies, just emancipated, would vote against their late lord and masters, at least for the first time. Besides, as Mrs. Chapman Catt had made very clear during her fateful visit to Denmark, the liveliest, the most reasonable, the most intellectual women in the world were deprived by the unjust laws of the country that wanted the Islands of the right to vote. . . . We *must* have the women's vote. Madame Gad helped to save the day.

" 'You will, in your annual *conférence,*' she said to me, 'explain the position of the American women, and your words will be reprinted, not only all over Denmark, but throughout Sweden and Norway. The editor of *Politiken* will give you his famous hall '*Politiken Hus,*' and your words will make good feeling.'

" 'I can honestly say,' I answered, 'that I want the women to vote. In fact, in my country, they have only to desire the suffrage badly enough to have it! It is the fault of their own sex, not ours, if they do not get it.'

"It was agreed that I should speak on the 'American Woman and Her Aspirations,' at *Politiken Hus,* on the evening of December 5th. . . . The hall was crowded. Sir Ralph Paget, who seldom went out, had come, and, at some distance—Sir Ralph was of all men the most anti-Prussian—were the Prince and Princess Wittgenstein. 'All Copenhagen,' Madame Gad said, which was equivalent to 'Tout Paris.' I did my best.

"At the reception afterwards at Admiral Urban Gad's, the ladies—some of them of great influence in politics—told me that I had said the right things. I had the next day a *bonne presse.* The provincial papers all over Scandinavia reprinted the most important parts of the discourse with approval, and letters of commendations from all parts of Denmark—from ladies—came pouring in.

"Time dragged; but the news from the provinces was consoling. The Foreign Office seemed still to be discouraged, and I am sure that Edward Brandes again wished that the Danish Antilles had suffered extinction."[85]

Although Dr. Egan had refused to adopt a gloomy attitude relative to the outcome of the plebiscite on December 14, yet he was agreeably surprised at the overwhelming victory of the administration. When the votes were counted it was discovered that there were some 283,694 yeas, and 157,596 nays.[86]

But there were still slight difficulties in the way of effecting the transfer of the islands. On December 16, Dr. Egan paid a visit to the Foreign Office, and found Mr. de Scavenius looking very worried. In the midst

"of alarms he had always retained a certain calm, which gave everybody confidence. When the petrels flew about his head and the storms dashed, he was astonishingly courageous. Today, he sighed. In spite of the plebiscite, he seemed to think that we were beaten. I was astonished. I had always thought that we had one quality, at least, in common—we liked embarrassing situations. I soon discovered the reason for this apparent loss of nerve.

[85] M. F. Egan, *Ten Years Near the German Frontier*, pp. 283-86.

[86] As early as 9 A. M. on December 15, Dr. Egan cabled to the Secretary of State that the vote was "approximately 284,000 for sale and 158,000 against." *For. Rel.*, 1917, p. 687.

" 'Would our Government agree to take less than the three Islands?'

"It was plain that the Opposition, not always fair, was tiring him and Brandes out: I could understand their position, and sympathize with their discouragement, but not feel it.

" 'To admit a new proposition on our part would be to interfere in the interior politics of Denmark,' I said. 'The plebiscite was arranged on the question of the treaty; it meant the cession of all the Danish Islands or nothing.' . . . De Scavenius approved of what I said. I believed that we would win, in spite of dire prophecies."[87]

On December 20, 1916, the vote was taken in the Folkething on the question of the transfer of the islands through the ratification of the treaty, and the vote stood, 90 yeas, and 16 nays. On the following day the Landsthing expressed approval of the treaty by a vote of 40 yeas and 19 nays. The King now hastened to ratify the treaty on December 22; President Wilson took similar action on January 16, 1917, and when on the following day ratifications were exchanged, a long and tedious chapter that had been started by Seward in January, 1865, was finally brought to a successful close.[88]

[87] M. F. Egan, *op. cit.,* pp. 287-88. See also New York *Times,* December 21, 22, 23, 1916.

[88] With reference to Secretary Lansing's personal opinion as to the value of the Danish islands see *For. Rel.,* 1917, pp. 692-94. Also, *Hearing before the Committee on Foreign Relations,* February 12, 1917, *Statement of Robert Lansing,* 64 Cong., 2 sess., pp. 3 ff. In addition to the articles we have already cited relative to the Danish West Indies and their acquisition by the United States, see Professor Brander

Matthews, in New York *Times,* July 30, 1916; Montgomery Schuyler, New York *Times,* August 1, 1916; Professor Roland G. Usher, *New Republic,* September 2, 1916, pp. 111-112; Eldred E. Jacobsen, *Review of Reviews,* March, 1917, pp. 275-80; M. R. Ryan, *The Catholic World,* May, 1917, pp. 219-23; and Edwin E. Slosson, *World Outlook,* June, 1917, pp. 15-17.

APPENDIX A

CONVENTION BETWEEN HIS MAJESTY THE KING OF DENMARK,

AND

THE UNITED STATES OF AMERICA,

Concerning the Cession of the Islands of St. Thomas and St. John in West Indies.

His Majesty the King of Denmark and the United states of America being desirous of confirming the good understanding which exists between them, have for that purpose appointed as Plenipotentiaries, his Majesty the King of Denmark, Count Christian Emil Juel Vind-Frijs, President of the Council of the Ministers and Minister for Foreign Affairs, Grandcross of the Order of Danebrog, and decorated with the Cross of honor of the same Order, and the President of the United States, George H. Yeaman, accredited as their Minister Resident to his said Majesty, and the said Plenipotentiaries having exchanged their full powers, which were found to be in due form, have agreed upon and signed the following articles:

Article I

His Majesty the King of Denmark agrees to cede to the United States by this Convention immediately upon the exchange of the ratifications thereof, the islands of St. Thomas and St. John, in the West Indies, with the adjacent islands and rocks, situated north of the 18th degree of north latitude.

His Majesty the King of Denmark will, however, not exercise any constraint over the people, and will therefore, as soon as practicable, give them an opportunity of freely expressing their wishes in regard to this cession.

ARTICLE II

In the cession of territory and dominion made by the preceding article are included the right of property of the crown of Denmark in all public lots and squares, vacant lands, and all public buildings, fortifications, barracks, and other edifices which are not private individual property. It is, however, understood that the Lutheran Congregations shall remain in possession of the churches which are now used by them, and that sums due the Danish treasury by individuals are reserved and do not pass by this cession.

Any government archives, papers and documents relative to the territory and dominion aforesaid, which may be now existing there, shall be left in possession of the agent of the United States appointed in accordance with Article IV; but an authenticated copy of such of them as may be required will be at all times given by the United States to the Danish Government, or to such Danish officers or subjects as may apply to them.

ARTICLE III

The inhabitants of the said islands shall be protected in their liberty, their religion, their property, and private rights, and they shall be free to remain where they now reside, or to remove at any time, retaining the property which they possess in the said islands, or disposing thereof and removing the proceeds wherever they please, without their being subjected on this account to any contribution, tax, or charge whatever. Those who shall prefer to remain in the said islands, may either retain the title and the rights of their natural allegiance, or acquire those of citizens of the United States. But they shall make their election within two years from the date of the exchange of ratifications of this convention; and those who shall remain in the said islands after the expiration of that term, without having declared their intention to retain their natural allegiance, shall be considered to have elected to become citizens of the United States.

ARTICLE IV

Immediately after the payment by the United States of the sum of money stipulated for in the fifth article of this Convention, His Majesty the King of Denmark will appoint an agent or agents for the purpose of formally delivering to a similar agent or agents, appointed on behalf of the United States, the territory, islands, property, and appurtenances which are ceded as above, including any fortifications or military posts which may be in the ceded territory, and for doing any other act which may be necessary in regard thereto. But the cession with the right of immediate possession is nevertheless to be deemed complete and absolute on the exchange of ratifications, without waiting for such formal delivery. Any Danish troops, which may be in the territory or aforesaid islands, shall be withdrawn as soon as may be reasonably and conveniently practicable.

ARTICLE V

In consideration of the cession aforesaid, the United States agree to pay, at the treasury in Washington, within three months after the exchange of the ratifications of this convention, to the diplomatic representative or other agent of His Majesty the King of Denmark, duly authorized to receive the same, seven millions five hundred thousand dollars, in gold.

The cession conveys to the United States the said islands and appurtenances in full and entire sovereignty, with all the dominion, rights and powers which Denmark now possesses and can exercise in them, free and unincumbered by any grants, conditions, priviliges or franchises in any way affecting or limiting the exercise of such sovereignty.

ARTICLE VI

When this convention shall have been duly ratified by His Majesty the King of Denmark, by and with the consent of the Rigsdag on the one part, and on the other by the President of the United States, by and with the advice and consent of the Senate, the ratifications shall be exchanged at Washington, within four months from the date hereof, or sooner if possible.

In faith whereof the respective Plenipotentiaries have signed this convention and thereto affixed the seals of their arms.

Done at Copenhagen, the 24th of October, in the year of our Lord one thousand eight hundred and sixty-seven.

GEO. H. YEAMAN, [L. S.]

C. E. JUEL-VIND-FRIJS, [L. S.]

APPENDIX B

CONVENTION BETWEEN THE UNITED STATES AND DENMARK FOR THE CESSION OF THE DANISH WEST INDIES

SIGNED AT WASHINGTON, JANUARY 24, 1902. RATIFICATION ADVISED BY THE SENATE FEBRUARY 17, 1902. RATIFIED BY THE PRESIDENT, MARCH 1, 1902.

The United States of America and His Majesty the King of Denmark being desirous of confirming the good understanding which exists between them, have to that end appointed as Plenipotentiaries,

The President of the United States:

John Hay, Secretary of State of the United States; and His Majesty the King of Denmark:

Mr. Constantin Brun, Commander of Dannebrog and decorated with the Cross of Honor of the same Order, His Majesty's Chamberlain and Envoy Extraordinary and Minister Plenipotentiary at Washington; who, having mutually exhibited their full powers, which were found to be in due form, have agreed upon the following articles:

ARTICLE I

His Majesty the King of Denmark agrees to cede to the United States immediately upon the exchange of the ratifications of this convention the Islands of Saint Thomas, Saint John and Sainte Croix, in the West Indies, with the adjacent Islands and rocks, comprising in said cession all title and claims of title to the territories in and about said islands over which the Crown of Denmark now exercises, asserts or claims jurisdiction.

This cession conveys to the United States the said Islands and appurtenances in full sovereignty, entire and unincumbered except as stipulated in the present Convention, with all the dominion, rights and powers which Denmark now possesses, exercises, asserts and claims therein; it being however understood and agreed that the consummation of said cession does not import the transference to the United States of the financial claims now held by Denmark against the Colonial treasuries of the Islands, it being agreed that these claims are altogether extinguished in consequence of the cession. And it is moreover understood and agreed, that the United States will assume and continue to discharge from the time of the cession the obligations heretofore incumbent upon the Danish Government towards the St. Thomas Floating Dock Company and the West India and Panama Telegraph Company.

No responsibility of any kind whatever is incumbent on the Danish Government, nor on the United States Government, as to the guaranty which, conformably to the ordinance of June 16, 1876, the Colonial treasury of Sainte Croix has assumed with regard to the payment of an interest of five per cent per annum to the holders of shares of the "Sainte Croix Fallessukkerkogerier" Company limited.

ARTICLE II

The aforesaid title conveys to the United States the absolute fee and ownership of all public, Government or Crown lands, public buildings, ports, harbors, fortifications, barracks, and all other public property of every kind and description belonging to the Government of Denmark, together with every right and appurtenance thereunto appertaining: it being however agreed that the arms and military stores existing in the islands at the time of the cession and belonging to the Government of Denmark shall remain the property of that Government and shall, as soon as circumstances will permit, be removed by it, unless they, or parts thereof, may before have been bought by the Government of the United States upon a special agreement made with the Government of Denmark; it being however understood that flags and colors, uniforms and such arms or military objects as are marked as being the property of the Danish Government shall not be included in such purchase.

It is moreover agreed and understood: first, that the congregations belonging to the Danish National Church shall remain in possession of the churches which are now used by them, together with the parsonages appertaining thereunto, and secondly, that sums due to the Danish treasury by individuals are reserved and do not pass by this cession; and where the Danish Government shall at the time of the cession hold property taken over by the Danish Treasury for sums due by individuals, such property shall not pass by this cession, but the Danish Government shall sell or dispose of such property and remove its proceeds within two years from the date of the exchange of ratifications of this convention, the United States Government being entitled to sell by public auction, to the credit of the Danish Government, what may not have been sold before expiration of the said term of two years.

The Danish Government retains the claims held by the same as a creditor against the "Ste. Croix Fallessukkerkogerier" Company limited; should that Government acquire the ownership of property belonging to this Company in the island of Ste. Croix, the above provision regarding a sale within two years shall apply to such property; the two years however to begin from the date of the acquirement of ownership of said property which shall be within three years from the exchange of the ratifications of the present treaty.

Any Government archives, papers and documents relative to the islands ceded and the dominion of the same, which may now be existing there, shall pass by this cession, but an authenticated copy of such documents or papers as may be required will be at all times given by the United States to the Danish Government or to such properly authorized Danish officers or subjects as may apply for them.

ARTICLE III

Danish subjects residing in said islands may remain therein or may remove therefrom at will, retaining in either event all their rights of property, including the right to sell or dispose of such property or its proceeds; and in case they remain in the islands, they shall continue until otherwise provided, to enjoy all the private, municipal and religious rights and liberties secured to them by the laws now in force. If the present laws are altered, the said inhabitants shall not thereby be placed in a less favorable position in respect to the above mentioned rights and liberties than they now enjoy. Those who remain in the islands may preserve their allegiance to the Crown of Denmark by making, before a court of record, within two years from the date of the exchange of ratifications of this convention, a declaration of their decision to preserve such allegiance, in default of which declaration they shall be held to have renounced it and to have accepted allegiance to the United States; but such election of Danish allegiance shall not, after the lapse of the said term of two years, be a bar to their renunciation of their preserved Danish allegiance and their election of allegiance to the United States and admission to the nationality thereof on the same terms as may be provided according to the laws of the United States, for other inhabitants of the islands.

The civil rights and the political status of the inhabitants of the islands shall be determined by the Congress, subject to the stipulations contained in the present convention.

Danish subjects not residing in the islands but owning property therein at the time of the cession shall
retain their rights of property, including the right to
sell or dispose of such property, being placed in this
regard on the same basis as the Danish subjects residing in the islands and remaining therein or removing
therefrom to whom the first paragraph of this article
relates.

Article IV

Formal delivery of the territory and property ceded
as aforesaid shall be made immediately after the payment by the United States of the sum of money stipulated in the fifth article hereof; but the cession with
the right of immediate possession is nevertheless to
be deemed complete on the exchange of the ratifications of this convention, and any Danish troops which
may be in the islands aforesaid shall be withdrawn as
soon thereafter as may be practicable, but not later
than six months after the said exchange; it being
however understood that if those persons, after having terminated their Danish service, do not wish to
leave the islands, they shall be allowed to remain there
as civilians.

The Colonial Treasury shall continue to pay the
yearly allowances now given to heretofore retired
functionaries appointed in the Islands but holding no
Royal Commissions, unless those allowances may have
until now been paid in Denmark.

Article V

In full consideration of the cession of said islands
in full sovereignty, entire and unincumbered except
as stipulated in the present Convention, the United
States agrees to pay, within ninety days from the date
of the exchange of ratifications of this convention, in
the City of Washington to the diplomatic representative or other agent of His Majesty the King of Den-

mark, duly authorized to receive the money, the sum of five million dollars in gold coin of the United States.

ARTICLE VI

In case of differences of opinion arising between the High Contracting Parties in regard to the interpretation or application of this convention, such differences, if they cannot be regulated through diplomatic negotiations, shall be submitted for arbitration to the permanent court of arbitration at The Hague.

ARTICLE VII

The ratifications of this Convention shall be exchanged at Washington, within six months from the date hereof, after it shall have been ratified by both the High Contracting Parties according to their respective procedure.

In faith whereof the respective plenipotentiaries have signed and sealed this convention, in the English and Danish languages.

Done at Washington the 24th day of January in the Year of our Lord one thousand nine hundred and two.

JOHN HAY (Seal)
C. BRUN   (Seal)

APPENDIX C

CONVENTION BETWEEN THE UNITED STATES AND DENMARK FOR THE CESSION OF THE DANISH WEST INDIES

Signed at New York, August 4, 1916; Ratification Advised by the Senate, September 7, 1916; Ratified by the President, January 16, 1917; Ratified by Denmark, December 22, 1916; Ratifications Exchanged at Washington January 17, 1917; Proclaimed, January 25, 1917.

Treaty Series No. 629

BY THE PRESIDENT OF THE UNITED STATES OF AMERICA

A PROCLAMATION

Whereas a Convention between the United States of America and Denmark providing for the cession to the United States of all territory asserted or claimed by Denmark in the West Indies, including the islands of St. Thomas, St. John and St. Croix, together with the adjacent islands and rocks, was concluded and signed by their respective Plenipotentiaries at the City of New York on the fourth day of August, one thousand nine hundred and sixteen, the original of which Convention, being in the English and Danish languages, is word for word as follows:

The United States of America and His Majesty the King of Denmark being desirous of confirming the good understanding which exists between them, have to that end appointed as Plenipotentiaries,

The President of the United States:

Mr. Robert Lansing, Secretary of State of the United States, and His Majesty the King of Denmark:

Mr. Constantin Brun, His Majesty's Envoy extraordinary and Minister plenipotentiary at Washington, who, having mutually exhibited their full powers which were found to be in due form, have agreed upon the following articles:

ARTICLE I

His Majesty the King of Denmark by this convention cedes to the United States all territory, dominion and sovereignty, possessed, asserted or claimed by Denmark in the West Indies including the Islands of Saint Thomas, Saint John and Saint Croix together with the adjacent islands and rocks.

This cession includes the right of property in all public, government, or crown lands, public buildings, wharves, ports, harbors, fortifications, barracks, public funds, rights, franchises, and privileges, and all other public property of every kind or description now belonging to Denmark together with all appurtenances thereto.

In this cession shall also be included any government archives, records, papers or documents which relate to the cession or the rights and property of the inhabitants of the Islands ceded, and which may now be existing either in the Islands ceded or in Denmark. Such archives and records shall be carefully preserved, and authenticated copies thereof, as may be required shall be at all times given to the United States Government or the Danish Government, as the case may be, or to such properly authorized persons as may apply for them.

ARTICLE 2

Denmark guarantees that the cession made by the preceding article is free and unencumbered by any reservations, privileges, franchises, grants, or possessions, held by any governments, corporations, syndicates, or individuals, except as herein mentioned. But it is understood that this cession does not in any respect impair private rights which by law belong to the peaceful possession of property of all kinds by private individuals of whatsoever nationality, by municipalities, public or private establishments, ecclesiastical or civic bodies, or any other associations having legal capacity to acquire and possess property in the Islands ceded.

The congregations belonging to the Danish National Church shall retain the undisturbed use of the churches which are now used by them, together with the parsonages appertaining thereunto and other appurtenances, including the funds allotted to the churches.

ARTICLE 3

It is especially agreed, however, that:

1) The arms and military stores existing in the Islands at the time of the cession and belonging to the Danish Government shall remain the property of that Government and shall, as soon as circumstances will permit, be removed by it, unless they, or parts thereof, may have been bought by the Government of the United States; it being however understood that flags and colors, uniforms and such arms or military articles as are marked as being the property of the Danish Government shall not be included in such purchase.

2) The movables, especially silver plate and pictures which may be found in the government buildings in the islands ceded and belonging to the Danish Government shall remain the property of that Government and shall, as soon as circumstances will permit, be removed by it.

3) The pecuniary claims now held by Denmark against the colonial treasuries of the islands ceded are altogether extinguished in consequence of this cession and the United States assumes no responsibility what-

soever for or in connection with these claims. Excepted
is however the amount due to the Danish Treasury in
account current with the West-Indian colonial treasuries pursuant to the making up of accounts in consequence of the cession of the islands; should on the
other hand this final accounting show a balance in
favour of the West-Indian colonial treasuries, the
Danish Treasury shall pay that amount to the colonial
treasuries.

4) The United States will maintain the following
grants, concessions and licenses, given by the Danish
Government, in accordance with the terms on which
they are given:

a. The concession granted to "Det vestindiske Kompagni" (The West-Indian Company) Ltd. by the communications from the Ministry of Finance of January
18th 1913 and of April 16th 1913 relative to a license
to embank, drain, deepen and utilize certain areas in
St. Thomas Harbor and preferential rights as to commercial, industrial or shipping establishments in the
said Harbor.

b. Agreement of August 10th and 14th, 1914 between the municipality of St. Thomas and St. John
and "Det vestindiske Kompagni" Ltd. relative to the
supply of the city of Charlotte Amalie with electric
lighting.

c. Concession of March 12th 1897 to "The Floating Dock Company of St. Thomas Ltd.", subsequently
transferred to "The St. Thomas Engineering and Coaling Company Ltd." relative to a floating dock in St.
Thomas Harbor, in which concession the maintenance,
extension, and alteration of the then existing repairing
slip are reserved.

d. Royal Decree Nr. 79 of November 30th 1914
relative to the subsidies from the colonial treasuries of
St. Thomas and Sainte Croix to "The West India and
Panama Telegraph Company Ltd."

e. Concession of November 3rd, 1906, to K. B.
Hey to establish and operate a telephone system on St.

Thomas island, which concession has subsequently been transferred to the "St. Thomas Telefonselskab" Ltd.

f. Concession of February 28th 1913 to the municipality of Sainte Croix to establish and operate a telephone system in Sainte Croix.

g. Concession of July 16th 1915 to Ejnar Svendsen, an Engineer, for the construction and operation of an electric light plant in the city of Christiansted, Sainte Croix.

h. Concession of June 20th 1904 for the establishment of a Danish West-Indian bank of issue. This bank has for a period of 30 years acquired the monopoly to issue bank-notes in the Danish West-India islands against the payment to the Danish Treasury of a tax amounting to ten percent of its annual profits.

i. Guarantee according to the Danish supplementary Budget Law for the financial year 1908-1909 relative to the St. Thomas Harbor's four percent loan of 1910.

5) Whatever sum shall be due to the Danish Treasury by private individuals on the date of the exchange of ratifications are reserved and do not pass by this cession; and where the Danish Government at that date holds property taken over by the Danish Treasury for sums due by private individuals, such property shall not pass by this cession, but the Danish Government shall sell or dispose of such property and remove its proceeds within two years from the date of the exchange of ratifications of this convention; the United States Government being entitled to sell by public auction, to the credit of the Danish Government, any portion of such property remaining unsold at the expiration of the said term of two years.

6) The Colonial Treasuries shall continue to pay the yearly allowances now given to heretofore retired functionaries appointed in the islands but holding no Royal Commissions, unless such allowances may have until now been paid in Denmark.

ARTICLE 4

The Danish Government shall appoint with convenient despatch an agent or agents for the purpose of formally delivering to a similar agent or agents appointed on behalf of the United States, the territory, dominion, property, and appurtenances which are ceded hereby, and for doing any other act which may be necessary in regard thereto. Formal delivery of the territory and property ceded shall be made immediately after the payment by the United States of the sum of money stipulated in this convention; but the cession with the right of immediate possession is nevertheless to be deemed complete on the exchange of ratifications of this convention without such formal delivery. Any Danish military or naval forces which may be in the islands ceded shall be withdrawn as soon as may be practicable after the formal delivery, it being however understood that if the persons constituting these forces, after having terminated their Danish service, do not wish to leave the Islands, they shall be allowed to remain there as civilians.

ARTICLE 5

In full consideration of the cession made by this convention, the United States agrees to pay, within ninety days from the date of the exchange of the ratifications of this convention, in the City of Washington to the diplomatic representative or other agent of His Majesty the King of Denmark duly authorized to receive the money, the sum of twenty-five million dollars in gold coin of the United States.

ARTICLE 6

Danish citizens residing in said islands may remain therein or may remove therefrom at will, retaining in either event all their rights of property, including the right to sell or dispose of such property or its proceeds; in case they remain in the Islands, they shall continue until otherwise provided, to enjoy all the private, municipal and religious rights and liberties secured to them by the laws now in force. If the present laws are altered, the said inhabitants shall not thereby be placed in a less favorable position in respect to the above mentioned rights and liberties than they now enjoy. Those who remain in the islands may preserve their citizenship in Denmark by making before a court of record, within one year from the date of the exchange of ratifications of this convention, a declaration of their decision to preserve such citizenship; in default of which declaration they shall be held to have renounced it, and to have accepted citizenship in the United States; for children under eighteen years the said declaration may be made by their parents or guardians. Such election of Danish citizenship shall however not, after the lapse of the said term of one year be a bar to their renunciation of their preserved Danish citizenship and their election of citizenship in the United States and admission to the nationality thereof on the same terms as may be provided according to the laws of the United States, for other inhabitants of the islands.

The civil rights and the political status of the inhabitants of the islands shall be determined by the Congress, subject to the stipulations contained in the present convention.

Danish citizens not residing in the islands but owning property therein at the time of the ceession, shall retain their rights of property including the right to sell or dispose of such property, being placed in this regard on the same basis as the Danish citizens residing in the islands and remaining therein or removing therefrom, to whom the first paragraph of this article relates.

ARTICLE 7

Danish subjects residing in the Islands shall be subject in matters civil as well as criminal to the juris-

diction of the courts of the Islands, pursuant to the
ordinary laws governing the same, and they shall have
the right to appear before such courts, and to pursue
the same course therein as citizens of the country to
which the courts belong.

ARTICLE 8

Judicial proceedings pending at the time of the
formal delivery in the islands ceded shall be determined
according to the following rules:

(1) Judgments rendered either in civil suits between
private individuals, or in criminal matters, before the
date mentioned, and with respect to which there is no
recourse or right to review under Danish law, shall be
deemed to be final, and shall be executed in due form
and without any renewed trial whatsoever, by the competent authority in the territories within which such
judgments are to be carried out.

If in a criminal case a mode of punishment has been
applied which, according to new rules, is no longer
applicable on the islands ceded after delivery, the
nearest corresponding punishment in the new rules
shall be applied.

(2) Civil suits or criminal actions pending before
the first courts, in which the pleadings have not been
closed at the same time, shall be confirmed before the
tribunals established in the ceded islands after the
delivery, in accordance with the law which shall thereafter be in force.

(3) Civil suits and criminal actions pending at the
said time before the Superior Court or the Supreme
Court in Denmark shall continue to be prosecuted
before the Danish courts until final judgment according
to the law hitherto in force. The judgment shall be
executed in due form by the competent authority in the
territories within which such judgment should be
carried out.

Article 9

The rights of property secured by copyrights and patents acquired by Danish subjects in the Islands ceded at the time of exchange of the ratifications of this treaty, shall continue to be respected.

Article 10

Treaties, conventions and all other international agreements of any nature existing between Denmark and the United States shall eo ipso extend, in default of a provision to the contrary, also to the ceded islands.

Article 11

In case of differences of opinion arising between the High Contracting Parties in regard to the interpretation or application of this convention, such differences, if they cannot be regulated through diplomatic negotiations, shall be submitted for arbitration to the permanent Court of Arbitration at the Hague.

Article 12

The ratifications of this convention shall be exchanged at Washington as soon as possible after ratification by both of the High Contracting Parties according to their respective procedure.

In faith whereof the respective plenipotentiaries have signed and sealed this convention, in the English and Danish languages.

Done at New York this fourth day of August, one thousand nine hundred and sixteen.

[Seal]   Robert Lansing
[Seal]   C. Brun

And whereas in giving advice and consent to the ratification of the said Convention, it was declared by the Senate of the United States in their resolution that "such advice and consent are given with the understanding, to be expressed as a part of the instrument of ratification, that such Convention shall not be taken and construed by the High Contracting Parties as imposing any trust upon the United States with respect to any funds belonging to the Danish National Church in the Danish West Indian Islands, or in which the said Church may have an interest, nor as imposing upon the United States any duty or responsibility with respect to the management of any property belonging to said Church, beyond protecting said Church in the possession and use of church property as stated in said Convention, in the same manner and to the same extent only as other churches shall be protected in the possession and use of their several properties";

And whereas it was further provided in the said resolution "That the Senate advises and consents to the ratification of the said Convention on condition that the attitude of the United States in this particular, as set forth in the above proviso, be made the subject of an exchange of notes between the Governments of the two High Contracting Parties, so as to make it plain that this condition is understood and accepted by the two Governments, the purpose hereof being to bring the said Convention clearly within the Constitutional powers of the United States with respect to church establishment and freedom of religion";

And whereas this condition has been fulfilled by notes exchanged between the two High Contracting Parties on January 3, 1917;

And whereas the said Convention has been duly ratified on both parts, and the ratifications of the two Governments were exchanged in the City of Washington, on the seventeenth day of January, one thousand nine hundred and seventeen;

Now, therefore, be it known that I, Woodrow Wilson, President of the United States of America, have caused the said Convention to be made public, to the end that the same and every article and clause thereof may be observed and fulfilled with good faith by the United States and the citizens thereof, subject to the said understanding of the Senate of the United States.

In testimony whereof, I have hereunto set my hand and caused the seal of the United States to be affixed.

Done at the City of Washington this twenty-fifth day of January in the year of our Lord one thousand nine hundred and seventeen, and of the Independence of the United States of America the one hundred and forty-first.

[SEAL]

By the President: WOODROW WILSON.
  ROBERT LANSING,
    Secretary of State.

DECLARATION

In proceeding this day to the signature of the Convention respecting the cession of the Danish West-Indian Islands to the United States of America, the undersigned, Secretary of State of the United States of America, duly authorized by his Government, has the honor to declare that the Government of the United States of America will not object to the Danish Government extending their political and economic interests to the whole of Greenland.

ROBERT LANSING.

New York, August 4, 1916.

INDEX

[1] Spelled by U. S. Department of State as Schested. See For. Rel. 1917, pp. 473, 479-481, 483-487, 490-493. For the sake of convenience when quoting from Foreign Relations, I have used the spelling Schested.